80° DAM

Da ✓ P9-DFW-722

Around the world in 80 books.

PRICE: $25.00 (3798/anf   )

AROUND

THE

WORLD

IN

80 BOOKS

AROUND
THE
WORLD
IN
80 BOOKS

David Damrosch

PENGUIN PRESS

NEW YORK

2021

PENGUIN PRESS
An imprint of Penguin Random House LLC
penguinrandomhouse.com

LIBRARY OF CONGRESS CONTROL NUMBER: 2021944860

Printed in the United States of America
1   3   5   7   9   10   8   6   4   2

Designed by Alexis Farabaugh

Contents

CHAPTER TWELVE

Brazil–Colombia: Utopias, Dystopias, Heterotopias

CHAPTER THIRTEEN

Mexico–Guatemala: The Pope's Blowgun

CHAPTER FOURTEEN

The Antilles and Beyond: Fragments of Epic Memory

The Voyage Out

In the spring of 1968, my ninth-grade English teacher, Miss Staats, gave me the book that changed my life: Laurence Sterne's comic masterpiece, *The Life and Opinions of Tristram Shandy, Gentleman*. I put aside *The Lord of the Rings*, which I was then reading for the sixth or seventh time, and fell into an entirely new world: not only the lively landscape of eighteenth-century England, with its snuff-boxes and horse-drawn carriages, its fops, rakes, and glances half-hidden behind lacy fans, but also a fictional realm that I'd never imagined. Sterne reveled in the infinite possibilities of the modern novel, a form so new that its very name announced its novelty. He loved to interrupt his narrative with black or marbled pages, and he inserted a dedication, eight chapters in, offered for sale to the highest bidder. Sterne poured the entire world into his tale of the Shandy family's misadventures, in a heady mix of social satire and philosophical speculation, enlivened by verbal hijinks and sly sexual innuendo. I was entranced. Where had such writing *been* all my life—all fifteen years of it? Where could I find more books like it?

Tristram himself served as my guide. Among the many opinions that crowd his life story, he speaks at one point of "my dear Rabelais, and dearer Cervantes."[1] I didn't know anything about either of these gentlemen, but if they were good enough for Tristram Shandy, they'd be good enough for me. In the bookstore next to my school bus stop I found the thick black Penguin paperbacks of *Gargantua and Pantagruel* and *Don Quixote*, in the solid translations of that era by J. M. Cohen. Both authors more than lived up to their billing, and by midsummer I was hungry for more. But where to go next? Anticipating Amazon's algorithms today, at the back of their books Penguin offered a selection of titles likely to appeal to readers of the book they'd just finished. I was eager to find another rollicking Rabelaisian satire, so I settled on a likely title: *The Divine Comedy*. I soon discovered that Dante's visionary epic wasn't exactly the knee-slapper I'd been hoping for, but his cosmic vision and his melancholy eloquence drew me in. As summer waned and the new responsibilities of tenth grade approached, I decided that I was ready for another deeply serious and otherworldly work. Bidding farewell to the pulsating celestial rose at the heart of Dante's surprisingly sensuous paradise, I came upon the perfect title in the back of my Penguin *Paradiso*, Nikolai Gogol's *Dead Souls*— only to discover that this was the sparkling satire I'd expected from Dante. Bliss was it in that dawn to be alive, as Wordsworth would say, but to be a young reader was very heaven.

Literature's pleasures can have real-world benefits, both personal and political. I came of age as the Vietnam War was winding down, but eighteen-year-olds were still being drafted in considerable numbers. When it came time to register for the draft as a high school senior, I mounted a case for designation as a conscientious objector, and I bolstered my application with a satirical story I'd written about guns that turn on their users. I received the designation, quite possibly only because my local draft board had plenty of more likely prospects to fill their quota, but I felt that I'd been able to enlist the power of literature in making my appeal. The next year, as a college freshman, I had definitive evidence of the value of reading. Early in the fall semester, I saw a sign for an audition that night for a production of Gilbert and Sullivan's operetta *Trial by Jury*, and I wanted to try out for the chorus, even though I hadn't yet done the reading for my class the next day on Plato's *Republic*. But I had read *The Republic* a couple of years before, and I decided that my limited recollections would do, so I went ahead with *Trial by Jury*. This proved to be a non-Platonic choice in more ways than one, since in the chorus I met an alto with a lovely smile. When I teach a great books course today, I tell my students that I have visual proof that reading Plato can change your life, and I show a photo of my wife, Lori, and myself, three and a half decades after that memorable autumn, with our three kids at our older daughter's college graduation. Our life's journey began thanks to reading Plato, or more precisely thanks to *having read* Plato; we never know when a book may prove to be a life-changing experience.

Since then, I've devoted myself to exploring ancient and modern literatures. Long focused on a handful of European literatures, the realm of world literature now encompasses a host of classic works, from *The Epic of Gilgamesh* to *The Tale of Genji* and the Mayan *Popol Vuh*, that were never found on syllabi outside specialized area studies programs, while the Nobel and Booker prizes are given to contemporary writers as varied as China's Mo Yan, Turkey's Orhan Pamuk, Poland's Olga Tokarczuk, and Oman's Jokha Alharthi. I've written a good deal about these changes, but apart from a book on *Gilgamesh*, I've addressed myself to students and to scholars. More recently, however, I began to think about how I might introduce a broader readership to the expansive landscape of literature today, both in Europe and beyond. What kind of story to tell, and how to give it a satisfying shape?

Literary works are the product of two very different worlds—the world of the writer's experience, and the world of books. These offer the resources that writers use, and transform, in order to process their often chaotic and painful experience into lasting and pleasurable form. The present project is no exception. It draws on my experiences in giving talks in some fifty countries around the world, and it equally takes shape from a variety of literary explorations and fictional adventures. The first movie I ever saw, at age three in 1956, may have been the wide-screen version of Jules Verne's *Around the World in 80 Days*, starring David Niven as the obsessively punctual Phileas Fogg and the Mexican comedian Cantinflas as his servant Jean Passepartout. I also had in mind Harold Bloom's eloquent, idiosyncratic paean to great books, *The Western Canon*, though to survey today's global landscape, I wanted a larger cast of characters than his select set of twenty-six writers. Verne's tally of eighty seemed about right, a capacious but still manageable number of works to discuss. Drawing on my experiences abroad, I decided to loosely mimic Phileas Fogg's route from London eastward through Asia, across the Pacific to the Americas, and finally back to London. I would recall, and often actually revisit, a group of particularly memorable locations and the books I associate with them, both to see how literature enters the world and to think about how the world bleeds into literature.

In January of 2020, I was plotting my itinerary, building it around upcoming talks and conferences. Then came Covid-19. I managed to get in a trip to Muscat in February, but in rapid succession events got cancelled in Chicago, Tokyo, the Netherlands, Heidelberg, Belgrade. So much for going around the world anytime soon. But then again, what was I *thinking*? It was Phileas Fogg, not his creator, who traveled the world by steamship, train, hot air balloon, elephant, and stagecoach. Verne never ventured beyond Europe throughout his long life, and he didn't even set foot outside Paris during the months in 1872 when he wrote his novel. He didn't need to, as he could encounter the world in his cosmopolitan world capital; the idea for the book came to him in a Paris café, where he read a newspaper account of new railway lines and steamship routes that could make it possible for someone to go around the world in eighty days.

Sitting in cafés wasn't going to be in the cards for me under Covid-19 restrictions, but then another literary model came to mind: Xavier de Maistre's little masterpiece, *Voyage autour de ma chambre*—"Voyage Around My Room."[2] De Maistre was a young French aristocrat serving in the Piedmontese army in 1790 when he was punished for taking part in a duel. The judge sentenced him to house arrest for forty-two days—really a quarantine, in its root sense of forty days of sequestration—to give time for the fever of his impulsive anger to subside. Unable to spend his customary evenings drinking with friends, gambling at cards, and flirting with Italian enchantresses, de Maistre decided to treat his room as a miniature world. Parodying the "Grand Tour" that wealthy young men of his era would undertake around Europe—the eighteenth-century equivalent of a gap year—he wrote a series of vivid vignettes based on everything around him in his room, from books to paintings to furniture. I could do the same, and so I invited readers to travel with me on the world-wide web for sixteen weeks from May through August 2020, exploring a worldly locale through five books each week. I delved into a different book each Monday through Friday, taking the weekends off in hopes of maintaining the fiction of a "work week" and "weekends" during the collapse of time under Covid sequestration. This book is the result of that exploration.

Phileas Fogg's journey was shaped by the trade routes—and the Orientalist fantasies—of the British Empire, but today we can cast our net more widely, and so we'll be going to Eastern Europe, Africa, and Latin America as well as to several of Fogg's destinations. Jules Verne serialized his novel in a Paris paper, and his avid readers traced each stage of Phileas Fogg's journey on maps, placing bets on where he'd go next and whether he'd return on time to his London club, where he'd rashly wagered his entire fortune that he could return within eighty days. Fogg's success results from his extreme precision. His clocks all have to chime the hour at the same instant, and Passepartout must bring his master tea and toast every morning at 8:23; he'd be sacked if he heated Fogg's shaving water two degrees below its "statutory" level. Above all, the pair must girdle the globe within eighty days, not a day or even a minute more, a task that Fogg triumphantly accomplishes. So too, this book offers a journey through eighty books across sixteen world locales, though in place of Fogg's hot air balloons and elephants, we'll be traveling via Penguins and other editions of our books.

Around the World in 80 Books explores works that have responded to times of crisis and deep memories of trauma. Not that the books in question are all doom and gloom. Though *The Decameron*'s young men and women have fled the plague in Florence to shelter in place outside the city, the hundred tales they tell are mostly comic and satiric in nature. We too need literature as a refuge in troubled times. When our external activities are curtailed, reading fiction and poetry offers a special opportunity—free from the carbon footprint of long-haul flights—both for pure pleasure and for deep reflection on our lives and the social and political struggles that surround us, as we navigate our world's turbulent waters with the aid of literature's maps of imaginary times and places.

The writers we'll be encountering have drawn both on their home culture and on traditions beyond their own. Virginia Woolf was in rivalrous dialogue with her contemporaries Joseph Conrad and Arnold Bennett in London, and with her English predecessors from Dickens and Jane Austen back to Richardson and Sterne. Yet she also read Chekhov (in Russian), Proust (in French and in English), and Sophocles (in Greek), and in her diary she described "going to bed with Arthur Waley"—meaning not the man himself but his pioneering translation of *The Tale of Genji*. Many of the writers treasured at the heart of our national traditions have drawn extensively on foreign sources. Even when a work is written in a purely local context, if it travels beyond its borders it enters into a new set of literary relations, and we'll often be looking at ways in which later writers have revisited and reworked classic texts in very different circumstances.

While the pandemic provided a particular occasion for framing this project, a still more troubling, and likely more lasting, phenomenon in many parts of the world is the rise of ethnic nationalism, isolationism, and the fear of people or ideas crossing borders. Even more widespread is the siloing of political discourse and cultural or religious perspectives; we are all finding it more and more difficult to really listen to viewpoints we don't already agree with. In such times, literature offers us unique opportunities to resist what Chimamanda Adichie calls "the danger of a single story." Not that writers ever simply reflect some pure ethnic or national identity, but we can learn from the ways they *refract* their experience into new perspectives on the world.

There's been a good deal of debate in recent years about the obstacles that stand in the way of a genuine appreciation of foreign works, including the highly selective processes by which writers enter world literary space—a cultural landscape of considerable inequality, grounded in centuries of national and imperial conflict and reinforced today by the globalization of the world market and the neoimperial dominance of global English. All of us who want to venture beyond the boundaries of our own country need to be vigilant in not succumbing to reductive cultural stereotypes, whether reflexively negative or patronizingly positive, and we need to push back against market mechanisms that limit the variety of works available to us. This book is intended as an intervention in this process. I hope that the range of books I take up, and the varied approaches to them here, can illustrate the opportunities that an expanding literary canon offers us to open out our world.

A full picture of world literature today includes compelling contemporary works as well as perennial classics, poetry and drama as well as novels, hardbitten crime fiction as well as haunting fantasy worlds, philosophical and religious texts, and the formative works that introduce children to the world they're entering. Taken together, these eighty works can help us gain perspective on problems that are very much with us today, whether the rising economic inequality that Thomas More designed *Utopia* to combat, the politicization of religion that Salman Rushdie dissects in his stories, or the patriarchal structures within and against which many of our books' heroines have to struggle, from the work of Murasaki Shikibu a millennium ago to Margaret Atwood and Jokha Alharthi today.

Literature lives in its language, and when we look beyond our borders, the question of translation soon arises. How worthwhile is it to read a work when we don't know the language it was written in? Certainly we should all learn languages beyond the one or two we've grown up with, but we'll never get far in the world today if we confine ourselves to the few languages we can actually read. Having utterly failed to learn more than a fraction of the languages that I wish I knew, I live with this question on a daily basis. At the same time, translations offer a powerful impetus to learning new languages. When I teach a world literature course, my utopian hope is that each student will, unpredictably, come to feel that they can't live another year without studying a language they'd never thought about learning. It was reading Dante and Calvino in translation that inspired me to study Italian; reading Aztec poetry—in an English translation of a Spanish translation—impelled me to study Nahuatl.

In the following pages, we'll encounter the intertwined problem of translation and untranslatability in specific instances, from *The Thousand and One Nights* to Persian ghazals to the Auschwitz-haunted poetry of Paul Celan. But even as we explore the limits of translatability, we should be aware that we're living in a golden age of translation, with more and better translations being published than ever before. Many of our eighty authors, indeed, were significant translators themselves, sometimes of other writers taken up here: Celan translated Kafka, Julio Cortázar translated Marguerite Yourcenar, Yourcenar translated James Baldwin. One of the principles of selection for these eighty works is that they're all available in excellent translations, and in the case of multiply translated works we have the opportunity to consider what kinds of excellence a given translation may offer.

A successful translation recreates a work for a new time and a new audience, and skillful translators find creative ways to convey a work's power and beauty using the resources of their own language; influential translations can spur innovation in the host language itself. It remains true that reading Dante in English isn't the same as reading him in Italian, but it's also the case that reading *La Divina Commedia* in Italian today isn't the same experience as Boccaccio had when he read it in the mid-1300s. Few readers these days will be particularly attuned to Dante's dialogues with Provençal poets or his quarrels with Florentine politicians; we now read him in a new set of relations, from Primo Levi reciting his verses in Auschwitz to Derek Walcott adapting his *terza rima* to portray the lives of Creole-speaking fishermen in the Caribbean.

Like Phileas Fogg's journey, this project is based on a very personal itinerary, only partially overlapping with what another literary traveler would create. I myself could readily have constructed a very different set of books, and locales, from Reykjavik to Moscow to Bangkok and beyond. The itinerary I've settled on gives *one* version of world literature, not the uniform order of some globalized "one-world" literature. Each chapter centers on a city or region that has produced a significant body of great writing, and is further focused on a particular theme: how writers create cities and how cities create writers; the legacies of war in Europe and of empire elsewhere; questions of migration and diaspora; and the living heritage of poetic and storytelling traditions from Homeric epics to Japanese haiku to the nested tales of *The Thousand and One Nights*.

Within each chapter's common settings and themes, we'll explore the creative variety with which our authors construe their homeland and their heritage, often in dramatically different ways within a single culture. We readers in turn use their works for purposes of our own, and I periodically take examples from my own experience to suggest how literature can inform our sense of ourselves and our world, particularly in difficult times. These eighty works aren't intended as a permanent listing of "the books and school of the ages," to recall the subtitle of Bloom's *The Western Canon*. What I've chosen are particularly *worldly* works, written by authors who are reflecting on the world around them and the wider world beyond their borders, either as their characters venture abroad or as the outside world impinges upon them. Through unexpected encounters and sometimes surprising twists, turns, and juxtapositions, I hope that you will find fresh ways to look at long-familiar works, together with some exciting new discoveries.

Enough for now; eighty books await us. As Apuleius of Madaura said at the start of his border-crossing masterpiece, *The Golden Ass*, nearly two thousand years ago, *Lector, intende: laetaberis*: Attend, reader, and you will find delight.[3]

CHAPTER ONE

London: Inventing a City

1. Virginia Woolf: *Mrs. Dalloway*

After making his round-the-world wager with his friends at the Reform Club, Phileas Fogg strides to his home at 7 Savile Row, several blocks away, to collect some clothes and his newly hired French servant, Jean Passepartout. Halfway there, he crosses the route that would be taken by Clarissa Dalloway fifty years later (had she, or he, actually existed), on her way to nearby Bond Street to buy flowers for her party that evening. Woolf begins her novel with Clarissa's meditative stroll, which becomes a kind of hymn to the joys of London:

> Such fools we are, she thought, crossing Victoria Street. For Heaven only knows why one loves it so, how one sees it so, making it up, building it round one, tumbling it, creating it every moment afresh; but the veriest frumps, the most dejected of miseries sitting on doorsteps (drink their downfall) do the same; can't be dealt with, she felt positive, by Acts of Parliament for that very reason: they love life. In people's eyes, in the swing, tramp, and trudge; in the bellow and the uproar; the carriages, motor cars, omnibuses, vans, sandwich men shuffling and swinging; brass bands; barrel

organs; in the triumph and the jingle and the strange high singing of some aeroplane overhead was what she loved; life; London; this moment of June.[1]

Mrs. Dalloway is one of the most localized of books, taking place on a single day in June 1923 within a few fashionable neighborhoods of central London. It might have seemed more logical to begin our journey with Woolf's picaresque, uncanny *Orlando*, whose hero has an affair with a Russian princess before changing sex in Constantinople and becoming the book's heroine. Or with the globe-spanning Joseph Conrad, with novels set in Malaysia and Latin America, whose *Heart of Darkness* takes us from London to the Belgian Congo and back again. Yet I've preferred to begin with a novel set squarely in London, not only because this is our point of departure but because *Mrs. Dalloway* shows London becoming the world city it is today. Clarissa's former suitor, Peter Walsh, has returned from India in order to arrange a divorce; her daughter's tutor and possible lover, Miss Kilman, feels radically out of place in an England that only recently was locked in a life-or-death struggle with her native Germany; and the Italian war bride Rezia struggles to adapt to London life and to rescue her shell-shocked husband, Septimus Warren Smith, from the brink of suicide.

The world has certainly come home to London, most ominously in the form of World War I, whose aftershocks resonate throughout the city and through the novel. Even as Clarissa enjoys "life; London; this moment of June," she also hears "the strange high singing of some aeroplane overhead." This turns out to be a sky-writing biplane advertising a product that people on the ground try to make out (toffee? Glaxo milk powder?). Yet the plane's approach seems oddly like an air raid, its effects almost fatal:

Suddenly Mrs. Coates looked up into the sky. The sound of an aeroplane bored ominously into the ears of the crowd. There it was coming over the trees, letting out white smoke from behind, which curled and twisted . . .

Dropping dead down the aeroplane soared straight up, curved in a loop,
raced, sank, rose . . . and again, in a fresh space of sky, began writing a K,
an E, a Y perhaps?

"Glaxo," said Mrs. Coates in a strained, awe-stricken voice, gazing straight
up, and her baby, lying stiff and white in her arms, gazed straight up. (20)

Sky-writing had actually been invented that year by the aptly named Major
Jack Savage, recently retired from the Royal Air Force; he wrote his aerial advertisements using airplanes decommissioned from the RAF after the
war's end.[2]

Mrs. Dalloway is haunted by the chaos that lies just outside the comfortable
boundaries of Clarissa's upper-class environment. Anything at all can shake
the foundations of a still fragile postwar world. As the biplane flies overhead,
a curtained limousine glides along Bond Street, causing a stir of excitement, though no one can see who is inside the car as it heads to Buckingham
Palace. Its discreet glamour stirs patriotic sentiments in prosperous gentlemen
and an impoverished flower-seller, but also thoughts of loss and even a
near-riot:

in all the hat shops and tailors' shops strangers looked at each other and
thought of the dead; of the flag; of Empire. In a public house in a back street
a Colonial insulted the House of Windsor which led to words, broken beer
glasses, and a general shindy, which echoed strangely across the way in the
ears of girls buying white underlinen threaded with pure white ribbon for
their weddings. For the surface agitation of the passing car as it sunk grazed
something very profound. (18)

A few blocks away in Regent's Park, worried sick about her husband's erratic
behavior, Rezia senses England's entire civilization dropping away, leaving her
in a primeval wasteland:

"For you should see the Milan gardens," she said aloud. But to whom?

There was nobody. Her words faded. So a rocket fades. Its sparks, having grazed their way into the night, surrender to it, dark descends, pours over the outlines of houses and towers; bleak hillsides soften and fall in . . . as perhaps at midnight, when all boundaries are lost, the country reverts to its ancient shape, as the Romans saw it, lying cloudy, when they landed, and the hills had no names and rivers wound they knew not where—such was her darkness . . . (23–4)

In *Heart of Darkness*, Conrad's hero, Marlow, had already compared the European scramble for Africa with the Roman conquest of a dank and primitive England: "marshes, forests, savages,—precious little to eat fit for a civilized man, nothing but Thames water to drink."[3] Woolf brings the comparison home. Amid all of Clarissa's upper-class comforts (the irises and delphiniums, the dove-grey gloves, the Prime Minister dropping by her party) her London bears more than a passing resemblance to Conrad's heart of darkness. Even Mr. Kurtz's famous last words—"The horror! The horror!"—are echoed in a mounting crescendo in the novel's opening pages. First, Clarissa recalls "the horror of the moment" when she learned of Peter Walsh's impending marriage; then the shell-shocked Septimus feels "as if some horror had come almost to the surface and was about to burst into flames," and finally nineteen-year-old Maisie Johnson, newly arrived from Scotland seeking employment, is disturbed by Septimus's behavior, and she wishes she'd never come to town: "Horror! horror! she wanted to cry. (She had left her people; they had warned her what would happen.) Why hadn't she stayed at home? she cried, twisting the knob of the iron railing" (8, 15, 27).

Virginia Woolf was a lifelong Londoner, but she was also a citizen of a wider literary world. She was studying Russian when she began work on the novel, and she read Sophocles and Euripides in Greek as she finished it. She also took a close, quizzical interest in foreign-born writers on the English scene, including Conrad, Henry James, and her friend T. S. Eliot. In her essay collection *The Common Reader* (published in the same year as *Mrs. Dalloway*) she wrote that "instances will occur to everybody of American writers in particular who have written with the highest discrimination of our literature and of ourselves; who have lived a lifetime among us, and finally have taken legal steps to become subjects of King George. For all that, have they understood us, have they not remained to the end of their days foreigners?"[4]

A feminist, a socialist, and a pacifist in a largely patriarchal, capitalist, and imperialist England, Woolf herself often felt like a foreigner at home. A slyly subversive streak, though, ran through her commitment to pacifist anti-imperialism. In 1910 she donned a cross-dressing disguise to join her brother Adrian and several friends in an Ethiopian "state visit" to the warship HMS *Dreadnought*, anchored in Portsmouth (Figure 1). The visitors were welcomed with an honor guard and given a tour of the ship; they expressed their admiration with cries of "Bunga! Bunga!" Conversing in a gibberish made up of Latin and Greek, they bestowed bogus military honors on the clueless officers and returned to London unexposed. The Royal Navy was deeply embarrassed when the friends published an account of the hoax, complete with a formal

1. The Dreadnought *hoaxers*

photo of the delegation, in the London *Daily Mirror*. (Woolf is the hirsute gentleman on the left.)

The foreign and the familiar constantly intermingle in Woolf's work. In *The Common Reader*, she describes the disorienting strangeness of Chekhov, Dostoevsky, and Tolstoy, yet she drew deeply on their work to find resources not available to her in Victorian fiction. Her description of Chekhov's stories could be an account of *Mrs. Dalloway* itself: "Once the eye is used to these shades, half the 'conclusions' of fiction fade into thin air; they show like transparencies with a light behind them—gaudy, glaring, superficial . . . In consequence, as we read these little stories about nothing at all, the horizon widens; the soul gains an astonishing sense of freedom" (186). *Mrs. Dalloway* is imbued as well with Woolf's admiration for Proust ("My great adventure is really Proust. Well—what remains to be written after that?"[5]). She was more ambivalent about Joyce's *Ulysses*, which she described in print as "a memorable catastrophe"[6] and in private as "merely the scratching of pimples" on a hotel's bootboy.[7] Devising her own version of Joyce's stream-of-consciousness technique, and like him adapting the ancient Greek unities of time and place for her novel, Woolf draws on Sophocles and Euripides as well as on Chekhov, Conrad, Eliot, Joyce, and Proust.

Yet her London isn't the "unreal city" of Eliot's *Waste Land* but an intensely present world. Woolf's shifting, glancing sentences emphasize nuance and openness to experience, not the imposing mastery of her male counterparts. As she wrote in her great essay *A Room of One's Own*, in most men's writing "a shadow shaped something like the letter 'I' often falls across their pages."[8] As Clarissa walks to Bond Street to buy her flowers, she reflects that "her only gift was knowing people almost by instinct" (9). She loves London's "hosts of people; and dancing all night; and the wagons plodding past to market . . . what she loved was this, here, now, in front of her; the fat lady in the cab" (9). No one has ever surpassed Woolf's ability to create scenes in which the most serious concerns—world war, madness, the unbridgeable gaps between men and women—emerge from "this, here, now."

Yet Woolf shows us the here and now on the threshold of death, and she sees

London almost with an archaeologist's eye. When the curtained limousine glides down Bond Street

> there could be no doubt that greatness was seated within . . . the enduring symbol of the state which will be known to curious antiquaries, sifting the ruins of time, when London is a grass-grown path and all those hurrying along the pavement this Wednesday morning are but bones with a few wedding rings mixed up in their dust and the gold stoppings of innumerable decayed teeth. The face in the motor car will then be known. (16)

Woolf's panoramic framing of her local scenes fueled the book's circulation out into the world, embraced by readers around the globe who wouldn't be able to locate Bond Street or even London on a map. In 1998, in *The Hours*—Woolf's original title—Michael Cunningham set the story in Los Angeles and Greenwich Village. Writing on a different continent and for a new generation, Cunningham expanded on the theme of same-sex desire that Woolf had only hinted at in the troubled figure of Miss Kilman and in Clarissa's early crush on the free-spirited Sally Seton, whose ardent kiss she vividly recalls decades later. But Woolf's subtly subversive book was never confined to its immediate time and place. The most local of novels, *Mrs. Dalloway* is also one of the most worldly books ever written: a long day's journey into life; London; this moment of June.

2. Charles Dickens, *Great Expectations*

In "David Copperfield," an essay she published the same year as *Mrs. Dalloway*, Virginia Woolf tried to come to terms with her lifelong ambivalence toward Dickens's work. In place of the intricacies of human emotions, she says, what we remember from his novels

> is the ardour, the excitement, the humour, the oddity of people's characters; the smell and savour and soot of London; the incredible coincidences which

hook the most remote lives together; the city, the law courts, this man's nose, that man's limp; some scene under an archway or on the high road; and above all some gigantic and dominating figure, so stuffed and swollen with life that he does not exist singly, but seems to need for his own realization a host of others.[9]

She remarks that "there is perhaps no person living who can remember reading *David Copperfield* for the first time" (75). Dickens wasn't really an author any more, she says, but "an institution, a monument, a public thoroughfare trodden dusty by a million feet" (76)—probably trodden simultaneously by the host of his characters and by his millions of readers.

Few writers and their cities have ever been so closely linked as Dickens and London. To this day, a host of guidebooks and websites invite you to take walking tours through "Dickens's London." Dozens of locales are on view, including the Old Curiosity Shop at the center of the novel of that name, now "immortalized by Charles Dickens," as the façade proudly declares in faux-Gothic lettering. Certainly in my own case, long before I ever got there, the London of my early imagination was largely Dickens's creation, in a literary embodiment of Oscar Wilde's claim that London's fogs had actually been invented by the Impressionists. As he asked in his brilliant essay "The Decay of Lying": "Where, if not from the Impressionists, do we get those wonderful brown fogs that come creeping down our streets, blurring the gas-lamps and changing the houses into monstrous shadows?" He allows that "there may have been fogs for centuries in London. I dare say there were. But no one saw them . . . They did not exist until Art had invented them."[10] Wilde, however, wouldn't have joined a Dickens tour, as he was put off by Dickens's sentimentality. As he famously declared about *The Old Curiosity Shop*'s tragic little heroine, "One must have a heart of stone to read the death of Little Nell without laughing."[11]

Virginia Woolf too wasn't content to live in Dickens's London, as she and her friends were intent on inventing a city—and a mode of writing—more to their liking. As she notes with some asperity in her essay on *David Copperfield*, "His sympathies, indeed, have strict limitations. Speaking roughly, they fail him whenever a man or woman has more than two thousand a year, has been to the university, or can count his ancestors back to the third generation" (77), and she misses the emotional complexity that was foregrounded in the work of George Eliot and Henry James. At the same time, she sees in Dickens the seeds of the active readerly involvement that she was seeking to create on her own terms. Dickens's "fecundity and apparent irreflectiveness," she says, "have a strange effect. They make creators of us, and not merely readers and spectators . . . Subtlety and complexity are all there if we know where to look for them, if we can get over the surprise of finding them—as it seems to us, who have another convention in these matters—in the wrong places" (78–9).

Dickens's later works actually have a good deal more artistry and psychological complexity than we find in early novels such as *Nicholas Nickleby* and *David Copperfield*. It's interesting that Woolf chose to focus on the early Dickens, rather than mature masterpieces such as *Bleak House* and *Great Expectations*, which were perhaps a little too close for comfort. It is these works that I've found to repay repeated reading, in a way that his earlier novels don't.

Over the years, I've acquired no fewer than five copies of *Great Expectations*, and each of them embodies a different way to read it. One old version is part of a multivolume *Collected Works of Charles Dickens*. Here the proper context for reading the novel is the author's entire oeuvre. The Victorians loved to buy such collections, which they could binge-read during long winter evenings. Dickens oversaw an edition of his collected works in 1867, but his readers had first encountered his novels in their era's version of weekly TV series. He published *Great Expectations* in his magazine *All the Year Round* in weekly installments over the course of nine months in 1860–61, working to his weekly schedule as intently as Phileas Fogg would do a dozen years later in going around the world.

In the decades following Dickens's death, his novels came to be regarded as popular entertainment, particularly suited for young readers. One of my copies of *Great Expectations* was published in New York sometime around the turn of the century (the copy is undated) in a series of "BOOKS FOR BOYS." At the back of the book the publisher advertises two dozen other works in the series, including such tempting titles as *Tom the Bootblack*, *Dan the Newsboy*, and *Wrecked on Spider Island*. Growing up in Maine, I'm sure I would have enjoyed *Jack, the Hunchback*, "the story of a little hunchback who lived on Cape Elizabeth, on the coast of Maine. His trials and successes are most interesting."

Dickens's stock revived in mid-century, when a generation of New Critics began to probe more deeply into his artistry. My next copy of the novel, published in 1963, was a "Signet Classic," adorned with a spooky image of the convict Magwitch hiding in the cemetery where Dickens's hero, Pip, meets him at the start of the novel. This version features a laudatory afterword by the British novelist Angus Wilson, and the back cover emphasizes that "*Great Expectations* is at once a superbly constructed novel of spellbinding mystery and a profound examination of moral values." So different publishers over the years have presented the world with distinctively different *Great Expectations*, and a work can change at the hands of a single publisher, as times and tastes change. Figure 2 shows my copies of two Penguin editions, the first of which I read as a college freshman in 1971, and the second of which I used when teaching the novel in the late 1990s.

Both editions are geared toward an academic market as much as to general

2. *Changing* Expectations

readers. They are amply annotated and come complete with introductions by prominent scholars and bibliographies for further reading. With all these similarities, the covers are significantly different. The older edition features an 1860 painting by J. M. W. Turner, entitled *A country blacksmith disputing upon the price of iron, and the price charged to the butcher for shoeing his poney.* This image evokes the forge of little Pip's great friend and protector Joe Gargery, situating the novel in terms of a realistic slice of life in mid-Victorian England. By contrast, the more recent cover features a ghostly landscape by the German Romantic painter Caspar David Friedrich, *The Cemetery Entrance* (1825). Removed from Dickens's novel both in time and place, Friedrich's mist-filled "deathscape" (as one art historian has described it) suggests the ghostly Miss Havisham's Satis House, rather than the modest churchyard where young Pip tries to discern his parents' characters by studying their tombstones, where "the shape of the letters on my father's, gave me an odd idea that he was a square, stout, dark man, with curly black hair."[12]

The multiple versions of the novel, from a boy's adventure story to a slice of life in old England to a proto-Symbolist landscape, are intertwined for me with my own life's story. Having first encountered *Great Expectations* at something like little Pip's age when the novel begins, I then studied it in college, at roughly the age when Pip moves to London as a young man after inheriting the fortune that he believes was bequeathed to him by the eerie Miss Havisham. I then taught the novel at around the age when the thirty-something Pip writes down his life story. Another thirty years later, I am now a decade older than Caspar David Friedrich when he painted the Dresden cemetery (for which he'd actually designed the towering entrance gate), and two decades older than Dickens was when he wrote the novel. But every time I open *Great Expectations*, I am back with little Pip, as he is about to receive his "first most vivid and broad impression of the identity of things . . . on a memorable raw afternoon towards evening," when the startling figure of Magwitch emerges from among the graves by the churchyard porch. Pip and I are ready to begin our life's journey once again.

3. Arthur Conan Doyle, *The Complete Sherlock Holmes*

Few literary characters have so successfully imposed themselves on the world as Sherlock Holmes. According to the *Guinness Book of World Records*, he has been portrayed on television and in film more often than any other character in the history of literature. Any number of writers have adopted him and his faithful sidekick, Dr. Watson, either openly or in thinly disguised reworkings, as in Umberto Eco's massively bestselling *The Name of the Rose*, with its medieval detective William of Baskerville and the naïve Adso of Melk as his Watson. Beyond his proliferating literary afterlife, Sherlock has also materialized in London itself. In a recent BBC poll of British teenagers, over half of the respondents believed that Holmes was an actual person. Even though, technically speaking, Sherlock never existed, you can visit his lovingly recreated sitting room at 221B Baker Street, which is now the Sherlock Holmes Museum, complete with a plaque above the entrance, listing the years in which he was supposedly in residence there:

221B

SHERLOCK HOLMES

CONSULTING DETECTIVE

1881–1904

If Holmes and Watson enjoy an exceptional worldwide presence today, their vitality doesn't owe much to the psychological complexity that gives Clarissa Dalloway such resonance in our minds. Virginia Woolf, indeed, couldn't stand Conan Doyle's stories. As she remarked in an essay on her rival Arnold Bennett: "A character may be real to Mr. Bennett and quite unreal to me . . . he says that Dr. Watson in Sherlock Holmes is real to him: to me Dr. Watson is a sack stuffed with straw, a dummy, a figure of fun."[13]

Still less can the vividness of Sherlock's world have to do with richly detailed descriptions of London. In the inaugural tale, *A Study in Scarlet*, when Holmes and Watson make the pivotal decision to move in together at 221B Baker Street, all we're told is that their apartment "consisted of a couple of comfortable bedrooms and a single large airy sitting-room, cheerfully furnished, and illuminated by two broad windows."[14] The cheerful furnishings don't merit any description, while the view from the broad windows is dreary enough to drive Sherlock to drugs. In *The Sign of the Four*, explaining his recourse to cocaine when he doesn't have a case to enliven his life, Holmes tells Watson, "What else is there to live for? Stand at the window here. Was ever such a dreary, dismal, unprofitable world? See how the yellow fog swirls down the street and drifts across the dun-coloured houses. What could be more hopelessly prosaic and material?" (1:93).

Conan Doyle's world is only partly built out of fragments of prosaic material reality; even more, it is a world of stories upon stories. Early in *A Study in Scarlet*, Holmes critiques the detective stories of Edgar Allan Poe (whose Inspector Dupin "was by no means such a phenomenon as Poe seemed to imagine") and the French writer Émile Gaboriau, whose Monsieur Lecoq "was a miserable bungler" (1:24–5). What sets Holmes apart is his ability to deduce the story behind any person or object, however plain. In *The Sign of the Four*, he demonstrates this skill by examining Watson's pocket watch. The watch seems devoid of any distinctive features, but to Sherlock's eye it reveals an entire tale of a brother's wasted life and eventual death from alcoholism. Watson is dismayed to have Sherlock divine so much about his lost brother—whose existence he'd never even mentioned—and Sherlock is momentarily embarrassed: "'My dear doctor,' said he kindly, 'pray accept my apologies. Viewing the matter as an abstract problem, I had forgotten how personal and painful a thing it might be to you'" (1:93).

Writers often allude to events outside the scope of their work, suggesting that their story isn't just taking place on some cardboard stage set. In "The Adventure of the Sussex Vampire," Sherlock refers to a series of never-published cases, including one involving "the giant rat of Sumatra, a story for which the world is not yet prepared." Here Holmes gestures toward a life more fully lived outside the story's boundaries, or more precisely a "case-book" of tales outside the story of "the Sussex Vampire." He is leafing through his casebook looking for guidance, as he doubts that he can handle the situation he is being asked to investigate: a young mother has been discovered sucking blood from her baby's neck. "But what do we know of vampires?" he asks Watson; "really we seem to have been switched on to a Grimm's fairytale" (2:1034). "Switched" is a railway metaphor here, not an electrical one: Holmes fears that he may be getting diverted onto a horror-story track, derailed from his customary genre of rationally solvable crimes. Fortunately, as he tells Watson at the story's end, he arrived at the solution thanks to "the train of reasoning which passed through my mind in Baker Street" (2:1043), before they boarded the 2:00 train at Victoria Station to head out to Sussex.

Conan Doyle has enhanced his tale's worldliness through a metafictional reference to a nonexistent tale involving an imaginary species on the other side of the globe. The world may not have been prepared to read a Sherlock Holmes story more outré yet than one about a vampire mother, but Conan Doyle had fully prepared the world for the *idea* of a story involving a giant rat of Sumatra—so successfully, in fact, that at least a dozen later writers have written the story for him. And more than that: in 2007, when a new species of large rodent was discovered in Papua New Guinea, the find was announced by *The New York Times* in an article entitled "The Giant Rat of Sumatra, Alive and Well,"[15] even though the reporter had to admit that Papua New Guinea is located "a few islands too far to the right"—in actual fact, nearly 3,000 miles away.

Giant rats may one day turn up in Sumatra itself—smuggled in, if necessary, by devoted Holmesians—but we know that no vampires will ever be unearthed in Sussex. Though the mother declares that Holmes seems to have magical powers, the great detective has discovered an earthly explanation for her bizarre behavior (sucking out curare with which a jealous stepsibling is trying to poison his tiny rival). As Holmes says to Watson, "This agency stands flat-footed upon the ground, and there it must remain. The world is big enough for us. No ghosts need apply" (2:1034). The worldwide network of the Baker Street Irregulars testifies to his devotees' desire to fit his world to the dimensions of our own, even though they privately know that there is no long-lost casebook in a steamer trunk somewhere, beyond the actually existing canon of four novels and fifty-six tales.

Sherlock is the only "private consulting detective" in the world; his unique skill is to make sense of the stories that other detectives can't unravel. Often he performs this feat without stirring from the socially distanced seclusion of his rooms. Sherlock made few friends in college and dropped out after two years, he never joins a police force, he declines a knighthood, he has no steady income whatever. Stories are the only things that save him from a downward spiral into addiction.

For his part, Watson is a man whose active life is over, after being almost fatally wounded in the second Anglo-Afghan War. As he tells us on the first page of *A Study in Scarlet*, "The campaign brought honours and promotion to many, but for me it had nothing but misfortune and disaster." He received his career-ending injury quite specifically "at the fatal battle of Maiwand." This was a humiliating defeat in July 1880 in which the British lost nearly a thousand soldiers. Disabled by his injury and emaciated from enteric fever, Watson returns, he tells us, "to London, that great cesspool into which all the loungers and idlers of the Empire are irresistibly drained" (1:15). Though Conan Doyle was writing at the height of Britain's imperial expansion, Watson's London sounds like the distant backwater of a collapsing empire. But he finds a new life with Sherlock, who desperately needs him—not as a gay lover (as some later writers have imagined) but as a storyteller. When the King of Bohemia appears at their rooms in "A Scandal in Bohemia" and requests a private consultation, Watson plans to step out, but Holmes insists that the wounded doctor-turned-writer has to remain: "Stay where you are. I am lost without my Boswell" (1:164). In a world whose medical, social, and political orders all seem to be on the verge of collapse, we are lost without our storytellers.

4. P. G. Wodehouse, *Something Fresh*

One of the most popular novelists of the twentieth century, Pelham Grenville Wodehouse revolutionized the comic novel during his seventy-five-year career, using a riotous, multilayered prose style to create a world of bumbling aristocrats, masterful servants, strong young women, eminent loony-doctors, and imperious aunts. To invent his farcical London and its associated country estates, Wodehouse first had to invent himself. Born in 1881, he was soon taken to Hong Kong, where his father was a colonial magistrate. At age two, Wodehouse was shipped back to England and was raised by aunts and uncles. He had almost three dozen of them all told, and aunts and uncles figure more prominently in his fiction than distant mothers and fathers. In 1900, shortly before he was to follow an older brother to Oxford, his father suffered sunstroke and had to retire on disability. Like T. S. Eliot a few years after him, Wodehouse got a job as a bank clerk and began writing incessantly at night. In 1902 he was offered a five-week job writing a humorous newspaper column while the regular columnist went on summer vacation; forced to choose between the bank and this temporary job, Wodehouse left the bank, never to return.

He began visiting New York in 1909, seeking to make a place for himself in the larger American publishing market, and hoping to write for the Broadway stage as well. He was in New York when World War I began and stayed there through the war. By 1917 he'd become the most active writer on Broadway, with a remarkable total of five shows performing simultaneously—a record never surpassed before or since. Wodehouse's theatrical involvements had a pivotal effect on his fiction. He later wrote that "I believe there are only two ways of writing a novel. One is mine, making the thing a sort of musical comedy without music, ignoring real life altogether; the other is going right down deep into life and not caring a damn."[16]

This self-deprecating statement understates his stories' grounding in reality, reinforced by his attention to stagecraft—the movement of real bodies and the handling of props on stage—and the fundamental realities of economic need and family pressures are always waiting in the wings. His works are full of clueless younger sons whose fathers resent having to support them, and the sons are half-aware of their paralytic immaturity—Bertie Wooster and his friends belong to a club called The Drones. These passive youths are balanced by scrappy heroines who take them in hand as they make their way in the world, in very modern scenarios of self-creation and advancement.

Together with the theater, detective fiction was a perennial source of inspiration for Wodehouse. In 1975, at age ninety-four, he wrote an introduction to an edition of Conan Doyle's *The Sign of the Four*. There he declared: "When I was starting out as a writer—this would be about the time Caxton invented the printing press—Conan Doyle was my hero. Others might revere Hardy and Meredith. I was a Doyle man, and I still am."[17] In the years before World War I he became friends with his hero, and they regularly played cricket together. Wodehouse's most famous characters, the feckless young Bertie Wooster and his brilliant "gentleman's gentleman," Jeeves, regularly echo Holmes and Watson, with an awed Bertie recounting Jeeves's abilities to solve mysteries and resolve every kind of personal dilemma. Appropriately, Bertie is never happier than when curled up with *The Man with the Missing Toe* or *The Mystery of the Pink Crayfish*. Jeeves, on the other hand, confesses that "my personal tastes lie more in the direction of Dostoevsky and the great Russians."[18] Elsewhere, he cautions Bertie against a recommendation from a fiancée who's trying to improve his mind: "You would not enjoy Nietzsche, sir. He is fundamentally unsound."[19]

Wodehouse's farcical realism reached its first full flowering in his early bestseller, *Something Fresh* (1915, published in the USA as *Something New*). Drawing on his own experience as a struggling writer, Wodehouse tells the tale of Ashe Marson, who is caught on the treadmill of writing the monthly "Adventures of Gridley Quayle, Detective" for the Mammoth Publishing Company: "The unholy alliance had been in progress now for more than two years, and it seemed to Ashe that Gridley grew less human each month. He was so complacent and so maddeningly blind to the fact that only the most amazing luck enabled him to detect anything. To depend on Gridley Quayle for one's income was like being chained to some horrible monster."[20] Ashe's fortunes change when he is invited to the country estate of Clarence, Earl of Emsworth, whose chief love is his prize pig, the Empress of Blandings. At Blandings, Ashe meets another struggling hack writer, Joan Valentine, who cranks out tales of lords and ladies for women's magazines. Ashe and Joan succeed in pooling their talents—and their genres—to solve a ludicrous mystery at Clarence's country house; their fortune, and their love life, is assured.

Over the years, Wodehouse developed long series of stories and novels featuring his favorite characters and settings, particularly Lord Emsworth's Blandings Castle and Bertie and Jeeves's London flat. As early as 1928, a reviewer accused Wodehouse of self-plagiarism, a charge that Wodehouse hilariously took up in a preface to his next novel: "A certain critic—for such men, I regret to say, exist—made a nasty remark about my last novel that it contained 'all the old Wodehouse characters under different names.' With my superior intelligence I have outgeneralled the man this time by putting in all the old Wodehouse characters under the same names. Pretty silly it will make him feel, I rather fancy."[21]

Writing steadily into his nineties, Wodehouse continued to rework his characters and situations with undiminished zest. Increasingly, his novels play openly with the pleasures of their own conventions. Having intimidated Bertie Wooster in several novels over the years, in 1960 the formidable psychiatrist Sir Roderick Glossop shocks Bertie when he turns up disguised as a butler named Swordfish. Yet Bertie shouldn't have been so surprised, since twenty-five years earlier he and Sir Roderick had disguised themselves together as traveling minstrels (*Thank You, Jeeves*). Conversely, in *Uncle Fred in the Springtime* (1939), the Earl of Ickham stays at Blandings Castle disguised as Sir Roderick himself.

Like Count Westwest's domain in Kafka's *The Castle*, Blandings Castle is observed with an almost ethnographic fascination. Both are arcane, self-enclosed societies whose rules are gradually laid bare for the observer, who is often an intruder or an imposter. In a preface to a reissue of *Something Fresh* in 1972, an eighty-nine-year-old Wodehouse noted that "Blandings had impostors the way other houses have mice." He added that "it is about time that another was coming along; without at least one impostor on the premises, Blandings Castle is never itself."[22] Like Kafka's symbolist locales, Wodehouse's farcical settings lie somewhere between the realms of fantasy and realism, providing an intermediate ground on which the system can evolve according to its own internal logic, even as it refers obliquely back to the world we know.

Wodehouse's ninety-eight books have been translated into dozens of languages and have sold tens of millions of copies. He is an immensely popular author, yet he wasn't a man of the people, either in origin or in his themes. His writing is anti-modernist, yet like T. S. Eliot and James Joyce he mingles high and low styles, music-hall lyrics and Shakespeare. Wodehouse enjoyed playing on his in-between status. In a 1926 story called "The Clicking of Cuthbert," a gloomy Russian novelist named Vladimir Brusiloff is making a lecture tour in America. His novels are "grey studies of hopeless misery," where "nothing happens until a peasant commits suicide on page 380," but Brusiloff rejects a comparison to his socialist-realist contemporaries, Sovietski and Nastikoff. "No novelists any good except me," Brusiloff insists, his words emerging from the dense undergrowth of his beard: "Sovietski—yah! Nastikoff—bah! I spit me of zem all. No novelists any good except me. P. G. Wodehouse and Tolstoy not bad. Not good, but not bad. No novelists any good except me."[23] Courteously giving his creator pride of place over Tolstoy, Vladimir Brusiloff enshrines Wodehouse at the heart of world literature.

5. Arnold Bennett, *Riceyman Steps*

When Clarissa Dalloway ventured out to Bond Street on June 13, 1923, to buy the flowers for her party that evening, she was walking through a very different London than the one portrayed that year by Arnold Bennett in his masterpiece, *Riceyman Steps*. Bennett's novel won the important James Tait Black

Prize, which was awarded the next year to Woolf's friend E. M. Forster for *A Passage to India*. But the widely popular Bennett was a harder sell in the rarefied precincts of Bloomsbury. Looking back at Bennett's novel as she began *Mrs. Dalloway*, Woolf complained in a letter to a friend, "I have to read *Riceyman Steps* in order to consolidate a speech which I have to make, and I'm drowned in despair already. Such dishwater! Pale thin fluid in which (perhaps, but I doubt it), a leg of mutton once swam."[24]

Woolf was put off not just by Bennett's straightforward style but by the social themes he developed in working-class settings. The difference between the books is well conveyed by the covers of my paperback copies (Figure 3). The Harcourt edition of *Mrs. Dalloway* shows a meditative, psychologically fraught Clarissa choosing her roses, with a ghostly figure faintly visible at her chest that suggests her early almost-lover Sally Seton. By contrast, Penguin's *Riceyman Steps* shows a bustling scene in the neighborhood where the novel is set, with modest houses and shops in the foreground and the imposing bell tower of the St. Pancras railway station shimmering on the horizon.

The speech that Woolf was writing became her essay "Mr. Bennett and

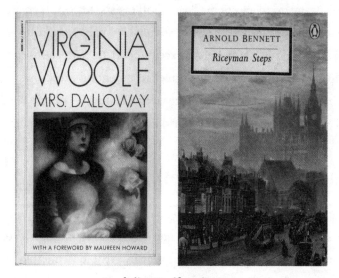

3. Symbolist Woolf, realist Bennett

Mrs. Brown," in which she makes her case against her older rivals Bennett, H. G. Wells, and John Galsworthy. She takes them as the leading representatives of commercial middlebrow fiction, purveying tales of social strife with too little attention to depth of character or perfection of style. Her irritation against Bennett in particular had been sparked by a review essay, "Is the Novel Decaying?," that he'd written in March of 1923 on the rising generation of modernists. There, he singled out Woolf for condescending praise:

> I have seldom read a cleverer book than Virginia Woolf's *Jacob's Room*, a
> novel which has made a great stir in a small world. It is packed and bursting
> with originality, and it is exquisitely written. But the characters do not
> vitally survive in the mind, because the author has been obsessed by details
> of originality and cleverness. I regard this book as characteristic of the new
> novelists who have recently gained the attention of the alert and the curious;
> and I admit that for myself I cannot yet descry any coming big novelists.[25]

In her essay, Woolf engineered one of the most devastating take-downs in the history of modern literature. She recounts a train ride in which she observes a modest little working-class woman, whom she names "Mrs. Brown," whose thoughts and troubles she begins to imagine for us. (In view of her scorn for Conan Doyle, it is ironic that she unfolds Mrs. Brown's life story with an altogether Sherlockian attention to suggestive details.) Her theme is that Bennett and company are too concerned with preaching about social issues to give us a living portrait of such a person, "to realize her character, to steep oneself in her atmosphere." Worse still, on closing one of their novels, "it seems necessary to do something—to join a society or, more desperately, to write a cheque. That done, the restlessness is laid, the book finished; it can be put upon the shelf, and need never be read again." By contrast, a great work such as *Tristram Shandy* or *Pride and Prejudice* "is complete in itself; it is self-contained; it leaves one with no desire to do anything, except indeed to read the book again, and to understand it better."[26]

So successful was Woolf's attack that Bennett's stock plummeted on the critical market, and even in the book trade. As I write, the highest price listed on abebooks.com for a first edition of *Mrs. Dalloway*, with the dust jacket designed by her sister, Vanessa, is £39,500 (or $56,671, plus $35 for shipping to the U.S.). For *Riceyman Steps*? Top price: £532 ($763), barely 1 percent of Woolf's. Or suppose you want the novel that to me is his other greatest work, *Clayhanger*. Top price for the first edition? £25 ($35). Published in 1910—sadly, just before human character changed "on or about December, 1910," according to Woolf's famous pronouncement in her essay—it is the first novel ever written, so far as I know, about the degenerative disease that Alois Alzheimer had first diagnosed in 1907. And Bennett isn't just illustrating some medical problem; he gives a penetrating psychological portrait of the shifting power relations between young Clayhanger and his father, as the patriarch succumbs to the inexorable progress of the disease.

Set in 1919, *Riceyman Steps* is a deeply moving study of the corrosive effect of miserliness on a lower-middle-class husband and wife, counterpointed against the struggles of their loyal servant Elsie to make do as she tries to deal with her husband, who has returned from the Great War in a state of shell shock. This of course is the very theme that Woolf takes up in *Mrs. Dalloway* through the shell-shocked Septimus Warren Smith and his war bride, Rezia, in terms far closer to Bennett's than you'd have guessed from her essay.

Woolf's world is chock-a-block with artists and aesthetes, from the abstract painter Lily Briscoe and the poet Augustus Carmichael in *To the Lighthouse* to the gender-shifting Orlando who takes 300 years to write his / her masterpiece. Bennett turned out his fiction with clockwork regularity, and his world isn't that of artists but of the commercial life around them. Clayhanger's father is involved with books, not as an author but as the founder of his town's first steam-powered printing shop; *Riceyman Steps'* miserly protagonist, Henry Earlforward, owns a dusty second-hand bookstore in Clerkenwell, a London neighborhood of small manufacturing, distilleries, and printing shops. Physical constraints dominate the novel, from the pinched conditions of the used-book trade to the uterine fibroids that assail Henry's wife, Violet.

When we explore literary London, we are really entering a series of Londons, constructed on different principles and with differing materials. These Londons are often at war with each other, though sometimes they overlap more than the combatants themselves would like to admit. We need multiple Londons to help us deal with the shell shock induced by diseases, wars, and warring voices today. We also need multiple cities, countries, languages. Our next stop will be Paris, but actually we're already there. Bennett had lived in Paris periodically since 1903, and the troubled marriage at the heart of *Riceyman Steps* may reflect the recent collapse of his marriage to his French wife. He'd long been a devotee of French literature; as he wrote in 1898, "it seems to me that only within the last few years have we absorbed from France that passion for the artistic shapely presentation of truth, and that feeling for words as words, which animated Flaubert, the Goncourts, and Maupassant."[27] The shapely presentation of truth, and of fiction and outright lies, has never been more brilliantly conveyed than in the words of Marcel Proust, who will provide our point of entry into Paris.

CHAPTER TWO

Paris: Writers' Paradise

6. Marcel Proust, *In Search of Lost Time*

So many writers have immortalized Paris—and Paris has immortalized so many writers—that no one writer can loom as large as Dickens in London, Joyce in Dublin, or Murasaki Shikibu in Kyoto. But for me, Paris is Proust, and I'm hardly alone. Any number of books seek to bring us back into Proust's world, with period photos of streetscapes and portraits of the "real" people behind Proust's characters. My favorite in the "Proust's Paris" genre is an album whose cover shows a dashing young Marcel—the actual one, not the fictional one—pretending to serenade a young lady friend, his tennis racquet serving as a guitar (Figure 4).

If Proust's *recherche du temps perdu* recovered lost time for him, it now has the power to recover his life and times for us. And so we can buy a coffee-table book that pairs passages from Proust with photographs by the Parisian flâneur Eugène Atget, and imagine ourselves there. The impulse to seek out "the originals" of Proust's locales is so powerful that his family's summer town of Illiers, the model for the novel's Combray, has actually been renamed "Illiers-Combray." Yet we shouldn't forget that all these locales, and the people and things that populate them, have been transmuted into something far richer and more evocative than they'd originally been. After World War I broke out,

4. Paris recovered

Proust moved Combray away from the region of Illiers, so as to put the town in the path of combat. Or consider the famous "petite madeleine," whose taste sets in motion Marcel's quest in search of lost time:

> Many years had elapsed during which nothing of Combray, save what lay in the theatre and the drama of my going to bed there, had any existence for me, when one day in winter, on my return home, my mother, seeing that I was cold, offered me some tea, a thing I did not ordinarily take. I declined at first, and then, for no particular reason, changed my mind. She sent out for one of those squat, plump little cakes called "petites madeleines," which look as though they had been moulded in the fluted value of a scallop shell. And soon, mechanically, dispirited after a dreary day with the prospect of a depressing morrow, I raised to my lips a spoonful of the tea in which I had soaked a morsel of the cake. No sooner had the warm liquid mixed with the crumbs touched my palate than a shiver ran through me and I stopped,

intent upon the extraordinary thing that was happening to me. An exquisite pleasure had invaded my senses, something isolated, detached, with no suggestion of its origin . . . I had ceased now to feel mediocre, contingent, mortal. Whence could it have come to me, this all-powerful joy?[1]

Appropriately, this scene reappeared in April 2020 in a Covid-inspired podcast, "Quarantine Quill: Daily Writing Prompts for Our Pandemic Times," hosted by Anna Polonyi of the Paris Institute for Critical Thinking. Episode 26 is called "Reclaiming the Physical and Proust's Tea-Soaked Madeleine."[2] Polonyi reads the famous passage and talks about the importance of retaining our connection to the physical world, then prompts her listeners to write a description of how things taste.

And yet that emblematic moment of reflective sensuality is not what Proust himself experienced. An evidently factual version of the moment appears at the beginning of his early essay "Contre Sainte-Beuve," in which he argued that writers should go deeper than surface observations of the social world. In this first version of the revelatory moment, Proust's cook (not his mother) brings him an ordinary cup of tea, not an elegant lime-blossom *tisane*, into which he dips . . . a *piece of toast*: "and at the moment when I put the piece of toast in my mouth and when I had the sensation of its softness penetrated with the flavor of tea against my palate, I had a feeling of trouble, of the scene of geraniums, of orange trees, a sensation of extraordinary light, of joy . . ."[3] We can see the essence of Proust's art in the transformation of a dry slice of *pain grillé* into the luminous, moist, feminine *petite madeleine*, around whose shape, flavor, and history he will weave an entire web of associations.

Yet the profound distance between Proust's lived experience and his novel's artistry doesn't mean that we're wrong to counterpoint Proust's fictional Paris with the real one, or Combray with Illiers, so long as we don't insist on a direct, literal correspondence. In the final paragraphs of *Swann's Way*, the first volume of the *Recherche*, an older Marcel returns to Paris's Bois du Boulogne, where he is chagrined to find no traces of Odette de Crécy and the other elegant ladies who used to promenade there in his youth. "Alas!" he exclaims, "there was nothing now but motor-cars driven each by a moustached mechanic, with a tall footman towering by his side" (576). In the volume's closing lines, he concludes:

> The places we have known do not belong only to the world of space on which we map them for our own convenience. They were only a thin slice, held between the contiguous impressions that composed our life at that time; the memory of a particular image is but regret for a particular moment; and houses, roads, avenues are as fugitive, alas, as the years. (579–80)

Marcel, however, is wrong, though it will take him more than two thousand pages to realize his mistake. But we can already glimpse his error, if we know that the late love of Proust's life was his chauffeur and secretary, Alfred Agostinelli. In 1913 Agostinelli typed out the manuscript of *Swann's Way* for publication, but soon afterward he tore himself away and left for the south of France. He started taking flying lessons, but then died in a tragic accident—if it was an accident. He had registered for his lessons under the name "Marcel Swann."

In his melancholy visit to the Bois du Boulogne, the fictional Marcel has no idea that in the very moment when he longs for a vision of his first erotic attachment, his author's lost love is standing in front of him, ready to transport him away.

At the end of his long quest, in *Time Regained* Marcel remarks that "the true paradises are the paradises that we have lost."[4] Paris has been a paradise for generations of writers, though often it's a paradise they've gained after losing their early illusions or their actual homeland. And yet, as we'll see in the coming selections, they can find themselves again in a Paris regained as they follow in the doubled footsteps of Marcel Proust and of Proust's Marcel.

7. Djuna Barnes, *Nightwood*

When Arnold Bennett moved to Paris in 1903 he settled in the Montparnasse neighborhood, where you couldn't throw a brioche without hitting an avant-garde painter or writer. Gertrude Stein arrived that same year, settling across the river in the Rive Gauche; Picasso had moved up from Barcelona three years earlier. In the years that followed, many more came from around the world, including James Joyce in 1920, Djuna Barnes and Ernest Hemingway in 1921, the Guatemalan surrealist (and future Nobel laureate) Miguel Ángel Asturias in 1923, the Senegalese poet and future prime minister Léopold Sédar Senghor in 1928—the list goes on and on. Some were fleeing political oppression or merely provincial stagnation, others were looking for artistic inspiration or simply for cheap rents. Still others were drawn by bohemian freedoms from normative gender roles, including Gertrude Stein and the playwright Natalie Barney, both of whom established long-running artistic salons.

Few of these new arrivals were more adventurous, sexually and artistically, than Djuna Barnes. Born in 1892 in upstate New York, she had established herself in Greenwich Village as a writer, illustrator, and journalist. Her quirky, probing interviews featured such varied personalities as Coco Chanel, the evangelist Billy Sunday, and a female gorilla at the Bronx Zoo. Throughout the 1920s she was a prominent member of the Parisian expatriate artworld, and her drawings include edgy portraits of both Stein and Joyce (Figure 5).

Like Proust's *Recherche*, *Nightwood* is a highly autobiographical work. It is built around Barnes's tortuous love affair with the American sculptor and silverpoint artist Thelma Wood. She appears in the novel under the name of Robin Vote, while Barnes becomes Robin's lover, Nora Flood, who hopes to recreate in Paris the "paupers' salon" she'd hosted in America "for poets, radicals, beggars, artists, and people in love."[5] Their relationship itself is described in artistic terms: "In Nora's heart lay the fossil of Robin, intaglio of her identity, and about it for its maintenance ran Nora's blood" (80).

5. *Djuna Barnes, portraits of Stein and Joyce*

Very different in tone from Hemingway's nostalgic *A Moveable Feast*, Barnes's masterpiece gives a darkly ironic portrayal of the Left Bank's louche denizens, most of them castaways from emotional shipwrecks elsewhere. Robin and Nora become involved with a displaced Viennese aesthete and self-styled Baron, Felix Volkbein, who frequents a ragtag circus run by the sexually ambiguous Frau Mann. At the center of the novel is the Irish-American Doctor Matthew O'Connor, an unlicensed abortionist, a kleptomaniac, a cross-dresser, and an inveterate talker. The other characters turn to him for advice on their always failing love lives, and long stretches of the novel take the form of Matthew's cascading monologues. As he says, "the Irish may be as common as whale-shit—excuse me—on the bottom of the sea—forgive me—but they do have imagination" (53). Yet as he later warns one of his listeners, "I have a narrative, but you will be put to it to find it" (122).

Barnes struggled to shape her experience into a form that could embody her restless, directionless life. She gradually found her narrative by rewriting the works of her older contemporaries, especially Proust and Joyce. Felix Volkbein, eternal Wandering Jew and art collector, is a cross between Joyce's Leopold Bloom and Proust's Charles Swann, while the aging medical student and compulsive talker Matthew O'Connor is part Buck Mulligan and part Baron de Charlus. In place of Proust's drama of recovered memory, Barnes stages the predicament of people who can't forget the traumas that eat away at them. After Robin has definitively left Nora after many infidelities, Nora despairs that they couldn't manage to have "forgotten our lives in the extremity of memory, moulted our parts, as figures in the waxworks are moulted down to their story, so we would have broken down to our love" (185).

Barnes directly evokes Proust's novel, via its English title, when Matthew remarks:

The wise men say that the remembrance of things past is all that we have for a future, and am I to blame if I've turned up this time as I shouldn't have been, when it was a high soprano I wanted, and deep corn curls to my bum, with a womb as big as the king's kettle, and a bosom as high as the bowsprit of a fishing schooner? And what do I get but a face on me like an old child's bottom—is that a happiness, do you think? (115)

As Matthew says of Jenny Petherbridge, yet another woman whom Robin has abandoned: "Looking at her quarters with harrowing, indelicate cries; burying her middle at both ends, searching the world for the path back to what she wanted once and long ago! The memory past, and only by a coincidence, a wind, the flutter of a leaf, a surge of tremendous recollection goes through her, and swooning she knows it gone" (151).

Proust's Marcel triumphantly recovers lost time by reconstructing the vast structure of recollection. Barnes gives us a far more fragmented world and a far more tenuous tale. In place of Proust's luminous optical metaphors (the magic lantern, the kaleidoscope, the magnifying glass with which we can look into our hearts), Barnes's characters seek to pierce the night "with the great blind searchlight of the heart" (118). Speaking of Robin, who has abandoned him after the failure of their tumultuous marriage, Felix Volkbein says, "The more we learn of a person, the less we know" (137). Barnes's Paris is populated by damaged souls who never learn their lesson.

But that's also their greatest virtue, if they can come to accept who they are and embrace the fallen world as it is. The sole legacy of Felix and Robin's relationship is Guido, an autistic child whom Matthew O'Connor diagnoses as "maladjusted." But he adds: "Wait! I am not using that word in the derogatory sense at all: in fact my great virtue is that I never use the derogatory in the usual sense" (142). As he concludes late in the novel, "So I, Doctor O'Connor, say, creep by, softly, softly, and don't learn anything because it's always learned of another person's body" (173). A halfway house for the lost souls of "the lost generation," Paris is equally a place of memory and forgetting, a haunt for haunted storytellers.

8. Marguerite Duras, *The Lover*

Few Parisian writers were more creatively haunted by early trauma than Marguerite Duras, as she reworked the story of her transgressive love affair as a fifteen-year-old in colonial Vietnam. Born Marguerite Donnadieu in 1914 in what was then French Indochina, she grew up in a family at the low end of the expatriate social scale. Her widowed mother struggled to make ends meet for herself and her three children, their financial situation vastly worsened by a failed venture to start a rice plantation. Marguerite began a lifelong process of reinvention after she escaped to Paris for college in 1931. She shifted her studies from mathematics to law, and changed her name to that of her deceased father's village, and she began to make her way as a writer. After war broke out, she worked in Paris for the Vichy government, but she and her husband, Robert Antelme, secretly joined the Communist Party and the Resistance; he was arrested in 1944, and barely survived imprisonment in Buchenwald and Dachau. The marriage didn't survive.

During the war years Duras began to process her memories of growing up in an abusive household, where her mother and older brother regularly and viciously beat her, and where she found a glimmer of life beyond the family in a love affair with an older Oriental man. After her death in 1996, a wartime notebook was found among her papers, giving a seventy-page account of her childhood and adolescence. This account is evidently as factual as Proust's toast-in-tea anecdote in *Contre Sainte-Beuve*, and it enables us to trace the transformations that eventually led to her most famous work, *L'Amant* (*The Lover*), which won the 1984 Goncourt Prize. The novel's strongly autobiographical dimension is signaled by the frequent use of an early photograph of Duras herself on its cover. This photograph in turn became the model for the portrait of the unnamed heroine of the 1992 film version directed by Jean-Jacques Annaud, ambiguously played by Jane March, whose mother was of Vietnamese and Chinese heritage (Figure 6).

Yet *The Lover* is a work of fiction, and it wasn't even the first fictional version of Duras's early years. In 1950 she'd published *Un Barrage contre le Pacifique* (*The Sea Wall*), which tells the story of her interracial love affair at age fifteen, counterpointed against her mother's attempts to protect her rice fields from flooding seawater. Nor was *The Lover* the last version of the story. Duras was an accomplished playwright and screenwriter (best known for her screenplay for Alain Resnais's *Hiroshima, Mon Amour*), and she drafted the screenplay for the film version of *L'Amant*, but she withdrew from the project after disputes with Annaud. Displeased by his romanticized and eroticized version, she then rewrote her screenplay as *The North China Lover* (1991). So *The Lover* is one layer in a decades-long palimpsest, in which we can trace the fortunes of the fifteen-year-old girl, the thirty-year-old who wrote her

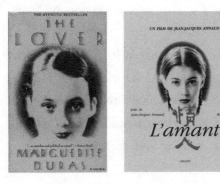

6. *Duras becomes her heroine*

33

wartime journal, and the middle-aged and then aging novelist. Already the opening paragraph of *The Lover* focuses on the passage of time inscribed on the narrator's body: "One day, I was already old, in the entrance of a public place a man came up to me. He introduced himself and said, 'I've known you for years. Everyone says you were beautiful when you were young, but I want to tell you I think you're more beautiful now than then. Rather than your face as a young woman, I prefer your face as it is now. Ravaged.'"[6]

In her wartime memoir Duras focuses largely on her mother, who is often depressed and who communes nightly with her dead husband, who tells her how to build the hopeless dikes against the ocean. Duras is unsparing in describing her mother's violence: "Since I was the smallest of her children and the easiest to control, I was the one Mama beat the most. She used to hit me with a stick and easily sent me spinning." Then her older brother got into the act: "Through some strange rivalry, he picked up the habit of beating me as well. The only question became who would beat me first."[7] Even so, Duras remembers her mother fondly, even with admiration: "She beat hard, she slaved hard, she was profoundly good, she was made for tempestuous destinies, for hacking her way in exploration through the world of emotions . . . My mother dreamed the way I have never seen anyone dream" (25–6).

As for her lover, Léo, he is the son of a wealthy Vietnamese landowner, and he approaches her when she is still only fourteen. Her mother welcomes the relationship for its financial benefits, always on the condition that Marguerite never actually sleep with him. Duras describes Léo as kind but ugly and unintelligent ("Léo was perfectly laughable and that pained me deeply"), and she mentions that "I only slept with him once and after two years of pleading" (26–7). In *The Sea Wall*, Léo has become "Monsieur Jo," son of a wealthy white planter. The story changed further in *The Lover*: now unnamed, the lover is Chinese, placing him socially above the actual Huynh Thuy Le, but well below the romanticized Monsieur Jo. He and the narrator engage in a passionate but emotionally distanced affair, making love daily in the secluded studio that he uses for his assignations. Now it isn't the mother but the Oedipally jealous brother who is the prime agent of abuse.

At several points in *The Lover*, Duras explicitly corrects the account she'd given in *The Sea Wall*: "So you see it wasn't in the bar at Réam, as I wrote, that I met the rich man with the black limousine, it was after we left the land by the dike, two or three years after, on the ferry, the day I'm telling you about, in that light of haze and heat" (27). The new version now becomes a work of historical fiction, as the aging author intersperses the Indochinese story with scenes set in wartime and postwar Paris:

> I see the war as I see my childhood. I see wartime and the reign of my elder
> brother as one . . . I see the war as like him, spreading everywhere, breaking
> in everywhere, stealing, imprisoning, always there, merged and mingled
> with everything, present in the body, in the mind, awake and asleep, all the
> time, a prey to the intoxicating passion of occupying that delightful territory,
> a child's body, the bodies of those less strong, of conquered peoples. Because
> evil is there, at the gates, against the skin. (62–3)

Strikingly, she now finds a deep connection between her youthful trauma and the war. "The story of my life doesn't exist," the narrator tells us at the outset. "There's never any center to it. No path, no line" (8). But we might also say that the story never ceases to exist, always coming to life in new forms. Even more fragmented and ambiguous than Djuna Barnes's *Nightwood*, Duras's lyrical palimpsest isn't so much a recovery as a rewriting of lost time. Political and erotic transgressions intertwine in this hallucinatory novel, as Duras rediscovers herself as a daughter, a lover, and a writer amid the Nazi occupation of Paris.

9. Julio Cortázar, *The End of the Game*

If Paris provided Marguerite Duras with the chance to endlessly rewrite her life story, Julio Cortázar found in Paris the place where he could rewrite everyone else. Born like Duras in 1914, he emigrated to Paris in 1951, after a series of attempts to establish himself as a jazz musician and as a writer in Buenos Aires. He went on to publish dozens of works, including novels, story collections, poetry, travelogues, and two volumes of essays and reviews published under the resonant title *La vuelta al día en ochenta mundos*—*Around the Day in Eighty Worlds*. He also made significant translations into Spanish, including *Robinson Crusoe*, the tales of Edgar Allan Poe, and Marguerite Yourcenar's *Memoirs of Hadrian*. Here I want to focus on his breakthrough story "Axolotl," which opens his first collection, *Final del Juego* (*The End of the Game*). This story stages Cortázar's discovery of his path as a writer in a very specific Parisian locale: in the 5th Arrondissement, in the spring of 1951, in an exhibition hall of the Jardin des Plantes.

To locate "Axolotl" squarely in the time and place of its composition doesn't mean reducing Cortázar to a merely French writer, much less an *almost* French writer—a grateful immigrant whose chief value is his testimony to the glory of the *ville lumière*. This is the impression given by a writer in *Le Monde*, in an article written in 2013 for the fiftieth anniversary of Cortázar's masterpiece, *Rayuela* (*Hopscotch*). He declares that the novel "is certainly one of the most beautiful homages ever made by an Argentine to the French capital," but he regrets that no streets have been named after Cortázar; "City Hall seems unaware of how many readers of *Rayuela* crisscross the city carrying in their head a sentimental map made of the itineraries taken by its characters."[8]

We may wonder just how many tourists are wandering around Paris, like some Hispanic Emma Bovarys, seeking to realize *Rayuela*'s map in their heads, and it isn't clear that the book's motley crew of low-life types really offer such a *bel hommage* to their adoptive city, which is only one of the transatlantic poles of Cortázar's hopscotching novel. Yet the Parisian setting is central to "Axolotl." The story's autobiographical narrator loves to bike over to the city's great botanical garden, to commune with the lions and panthers kept at the garden's Ménagerie. Here, he finds one day that the lions are gloomy and his favorite panther is asleep. On a whim, he heads into the aquarium building, where he becomes transfixed by the unwavering gaze of a tiny axolotl, a Mexican species of salamander. Returning repeatedly to commune with the "Aztec" axolotl, the narrator ends up becoming one with the little creature, trapped within the aquarium. In the story's final lines, either the narrator or the axolotl consoles himself that "he" who is now outside may one day write "all this about axolotls."[9]

"Axolotl" resonates with Ovid's *Metamorphoses* and with Kafka's *Metamorphosis*, and also with Dante; the axolotls float eternally in a "liquid inferno." A central reference is to Rainer Maria Rilke's poem "The Panther," also set in the Jardin des Plantes, where the poet takes inspiration from the panther's elemental force, expressed in the caged animal's gaze:

> His gaze, grown weary from the shifting bars
> passing back and forth, takes nothing in.
> There seem to him to be a thousand bars,
> and in behind the thousand bars, no world.

In Rilke's brilliant image, the spiritual power of the restlessly pacing panther is so great that it seems to be the bars that move back and forth. In the poem's final quatrain, the panther becomes an image of the modern poet, with his gaze theatricalized:

> Just now and then his eyelids' curtain lifts
> in silence; then an image enters in,
> goes through the tensile stillness of the limbs,
> and vanishes within the heart.[10]

Far less majestic than Rilke's panther, the uncanny little axolotl sucks the writer / viewer into its liquid inferno. Has the displaced Argentine writer been consumed by the greater force of European literature, reduced to endlessly rewriting his metropolitan predecessors?

The anxiety of rewriting a European predecessor is the central issue of another breakthrough Argentine story, published a dozen years earlier: "Pierre Menard, autor del Quijote," the first of Jorge Luis Borges's great *ficciones*. Hoping to become a modern Cervantes, the provincial French writer Pierre Menard considers converting to Catholicism, becoming fluent in sixteenth-century Castilian, forgetting the intervening centuries of European history, and in short, to "*be* Miguel de Cervantes."[11] He discards this plan as too easy, opting instead to try rewriting Cervantes while remaining himself. He produces fragments that are identical to passages in the *Quixote* but now have radically different meaning as his own production. Across the distance of 300 years, Borges's narrator declares, "The Cervantes text and the Menard text are verbally identical, but the second is almost infinitely richer" (94).

Going beyond Borges, in "Axolotl" Cortázar mobilizes not just one classic text but the entire European tradition from Ovid to Kafka, in order to free himself from the patron to whom he owed the greatest artistic and practical debts: Borges himself. As the story proceeds, the enigmatic axolotls start to sound notably Borgesian: "Obscurely I seemed to understand their secret will, to abolish space and time with an indifferent immobility" (5–6). The axolotls transfix him with a gaze that is strikingly described as *blind*: "Above all else, their eyes obsessed me . . . Their blind gaze, the diminutive gold disc without expression and nonetheless terribly shining, went through me like a message" (7) (Figure 7).

Cortázar had been writing in Buenos Aires for years without publishing, not wanting to appear before the public until he'd found his own voice. In 1949, he finally had his first mature work published: a closet drama entitled *Los Reyes*, a poetic meditation on the Minotaur in the Cretan labyrinth. The mentor

7. *"Their eyes obsessed me"*

who gave this work to the world was none other than Borges, who published it in a Buenos Aires journal. In the same year, Borges also published his collection *El Aleph*, which upstaged Cortázar with his own meditation on the Minotaur's labyrinth, "La casa de Asterión." Two years later Cortázar emigrated to Paris, and beginning with "Axolotl" he gradually made a path of his own through the Borgesian labyrinth. At the end of the story the narrator declares: "I am an axolotl for good now . . . And in this final solitude to which he no longer comes, I console myself by thinking that perhaps he is going to write a story about us, that, believing he's making up a story, he's going to write all this about axolotls."

These words can be compared to the ending of Borges's famous short parable "Borges y Yo" ("Borges and I"), written four years later, in which Borges expresses his uncertainty whether he or the figure named "Borges" is now writing his stories: "I am not sure which of us it is that's writing this page."[12] In questioning his authorial identity, Borges may also be expressing an ambivalence toward his growing influence on younger writers whose *beaux hommages* were threatening to upstage him by 1955, the year in which his blindness became complete. Which of the two writers is rewriting which? Perhaps both fictions could be given a common title: "Axolotl y Yo."

The multiplying reversals between consumer and consumed—narrator and axolotl, Kafka and Rilke, Paris and Buenos Aires, Borges and Cortázar—play out a shifting figure/ground reversal of the home and the world. Even when an epidemic limits our ability to hopscotch between home and anywhere else, we can both lose and find ourselves, like Cortázar, in the many worlds that may enter into a single short story. The world in a grain of sand, as William Blake would say; or in an aquarium, in the Jardin des Plantes, in the spring of 1951.

10. Georges Perec, *W, or the Memory of Childhood*

Fleeing rising anti-Semitism in Poland in the 1920s, Perec's grandparents brought their respective families to Paris. They settled in a largely Jewish working-class neighborhood, where Perec's parents, Icek and Cyrla, met and married. Cyrla started a hairdressing salon, while Icek worked as a foundryman; their son, Georges, was born in 1936. The young family's new life didn't last long. Icek enlisted in the French army when war broke out, joining via the Foreign Legion as he still had Polish citizenship; he was killed in action in 1940. Cyrla managed to get her son taken into hiding by the Red Cross before she was deported to Auschwitz, where she was murdered. Young Georges spent the war years being shuttled about in a series of safe houses; he was adopted by an aunt and uncle when the war ended. He excelled in school and earned a degree in sociology at the Sorbonne, then took a job as an archivist in a science library and began writing on the weekends.

Perec had early international success with a prize-winning novel, *Les Choses* (*Things*), which he described as "a sociology of the quotidian," in which his characters are dominated by the material objects around them. He then began *Un homme qui dort* (*A Man Asleep*)—his title taken from Proust—in which he went a step beyond Julio Cortázar by rewriting Borges by *not* rewriting him. As he told an interviewer, "Obviously, my aim is not to rewrite *Don Quixote*, like Borges's Pierre Menard, but I do want, for instance, to remake my favorite Melville story, 'Bartleby the Scrivener' . . . to write it again, not as a pastiche but to make another one, really the same 'Bartleby,' but a little more . . . as if I had invented it myself."[13] The result was a text made up almost entirely of quotations from other writers, including Proust, Borges, Melville, Dante, and many more. As he wrote while struggling to complete the book: "Only complete discontinuity—fragments—can save me! But it bugs me! It bugs me!"[14]

Perec joined an avant-garde group of writers and mathematicians who met together under the name "Oulipo," short for "Ouvroir de littérature potentielle" (Workshop of Potential Literature). Founded in 1960 by the former surrealist Raymond Queneau, the group sought compositional models in mathematics and games, and Perec began to bring "complete discontinuity" under control through rigorous constraints. His magnum opus, *La Vie mode d'emploi* (*Life: A User's Manual*, 1978), employs an elaborate system of preset devices, as we skip around the ninety-nine rooms of a Parisian boarding house using the moves of a knight in chess. Another novel, *La Disparition* (brilliantly translated by Gilbert Adair as *A Void*), is written entirely without the most common letter in the alphabet, the letter "e." A plaque on a square named for him honors this achievement:

PLAC

G ORG S

P R C

CRIVAIN FRANÇAIS 1936–1982

He followed this tour de force with *Les Revenentes*, a novella written using *only* words with the vowel "e."

Perec set most of his works in Paris, always approaching his city from unusual angles. In *An Attempt at Exhausting a Place in Paris* (1975), he describes everything he sees during a few days sitting in the little square between the Église de Saint-Sulpice and the Café de la Mairie—the very café, I'm pleased to say, that Doctor Matthew O'Connor loved to haunt in *Nightwood*. Perec meticulously describes everything from pigeons to passersby to the weather: everything, he said, that artists and writers had always left out of their portrayals of Paris. That same year, he published his remarkable *W, or the Memory of*

Childhood. This work consists of alternating chapters that seem radically different in kind. Italicized chapters describe a utopian community located on "W," an island off the coast of Tierra del Fuego, where life is organized around an endless series of Olympic-style games. In between these chapters come sober autobiographical chapters in which Perec tries to remember his parents and his wartime childhood.

The utopia of W is both Olympian and Oulipian, with competitions between the island's four towns rigorously organized along mathematical lines. By contrast, as Perec says in a prefatory note, the autobiographical chapters constitute "a fragmentary tale of a wartime childhood, a tale lacking in exploits and memories, made up of scattered oddments, gaps, lapses, doubts, guesses and meagre anecdotes."[15] Far from performing a Proustian recovery of time past, Perec asserts that "I have no childhood memories" (6). The book is dotted with expressions such as "a hazy recollection" and "I have no visual memory of it." Like Duras in *The Lover*, he tries to prompt his memory by scrutinizing the few photographs that have survived from his early years, but we aren't shown the photographs, and they never lead to any definite understanding.

The book is pregnant with meaning, but we have to construct it ourselves, filling in the gaps as best we can and reflecting on the interplay between the autobiography and the island tale. Perec says that "W" is based on a fantasy that he'd spun out when the war ended, but what begins as a wishful child's tale soon grows dark. The island's ideology rewards only victory ("All hail to the victorious! Woe betide the vanquished," 89), and the many losers are punished in ever more horrible ways. Their fates are governed by a Kafkaesque legal system: "The Law is implacable, but the Law is unpredictable. The Law must be known by all, but the Law cannot be known" (117). Children are brought up in a communal dormitory behind electrified barbed wire. Most girl babies are killed, while those who are allowed to grow up participate only in one kind of competition, the Atlantiads, in which they are pursued by men and then raped.

In the penultimate autobiographical chapter, Perec recalls being brought back to Paris after Liberation, at age nine. He can no longer recall Liberation, but he does remember being taken to an exhibit on the Nazi concentration camps. Now he finally has a clear memory, not of an event but of a photograph: "I remember the photographs of the walls of the gas chambers showing scratchmarks made by the victims' fingernails, and a set of chessmen made from bits of bread" (158).

Perec once described himself as "a man of letters," referring to his continual play with the alphabet. In one passage in *W*, he dissects the letter "W" (pronounced *double-vé* in French) as the sign of doubleness, then offers a meditation on the transformations that can turn a V into an X (when it's mirrored vertically) as well as a W (when it's doubled horizontally). The X in turn can be extended or redoubled, both into the Nazi swastika and into the Star of David. In Perec's *W*, the *double-vé* becomes a doubled life—a *double-vie*, we might say. His book connects fantasy and autobiography, playtime and the Holocaust, Paris and Auschwitz, the life he had and the life his mother lost. "She saw the country of her birth again before she died," Perec comments. "She died without understanding" (33).

As it happens, the country of Cyrla's birth is also where my great-great-grandfather Leopold was born, but that's a story for another day—and for our next chapter.

CHAPTER THREE

Kraków: After Auschwitz

11. Primo Levi, *The Periodic Table*

I went to Kraków several years ago to give a talk at the annual Conrad Festival there, and it would be natural to suppose that he must have been a native son. Yet he wasn't born in Kraków, never wrote about the city, and lived there only for a few years as an adolescent before he ran away to join the French merchant marine, long before he finally became a writer in his third or fourth language, English. He was never even a Polish citizen, as he was born under the Russian Empire and eventually took British citizenship. But even as writers can invent imaginary worlds, cities can create an imagined literary heritage, and Conrad's fame as a world author has made him a good choice for their international festival.

In coming to Poland, I was retracing a key part of my own heritage. My great-great-grandfather Leopold Damrosch was born in 1832 in Poznań, 300 miles northwest of Kraków. He too was never a Polish citizen; he was a German Jew in what was then a Prussian dependency. He lived in Posen, as the Germans called the city, until he left for Berlin in 1850. He became Liszt's first violinist and later came back to Wrocław, halfway between Poznań and Kraków, to conduct the city's orchestra, before emigrating to New York to further his conducting career after a hoped-for post in Vienna went instead to Anton

Rubinstein. He spoke of America as "das Land der Zukunft" (the land of the future), and so it was for his family. Less so for Leopold himself: he died at age fifty-two of pneumonia brought on by overwork while conducting a full season at the newly founded Metropolitan Opera, where he introduced the work of his friend Richard Wagner—interestingly, together with Fromental Halévy's opera *La Juive*. A portrait published when he died shows a heartbroken Muse holding his violin, its strings broken (Figure 8).

During my stay in Poland, I couldn't help imagining what it would have been like if he'd never left. What if I'd grown up in postwar Poznań, eating sausages instead of Big Macs, and reading Conrad in Polish translation? I knew, of course, that if Leopold had stayed, he'd have had an entirely different line of descendants, but my father was named after him, and as I walked through Leopold's former neighborhoods, it was tempting to imagine this alternative history.

8. Puck *magazine portrait of Leopold (1885)*

9. Poznań old town, 2013

But then, when my hosts were driving me to Kraków, we passed the town of Oświęcim: Auschwitz. If the Damrosches had never left, that is where we would have ended up.

10. Auschwitz gate, 1948

A flood of Holocaust testimonies began to appear soon after the war ended, often blending memoir and fiction. Primo Levi's *The Periodic Table* (1975) is just such a work. As with Marguerite Duras's multiple rewritings of her Indochinese years, Levi kept returning to the year of his imprisonment in 1944–5, seeking new ways to record and make sense of his experience. In 1947 he published *Se questo è un uomo* (*If This Is a Man*, also translated as *Survival at Auschwitz*), then revised it in 1958. This was followed by *The Reawakening* (1965), describing his roundabout and painful return to Italy, then by *The Periodic Table* and two novels and a steady output of poetry and short stories. Finally came *The Drowned and the Saved* in the year before his death in 1987—by accident? by suicide?—from a fall down the stairwell of his building.

Levi was a chemist, but *If This Is a Man* already shows a highly literary sensibility. In the most famous chapter, "The Canto of Ulysses," as Levi walks with a friend to get the day's soup for their barracks, he begins reciting what he can recall of the *Inferno*'s twenty-sixth canto. There Dante and Virgil meet Ulysses, who describes his fatal quest for knowledge beyond the known world, until he drowns after his ship passes beyond the Straits of Gibraltar. Levi takes comfort in his ability to remember many lines of the canto, and he's grateful for his friend's willingness to listen to his interpretation:

> it is vitally necessary and urgent that he listen, that he understand this "as pleased Another" before it is too late; tomorrow he or I might be dead, or we might never see each other again, I must tell him, I must explain to him about the Middle Ages, about the so human and so necessary and yet unexpected anachronism, but still more, something gigantic that I myself have only just seen, in a flash of intuition, perhaps the reason for our fate, for our being here today...[1]

Literature provides a lifeline to the prisoners' humanity. As he remarks, "precisely because the Lager was a great machine to reduce us to beasts, we must not become beasts; that even in this place one can survive, and therefore one must want to survive, to tell the story, to bear witness; and that to survive we must force ourselves to save at least the skeleton, the scaffolding, the form of civilization" (39).

Levi finds in Dante's epic more than an experience of reading: it is a spur to writing, to tell his story and bear witness. Yet in his late essay collection *The Drowned and the Saved*, rereading his chapter on Ulysses written forty years before, he gives a measured, even melancholy, account: "Culture was useful to me. Not always, at times perhaps by subterranean and unforeseen paths, but it served me well, and perhaps it saved me." The repetition of "perhaps" in this sentence is telling. Significantly, he adds that equally valuable in Auschwitz was "the help I got from my trade as a chemist." He says that his scientific training had given him "an ill-defined patrimony of mental habits," above all "the habit of never remaining indifferent to the individuals that chance brings before me. They are human beings but also 'samples,' specimens in a sealed envelope to be identified, analyzed, and weighed."[2]

Levi's blending of moral passion and meticulous observation reaches its height in *The Periodic Table*. Each of its essay-stories centers on a chemical element he'd dealt with during his career. Levi describes each element with precision and also a kind of personified human interest, and he connects each to an episode from his life before, during, or after Auschwitz. What mathematics was for Perec, chemistry was for Levi, a way of ordering the nearly inexpressible. Until I reread the book for this project, I'd forgotten that it bears a striking resemblance to Perec's *W*, coincidentally published in the same year. At the center of *The Periodic Table*'s memoir-essays are two short stories, printed in italics like the tales of Perec's dystopian island. The second of these tales, "Mercury," actually describes an imaginary Desolation Island, complete with a sketched map. "The loneliest island in the world,"[3] Desolation Island becomes the scene for a drama of abandonment and infidelity, then a recovery of new life and a combinatory redistribution of men and women, in a redeemed version of the fascistic sexual politics on Perec's "W."

In a subsequent chapter, "Chromium," Levi describes recording his wartime experiences in the months following his return from Auschwitz, at the same time as he is untangling a German company's falsification of records of adulterated chemicals shipped to his firm. He works through the problem by "drawing on good inorganic chemistry, that distant Cartesian island, a lost paradise for us organic chemists" (157). In the book's final chapter, "Carbon," Levi goes farther back into his past, again resembling Perec revisiting his childhood fantasy of W. Levi says that his "first literary dream" had been to write a tale of the transformations of an atom of carbon as it would voyage from the earth through the air, going around the world not once but three times and then ending up in the writer's own brain. Levi now retells this unwritten tale, and in the book's concluding sentence, the carbon molecule guides "this hand of mine to impress on the paper this dot, here, this one" (233). Brought to life in literature, the atom of carbon, building block of all earthly life, is transformed into the period that ends *The Periodic Table*.

12. Franz Kafka, *The Metamorphosis and Other Stories*

Perec's Auschwitz-based "W" was governed by Kafkaesque laws, at once implacable and arbitrary. Along with Dante, Kafka is a prime source text for both Perec and Levi, as his works have become deeply linked to the events they seem in retrospect already to have experienced. What does it mean to read Kafka in a post-Auschwitz world? Whereas Duras, Perec, and Levi repeatedly rewrote their early lives, with Kafka we have a writer who constantly envisioned his death. Throughout his oeuvre, one authorial stand-in after another dies, from Georg Bendemann sentenced to death by his father in "The Judgment" and Gregor Samsa expiring—to his family's relief—at the end of *The Metamorphosis*, all the way to Josephine the Singer in Kafka's final story, completed shortly before his own death in June 1924. If Kafka's collected works were murder mysteries, the only question would be: Who *didn't* do it?

None of these deaths is caused by the Nazis, whose rise to power was just a gleam in Hitler's eye when Kafka died. Kafka's work was marked by the rising anti-Semitism in his lifetime, but this element coexists in his work with dynamics within his family and his own psyche. As he mordantly remarked in his *Diary*, "What have I in common with the Jews? I have hardly anything in common with myself."[4] After Auschwitz, however, it is impossible to read his works without an intense awareness of where Europe's cultural-political trends were soon to lead. Kafka's older sisters Elli and Valli were deported to the Łódź ghetto, where they died. His favorite sister, Ottilie, was sent to Theresienstadt, and then in October 1943 she volunteered to accompany a transport of children to Auschwitz, where they were all murdered two days after their arrival.

As Walter Benjamin remarked in his essay "The Storyteller," "Death is the sanction of everything that the storyteller can tell . . . The nature of the character in a novel cannot be presented any better than is done in this statement, which says that the 'meaning' of his life is revealed only in his death."[5] For Benjamin, this is a positive thing: "What draws the reader to the novel is the hope of warming his shivering life with a death he reads about." Yet how much warmth can we draw from all those deaths in Kafka's work, when we read him in the aftermath of the deaths that Ottilie and 1,300,000 others suffered in Auschwitz alone?

As in Primo Levi, we can find in Kafka a multifaceted accounting of the forces that can shatter a family, a nation, a civilization, but these destructive forces are countered by moments of clear vision, of humanity, and of ironic humor that can give strength even in terrible circumstances. In 1910 Kafka put the onus on the repressive, two-dimensional father in "The Judgment," but he rapidly expanded his focus and deepened his understanding. In *The Metamorphosis* (1915) Gregor Samsa suffers from his family's dependence on his income, but he also assumes a quasi-dictatorial role in the household. He resents having to take on the responsibility of paying down his father's business debt— *Schuld*, in German, which also means "guilt." His sudden transformation into the famous "gigantic vermin" lets him turn his back on the family, but it also becomes a way to reinforce his centrality in the household, where everyone has to tiptoe around, not daring to confront him.

The entire episode may reflect a mental breakdown, but it can also be a wish-fulfillment dream, in a story marked by a dreamlike warping of time. This possibility is raised, with Kafka's characteristic irony, by Gregor's very denial: "It was no dream."[6] Gregor is less an innocent victim than a frustrated tyrant. Already before his transformation, he intends to play the lordly gift-giver by sending his sister to music school, that classic route to upward mobility for assimilated Jews like my great-great-grandfather—never mind that she is hopelessly incompetent as a violinist. Even after Auschwitz, we should remember that when Kafka read the story aloud to his friends, he had to pause several times, overcome with laughter. To paraphrase Oscar Wilde on Dickens, one of Kafka's favorite authors: One would need a heart of stone to read the death of little Gregor without laughing.

In Kafka's emblematic story "In the Penal Colony" (1914), a prisoner is condemned to be executed by a machine that tattoos his punishment on his back. The victim will be enlightened at the very moment of death, and then the machine will hurl his corpse into a pit, as the presiding officer proudly explains to the visiting narrator. Many commentators have very reasonably seen this horrific machine as a prophecy of what Primo Levi calls the "complex machinery" of the extermination camp system. Yet "In the Penal Colony" doesn't tell a simplistic story of victimizer and victim. Certainly the hapless prisoner, unjustly condemned by arbitrary authority, is another version of Kafka's semi-autobiographical Georg, Gregor, and Joseph K. Yet the "traveling researcher" (*Forschungsreisender*) is another stand-in for our author. An outsider who is studying penal colonies, he is someone who can't be caught up too deeply into the action or even be blamed for his inaction when he doesn't intervene. Yet again, the real artist is the colonial officer, proud architect and operator of the murderous machine. He is devoted to his elaborate tattoo-machine even if the results—like modernist narratives—are incomprehensible to the ordinary viewer or reader. In a culminating irony, the machine ends up murdering its maker, who suicidally takes the prisoner's place, a denouement that intimately links officer, prisoner, and visitor. And what of us readers? Can we find an alternative to the characters' options of victimhood, complicity, or flight?

Kafka's final story, "Josephine the Singer, or the Mouse Folk," written as he was dying of tuberculosis, represents his most profound statement on art in dangerous times. Josephine gathers her people around her to inspire them with her songs, but these gatherings also make it easier for their enemies to find the mice and fall upon them. She believes that she comforts her people with her glorious songs, but perhaps she only annoys them with her pitiful "piping." At the end, Josephine disappears; has she died, or has she deserted her people? As Hamlet might say, "the rest is silence," though in Josephine's case it isn't clear whether she was making any audible sounds to begin with. As the—devoted? hostile?—narrator concludes:

> So perhaps we shall not miss so very much after all, while Josephine, for her part, delivered from earthly afflictions, which however to her mind are the privilege of chosen spirits, will happily lose herself in the countless throng of the heroes of our people, and soon, since we are no historians, will be accorded the heightened relief of being forgotten along with all her brethren. (281)

What might have seemed somewhat baroque artistic parables in the 1920s gained a new realism with the war, and they found a worldwide audience soon afterward. Memory and forgetting, speech and silence intertwine in Kafka's work and in the increasing throng of writers who have followed his vanishing footsteps. What Dante was to Primo Levi, Kafka became for Paul Celan.

13. Paul Celan, *Poems*

Like Kafka, Celan was born in a doubly minor community, among the German-speaking Jews in Cernăuți / Czernowicz in the short-lived Kingdom of Romania created as part of the breakup of the Austro-Hungarian Empire at the end of World War I. Like Kafka, Celan had an intense interest in a Hebrew and Yiddish heritage from which he was significantly estranged, and again like Kafka, his primary loyalty remained to the German language and literary tradition, even as he learned the languages of the wider community: Czech in Kafka's case, Russian and Romanian for Celan.

Celan discovered Kafka while still a student and aspiring poet in the 1930s, before leaving for an abortive course of medical studies in France in 1938. Returning to Czernowicz in 1939, he began studying literature, until his community's life was overturned by the Nazi takeover. His parents were deported in June 1942; his father died of typhus in a labor camp, and his mother was shot. Celan was desolated by their deaths, and he was afflicted with guilt at not having persuaded them to go into hiding with him. Celan himself was soon rounded up, and he survived a year and a half in a labor camp until the Russians drove out the Nazis in 1944. He spent two years in Bucharest, and translated several of Kafka's stories and parables into Romanian, at a time when Kafka was only just beginning to be known anywhere. In 1947 the Communists came to power and Celan moved to Paris, where he worked as a translator and composed his increasingly influential poetry.

As his translator John Felstiner has remarked, Celan's oeuvre can well be described in terms of Kafka's statement about his own writerly predicament. German-Jewish writers, he told his friend Max Brod, "live beset by three impossibilities: the impossibility of not writing, the impossibility of writing in German, and the impossibility of writing differently, and we could add a fourth impossibility: the impossibility of writing at all."[7] During the war years Celan wrote "Todesfüge" ("Death Fugue"), one of the earliest and most famous of all poetic responses to the Holocaust. Primo Levi—who also translated Kafka—said that "I carry this poem inside me like a virus."[8]

> Black milk of daybreak we drink it at evening
> we drink it at midday and morning we drink it at night
> we drink and we drink
> we shovel a grave in the air where you won't lie too cramped

The poem ends with Death, "a Master from Germany," shooting a woman:

> he shoots you with shot made of lead shoots you level and true
> a man lives in the house your goldenes Haar Margarete
> he looses his hounds on us grants us a grave in the air
> he plays with his vipers and daydreams der Tod ist ein
>   Meister aus Deutschland
>
> dein goldenes Haar Margarete
> dein aschenes Haar Sulamith[9]

Here Celan's murdered mother, Fritzi, is doubly reborn, both as the betrayed heroine of Goethe's *Faust* and as the bride of the Song of Songs—a resonant biblical poem for many Jewish artists. My great-great-grandfather Leopold, in fact, had composed a choral piece based on it. The great painter Anselm Kiefer has used the concluding lines of "Todesfüge" to title a pair of stark paintings, in which the golden hair mingles with barbed wire. He has regularly returned to Celan, as in his vast painting, six feet high by fifteen feet wide, *Für Paul Celan: Aschenblüme* (ash-flowers, Figure 11), in which the corpses of burned books lie amid the stubble in a desolate landscape.

11. Anselm Kiefer, Für Paul Celan: Aschenblüme *(2006, detail)*

Celan increasingly pared down his verses to a state approaching silence. His late poems can be compared to Samuel Beckett's late writings, and more immediately to the haunting and haunted poetry of his friend Nelly Sachs. She'd fled with her mother to Sweden when the Nazis came to power; she won the Nobel Prize in 1966 for her poetry centered on wartime trauma. As she wrote to Celan in 1959: "Between Paris and Stockholm runs the meridian of pain and of comfort."[10] The next year, Celan gave the title "The Meridian" to his speech accepting a major award, the Büchner Prize. There he describes poetry as "a counter-word, a word that snaps the 'wire,' a word that no longer bows to 'history's loiterers and parade-horses,' it is an act of freedom. It is a step."[11] In a poem dedicated to Sachs, "Zürich, at the Stork" (1963), he recalled their conversations once they finally met after years of corresponding:

> Our talk was of your God, I spoke
> against him, I let the heart
> I had
> hope:
> for
> his highest, death-rattled, his
> wrangling word— (141)

Celan's late poems, like Sachs's, are both stripped bare and yet endlessly resonant:

> The shofar-place
> deep in the glowing
> text-void
> at torch height
> in the timehole:
>
> hear deep in
> with your mouth. (360–61)

In the German, Celan's invented word "text-void" (*Leertext*) plays on *Lehrtext*, "teaching text," used especially for Bible study.

Increasingly beset by depression, Celan was hospitalized several times before he drowned himself in the Seine in 1970, at age fifty. Yet to the end, his poems remained luminous. On receiving a prize in 1958, Celan said that following the horrors of the war,

> Reachable, near and not lost, there remained in the midst of the losses one thing: language. It, the language, remained, not lost, yes, in spite of everything. But it had to pass through its own answerlessness, pass through frightful muting, pass through the thousand darknesses of deathbringing speech. It passed through and gave back no words for that which happened; yet it passed through this happening. Passed through and could come to light again, "enriched" by all this. (395)

14. Czesław Miłosz, *Selected and Last Poems, 1931–2004*

As the Nazis hastily prepared to withdraw from Kraków in January 1945, they set up an extensive set of demolition charges, but at the last moment the general countermanded the order, and so the old center of town looks today much as it did in the late nineteenth century. This quality of the city, at once time-bound and timeless, suited Czesław Miłosz when he settled in Kraków toward the end of his long life. His poetry both reflects and transcends his personal experience and the times he lived through. Born in Lithuania in 1911, he began publishing poetry in 1931, and he was still publishing significant poems seventy years later, before his death at age ninety-three in 2004. His extraordinary literary longevity is probably matched, among our eighty authors, only by P. G. Wodehouse—a conjunction that isn't entirely inappropriate, as both writers spent much of their lives recreating a vanished world.

Growing up during the troubled interwar years, Miłosz became part of a group of poets in Vilnius who went by the name of "Catastrophists." Like Kafka, they could see what was coming. In "Six Lectures in Verse" (1985), Miłosz recalls his young self, "different, alien . . . a judge, observer," adding: "Thus the sickliness of adolescence / Divines the sickness of an era / That will not end well."[12] The Catastrophists' mentor was a pessimistic philosopher, Marian Zdziechowski (1861–1938), who'd moved to Vilnius after twenty years teaching at Kraków's Jagiellonian University. In a late poem, "Zdziechowski," Miłosz envisions him in those long-ago years:

> Here he walks to class on the streets of Kraków.
> With him his contemporaries: tulle, velvet, satin
> Touch the bodies of women that are like slender stalks
> Of the perverse flora of Art Nouveau.
> Glances and calls from inside the night.

He recalls meeting Zdziechowski not long before his death in 1938: "In a city taken from the Bolsheviks by the Polish cavalry, you waited, aware of 'the approaching end.' / . . . You died just in time, your friends whispered."[13]

Miłosz himself nearly died in the bombardment of Warsaw, but after a long trek southward on foot, he and his wife managed to take refuge in a village outside Kraków. After the war, he worked in Warsaw and served in the Polish diplomatic service, until the increasingly repressive Communist regime grew suspicious of his cosmopolitanism and his lack of devotion to the cause (though a socialist at that time, Miłosz was never a communist). In 1951 he went into exile in Paris, where he wrote *The Captive Mind*, a dissection of totalitarianism. From the 1950s through the 1970s his works were banned in Poland and were known only to a small number of admirers elsewhere. In 1960 he moved to Berkeley, California, where he taught Slavic literature for nearly three decades. When he was awarded the Nobel Prize in 1980, some of his colleagues learned for the first time that he also wrote poetry. He became an international celebrity and a public figure back in Poland, meeting with the Polish-born Pope

John Paul II and with Lech Wałęsa, and began dividing the year between Berke-ley and Kraków, where he settled permanently in 2000.

During his decades of exile, unable to return either to Poland or to Lithuania, he became centrally concerned with the problem of memory. In a moving poem, "On Parting with My Wife, Janina," written upon her death in 1986, he asks:

> How to resist nothingness? What power
>
> Preserves what once was, if memory does not last?
>
> For I remember little. I remember so very little.[14]

In his book-length poem *A Treatise on Poetry* (1957), he recalls Kraków's lit-erati, noting the loss of names that even he doesn't record:

> Kraków was tiny as a painted egg
>
> Just taken from a pot of dye on Easter.
>
> In their black capes poets strolled the streets.
>
> Nobody remembers their names today,
>
> And yet their hands were real once,
>
> And their cufflinks gleamed above a table.[15]

A quarter century later, in "Six Lectures in Verse" (1985), he names one very modest victim of the destruction of Warsaw:

> Still in my mind trying to save Miss Jadwiga,
>
> A little hunchback, librarian by profession,
>
> Who perished in the shelter of an apartment house
>
> That was considered safe but toppled down.
>
> And no one was able to dig through the slabs of wall,
>
> Though knocking and voices were heard for many days.
>
> So a name is lost for ages, forever,
>
> No one will ever know about her last hours.

He sets this memory against broad generalizations about history and fate:

> History is not, as Marx told us, anti-nature,
> And if a goddess, a goddess of blind fate.
> The little skeleton of Miss Jadwiga, the spot
> Where her heart was pulsating. This only
> I set against necessity, law, theory.[16]

Miłosz's final poems look back at the world from the threshold of the grave. "A Ninety-year-old Poet Signing His Books" (2002) begins on a note of comic triumph: "And so, after all, I've outlasted you, my enemies!" But the poet realizes that he can't take credit for having been saved from Auschwitz and from the Soviet gulag: "I don't see in this any merit of mine. / Providence shelters dimwits and artists." He realizes that "Now, in old age, I stand before witnesses / Who to the living are already unseen."[17]

Unusually among major modern writers, Miłosz was a religious thinker. He was ambiguously but powerfully connected to Catholicism, and to visionary poetic predecessors from Dante to William Blake. In his late poems he looks ahead to his imminent death with calm irony and a very tentative hope for a life to come. "Even if illusion / Unites us in this belief in life eternal, / We, dust, give thanks for the miracle of faithful dust."[18] Miłosz wasn't convinced that the world is ruled by a just God rather than by some more demonic force, but he retained a faith that, whatever else, this divinity must be a lover of poetry. In "Heavenly," a poem written at age ninety-two, he hopes that in heaven, like Socrates, he will

> be able to keep doing what I started on earth.
> That is, to strive unceasingly, to be striving itself,
> and never have my fill of touching
> the shimmering weave on the loom of the world.[19]

15. Olga Tokarczuk, *Flights*

Remarkably, Poland has been the homeland of no fewer than six Nobel laureates in literature. Four of the six, starting with Henryk Sienkiewicz in 1905, had close ties to Kraków, which has long been a cultural center rivaling or even surpassing Warsaw. The 1996 laureate Wisława Szymborska lived in Kraków from age eight until her death eighty years later, and as a student at Jagiellonian University, she became friends with Czesław Miłosz in 1945, the year she published her first poem. Today, Kraków is home to the Polish Book Institute, which encourages reading in Poland and promotes Polish writers abroad. The Institute has underwritten translations of a host of writers, including Szymborska, Miłosz, and Ryszard Kapuściński, and it helped fund Jennifer Croft's English translation of *Flights*. They awarded the result their "Found in Translation" prize in 2017, and the next year *Flights* won the Man Booker Prize in England, shortly followed by the Nobel for Tokarczuk in 2019 (awarded retroactively for 2018, after a year in which the Swedish Academy's deliberations were suspended during a scandal over sexual harassment). Following the award of the Nobel, more than 2,000 of Tokarczuk's readers lined up for a book signing at her publisher's offices in Kraków.

Flights is a particularly apt choice for our journey, as it could equally have been titled *Around the World in 116 Fragments*. The book's episodes range from a single sentence to thirty pages, many of them told by a narrator who travels incessantly. As she says, "my roots have always been shallow . . . I don't know how to germinate. I'm simply not in possession of that vegetable capacity."[20] Her entries form a kind of discontinuous travel diary, with reflections on luggage, on wi-fi, and on airport anomie. In one airport she sees an ad that she reproduces in Russian, and then translates for us: "Mobility is reality." She adds the deadpan comment: "Let us stress that it is merely an ad for mobile phones" (226).

Often our narrator describes chance encounters with people on airplanes and trains, and we get glimpses of their disordered lives. She is "drawn to all things spoiled, flawed, defective, broken," and to "anything that deviates from the norm" (17). Later she remarks: "Tales have a kind of inherent inertia that is never possible to fully control. They require people like me—insecure, indecisive, easily led astray. Naïve" (212). Unlike our eighty-book journey, her travels are decidedly not literary pilgrimages, which she mocks: "We know people who travel to Morocco through Bertolucci's films, to Dublin through Joyce, to Tibet through a film about the Dalai Lama. There is a certain well-known syndrome named after Stendhal in which one arrives in a place known from literature or art and experiences it so intensely that one grows weak or faints" (175). Her own travels aren't for the faint of heart: she visits medical museums around the world, where she is fascinated by the ways in which body parts are preserved and displayed. As she says at the first of these museums, "Each of my pilgrimages aims at some other pilgrim. In this case the pilgrim is in pieces, broken down" (19).

Stories are interspersed among the first-person narratives. One involves the chemical preservation of body parts. Another sequence involves letters written by a woman to the Holy Roman Emperor Francis II in 1796, begging him to return for burial the preserved corpse of her African father, which he'd stuffed and mounted in his cabinet of curiosities—an event that actually happened. A recurrent theme concerns people who deviate from their accustomed paths in life. A ferryboat operator can no longer stand the daily back-and-forth between the mainland and an island; he takes an entire load of passengers out to sea. Vacationing on the Croatian island of Vis in the Adriatic, a woman abandons her husband for two days, taking their toddler with her, then mysteriously reappears; unable to accept her vague explanations, the husband gradually descends into obsessive paranoia. *Flights* is furnished with several maps, but these never really orient us. The episode of the husband's search for his wife and child features a map that we'd assume shows the town where he's staying on the island (Figure 12). In actual fact, this is a detail of an old map of Saint Petersburg, and the water isn't the Adriatic Sea but the Neva River.

12. Faux-Adriatic Saint Petersburg (1850)

Yet the disorienting conjunctions invite us to begin the work of piecing together the narrative's body parts, as subtle connections are interwoven between history and fiction, myth and everyday reality, men and women, first- and third-person narratives. In her Nobel lecture, Tokarczuk gave eloquent expression to her view of literature's social importance:

> The world is a fabric we weave daily on the great looms of information, discussions, films, books, gossip, little anecdotes. Today the purview of these looms is enormous—thanks to the internet, almost everyone can take place in the process, taking responsibility and not, lovingly and hatefully, for better and for worse. When this story changes, so does the world. In this sense, the world is made of words.

She adds that tyrants and dictators have always known this, and that "he who has and weaves the story is in charge."[21]

Tokarczuk is a weaver of counter-narratives that resist easy closure, often involving alternative versions of the author herself. She is a committed vegetarian and an advocate for animal rights, but she hasn't gone as far as an angry character who is traveling the world to write a "Book of Infamy" of the mistreatment of animals by meat eaters. At the center of *Flights* is a story, itself entitled "Flights," in which a Russian woman, Annushka, lies awake at night, exhausted from the burden of caring for her disabled son and a shell-shocked veteran husband. "Over the world at night hell rises," the episode begins; "the nocturnal brain is a Penelope unraveling the cloth of meaning diligently woven during the day" (227). Annushka leaves home and rides the Moscow metro for days, then becomes homeless before eventually returning to her bleak apartment block. We don't know whether she goes back inside or not.

If Tokarczuk is a Penelope weaving her fragmentary narratives together, she is also a world-traveling Odysseus, whose voyages around the Mediterranean are shown in the novel's final map. In her Nobel speech, Tokarczuk says that

> All my life I've been fascinated by the systems of mutual connections and influences of which we are generally unaware, but which we discover by chance, as surprising coincidences or convergences of fate, all those bridges, nuts, bolts, welded joints and connectors that I followed in *Flights* . . . At base—as I am convinced—the writer's mind is a synthetic mind that doggedly gathers up all the tiny pieces in an attempt to stick them together again to create a universal whole.[22]

CHAPTER FOUR

Venice–Florence: Invisible Cities

16. Marco Polo, *The Travels*

Voyaging up the Adriatic from the island of Vis, we come to Venice, home to one of Olga Tokarczuk's greatest predecessors as a world traveler, Marco Polo. Venice has long been a home for many travelers and a destination for others. Late in *À la recherche du temps perdu*, Proust's Marcel is going to a party at the Parisian mansion of his friends the Guermantes, brooding about the many losses in his life and his inability to write. As he crosses the Guermantes' courtyard, he stumbles on a pair of uneven paving stones, and suddenly his mood changes: "Just as, at the moment when I tasted the madeleine, all anxiety about the future, all intellectual doubts had disappeared, so now those that a few seconds ago had assailed me on the subject of the reality of my literary gifts, the reality even of literature, were removed as if by magic."[1] The paving stones have brought about an involuntary recollection of his joy, years before, at visiting Saint Mark's Cathedral in Venice. Now, putting together this new recovery of time past with his early experience of the madeleine, he finally begins to see his way to the construction of his great "cathedral-novel." Like the young Marcel, I dreamed for years of visiting Venice, inspired both by its architecture and also by the depictions by writers ranging from Giacomo Casanova to John Ruskin to Proust. I'd taught the *Recherche* not long before I finally did get to Venice, and when I began to walk across the uneven paving stones of the cathedral's Baptistry, I actually did have an involuntary recollection of my own: a vivid memory of *reading* this passage in Proust.

The Venetians themselves have been great world travelers. None has been more influential than the merchant Marco Polo (1254–1324), whose book inspired Christopher Columbus to seek a westward route to Asia; he carried a copy with him on his epochal voyage in 1492. Fact and fiction intermingle in Polo's *Travels*. He'd voyaged along the Silk Road to Asia with his father and uncle in 1271 and had prolonged his travels for many years, entering the service of Kublai Khan, the Mongol emperor of China. When he finally returned to Venice in 1295, he brought back little material wealth but a vast trove of stories. There is no indication that he had any literary ambitions, but in 1298 he got caught up in a conflict between Venice and Genoa and was thrown into prison in Genoa. There he met a romance writer, Rustichello da Pisa, who knew good material when he heard it. He persuaded Polo to dictate his memoirs, and wrote them up in French, under the title *Livre des merveilles du monde* (Book of the Wonders of the World). The book circulated widely in manuscript— printing wouldn't be invented for another century and a half—and was translated into Latin as early as 1302. Soon cartographers were using Polo as a source for their maps.

Rustichello embellished Polo's stories to the point of inserting some episodes from romances of his own. Even apart from those additions, Polo's account is a remarkable mixture of first-hand observation, tall tales, and pure projection, as when he insists that Kublai Khan was "most desirous" to convert to Christianity. Here we can already see a major theme of the later literature of imperial conquest: the most enlightened natives are eager for Europeans to come and teach them the ways of truth. At the same time, Polo nonetheless records the Khan's rejection of an invitation: "On what grounds do you desire me to become a Christian?" Kublai asks Polo's father. "You see that the Christians who live in these parts are so ignorant that they accomplish nothing and are powerless."[2]

Polo himself is less interested in conversion than in commerce. With his merchant's eye, he is closely attentive to the workings of the salt trade, and we learn the cost of ducks in the Chinese capital (a bargain at six for the value of a Venetian groat). But we also hear of banquets where Kashmiri sorcerers send flagons of wine floating through the air to the emperor's hand. If the floating flagons would seem at home at Hogwarts, this is because J. K. Rowling is one of many writers who have mined Polo's *Travels* over the years. Coleridge's romantic fantasy of Xanadu conveys a radiant vision of Kubla Khan's stately pleasure-dome, set in a sexualized landscape complete with vast romantic chasm, bursting fountain, and dulcimer-playing damsel. Caught up in all this Oriental splendor, the poet will be transfigured: "Beware! Beware! / His flashing eyes, his floating hair! / . . . For he on honey-dew hath fed, / And drunk the milk of Paradise."[3]

"The milk of Paradise" is a transcendent image at the poem's end, a metaphor for the poetic imagination, but it originates in ethnographic fact: Marco Polo describes a ritual that the Khan would perform annually at Xanadu, scattering milk to the winds as an offering to the spirits guarding the land and its crops. Elsewhere Polo calls the capital Kin-sai a "heavenly city," though here he isn't referring to its spiritual qualities but to its many courtesans, who are "highly proficient and accomplished in the use of endearments and caresses, with words suited and adapted to every sort of person, so that foreigners who have once enjoyed them remain utterly beside themselves and so captivated by their sweetness and charm that they can never forget them" (216). Involuntary memories have a long history in world literature.

The most exotic journeys come to life when they're grounded in material reality: paradise is best supplied not with unheard-of elixirs but with milk. Yet the factual observations in the literature of travel are always filtered through the voyager's imagination, informed by the imaginative accounts the traveler already knows. Proust was guided through Venice by John Ruskin's *Stones of Venice*; Dante is guided through the Inferno by his great predecessor Virgil, whose own underworld account was informed by his master Homer. Traveling in this chapter from Venice to Florence and back—before we notionally leave Italy via the Aeroporto di Venezia–Marco Polo—we'll see how invisible cities become visible, and how visible cities become cathedral-novels, and in Dante's case the most sensuous of all heavenly visions.

17. Dante Alighieri, *The Divine Comedy*

We may think that it was only in modern times that cities began to be identified with prominent authors such as Charles Dickens, James Joyce, or Orhan Pamuk. The "national poet" was a nineteenth-century creation, and the celebrity author has become his contemporary heir. Yet as early as 1456, the Florentine painter Domenico di Michelino created his fresco *La commedia illumina Firenze*, "The *Commedia* illuminates Florence" (Figure 13). The fresco shows Dante proffering his poem to his city, enlightening its citizens about the Inferno that awaits the damned, and the upward trajectory of Mount Purgatory that will lead the good citizens of Florence up to heaven. But we can also take the painting's title in terms of the manuscript culture that hadn't yet been

13. Dante illuminating Florence (1456)

displaced by the movable type invented by Johannes Gutenberg half a dozen years before. Domenico's title reverses the usual relationship between text and illustration: rather than an illuminated manuscript furnished with scenes to illustrate the story, now Dante's great poem becomes the illumination of his city, making it visible to all the world. Domenico's painting further flatters his Florentine viewers, as we see from left to right the images of hell, purgatory, and . . . Florence itself, looking for all the world like the heavenly Jerusalem.

Like enlightenment, illumination is a visual as well as spiritual process, and travel writing has always had a major visual dimension. Dante's worldwide impact has much to do with his exceptional ability to make us *see* the vast underworld city of the Inferno and then Mount Purgatory and the ethereal realm of Paradise. Today, Dante's visualization of Hell is central to *Dante's Inferno*—the video game. The game's maker, Electronic Arts, commissioned designs from Wayne Barlowe, a writer and illustrator known for his fantasy work *Barlowe's Inferno* (1999). One admirer of both Dante and Barlowe wrote about this fruitful conjunction on a gaming website:

> Honestly, the attention to detail is simply fantastic. The walls made of trapped sinners, Minos shouting out verdicts in the background as you approach, the screams of sinners, a man calls out for Ulysses in the bowels of Charon's boat, the detailed backgrounds such as a giant skull spitting out the corpses of the damned at the start. It's simply on a massive, grand scale and if you've ever read Dante and lived to see his Hell brought to the big screen . . . you will NOT be disappointed playing this video game.[4]

As important as Dante's visual imagination is the soundscape of his endlessly resonant verses. Dante was creating a revolutionary new kind of Italian, seamlessly combining down-to-earth language and transcendent theological insight. He developed the project of creating a truly literary Italian in his treatise—written in Latin—*De vulgari eloquentia*. He probably composed this work sometime in 1302–5, after he was sent into exile following the defeat of

the "White Guelph" party to which he belonged, amid decades-long civil conflict in Florence. In *De vulgari* he makes the case for giving Italian the same
dignity accorded to Latin. This is a challenge not only because of the common-
ness of the "vulgar" language, but because there wasn't any such thing as "Italian." Instead, there were (and still are) a plethora of differing dialects; Dante
discusses fourteen, none free of faults to the poet's ear. He claims, for example,
that if the Genoese lost the ability to use the letter ʒ, they would be unable to
speak, "for ʒ forms the greater part of their vernacular, and it is, of course, a
letter that cannot be pronounced without considerable harshness."[5] (That said,
I'll admit that in my last book I cited an Italian critique of "la progressiva de-
nazionalizzazione del romanzo" purely for the pleasure of savoring four z's in
a single word.)

Interestingly, Dante doesn't see his own Tuscan dialect as superior to the
others. Though he declares that "I love Florence so much that, because I loved
her, I suffer exile unjustly," he asserts that his fellow Tuscans have been "rendered senseless by some aberration of their own," as they think theirs is the most
elegant dialect. The Tuscans are outstanding, he asserts, only in that they are
"the most notorious victims of this mental intoxication" (31). Dante's own poetry
will have to create the illustrious vernacular he seeks. The best way to appreciate
the force of his verses is simply to hear them in an eloquent performance.[6]

Here I'll give just one example of Dante's extraordinary ability to convey
profound emotion in a language of elevated simplicity. At the end of *Purgato-
rio*, Virgil can guide Dante no farther, as the precincts of heaven are closed to
even the most virtuous of pagans. Now it will be Dante's early love Beatrice
who will take him into paradise. When she appears in glory on the summit of
Mount Purgatory, Dante is overcome with the resurgence of his love for her.
He turns for comfort to Virgil, but finds him gone:

> volsimi a la sinistra col respitto
> col quale il fantolin corre a la mamma
> quando ha paura o quando elli è afflitto[7]

> I turned around and to my left, just as
> a little child will hurry to his mama
> whenever he's afraid or in distress

I don't believe that any poet before Dante could have used such homely terms—"fantolin" and, especially, "mamma"—with such serious force.

Losing Virgil as he has already lost Florence, Dante will regain his lost love Beatrice, but now on spiritual terms. And in new poetic terms, he will write the greatest of all responses to Virgil's *Aeneid*, incorporating the entire classical tradition and its reinvention in his time. All of us can read ourselves through reading Dante, much as he was doing with Virgil. Dante filled the Inferno with figures from classical antiquity and with many of his own former friends and enemies. Yet the *Commedia* isn't all about him. As Dante tells us in his opening line, he lost his way "Nel mezzo del cammin di *nostra* vita" (1:39)— in the midst of the path of *our* life. His hundred cantos offer us a gallery of cautionary and hopeful tales, landmarks from which we can plot the pathways of our own lives.

18. Giovanni Boccaccio, *The Decameron*

Among the first and greatest of the many writers who have been inspired to follow in Dante's footsteps was his fellow Florentine Giovanni Boccaccio (1313–75), who wrote an influential life of Dante not long after completing his *Decameron*. There he brought to Italian prose the range and depth that Dante had brought to verse, now with plague added to political unrest—an all too resonant combination as I write this entry in a disunited "United States" today.

In 1348, Boccaccio was working (when he had to) as a tax assessor in Florence, having drifted into law after giving up on his father's profession, banking. His real passion was writing, and he'd made a reputation as a poet and writer of prose romances, notably *Fiammetta* (1343), which has been described as the first psychological novel, based on his romance with a married

Neapolitan noblewoman. Writing in the first person after the end of the affair, Fiammetta tries to make sense of her infatuation with the seductive young Florentine. By 1348, at age thirty-five—Dante's age in 1300, when *The Divine Comedy* is set—Boccaccio was in the middle of his life's journey, ready for something new.

Then the Black Death came to Florence. The plague killed three quarters of the city's inhabitants, including Boccaccio's stepmother; his father died the next year. Boccaccio then began *The Decameron*. Together with Daniel Defoe's *Journal of the Plague Year* and Albert Camus's *La Peste*, Boccaccio's masterwork is regularly referenced today by people trying to make sense of the world turned upside down, and for good reason. Boccaccio begins his book with a harrowing account of the plague, with many details that seem taken from the pages of *The New York Times*. Between March and July, Boccaccio says, the plague killed 100,000 people in Florence. The plague often spread asymptomatically, and bodies piled up in the streets. Many Florentines turn to prayer, and some practice social distancing, while others throw caution to the winds, claiming "that an infallible way of warding off this appalling evil was to drink heavily, enjoy life to the full," and they try to "shrug the whole thing off as one enormous joke." The city closes its gates to outsiders, but the plague still spreads like wildfire, and before long "all respect for the laws of God and man had virtually broken down and been extinguished in our city."[8] Then as now, many wealthy citizens get out of town: "Some people callously maintained that there was no better or more efficacious remedy against a plague than to run away from it. Swayed by this argument, and sparing no thought for anyone but themselves, large numbers of men and women abandoned their city" (53). The poor, however, have nowhere else to go. "Being confined to their own parts of the city, they fell ill daily in their thousands, and since they had no one to assist them or attend to their needs, they inevitably perished almost without exception" (55).

These are moving words; but whose side is Boccaccio on? His seven

14. Illustration for The Decameron *(1903)*

noblewomen and three noblemen take the callous route, abandoning the city
to shelter in place at a country estate (Figure 14). In a strange anticipation of
today's two-week quarantines, they stay there for fourteen days, feasting and
telling stories, before they return home. Possibly the plague had started to di-
minish by then, but their expressed motive for returning is the fear that tongues
will wag if they stay away any longer: people in the city will wonder just what
the seven young beauties have been up to with the three guys in their luxurious
retreat. Perhaps our illustrator has had the same question: note the pair of bun-
nies he's placed in the foreground.

Boccaccio says that though his story begins with "the painful memory of
the deadly havoc wrought by the recent plague," what follows won't be "an
endless torrent of tears and suffering." He accounts for his disorienting shift
from tragedy to comedy by echoing the beginning of Dante's *Commedia*, in
which Dante finds himself lost in a dark wood at the base of a steep hill. Boccaccio reassures the "fairest ladies" who will be his readers: "You will be
affected no differently by this grim beginning than walkers confronted by a
steep and rugged hill, beyond which lies a beautiful and delectable plain." He
adds: "Believe me, if I could decently have taken you where I desire by some

other route, rather than along a path so difficult as this, I would gladly have done so" (49).

These lines recall Dante, but Boccaccio's pathway leads to a distinctly earthly paradise, and God himself is invoked for carnal purposes. In one tale, a clever woman bribes a greedy friar into unwittingly serving as her go-between with her lover. Enjoying each other "to the accompaniment of many a hilarious comment about the stupid friar's naïveté," the couple make love "until they very nearly died of bliss." The beautiful Filomena, who is telling this ribald tale, piously concludes: "I pray to God that in the bountifulness of His mercy He may soon conduct me, along with all other like-minded Christian souls, to a similar fate" (256). As Judith Serafini-Sauli has said, Boccaccio has replaced *The Divine Comedy* with a very human comedy of his own.[9]

Boccaccio concludes his massive compilation with an epilogue in which he gives ironic answers to the literary and moral objections that could be raised to his tales. He asserts that there is nothing improper in the use of such innocent terms as "*hole*, and *rod*, and *mortar*, and *pestle*, and *crumpet*, and *stuffing*" (829), and he notes that far more scandalous stories can be found in the sober Church chronicles. He's only telling the truth about human conduct, and he's being blamed "because in certain places I write the truth about the friars. But who cares?" He has no objection to being condemned as a writer of light, frivolous tales: "I assure those ladies who have never weighed me that I have little gravity. On the contrary, I am so light that I float on the surface of water" (832–3). This is hardly the whole truth, of course. After 800 pages devoted to liars and tricksters, we should know better than to believe our author when he denies any serious intent, any more than when he says that he just couldn't help introducing his collection with the horrors of the plague.

In fact, the two dimensions are deeply interconnected. In his preface, Boccaccio asserts that he had long suffered the fever of love, "whose warmth exceeded all others, and which had stood firm and unyielding against all the pressures of good intention, helpful advice, and the risk of danger and open scandal." But he finally recovered, "and thus what was once a source of pain has now become, having shed all discomfort, an abiding sensation of pleasure" (45). He has the antibodies, in other words. He can now aid new sufferers, helping them to understand "what should be avoided and likewise what should be pursued" (47). During his period of lovesickness, it was conversation that saved his life: "if ever anyone required or appreciated comfort, or indeed derived pleasure from it, I was that person . . . in my anguish I have on occasion derived much relief from the agreeable conversation and the admirable expressions of sympathy offered by friends, without which I am firmly convinced that I should have perished" (45).

Retelling the hundred tales enables Boccaccio to master his own losses, including that of his first love, "Fiammetta," whom he makes the "queen" of *The Decameron*'s fifth day, devoted to "the adventures of lovers who survived calamities or misfortunes and attained a state of happiness" (405). The tales' therapeutic effect is underwritten by their presentation: a regular dosage of ten tales per day, each day's tales linked by a common theme. Until I was preparing this entry, I'd forgotten that the friends even take two days off halfway through their storytelling sequence: as with any marathon, or any sixteen-week blog project, pacing is important. The hundred tales of *The Decameron* may be the world's first performance of a talking cure.

19. Donna Leon, *By Its Cover*

Literary pilgrims often seek out settings they've read about in a favorite author. The American crime-fiction writer Donna Leon lived in Venice for over thirty years, and made it the setting for her bestselling series featuring the reflective Commissario Guido Brunetti. I first encountered her work two decades ago when my wife and I rented an apartment along the Grand Canal, and we found a selection of her novels there. Somewhat alarmingly for Lori, an international lawyer, the one she picked up was *A Venetian Reckoning*, which opens with the death of an international lawyer. There is a limit to just how far one wants art to dovetail with life. Yet Donna Leon is a particularly good guide to her adoptive city, as she views it as both an insider and an outsider. Like Georges Perec's *An Attempt at Exhausting a Place in Paris*, her books reveal the everyday Venice that tourists never see, hidden in plain sight like Edgar Allan Poe's "Purloined Letter"—a story that Brunetti recalls having read.

Leon's Venice has a human scale and rhythm of life; in an essay on "My Venice," she extols the absence of automobiles in the city. In *By Its Cover*, no one uses any form of transportation in the entire first half of the novel; only then does Brunetti take a police boat when he's particularly pressed for time. The city he wanders through is a place of Proustian memories, with the difference that in Venice time past has never been lost:

> For Brunetti, springtime was a succession of scent memories: the lilacs in a courtyard over by Madonna dell'Orto; the bouquets of lily of the valley brought in by the old man from Mazzorbo, who each year sold them on the steps of the church of the Gesuiti . . . and the smell of fresh sweat from clean bodies pressed together on the now-crowded vaporetti, a welcome relief after a winter of the musty smell of jackets and coats worn too many times, sweaters unwashed for too long.[10]

In place of the rare experience of Marcel's evocative madeleines, Brunetti constantly encounters his favorite foods—the first softshell crabs of the year, a dish of fusilli with fresh tuna and capers and onions. Returning home late after a stressful investigation, he finds that his wife has left him a plate of quails, peas, and roasted new potatoes. As he gratefully reflects: "The woman might be a troublemaker, but she knew how to cook" (173).

Venice, however, is under threat. Bribery, corruption, and old patriarchal hierarchies hem the Venetians in on all sides. Officials extort bribes from casino owners who thereby avoid paying taxes; pedophile priests are quietly shuffled from one parish to another. Brunetti himself has experienced a degree of upward mobility, thanks to his good fortune in marrying Paola, daughter of a count and a contessa. But even after twenty years, his in-laws are only grudg-ingly beginning to accept him as one of the family, and his boss, the Vice-Questore, is enviously aware "that Brunetti had, by virtue of his marriage, slithered in among the nobility" (44).

Beset with internal problems, Venice is being overwhelmed by an external threat, which is invading the city much as the plague swept over Boccaccio's Florence. The modern plague is tourism. As the novel begins, Brunetti and a colleague are walking to a library from which rare books have been stolen. Suddenly they stop and gasp, "their human response to the otherworldly and impossible. Ahead of them was the stern of one of the newest, largest cruise ships. Its enormous rear end stared bluntly back at them, as if daring them to comment" (6). As Leon says in an essay entitled "Tourists,"

> They have, these countless millions, effectively destroyed the fabric of life
> known to the inhabitants of the city for a thousand years, have made life
> intolerable for residents for vast periods of the year, have led to the
> proliferation of shops that sell masks, plastic gondolas, tinted paper, sliced
> pizza, vulgar jester's hats, and ice cream, all but the last of which the
> residents do not want and no one on the planet needs.[11]

The internal and external threats reinforce each other, as the local officials are making money from their city's destruction. Outraged by the environmental degradation caused by the massive cruise ships, Brunetti reflects: "Weren't most of the men making these decisions Venetians? Hadn't they been born in the city? Weren't their children in the schools and university? They probably spoke Veneziano during their meetings" (9).

Ecological concerns increasingly figure in Leon's novels, and they can appear even in the description of a character: "She was tall and thin and, at first sight, had the look of one of those slender wading birds which were once so common in the *laguna*. Like theirs, her head was silver grey . . . Like those birds, she had broad black feet at the end of long legs" (17). The comedy of the description is shadowed by the undertone of loss of the wading birds that were *once* so common in the *laguna*.

By Its Cover dramatizes these concerns through the damage done to precious early printed books in the (fictional) Biblioteca Merula. Someone has been secretly tearing illustrations from old books—a process that Brunetti compares to rape. Particular damage has been done to a rare copy of *Delle navigationi et viaggi*, published in six volumes in the 1550s by Giovanni Battista Ramusio, "the greatest of printers of the greatest of printing cities" (31). Appropriately, Ramusio's compendium featured the first critical edition of Marco Polo's *Travels*, together with a set of Venetian accounts of travels to the Americas.

It turns out that the villain blends together the internal and external threats: he is an Italian who *pretends* to be a visiting American scholar. Discussing with Paola the violation of Italy's heritage—and a murder that ensues, almost as an afterthought—Brunetti alludes to Ray Bradbury's *Fahrenheit 451*, though, ironically, he can't recall the actual name of the book or its author. "If you get rid of all the books," he remarks, "you get rid of memory." His wife replies: "And culture, and ethics, and variety, and any argument that opposes what you choose to think" (115). Paola is a professor specializing in Henry James, and *By Its Cover* itself is an American woman's *Portrait of a Lady* in which old and new Italy, local and foreign characters, innocence and corruption, are deeply intertwined.

It is ironically appropriate that Donna Leon's own books now contribute to the very problems she dissects in them, as her readers flock to Venice to retrace Brunetti's footsteps and take selfies at the precinct house where he works—or where he would work, if he actually *existed*. Recommending one of the tours available for this purpose, *The Lonely Planet* informs us: "If you are a fan of Donna Leon and her mystery novels featuring Commissario Brunetti in Venice, you'll love this tour with a private guide who will take you to discover the most representative and fascinating sites of the series."[12] Righting this wrong is far beyond the Commissario's power, but there is one foreign visitor that can help: Covid-19. On the very day I wrote up this posting in June 2020, the front page of *The New York Times* featured an article on Venice. Its headline? "Picture Venice Bustling Again, Not with Tourists, but Italians: A Post-Pandemic Vision of What Could Be."[13]

I rest my case.

20. Italo Calvino, *Invisible Cities*

Invisible Cities forms a fitting frame to this chapter that began with Marco Polo. In his magical, unclassifiable book, Calvino imagines a series of contemplative conversations between Marco Polo and Kublai Khan in the emperor's twilit garden, during the years when Polo was (or claimed to have been) a roving ambassador for the Mongol emperor. He reports on the cities he has visited around China, describing them under headings such as "Cities and Signs," "Cities and Eyes," and "Cities and the Dead." The headings seem random at first, but if we look closely, we discover a subtle mathematical sequence. There are eleven headings in all, each of which appears five times, in a progressive spiral over the course of nine sections, on a pattern of *Cities and*: Memory 1, Memory 2, Desire 1, Memory 3, Desire 2, Signs 1, Memory 4, Desire 3, Signs 2, Thin Cities 1, and so on. Italicized dialogues between Marco Polo and Kublai Khan begin and end each section, in a version of the interweaving of the frame tale of Shahrazad and Shahryar with the stories she tells in *The Thousand and One Nights*.

Calvino had moved to Paris in 1967, and he soon became a member of the experimental "Oulipo" group that we've already encountered with Georges Perec. The mathematical structuring of *Invisible Cities* (1972) is classically Oulipian, but with a highly poetic cast. Each chapter is a gemlike prose poem describing an emblematic city, replete with imagery from Polo and from *The Thousand and One Nights*. Many of the cities are flagrantly fantastical locales. One city is made entirely of pipes and plumbing fixtures, in which nymphs bathe in the mornings. Another city is supported by a great net strung between

15. Karina Puente Frantzen, Valdrada City

two cliffs: "Suspended over the abyss, the life of Octavia's inhabitants is less uncertain than in other cities. They know the net will last only so long."[14]

The city of Valdrada is built alongside a lake, which mirrors it as Venice is mirrored in its lagoon and canals. Here Valdrada is shown as imagined by a Peruvian architect and illustrator, Karina Puente Frantzen (Figure 15). Interestingly, the image is subtly distorted, as the lower Valdrada doesn't actually reflect the upper one, or it does so in a kind of double mirroring: the reflected buildings on the lower left approximate those on the upper right, and the lower right roughly reflect those on the upper left.

Marco Polo tells Kublai Khan that

Valdrada's inhabitants know that each of their actions is, at once, that action and its mirror-image . . . Even when lovers twist their naked bodies, skin against skin, seeking the position that will give one the most pleasure in the other, even when murderers plunge the knife into the black veins of the neck and more clotted blood pours out the more they press the blade that slips between the tendons, it is not so much their copulating or murdering that matters as the copulating or murdering of the images, limpid and cold in the mirror.

He concludes: "The two Valdradas live for each other, their eyes interlocked; but there is no love between them" (53).

All the cities have women's names, and desire—mostly as envisioned by men—permeates them. Women lead pumas on leashes down the street; a group of men build a city inspired by a common dream of a naked woman fleeing them; lucky travelers can be invited to revel in odalisques' baths. We seem to be immersed in an Orientalist fantasy of Burtonian proportions, but then modern elements begin to crop up in this medieval landscape: dirigibles, radar antennae, skyscrapers. Modernity increasingly intrudes as the book progresses, and several of the later cities embody very contemporary problems, comparable to Donna Leon's ecological emphasis. One city is so overpopulated that no one can move an inch; another city is about to be crushed beneath the towering mountains of garbage cast up around it. By the book's end, New York and Washington DC (mentioned by name) have merged into a single "continuous city," as have Tokyo, Kyoto, and Osaka. Calvino's text crosses the borders between past and present, East and West, utopia and dystopia, viewing the modern world through multiple lenses of worlds elsewhere. As Calvino remarked in a discussion of the book, "The invisible cities [*città invisibili*] are a dream born in the heart of the unlivable cities [*città invivibili*], the continuous, uniform cities that keep on covering the globe."[15]

A true comparatist, Calvino's Marco never sees one city in isolation; all are linked in chains of signification and social meaning. He falls silent, though, when Kublai asks him if he has ever seen a city resembling the ancient Chinese capital of Kin-sai, which is notable for "the bridges arching over the canals, the princely palaces whose marble doorsteps were immersed in the water, the bustle of light craft zigzagging, driven by long oars, the boats unloading baskets of vegetables at the market squares, the balconies, platforms, domes, campaniles, island gardens glowing green in the lagoon's grayness" (85). As any Italian reader (and many a foreign tourist) would recognize, Kin-sai is a double of Venice. Marco insists that he's never seen any such place, but Kublai presses him, asking why he never speaks of his native city. "Marco smiled. 'What else do you believe I have been talking to you about?'" (86).

On the far side of the European imperial adventure, Xanadu and Kin-sai are no longer the exotic otherworlds where an Abyssinian damsel will captivate the traveler with her dulcimer, just as Abyssinia (Ethiopia) is no longer a colony of fascist Italy. Instead, Kublai's empire becomes an image of a post-imperial Europe: "an endless, formless ruin" (5), typified in Venice's tilting campaniles and slowly sinking palaces.

Marco's beloved city is crumbling even more swiftly in memory: "Memory's images, once they are fixed in words, are erased," he tells the Khan. "Perhaps I am afraid of losing Venice all at once, if I speak of it. Or perhaps, speaking of other cities, I have already lost it, little by little" (87). His loss, however, is his listener's gain: "Only in Marco Polo's accounts was Kublai Khan able to discern, through the walls and towers destined to crumble, the tracery of a pattern so subtle it could escape the termites' gnawing" (5–6).

Like Donna Leon's Venice, Calvino's cities are palimpsests, revealing hidden stories and layers of meaning for those who can discern the tracery of their subtle patterns. Venice is sinking, the ecosystem is collapsing, and violence is rising, but like Dante's *Commedia* and Boccaccio's *Decameron*, Calvino's novel offers us a pathway forward. More modest in scale than Dante's hundred cantos and Boccaccio's hundred tales, Calvino's nine sections are all the more carefully arranged, their ordered presentation set against the chaotic world they describe. As Marco tells Kublai Khan in the book's closing lines, with direct reference to Dante:

> The inferno of the living is not something that will be; if there is one, it is
> what is already here, the inferno where we live every day, that we form by

being together. There are two ways to escape suffering it. The first is easy for many: accept the inferno and become such a part of it that you can no longer see it. The second is risky and demands constant vigilance and apprehension: seek and learn to recognize who and what, in the midst of the inferno, are not inferno, then make them endure, give them space. (165)

CHAPTER FIVE

Cairo-Istanbul-Muscat: Stories within Stories

21. Love Songs of Ancient Egypt

Leaving Venice and journeying southeastward for three days, we come to Cairo, the first of a triad of Middle Eastern locales we'll visit in this chapter. Cairo must have been in Calvino's mind when he described his city of Eusapia. Loving life and fleeing care, the Eusapians have constructed a vast necropolis that mirrors their life above ground. The necropolis is furnished with "all the trades and professions of the living"—just as we see on the walls of Egyptian tombs and in the figurines buried there to supply the royal dead with *khet nefret nebet*—"every good thing." In Calvino's account, though, this artistic afterlife is a mixed blessing: "the Eusapia of the living has taken to copying its underground copy." It is even rumored that it was actually the dead who constructed the upper Eusapia in their own image, and "in the twin cities there is no longer any way of knowing who is alive and who is dead."[1]

Cairo is very much a double city in my experience, where you relish the treasures of the Egyptian Museum after the near-death experience of weaving through eight chaotic lanes of traffic to get there. For many years, I thought of Egypt as the timeless land of the transcendent art that I'd fallen in love with as a teenager at the Metropolitan Museum, just a few blocks away from my father's parish in those years. And in college I studied Middle Egyptian, not Arabic, and I had little awareness of contemporary Egyptian culture. But by the time I finally went to Cairo, to give a memorial lecture for my longtime Columbia colleague Edward Said, I had modern as well as ancient sites to visit. After exploring the great necropolis and pyramid complex at Sakkara on the edge of town, I sought out the narrow, bustling Midaq Alley, the setting for a novel of that name by Naguib Mahfouz. I then went for tea at el-Fishawy Café in the Khan el-Khalili souq, where Mahfouz used to write while drinking green tea (Figure 16).

The two Cairos could hardly be more different, but they are inseparably intertwined. Unlike Calvino's deathly Eusapia, though, it is liveliness that marks ancient and modern Egypt alike. The ancient Egyptians devoted so much attention to the afterlife because they never wanted the party to end. The vibrancy of their culture wasn't always perceived by the Orientalists who unearthed the papyrus scrolls placed in the tombs to entertain the dead and guide them in the afterlife. The compilation of spells gloomily known today as *The Book of the Dead* was actually titled *Sesh en Peret em Herew*, "The Book of Coming Forth by Day." The reliefs carved on tomb walls are filled with evocations of earthly life, and their artists took pleasure in capturing a fleeting

16. Morning in the Great Pyramid, afternoon at el-Fishawy

moment for all eternity. In a relief from the Fifth Dynasty, carved four and a half thousand years ago, a watchman and his guard baboon have caught a thief who is trying to steal some grain. Above the thief's head we see his plea to the guard: "YAH! Smite your baboon! Get the baboon off me!"

It was the several dozen surviving love poems that first drew me to Egyptian literature. These delightful lyrics, which are echoed in the biblical Song of Songs, are filled with evocations of the pleasures of love:

> Why need you hold converse with your heart?
> To embrace her is all my desire.
> As Amun lives, I come to you,
> my loincloth on my shoulder.[2]

In one poem, a woman declares that

> My heart remembers well your love.
> One half of my temple was combed,
> I came rushing to see you,
> and I forgot my hair. (305)

The poems were probably composed by men, but the ones in a woman's voice were likely sung by scantily clad women at banquets (Figure 17). In one poem, the speaker meets her handsome lover at the edge of the Nile, emblem of fertility and renewal:

> I found my lover at the ford,
> his feet set in the water;
> he builds a table there for feasts
> and sets it out with beer.
> He brings a blush to my skin
> for he is tall and lean. (324)

17. Egyptian musicians

The gods themselves underwrite the lovers' earthly passion. "I sail downstream in the ferry by the oarsman's stroke," one man declares,

> my bundle of reeds in my arms.
> I'll arrive at Memphis,
> and say to Ptah, Lord of Truth:
> Give me my girl tonight! (299)

These poems were placed in tombs in collections with titles like "The Poems of Great Delight." Clearly, you haven't lived until you've died in ancient Egypt.

Along with love poetry, ancient Egyptian literature includes a major body of wisdom literature and the earliest tales ever written. These include "The Story of the Shipwrecked Sailor" (c. 2000 B.C.E.), which has the first known use of nested tales. A commander is returning after an unsuccessful expedition up the Nile, deeply worried at the reception he'll get from the king. His lieutenant tells him not to worry, as things can always turn out better than expected; he proceeds to tell his tale of being shipwrecked on a distant island. There he meets a huge serpent, who reassures him: "Do not fear, do not fear, little one, do not turn pale. Indeed, God has allowed you to live. He has brought you here to this Island of the Ka, where there is nothing that is lacking" (50) (literally, "nothing that is not"—an intriguing assertion in a fictional work). The serpent then comforts the sailor by telling his *own* story of loss and recovery; this is now a story inside the story inside the frame tale. The serpent magically restores the sailor's ship and brings his crew back to life and sends them on their way. Yet human narrators may not have such power. The shipwrecked sailor's captain isn't comforted by this upbeat tale, and he snaps: "Who gives water to a goose on the morning it's to be slaughtered?" (53). The very earliest known frame tale is also the first story to question the power of storytelling itself.

22. *The Thousand and One Nights*

There are 1,001 *Thousand and One Nights*. No two manuscripts are alike, translations often differ radically, and different readers read them very differently. Ever since Antoine Galland published his pathbreaking translation of *Les mille et une nuits* (1704–17), hundreds of writers and artists have reimagined the *Nights* for their own times and their own purposes, from ballets to paintings to Kuwaiti comic books. Many of us first encountered the *Nights* as children—in some heavily bowdlerized version—and even then we could sense that we were entering a magical world centered on a Baghdad that never was. What I'd like to emphasize here is how grounded the *Nights* are in reality, and often specifically in Cairo.

A core of the tales was first composed in Persia (hence the Persian names in the frame tale, with Shahryar identified as a Sassanid king), but the *Nights* as we have them developed chiefly in two centers of storytelling: Damascus and Cairo. The relatively brief Syrian versions never tried to present a full thousand and one nights, a term that could indicate simply "a large number." Some prefer this lineage. Introducing his Norton translation, Husain Haddawy praises his favored fourteenth-century Syrian manuscript as the product of "a fortunately stunted growth." He dismisses the later and more expansive

Cairene tradition as having "produced an abundance of poisonous fruits that proved almost fatal to the original."[3]

But what does it even mean to speak of "the original" in a case like this? It is probably better to think of any translation as one among many possible versions, reinscribing the text (as the translation theorist Lawrence Venuti puts it) into a new cultural context for new readers.[4] Some readers will share Haddawy's preference for a spare and fairly sober *Arabian Nights*, while others will prefer a translation that tries to embody the *Nights'* generative expansiveness. As Jorge Luis Borges shrewdly remarked in an illuminating essay, "The Translators of the Thousand and One Nights," the tales don't convey some slice of Baghdad life but are "an adaptation of ancient stories to the low-brow or ribald tastes of the Cairo middle classes."[5] Like the different editions of *Great Expectations* that we looked at in the first chapter, the various translations of the *Nights* aim at different readers and offer different reading experiences. An ideal approach to the *Nights* might be to set aside the quest for "the best" translation altogether and sample different translations on different nights, an option made available within the Everyman edition edited by Wen-chin Ouyang, who selected tales from several different translations.[6]

Over the centuries many stories and poems were added to the early compilations. Some of the best-known tales, including those of Aladdin and Ali Baba, first appeared in Galland's version, supposedly supplied by his Syrian informant Hana Diab. A century later, the influential English translator Edward Lane gathered material in Cairo in the 1820s. Like Sir Richard Burton after him, he filled his edition with copious ethnographic notes, placing his readers in the scene. Lane was an artist as well as a translator, and in one sketch he shows a caravan entering the Khan el-Khalili souq (Figure 18). In a private joke, the gentleman smoking a shisha on the left is none other than Lane himself, dressed in Turkish garb. I like to think that after he finished his sketch, he would have headed into the recently established el-Fishawy Café for tea.

Many details in the *Nights* suggest that the tales as we have them are as much a product of Ottoman-era Cairo and Damascus as of Sassanid Persia or

18. Edward Lane at Khan el-Khalili

Abbasid Baghdad. Thus in "The Porter and the Three Ladies of Baghdad," when a woman buys a lavish array of supplies for a feast, these include Turkish quinces, Hebron peaches, Damascus lilies, Aleppo raisins, and pastry from Cairo, Turkey, and the Balkans—the kind of variety that a storyteller's listeners could see around them at a Cairo souq.

The woman who has hired the porter to carry her purchases invites him into the house that she shares with her two sisters. They all undress to bathe in a fountain and play a sexual guessing game, before feasting together as they tell stories and recite verses. They are interrupted by a knock on their door: three wandering dervishes, each blind in one eye, are asking for alms. The ladies invite them in, on condition that they entertain them with marvelous tales but not ask about anything that doesn't concern them. Then comes another knock on the door: this proves to be the caliph Haroun al-Rashid, wandering the city in disguise in the company of his vizier and his executioner. They too are invited in, and a feast of storytelling is underway. Paulo Lemos Horta, who teaches at NYU Abu Dhabi (and who is the author of *Marvellous Thieves*, an excellent book on the rival translators of the *Nights*), tells me that when he taught the story in North America, his students remarked on the improbability that the porter would encounter women turned into dogs and that the dervishes would meet ifrits with supernatural powers. By contrast, his Arab students in Abu Dhabi consider many of these details as fairly plausible, and they are astonished by a different aspect: "Three women, living alone without a man? How can this be?"

I've earlier described Boccaccio's *Decameron* as the world's first talking cure, yet Shahrazad was there ahead of him, as she cures King Shahryar of his murderous madness through her three-year course of narrative therapy. In the Syrian versions of the closing of the frame tale, the king praises her chastity, wisdom, and eloquence, and says that "repentance has come to me through her,"[7] but the later Cairo version is explicitly psychological. "O wise and subtle one," Shahryar says to her, "you have told me some things which were strange, and many that were worth reflection. I have listened to you for a thousand nights and one night, and now my soul is changed and joyful, it beats with an appetite for life. I give thanks to Him Who has perfumed your mouth with so much eloquence and has set wisdom to be a seal upon your brow!"[8]

The most fantastic tales can be mobilized for political as well as psychological effect. And more than that: today the physical book itself can play a political role, as we find in a striking museum installation by the Palestinian performance artist Emily Jacir. The melancholy inspiration for her project was the assassination in 1972 of Wael Zuaiter, a translator and Palestinian activist in Rome, who'd been implicated by Israel (incorrectly, his supporters say) in the slaying of Israeli athletes at the Munich Olympics. He was in the process of translating *The Thousand and One Nights* into Italian when agents of the Mossad killed him; on his body was found a volume of *Alf Laylah wa Laylah*, punctured by a bullet.

Emily Jacir was given this actual volume, and she responded by making an art project. She had a thousand blank books made, and filmed herself shooting a bullet through each of them, using a pistol of the same type used by the Mossad. She then created an installation at the 2006 Sydney Biennale, *Materials for a Film (Performance)*, with further versions in Venice and at the Guggenheim Museum in New York, where she lined a room with the thousand

19. Emily Jacir, Materials for a Film (Performance) *(2006)*

bullet-pierced books, as a memorial to all of the world's untold and untranslated stories. Outside the room, a wall displayed photographs of each page of the bullet-riddled volume of *Alf Laylah wa Laylah* (Figure 19). As Jacir remarked at the time of her Sydney exhibition, "I repeated the action of shooting the book as a performance. In *A Thousand and One Nights*, Scheherazade is constantly telling stories to survive."[9] Her installation is a moving tribute to a life cut short, and a testimony to the ongoing life of the *Nights*, brought to bear in new circumstances by a modern-day Scheherazade—Emily Jacir herself.

23. Naguib Mahfouz, *Arabian Nights and Days*

Born in 1911, Naguib Mahfouz wrote thirty-four novels, 350 short stories, dozens of movie scripts, and any number of journalistic pieces, in a seventy-year career up to his death at age ninety-four in 2006, though he wrote little after he was stabbed in 1994 by a pair of fundamentalists who accused him of

blasphemy. A lifelong resident of Cairo, he became his country's most prominent recorder of his city's life. An Egyptian nationalist, Mahfouz was an artistic internationalist. His work draws both on the growing tradition of the
Egyptian novel and on his love of Russian literature and of modernists including Proust, Joyce, and Kafka. The assassination attempt came in the wake
of the controversy that arose over Salman Rushdie's *Satanic Verses*, which was
published in 1988, the same year Mahfouz was awarded the Nobel Prize.
Though he criticized Rushdie's portrayal of Islam, Mahfouz defended his right
to artistic liberty and opposed the Iranian *fatwa* on his life, going so far as to
call the Ayatollah Khomeini a terrorist. His stance stirred up simmering anger
among Islamists who considered that his 1959 novel, *Children of Gebelawi*,
equated Judaism, Christianity, and Islam and promoted secular science over
religion.

For many years, Mahfouz had the double distinction of having some of his
works banned in the Arab world for religious reasons while other works were
banned on political grounds, first for his critiques of the Nasser regime and
then for his support of Anwar Sadat's peace treaty with Israel. His work was
relatively unknown in the Arab world before he received the Nobel, but his
books circulated widely thereafter, and following his death plans were drawn
up for a museum in his honor. A series of bureaucratic tangles and then disrup-
tions caused by the revolution of 2011 led to more than a decade's worth of
delays—a story that would have been a perfect satiric topic for Mahfouz—
before the museum finally opened.

Naguib Mahfouz's cultural and political commitments were grounded in the
deepest of all his engagements: with the Arabic language. In his Nobel accep-
tance speech, Mahfouz doesn't begin (as many laureates do) by acknowledging
his literary predecessors, nor by saying that the prize is really being given to
his country. Instead, he says that the Arabic language

is the real winner of the prize. It is, therefore, meant that its melodies should
float for the first time into your oasis of culture and civilization. I have great

hopes that this will not be the last time either, and that literary writers of my nation will have the pleasure to sit with full merit amongst your international writers who have spread the fragrance of joy and wisdom in this grief-ridden world of ours.[10]

Mahfouz's works encompassed the full sweep of ancient and modern Egyptian history, from early novels set in pharaonic times to the social realism of the *Cairo Trilogy* (1956–7) and then existentialist works and postmodernist meta-fictions in the 1960s through the 1980s. Like Salman Rushdie and Orhan Pamuk after him, he often deals with the pressures of Western modernity on his culture, though he shows little concern with characters feeling torn between East and West. In his Nobel lecture, Mahfouz describes himself as the product of two cultures: not East and West, but ancient and Islamic:

> I am the son of two civilizations that at a certain age in history have formed a happy marriage. The first of these, seven thousand years old, is the Pharaonic civilization; the second, one thousand four hundred years old, is the Islamic one. It was my fate, ladies and gentlemen, to be born in the lap of these two civilizations, and to absorb their milk, to feed on their literature and art.

He mentions Western culture as a later strand in his formation: "Then I drank the nectar of your rich and fascinating culture. From the inspiration of all this—as well as my own anxieties—words bedewed from me."

Mahfouz's ability to weave together politics and philosophical concerns, a premodern heritage and contemporary life, is nowhere better shown than in his 1979 novel, *Arabian Nights and Days*. It begins on the thousand and *second* day, with Shahrazad's father the vizier anxiously going up to the palace, wondering what will finally become of his daughter and the kingdom. He is overjoyed when Shahryar says that he's decided to keep Shahrazad as his wife: " 'Her stories are white magic,' he said delightedly. 'They open up worlds that invite reflection.'"[11] Mahfouz seems to be showing us the therapeutic power of storytelling, but it turns out that Shahrazad herself has a less positive view. When the vizier goes to congratulate her on her triumph, he finds her bitter: "'I sacrificed myself,' she said sorrowfully, 'in order to stem the torrent of blood.'" She continues: "Whenever he approaches me I breathe the smell of blood . . . How many virgins has he killed! How many pious and God-fearing people has he wiped out! Only hypocrites are left in the kingdom" (3–4).

This is not the cheerful (and still patriarchal) fantasy of a work like John Barth's story "The Dunyazadiad" (1972), in which the writer magically encounters a radiantly sexual Scheherazade and her foxy sister, Dunyazad, healing his midlife crisis and restoring him to literary and sexual potency. In Mahfouz's novel, Shahryar reveals that Shahrazad's stories have had only limited value for him. "I got my share of depression," he gloomily tells his vizier; "did Shahrazad's stories tell me of anything apart from death? . . . Peoples swallowed up by peoples, with a sole determined victor knocking finally at their door: the Destroyer of Pleasures." The vizier realizes that far from being healed by Scheherazade's tales, "his master had changed only superficially" (55). Shahryar remains a violent autocrat, and he appoints one henchman after another to bleed the people and to cement his hold on power. As his own chief of police wonders, "Where did Shahryar get these governors?" (31).

Mahfouz's contemporary political point is clear, and we're in a world that blends medieval fantasy and contemporary reality in ways comparable to Calvino's *Invisible Cities*. Shahryar rules over a very Cairo-like capital, and we find a surreal mixture of characters at the Café of the Emirs where people discuss the day's events. Customers include Ibrahim al-Attar the druggist, Ugr the barber and his son Aladdin, and Ragab the porter, whose crony Sindbad is tired of the city and is leaving to go back to sea. At the outset, they're thrilled that their daughters are now spared, thanks to Shahrazad and "those beautiful stories" (9). Yet Mahfouz's tale soon darkens. A genie entraps a merchant into performing a political assassination; distraught over the task he has to carry out, the merchant wanders the streets at night, but instead of encountering some marvelous story as Haroun al-Rashid would have done, he comes upon a ten-year-old girl whom he rapes and murders. Discussing this crime at the Café of the Emirs, his friend the druggist remarks, "If one regards the genie as far-fetched, the story becomes a riddle" (29). Even the merchant can't understand his impulsive brutality: "His soul had begotten wild things of which he had no experience" (19).

Throughout the book, characters seek to understand themselves and to avoid succumbing to conformity with a corrupt system. A few succeed in refusing to carry out the dictates of power, accepting their own destruction if necessary. At the end of the book, Shahryar himself abandons his throne in disgust: "He deposed himself, defeated before his heart's revolt at a time when his people had forgotten his past misdeeds. His education had required a considerable time." Wandering away from his city, he meets an angelic young girl who asks his name and his trade. He replies: "A fugitive from his past" (222–4).

Arabian Nights and Days is an extraordinary meditation on both the limitations and the ultimate power of storytelling. For us as for Shahryar, our education in storytelling requires a considerable time—in Egypt's case, seven thousand years.

24. Orhan Pamuk, *My Name Is Red*

What Dickens has been for London and Mahfouz for Cairo, Orhan Pamuk has become for Istanbul. A good index of a writer's identification with a city is a museum dedicated to the author's life and times. Such museums are typically set in the writer's onetime home or neighborhood, as with the Mahfouz Museum in Cairo and the Goethe Museum in Weimar. At times, an author can be upstaged by his most famous creation, as with the Sherlock Holmes Museum at 221B Baker Street. The James Joyce Museum in Dublin combines life and fiction: it's located in the Martello Tower in Sandycove on the outskirts of

Dublin, where Stephen Dedalus is living in *Ulysses*; the young James Joyce had stayed there for a grand total of six days in 1904. Pamuk, however, has gone these authors' museums one better with his Museum of Innocence, which he constructed as he was writing his novel of the same name. In the novel, Pamuk's hero, Kemal, has turned his home into a museum in memory of his lost love, his cousin Füsun. He has collected all sorts of everyday objects that he associates with their time together, and the novel takes the form of a tour of the house museum's exhibits. When he began the novel, Pamuk bought a run-down building in his neighborhood, and over the course of a decade he renovated it as he wrote the book, published in 2008. The resulting museum, which opened in 2012, has surrealist vitrines representing the novel's eighty-three chapters (Figure 20).

The top floor contains Kemal's attic bedroom, its walls lined with pages from the manuscript of the novel itself. On the ground floor, you'll find a museum store where you can buy reproductions of the heroine's butterfly earrings, as well as copies of Pamuk's novels in many languages. Pamuk trained as an architect, and throughout his adolescence he intended to become a

20. Pamuk in his Museum of Innocence

painter, before abruptly switching to writing novels; the Museum of Innocence combines all these sides of his personality.

Pamuk's longstanding fascination with art found its classic expression in *My Name Is Red* (1998), the book that made him a prominent global author. Set in the 1590s, it centers on struggles between Ottoman miniaturists loyal to the stylized traditions of Persian art and those who seek to adopt a Western mode of perspective-based realism. Constantinople is tensely balanced between Asia and Europe, like Italo Calvino's city of Octavia suspended from a web between two precipices. People sit on carpets from India, drinking tea in Chinese cups imported via Portugal, poised between a Middle Eastern past and a Western future.

In this swirling matrix of competing cultures, Italian-style painting is starting to supplant the great traditions of Islamic art, as people are captivated by the idea that portraits can convey their individuality (a new, Western-style value) instead of more general qualities of character and status. Traditionalists object. One storyteller sketches a tree that declares its satisfaction that it isn't shown in the new realistic style: "I thank Allah that I, the humble tree before you, have not been drawn with such intent. And not because I fear that if I'd been thus depicted all the dogs in Istanbul would assume I was a real tree and piss on me: I don't want to be a tree, I want to be its meaning."[12]

History is on the side of the Westernizing realists, and yet the miniaturists will never succeed if they simply try to be more Italian than the Italian painters they admire. *My Name Is Red* involves a search for a murderer among the Sultan's miniaturists; he proves to be a Westernizer who kills rivals opposed to the new style. Yet at the book's end, he realizes that his secret masterpiece—a self-portrait of himself as the Sultan—is a failure, a clumsy imitation of a poorly grasped technique. "I feel like the Devil," he confesses, "not because I've murdered two men, but because my portrait has been made in this fashion. I suspect that I did away with them so I could make this picture. But now the isolation I feel terrifies me. Imitating the Frankish masters without having attained their expertise makes a miniaturist even more of a slave" (399).

The murderous miniaturist has ended up an outcast, torn between two worlds he can never fully join. Yet *My Name Is Red* is an exuberant book, filled with high and low comedy amid the aching loneliness of unfulfilled romantic and cultural desires. Pamuk's novel is, in fact, the best answer to the problem it so trenchantly poses: it is a vibrant hybrid that recreates a vanished Ottoman past for present purposes. As Pamuk has said, he wrote about his own childhood by reversing the digits, changing the 1950s into the 1590s. He uses all the techniques of the Western novel and also transforms them in new ways; his book is divided into fifty-nine short chapters, each titled to announce its speaker: "I am Black," "I am Shekure," "I am a Tree." Anticipating the eighty-three vitrines of the Museum of Innocence, these miniature self-portraits link together to form a sweeping historical novel.

Like Naguib Mahfouz, Pamuk approaches Western culture with sovereign freedom. An essay on "Mario Vargas Llosa and Third World Literature" reads like a portrait of Pamuk himself. "If there is anything that distinguishes Third World literature," he writes, it is "the writer's awareness that his work is somehow remote from the centers where the history of his art—the art of the novel—is described, and he reflects this distance in his work." Yet far from being a disadvantage for the writer,

> this sense of being an outsider frees him from anxieties about originality. He need not enter into obsessive contest with fathers or forerunners to find his own voice. For he is exploring new terrain, touching on subjects that have never been discussed in his culture, and often addressing distant and emergent readerships, never seen before in his country—this gives his writing its own sort of originality, its authenticity.[13]

My Name Is Red has clear affinities with Mahfouz's work, including recurrent scenes set in a coffee house where the locals gather to discuss events and where a storyteller spins his tales. Having noted this similarity, I asked Pamuk about Mahfouz; he replied that he has an entire "Mahfouz library." He said that he likes the way Mahfouz worked in so many different narrative forms, "which makes him like me a sort of Shehrazat," and added: "You have to be a cunning Shehrazat if you want to survive and continue to write in my part of the world."[14] Appropriately for the theme of translation, in Turkey Scheherazade is reborn as Shehrazat.

Together with Persian poetry and art, *The Thousand and One Nights* is a frequent resonance in *My Name Is Red*. The heroine, Shekure, is a Scheherazade figure who is well aware that she is a storyteller inside a story. As she tells us: "Don't be surprised that I'm talking to you. For years I've combed through the pictures in my father's books looking for images of women and great beauties." Usually the women have their eyes shyly downcast, but a few of them look boldly out at the reader. Shekure says that

> I've long wondered about that reader . . . just like those beautiful women
> with one eye on the life within the book and one eye on the life outside, I,
> too, long to speak with you who are observing me from who knows which
> distant time and place. I'm an attractive and intelligent woman, and it pleases
> me that I'm being watched. And if I happen to tell a lie or two from time to
> time, it's so you don't come to any false conclusions about me. (43)

My Name Is Red explores the challenges to identity and cultural memory brought about by Westernization, and in the process Pamuk transcends the either/or choices perceived by the Westernizing murderer and the café storyteller's traditionalist tree. He lives at once in the Ottoman past and in the postmodern present, just as he lives both in Istanbul and beyond it, within and outside the pages of his fiction. In a direct expression of this doubled identity, the novel includes a boy named Orhan, son of Shekure, which is also the name of Pamuk's mother. In the novel's closing lines, Shekure bequeaths her story to her son, hoping that he'll make it into an illustrated tale, but she warns us not to take the result too literally: "For the sake of a delightful and convincing story, there isn't a lie Orhan wouldn't deign to tell" (413).

25. Jokha Alharthi, *Celestial Bodies*

If Naguib Mahfouz was right to say that his Nobel Prize was really being given to the Arabic language, it can equally be said that the 2019 Man Booker International Prize was given to Arabic writing in the *English* language—literally so, as the £50,000 prize was evenly divided between Jokha Alharthi and her translator, Marilyn Booth. This dual award is all the more appropriate as *Celestial Bodies* portrays life in a fully globalized Oman, even as the characters feel the pull of village life and its persisting premodern patterns, in a country where slavery was only abolished in 1970, eight years before Alharthi's birth. Her novel is already being translated into two dozen languages. Its sudden and unexpected success reflects the major role of international prizes in the formation of contemporary world literature. The novel's Arabic title *Sayyidat al-Qamar* would literally be translated as "Ladies of the Moon," and it is oddly appropriate that on the cover of the current American edition, the Booker insignia appears like the full moon on a heavenly trajectory overlaid on an Omani woman's body (Figure 21).

Along with the value of prizes, the novel's success shows the critical role that individual translators can have in championing a work. In the early 2000s,

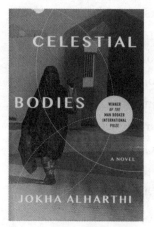

21. Celestial Booker award

Alharthi was living in Edinburgh with her husband and their young child. She had published a novel and a collection of short stories, but given the small Omani literary market she needed a secure profession, and so she was studying for a PhD in classical Arabic poetry; she subsequently became a professor of Arabic literature at Sultan Qaboos University in Muscat. Yet in Edinburgh she wasn't finding it congenial to write academic prose in English. As she has remarked in an interview,

> I was expected to write *fluent* English, and to write *fluent* essays, and I was like, I never did that! I *never* did that. So I just came back to the flat one night and got the baby to sleep, and just sat there with my laptop thinking about—not exactly Oman, but a different life, and a different language. And because I love my language so much, I felt the need to write in my own language.[15]

At the same time, she says that studying Arabic away from home allowed her to "get a different perspective" on her culture. Missing the warmth of her own language, she began to write a new novel. She showed the manuscript to Marilyn Booth, who was advising her on her dissertation; Booth loved it and offered to translate it. Finding a publisher for a work by a young Omani woman was difficult, and though it won a prize for the best Omani novel of 2010, the translation only appeared in 2018 from a small Scottish press. The book's fortunes changed dramatically when it won the Booker, one year after Olga Tokarczuk's *Flights*.

Alharthi's novel carries on the Arabic tradition of nested stories, now with multiple narrative perspectives, not unlike the perspectivism of Pamuk's multiple narrators. Her short chapters (fifty-eight in her case, fifty-nine in *My Name Is Red*), focus on three sisters and their families. Like the sisters in "The Porter and the Three Ladies of Baghdad," Alharthi's heroines are strong women, but they live in contemporary Omani reality; their fantasy worlds are formed in their imagination, and their dreams rarely come true. In the novel's opening sentence, "Mayya, forever immersed in her Singer sewing machine, seemed lost to the outside world."[16] She is daydreaming about a young man, having fallen in love just by a glimpse of him, after he's returned to Oman after years of study in London. But he doesn't seem to notice her, and she reluctantly accepts an arranged marriage. Then in a gesture of quiet rebellion, she names her daughter "London." The women of the village are baffled: "Does anyone name their daughter *London?* This is the name of a place, my dear, a place that is very far away, in the land of the Christians. We are all very, very surprised!" (8). Her husband is devoted to her, but when he asks if she loves him too, she laughs. "Where did you pick up those TV-show words? she asked. Or maybe it's the satellite dish out there. It's the Egyptian films, have they eaten up your mind?" (11).

Mayya's sisters have equally ambiguous success. Asma marries a self-centered artist and devotes herself to her many children; the third sister, Khawla, pines away for her first love, who has emigrated to Canada. She spurns offers of marriage, sure that he'll one day return and marry her. Surprisingly he does, but two weeks later he flies back to Montreal, in order to be with his girlfriend. A decade later, the Canadian girlfriend finally throws him out. "He came back. He found a good job in a company, and he began to get to know his wife and children" (204). But once their five children are grown, Khawla insists on getting a divorce: "It was just that she couldn't bear the past. Everything was calm and well-ordered now . . . She was at peace, so her heart stopped forgiving" (239).

Like Mahfouz and Pamuk, Alharthi writes within a literary framework that is both local and global. Her characters quote the pre-Islamic poet Imru al-Qays and the contemporary Mahmoud Darwish, but most people in her world know little of them. When the sisters' father gets enthralled by a free-spirited Bedouin woman, he quotes a verse from the tenth-century poet al-Mutanabbi, who describes his Bedouin beloved as a gazelle of the desert. The father's lover asks: "That's your friend, the one called al-Mutanabbi, the one you told me about?" She doesn't like the comparison: "Do I chew my words, then, like a gazelle chews her cud?" (178–9).

In interviews, Alharthi credits a wide range of favorite world writers, including Gabriel García Márquez, Yukio Mishima, and Anton Chekhov. In addition, the world of global English hovers in the background of a region with a long British colonial past. Mayya's husband, Abdallah, has reluctantly given in to the pressure to learn English: "In my own country! My Arab country, where restaurants, hospitals and hotels all announced that 'only English is spoken here'" (153). Later, when his daughter, London, now grown, waxes enthusiastic over a romantic gesture by her fiancé, her friend Hanan replies in English: "*So what?*" (231). When a disillusioned London breaks off the engagement, Hanan urges her to get over him: "London, come on! Hanan said to her. Life goes on. Where Ahmad's concerned, just hit Delete, okay? *Let it go*, she said, in English to underline her point" (185). Here, Hanan uses English in parallel with up-to-date computer lingo.

Jokha Alharthi is the first Arab writer to win the Booker, and she is also the first Omani woman to be translated into English. She lives in both worlds, and her website (jokha.com) has two versions, Arabic and English, and includes links to several of Alharthi's English-language apperances. The homepage of the Arabic version features an epigraph from *Celestial Bodies*: "Fi algharbat, kama fi alhub, nataearaf ealaa 'anfusina bishakl 'afdal" ("In alienation, as in love, we get to know ourselves better"). Alienation and freedom, poetry and prose, Oman and the wider world, are woven together in Alharthi's web of stories.

CHAPTER SIX

The Congo–Nigeria: (Post)Colonial Encounters

26. Joseph Conrad, *Heart of Darkness*

Since at least the time of Marco Polo, travelers have played an important role in representing regions to the wider world beyond their borders. A particularly influential account, whether factual or fictional, can have a lasting effect not only on distant readers but in the region itself, variously inspiring and infuriating later writers who may have a very different sense of their culture than the visitor has given the world. Both in its origin and in its reception by African writers, Joseph Conrad's most famous work shows the possibilities that open up, and the problems that can follow, when an outsider puts a place on the map of world literature.

Having left Poland at age sixteen to go to sea in 1874, Conrad made his career in the French and then British merchant marine before finally deciding in the mid-1890s to become a writer. In *Heart of Darkness* he wove a dense, hallucinatory web of words to transmute his raw experience of a river journey into a deeply unsettling portrayal of the descent of imperial ideals into madness. He had gotten a job in 1890 to pilot a steamboat on the Congo River for the company that King Leopold II of Belgium had set up to exploit the region's natural resources with the aid of forced labor. In the 1880s, Western powers accepted Leopold's control over what he dubbed the Congo Free State, aided by the promotional work of the journalist-explorer Henry Morton Stanley, who had become famous for locating the supposedly lost Doctor Livingstone in Central Africa.

Stanley dramatized his adventures in bestsellers such as *How I Found Livingstone* (1872) and *In Darkest Africa* (1890), copiously illustrated with maps, ethnographic engravings of native weapons and bare-breasted women, and with dramatic scenes of the great white man surmounting any and all obstacles. In the engraving shown here (Figure 22), he threatens to shoot a native bearer if he drops a precious box of papers when a rushing river threatens to sweep him away. ("All the men halted in their work while they gazed at their comrade who was thus imperilled by bullet and flood. The man himself seemed to regard the pistol with the greatest awe, and after a few desperate efforts succeeded in getting the box safely ashore."[1]) It's hard to know which is more astonishing: that this scene occurred, or that Stanley chose to boast about it and give it a full-page illustration.

"LOOK OUT, YOU DROP THAT BOX, I'LL SHOOT YOU."

22. Stanley saves his papers

Stanley served as King Leopold's principal agent in creating trading sta-
tions along the Congo River and establishing relations with tribal chieftains.
He detailed his success as colonial empire builder in *The Congo and the Founding of Its Free State* (1885), which is filled with praise of "the munificent and
Royal Founder of the Association Internationale du Congo."[2] This phrase appears in a chapter focused on the difficulties of dealing with native middlemen
in the ivory trade that was central to the economic exploitation of the colony.
In 1899, Conrad drew on Stanley's works for *Heart of Darkness*, as well as his
own experience as a steamboat captain. His hero, Charlie Marlow, says that
when he received his offer of employment, he was shown "a large shining map,
marked with all the colours of a rainbow," and he says that "I was going into
the yellow. Dead in the centre."[3] The Congo is indeed colored yellow in the
fold-out map at the end of Stanley's *In Darkest Africa* (Figure 23). Marlow ven-
tures upriver, "dead in the centre" of the map, in order to meet the mysterious
ivory trader Mr. Kurtz, only to find him dying amid horrific scenes of brutality
and the collapse of European ideals.

Readers have been sharply divided over what we find as we accompany
Marlow upriver. Do we really see Africa, or do we see Marlow's existential
vision of a dark night of the soul? Do we see the essential corruption of

23. "Into the yellow"

European imperialism, or more ambivalently the failings of an imperialism gone wrong, or are we being shown a primitivism so stark that Conrad reinforces the racist basis of imperialism even as he criticizes it? This last viewpoint was memorably advanced by Chinua Achebe in a 1977 essay entitled "An Image of Africa: Racism in Conrad's *Heart of Darkness*." Conrad, he charges, presents Africa as nothing more than

> a metaphysical battlefield devoid of all recognizable humanity, into which the wandering European enters at his peril. Of course, there is a preposterous and perverse arrogance in thus reducing Africa to the role of props for the breakup of one petty European mind. But that is not even the point. The real question is the dehumanization of Africa and Africans which this age-long attitude has fostered and continues to foster in the world. And the question is whether a novel which celebrates this dehumanization, which depersonalizes a portion of the human race, can be called a great work of art. My answer is: No, it cannot.[4]

Achebe offered an important corrective to readers' common glossing over the text's treatment of the African people who provide so threatening a backdrop for Marlow's adventures. At the same time, Achebe's critique also reflects a realist novelist's impatience with modernist ambiguities. Conrad forces us to experience Africa through Marlow's eyes, in a kind of literary Impressionism, yet Marlow is far from an objective observer. Conrad destabilizes Marlow's narrative authority at many points, undercutting any simple endorsement of the racial stereotyping in which Marlow as well as Kurtz so often indulge.

A key aspect of the novella is Conrad's use of a deeply ambiguous frame tale. The story begins not in Africa but on a pleasure yacht, the *Nellie*, anchored on the Thames outside London, and Marlow's "inconclusive tale" is recounted by a shadowy narrator who describes Marlow with an undercurrent of ironic disbelief. As dusk falls, Marlow is wrapped in growing obscurity even as he mistakenly tells listeners that "of course in this you fellows see more than I could then" (43). Though he criticizes Kurtz for setting up ivory as an idol to worship, Marlow sets himself up, the skeptical narrator observes, in "the pose of a Buddha preaching in European clothes and without a lotus-flower" (21). Conrad is doing something tricky with his hero: Marlow thinks of himself as some kind of Humphrey Bogart *avant la lettre*, but he appears to have the illusion that he has lost all his illusions.

Throughout the novella Conrad subtly satirizes Marlow's imperial machismo, beginning with his early embarrassment that he has to ask a well-connected aunt to get him his Congo assignment (as Conrad himself, in fact, had done): "I, Charlie Marlow, set the women to work—to get a job. Heavens!" (23). At the end, back in England after Kurtz's death, Marlow visits Kurtz's fiancée to offer his condolences. When she begs to know her beloved's last words, Marlow no longer looks like a commanding figure of disillusioned knowledge: "I felt like a chill grip on my chest. 'Don't,' I said in a muffled voice" (94). Instead of the voice of authority, Marlow sounds like someone resisting a rape attempt. Under this pressure, he can't bear to uphold his usual standard of truth-telling: rather than reveal Kurtz's true final words—"The horror! The horror!"—he claims that Kurtz said her name at the end. Having gotten what she wants from him, Kurtz's fiancée—whose name we're never told—gives a cry of triumph and dismisses him.

Conrad exploits racist stereotypes of Africa, not to counter them as Achebe will do, but to show how thin the line can be between supposedly enlightened European self and African Other. At the start of the story, Conrad undercuts the imperial enterprise by making Roman Britain an early-day Africa: "And this also has been one of the dark places of the earth," Marlow says at the outset of the story, as the sun sets over London. He evokes the grim experience of an imagined Roman legionnaire voyaging up the Thames, "going up this river with stores, or orders, or what you like. Sand-banks, marshes, forests, savages,—precious little to eat fit for a civilized man, nothing but Thames water to drink . . . cold, fog, tempests, disease, exile, and death—death skulking in the air, in the water, in the bush. They must have been dying like flies here" (20). England mirrors "darkest Africa," and night is falling on London as Marlow tells his tale. His return from a foreign continent has revealed to him the inextricable mix of civilization and barbarism at the heart of the British Empire.

27. Chinua Achebe, *Things Fall Apart*

By far the most famous work of African literature—with twenty million copies sold in fifty-seven languages—*Things Fall Apart* (1958) describes tensions within the Ibo village of Umuofia before the advent of the Europeans, but things really start to fall apart when Protestant missionaries arrive. The ensuing religious struggle leads to a European crackdown, and the novel ominously closes with the District Commissioner's decision to include the conflict in his planned book, *The Pacification of the Primitive Tribes of the Lower Niger*. The anticolonial theme could hardly be clearer, but this isn't the only way the book has been read. In marked contrast, my Random House edition from 1994 performs the surprising feat of presenting the book without a single mention of race or empire. The front cover offers a quotation from Nadine Gordimer praising Achebe as "gloriously gifted with the magic of an ebullient, generous, great talent," while on the back cover we're told: "A simple story of a 'strong man' whose life is dominated by fear and anger, *Things Fall Apart* is written with remarkable economy and subtle irony. Uniquely and richly African, at the same time it reveals Achebe's keen awareness of the human qualities common to men of all times and places."

A third level of reading is linguistic. This understanding builds on Achebe's 1962 essay "The African Writer and the English Language." There he argues for the value of writing in English or French instead of the less widely read indigenous languages. "Let us give the devil his due: colonialism in Africa disrupted many things," he says, but "it did bring together many peoples that had hitherto gone their several ways. And it gave them a language with which to talk to one another. If it failed to give them a song, it at least gave them a tongue, for sighing." He concludes that "for me there is no other choice. I have been given this language and I intend to use it."[5] At the same time, he stresses the need to remake English in the process. In *Things Fall Apart*, Achebe's portrayal of African society from within is closely linked to his project of creating an English prose infused with oral tales and proverbs. His blending of standard written English with African orality had a major impact on later writers, as we'll see with Wole Soyinka and Georges Ngal.

A reading of *Things Fall Apart* can combine the colonial, the universal, and the linguistic dimensions, but individual readers may bring additional perspectives as well. In my case, I approach Achebe's novel not only as a student of language and literature but also through a more specific identity: as the son of an Anglican missionary. *Things Fall Apart* is set in the 1890s, but missionary evangelism didn't end then, and the conditions of village life that Achebe describes often tally with my father's descriptions of life among the Igorot mountain people in the Philippines in the 1930s and 1940s.

From an informal memoir that my father put together at the end of his life, it appears that his motive in heading out across the Pacific, on graduating from seminary in New York at age twenty-five, was less religious fervor than a desire to get away from his feckless father and domineering mother. This desire was reinforced by "a romantic streak in my make-up, which finds in far-off places a sense of fascination." He mentions "the sound of the great whistles of the ocean liners berthed near the Seminary," and says that "they aroused in me a strong Wanderlust, which demanded fulfillment." His excitement as he began his journey, a Bible in his hand and a gleam in his eye, is palpable in a photo taken by his cousin Leopold Mannes—a precocious scientist as well as a concert violinist—using the new Kodachrome film he'd invented while still in high school. Seven thousand miles from the East Coast, my father could become his own Leopold as well as his own Damrosch.

Three years later, my mother sailed out from Seattle to meet him, set up by mutual family friends, and they became engaged three weeks after her arrival; a studio photograph taken in Bontoc shows the young couple about to embark

24. *The young missionaries*

on their new life (Figure 24). Posted to remote villages in the Mountain Province north of Manila, my father became fluent in one of the Igorot languages (unusually for missionaries of his era), and he'd spend hours with village leaders, discussing everything from theology to medicine to a prime common interest, the weather. For her part, my mother found communities of strong women in Bontoc and Baguio. An aspiring artist, she loved to sketch Igorot women in their intricately woven skirts. In the watercolor shown here (Figure 25), three women stride along mountain paths, one with her skirt showing off a muscular leg, another with a pipe in her mouth, the third unencumbered by her advanced pregnancy.

This parental history might seem an anachronistic and politically dubious way for a white reader to enter Achebe's novel today, and yet it is precisely this dimension of the book that is closest to his own experience. Born in 1930—just seven years before my father headed out to the Philippines—Achebe was the son of an enthusiastic convert who taught in a mission school. After studying

25. Mountain Province women (c. 1949)

English and theology in college, he taught in an evangelical school not far from his birthplace in Ogidi. Just as in the novel, the villagers had allowed the school to be built in a "bad bush" area, a region of disease and malevolent spirits. After several months there, he moved to Lagos to take a job with the Nigerian Broadcasting Service, where he prepared scripts for delivery over the radio.

Achebe's experience at the Merchants of Light School is reflected in the mission established by the good evangelist Mr. Brown. Unlike his far more rigid successor Mr. Smith, Brown is tolerant of local customs and doesn't overplay his hand, as he combats what he sees as primitive superstition and tribal violence. As my father says in his memoir, the mountain tribes were already being given "the inevitable worst of our civilization"—he mentions hard liquor, and exploitation by the lowlanders—and he considered that "we were trying to bring them what we thought to be the best of it." In the Philippines as in Nigeria, building churches went hand in hand with constructing schools and medical clinics. In *Things Fall Apart* the Christian message of universal brotherhood is particularly appealing to people on the margins of village life, and early converts include women who'd given birth to twins, which were traditionally viewed as evil and were abandoned in the forest to die.

Achebe's hero, Okonkwo, is a great man with a tragic flaw, which is as much Freudian as Greek. Ashamed of his ne'er-do-well father, Okonkwo is obsessed with manliness, and he scorns any behavior that he sees as effeminate or womanly. He beats his wives and children on little provocation, and in a shocking scene he takes part in the execution of his own foster son: "As the man who had cleared his throat drew up and raised his machete, Okonkwo looked away. He heard the blow. The pot fell and broke in the sand. He heard Ikemefuna cry, 'My father, they have killed me!' as he ran towards him. Dazed with fear, Okonkwo drew his machete and cut him down. He was afraid of being thought weak."[6] This event is a factor in the conversion of his beloved oldest son, Nwoye, who changes his name to Isaac and becomes estranged from his father. Achebe said in a 2008 interview "that Okonkwo is paying the penalty for his treatment of women, and that all his problems, all the things he did wrong, can be seen as offenses against the feminine."[7]

Okonkwo's rejection of the feminine has literary as well as moral consequences. He pays little heed to the tales and proverbs that women love to tell. Instead, wanting his sons to grow up as tough men, he "encouraged the boys to sit with him in his *obi*, and he told them stories of the land—masculine stories of violence and bloodshed." But his firstborn son isn't so sure. "Nwoye knew that it was right to be masculine and to be violent but somehow he still preferred the stories his mother used to tell" (53). Her stories pave the way for his future openness to conversion. In Achebe's own case, the tales that his mother and grandmother told him as a boy became the basis for his revolutionary practice as a novelist, after he'd honed his skills in a very different oral medium: radio.

In his art as in his life, Achebe sought a complementary interplay of cultures and perspectives. He often quoted an Ibo proverb: *"Wherever something stands, something else will stand beside it."* As he commented in 1988: "There is no one way to anything. The Ibo people who made that proverb are very insistent on this—there is no absolute anything. They are against excess—their world is a world of dualities . . . If there is one God, fine. There will be others as well. If there is one point of view, fine. There will be a second point of view."[8] And following his immensely influential novel, a third point of view, and a fourth, and many more to come.

28. Wole Soyinka, *Death and the King's Horseman*

In 1961, a quarter century before he became Africa's first winner of a Nobel Prize for literature, a young Wole Soyinka performed in a radio play version of *Things Fall Apart*. A year later, he attended the conference at Makerere University College in Uganda where Achebe gave his address on the African writer and the English language. In *Death and the King's Horseman* (1975), Soyinka brings many of Achebe's themes to the stage, developing them for the rapidly globalizing postcolonial world of the 1970s. The play's global footprint is increasing today in a newly expanding mediascape. A Netflix film version of the play was announced in June 2020, together with a series based on a Nigerian woman's debut novel. In a news release about the production, Soyinka was quoted as expressing his pleasure that the producer is a woman: "In a creative industry which, even in pioneering countries, is so male dominated, it is always a delight to see robust challenges offered by the female gender, and of attestable quality. Mo Abudu's incursion into this arena as film and television producer has been especially stimulating. It becomes part of one's sense of achievement, if one has contributed, however minutely, to the creation of an enabling environment."[9]

Like *Things Fall Apart*, Soyinka's play centers on a powerful but flawed hero who comes into conflict with a colonial administration hostile to local religious customs, and the hero's patriarchal obsessions run counter to the perspectives of the women around him. The play also dramatizes a clash of generations as well as of cultures, hinging on a son's shocking death. Yet *Death and the King's Horseman* combines many different literary strands, and it is based on an actual event. In 1946, when a Yoruba king died, the king's companion and counselor Elesin, known as the Horseman of the King, prepared to commit suicide as commanded by tradition, in order to accompany his king into the afterlife. Nigeria was still a British colony, and the colonial District Officer placed Elesin under arrest in order to prevent the ritual suicide from taking place. This act of mercy backfired when Elesin's eldest son committed suicide in his father's place.

A friend of Soyinka, Duro Ladipo, had already written a play on this theme in Yoruba under the title *Oba Waja*, "The King Is Dead." This short, polemical play unambiguously blames the tragedy on the English imperialists who have denied Elesin his proper role in the immemorial social and cosmic order. As he laments in sexualized language, "My charms were rendered impotent / By the European; / My medicines have gone stale in their calabash."[10] Soyinka developed a far more complex play, drawing on traditional Yoruba drama, in which music, song, and dance convey much of a work's meaning. Soyinka also builds on the traditions of Greek tragedy, with a group of market women, led by the feisty Iyaloja, serving as his version of a Greek chorus. Two years earlier, Soyinka had published an adaptation of Euripides, *The Bacchae: A Communion Rite*, in which he boldly associated Greek tragedy and Christian sacrifice: the tearing apart of King Pentheus by the ecstatic Bacchantes becomes a version of the sacrament of communion.

Soyinka's Elesin has much in common with Sophocles' Oedipus. Both are faced with the need to carry through an ancestral pattern that other characters—Oedipus's wife, Jocasta, District Officer Pilkings in Soyinka—wish to relegate to ancient history. In both plays, the life of the community requires the hero's self-sacrifice. *Death and the King's Horseman* also ends with a Sophoclean combination of reversal and recognition, complete with dialogue concerning vision and blindness. Elesin's son Olunde is deeply disappointed when he discovers that his father hasn't committed suicide as he should have.

Elesin reacts to Olunde's palpable disgust by crying, "Oh son, don't let the sight of your father turn you blind!"[11] The son's blinding insight into his father's failure is doubled with the father's reciprocal, devastating vision of his son's success, when Olunde's body is displayed to him in the final scene.

Soyinka's play can also be compared to Shakespeare's tragedies. Unable to free himself from earthly attachments, Elesin has delayed his suicide in order to consummate a last-minute marriage, much as King Lear tries to retain a sizeable retinue even after giving the kingdom over to his three daughters. Echoes of *Hamlet* can be heard as well. Soyinka has Olunde returning from medical school in England—a modern equivalent to Hamlet's philosophy studies in Germany—to try to heal the murderous disorder he finds at home. Like the young Hamlet, Olunde loses his own life in the process.

Soyinka takes further Conrad's overlaying of Africa and England. In *Heart of Darkness* Marlow connects the Congo River and the Thames; now, one of the market women asks: "Is it not the same ocean that washes this land and the white man's land?" (28). Soyinka complicates the theme of the intertwining of civilization and barbarism by shifting the story from its occurrence in 1946 back into the midst of World War II. When Jane expresses her horror at the prospect of Elesin's ritual suicide, Olunde retorts, "Is that worse than mass suicide? Mrs. Pilkings, what do you call what those young men are sent to do by their generals in this war?" (44).

Like *Things Fall Apart*, Soyinka's play portrays the tragedy of a community struggling to uphold its traditions in the face of colonial domination. Yet Nigeria's situation in 1975 was very different from 1958, when Achebe was writing on the cusp of independence. A parliamentary government was established in 1960, but it was overthrown in a military coup in 1966, and growing ethnic and economic conflicts led to the Nigerian-Biafran civil war of 1967–70. Soyinka suffered two years of imprisonment on charges of aiding the Biafran cause, then went into exile in England, where he wrote his play. Though Soyinka set the action back in the colonial period, Elesin's attempt to satisfy his personal desires by evoking traditional customs echoes comparable efforts by Nigeria's military leaders in the 1970s—a similarity we'll see in Georges Ngal's work as well.

Building on Achebe's call for African writers to reinvent the English language, Soyinka uses English as both a resource and a weapon. Pilkings and his fellow administrators use blunt language with their African subordinates, who often speak in a creolized English ("Mista Pirinkin, sir") that registers their lower status in the colonial hierarchy. But Soyinka plays with the politics of language among his African characters as well. When the Nigerian Sergeant Amusa goes to arrest Elesin to prevent his suicide, the market women block his path. After mocking him sexually, they take on British accents: "What a cheek! What impertinence!" (28). They then stage a little play within the play, acting the roles of self-satisfied colonialists: "I have a rather faithful ox called Amusa"; "Never known a native to tell the truth" (30). Amusa is reduced to a stammering pidgin: "We dey go now, but make you no say we no warn you" (31).

Yet even though he is working for the colonists, Amusa retains a deep-seated respect for his culture's traditional values, and he is horrified when Pilkings and his wife, Jane, don Yoruba *egungun* costumes for a costume ball. The *egungun* are the spirits of the dead, full of uncanny power (Figure 26). Amusa pleads with Pilkings, "I beg you sir, what you think you do with that dress? It belong to dead cult, not for human being" (19). Pilkings only mocks Amusa for giving credence to such "mumbo-jumbo."

The position of Jane Pilkings is particularly interesting in this war of races, genders, and words. Though she is loyal to her often obtuse husband, she makes genuine efforts to understand what's really going on, and she gradually becomes aware of parallels between the natives and herself as a woman within a patriarchal society. As she and Pilkings prepare to head off to the costume ball, hearing the ominous sound of drumming in the distance, she hints that he may not have been handling the problem of Elesin "with your usual

26. Egungun *costume*

brilliance—to begin with that is." Pilkings impatiently replies: "Shut up woman and get your things on," to which she responds in the language of a native servant: "Alright boss, coming" (27).

Once Olunde arrives, he tries to make Jane see the logic of his father's planned self-sacrifice, but here we see the limits of her understanding: "However cleverly you try to put it," she says, "it is still a barbaric custom. It is even worse—it's feudal!" (43). Her shift from the charge of barbarism to feudalism is telling: like Marlow comparing the modern Congo to Roman Britain, Jane associates modern-day Nigeria with medieval Europe. Yet Conrad never suggests that there's any problem with such an anachronistic view of Africa, whereas the thoroughly modern medical student Olunde shows us that African customs can't be pigeonholed as medieval barbarity. In Soyinka's work, we see the deep interconnectedness of ancient and modern, African and Western culture, embodied in a masterpiece of locally rooted world literature.

29. Georges Ngal, *Giambatista Viko,* or *The Rape of African Discourse*

In 1975, the same year that Wole Soyinka published *Death and the King's Horseman*, the Congolese novelist and academic Georges Ngal explored re-lated issues of language and identity in his brilliant novella *Giambatista Viko,* but in a satiric rather than tragic mode. Ngal's self-obsessed antihero is an African intellectual who is eager to make a name for himself on the world stage. Viko belongs to an institute of African studies that is riven between Europe-centered cosmopolitans and xenophobic Afrocentrists who reject Western culture out of hand. He has been struggling for two years to write the great African novel, a work that he longs to finish so that he can be invited to conferences in Paris and Rome. Yet instead of writing he spends his time on the phone with his disciple and sidekick Niaiseux ("Simpleton"), scheming against his Africanist colleagues, developing a cutting-edge theory of writing, and looking for ways to pad his résumé.

Viko knows that he has to produce a major work if he is to achieve his goal of becoming "the Napoleon of African letters,"[12] but like Achebe and Soyinka he knows that it's no simple matter to blend African and European cultures. Casting about for inspiration, he recalls the *New Science* of his namesake, the Italian humanist Giambattista Vico, whose 1725 treatise asserted that all lan-guage began in the poetic cries of primitive people. Inspired, Viko decides that he can use orality as his ticket to international fame, using an extravagantly experimental style: "abrupt opacities here, profound transparencies there . . . Punctuation? Don't even mention it!" (45–6).

His goal is within his grasp; but then disaster strikes. The Afrocentrists gain the upper hand at his institute, and they go public with a series of accusations against him: of plagiarism; of sexual indiscretions with a visiting Italian femi-nist; and above all, of betraying Africa by plotting to prostitute the mysteries of oral culture for Western exploitation—the "rape of African discourse" of the novel's subtitle. Outraged, a group of tribal elders arrests Viko and Niai-seux. They stage a show trial, which concludes by sentencing the two to wander around Central Africa, recovering their connection to native life.

A trenchant satire of problems of identity in a globalizing world, *Giambatista Viko* is a pathbreaking exploration of the vexed relations between metropolitan centers and peripheral former colonies. Ngal's own life has spanned the globe, with periods spent living and teaching in Africa, Europe, and North America. He was born in 1933 in what was still the Belgian Congo and came of age during the country's struggle for independence. Bilingual in French and in one of the several Bantu languages, he studied philosophy and theology in Jesuit schools. In an interview in 1975, he said that his teachers possessed "a liberal and humanistic spirit. In their students this developed a contestatory, critical, and anti-conformist spirit; something extraordinary beneath the colonial sky."[13] After earning a doctorate in Switzerland with a thesis on the Caribbean poet Aimé Césaire, he returned in 1968 as a professor of Francophone literature at his alma mater, and then at the University of Lubumbashi. There, one of his colleagues was the novelist and critic Valentin-Yves Mudimbe, with whom he developed a rivalrous friendship. Ngal spent two years lecturing and teaching abroad during 1973–5, and it was then that he began his novel, which he completed upon his return to Lubumbashi.

As Ngal worked on *Giambatista Viko*, his antihero took on various personal traits of Mudimbe, both in appearance and in his love of surrounding himself with disciples. Mudimbe himself had published a well-regarded novel two years before, *Entre les eaux* (*Between Tides*), whose hero is also caught between African and Western culture, Catholicism and revolutionary action. But far from appreciating Ngal's satiric treatment of similar themes, Mudimbe took the book personally, and he actually lodged a legal complaint, accusing him of defamation. Remarkably, then, like his own hero Ngal found himself subject to legal action by his university rival. This could be called a situation of life imitating art, though more precisely Mudimbe was accusing Ngal's *art* of too closely mirroring *life*.

The academic conflicts in the 1970s reflected the tumultuous politics of the country as a whole. Following decolonization in 1960, the leaders of the newly independent Democratic Republic of the Congo were divided between Westernizers and African-centered nationalists who wished to break with colonial times and emphasize African cultural identity. Several chaotic years ensued after the Marxist prime minister Patrice Lumumba was assassinated by opponents supported by Belgium and by the American CIA. Finally in 1965 power was seized by the army's chief of staff, Joseph-Désiré Mobutu, who held power for over thirty years, murdering many opponents and enriching himself and his cronies. He renamed the country Zaire and promoted "Zaïrization," requiring his citizens to adopt African names in place of the European names they'd often been given at birth. He dropped his own name of Joseph-Désiré and became Mobutu Sese Seko Nkuku wa za Banga ("all-conquering warrior, who goes from triumph to triumph"). As a result of this policy, during the 1970s Ngal didn't publish under his baptismal name, Georges, which he replaced with the symbolic name Mbwil a Mpang, "spiritual leader from Mpang."

Giambatista Viko says nothing about national politics, but the tribal elders' show trial, and their brutal methods of punishment, clearly echo the regime's practices. Yet Ngal's satire extends to his own protagonist, hilariously dissecting Viko's vanity, his self-promotion, and his unstable mixture of insecurity and megalomania. Viko is a surprisingly sympathetic character, embodying very real tensions experienced by people with a foot in each of two different cultures. These tensions yield literary innovations both in style and in content. Viko's search for an orally infused French responds to Achebe's call for the reinvention of the old colonial languages in African terms. Ngal shared with Achebe and Soyinka a deep fascination with indigenous oral styles and performative modes of storytelling, and his hero seeks to forge a path between conformism and creativity, French structuralism and tribal lore, independence and authoritarianism, and to make his Afro-Italian name truly his own.

Translation is a key element of Viko's strategy for achieving worldwide fame. As he tells Niaiseux:

No *savant* today can get by without a knowledge of several international languages. To know English—not to mention French, that goes without saying—Spanish, Russian, that's good. Japanese, that's even better; Chinese is ten times better, since the future, the key to the future, belongs to Asia, especially to China. The Westerners are terribly afraid of the Yellow Peril, but how long can they hope to hold out? They know how to combat yellow fever, arrest its spread. But they can't do a thing against the Yellow Peril. Translations! That will pad the list of my publications.

Not that Viko knows Japanese or Chinese himself; he plans to ask his visiting colleagues Sing-chiang Chu and Hitachi Huyafusia-yama to translate some of his articles. He hopes to get the essays published with the translators' names suppressed, so as to give the impression that he has done his own translations. Marxist that he is, Viko has a passing qualm about the ethics of exploiting his colleagues' labor in this way, but Niaiseux reassures him that "deontologically speaking, it isn't intellectual dishonesty" at all, but simple collegiality (45).

Giambatista Viko is a compelling meditation on the perils of artistic creation in a world of unequal power relations, where vanity, self-defensiveness, and a will to power pervade every group. As such, Ngal's novella gave no comfort to any side in the decolonization and postcolonial debates of the 1970s and 1980s, and until now it has only been available in French. I've long said that it ought to be translated, and finally I decided to put my time where my mouth is. *Giambatista Viko, or The Rape of African Discourse* is now in press, both in English and in French, in the Modern Language Association's "Texts and Translations" series. It is a novel whose time has come.

30. Chimamanda Ngozi Adichie, *The Thing Around Your Neck*

Born in Enugu in southeastern Nigeria, not far from Chinua Achebe's birthplace, Chimamanda Adichie came to the United States for college, and since then she has divided her time between the two countries. Deeply if somewhat ambivalently indebted to Achebe, she develops comparable themes from a woman's perspective in the fully globalized world that Soyinka and Ngal were just beginning to portray in the mid-1970s. She was thirty-two when she published her short-story collection *The Thing Around Your Neck* in 2009, but by then her two previous books—*Purple Hibiscus* (2003) and *Half of a Yellow Sun* (2006), about the Nigerian–Biafran civil war—had already been translated into thirty languages. In 2013 her TED talk "We Should All Be Feminists" was sampled by Beyoncé on her album *Flawless*.

Shortly after she published *The Thing Around Your Neck*, Adichie gave a TED talk on "The Danger of a Single Story," which has been viewed more than twenty-four *million* times. There she stresses the importance of the differing perspectives that fiction can give us—if we can find different kinds of writing. Daughter of a professor and a university administrator, she was an early reader:

> And what I read were British and American children's books. I was also an early writer. And when I began to write, at about the age of seven, stories in pencil with crayon illustrations that my poor mother was obligated to read, I wrote exactly the kinds of stories I was reading. All my characters were white and blue-eyed. They played in the snow. They ate apples . . . Now, this despite the fact that I lived in Nigeria. I had never been outside Nigeria. We didn't have snow. We ate mangoes.

Her sense of what she could write changed when she discovered African fiction (she names Chinua Achebe and the Francophone writer Camara Laye). She says that "I went through a mental shift in my perception of literature," and she started "to write about things I recognized. So what the discovery of African writers did for me was this: It saved me from having a single story of what books are."[14] Her own stories offer multiple perspectives. They take place in America as well as Nigeria, and often a single story features a decisive change in perspective.

Adichie's writing combines revelation and restraint. In the opening story, "Cell One," the narrator's brother shows his character by *not* making a story of his treatment by brutal guards while in jail: "Nnamabia did not say what had happened to him in Cell One . . . It would have been so easy for him, my charming brother, to make a sleek drama of his story, but he did not."[15] The stories probe the moral and psychological consequences of decisions made or not made, as women deal with disappointing marriages, or a husband mourns the death of his wife whose ghost comforts him at night. A woman's child is accidentally shot by policemen who break into their home looking for her husband, a critic of the regime. The bereaved mother is now at the American embassy, seeking a visa so as to join her husband, who has fled abroad. The story turns on her refusal to play up the tragedy of her boy's murder in order to win over a skeptical consular official; she decides to stay in Nigeria, to tend his grave.

Adichie's stories have a strongly political cast, whether in terms of national or gender politics. As she said in a 2005 interview: "In a place of scarce resources made scarcer by artificial means, life is always political. In writing about that life, you assume a political role."[16] But she hasn't wanted to be read only through a political lens. As she remarked a few years later: "Whatever I write, somebody is somehow going to find a way to show that I'm really writing about political oppression in Africa. Often I'm asked, 'Were you trying to use that as a metaphor for the politics of your country?' And I think, 'Well, no. No, it was a story about a woman and a man. It was not about bloody political oppression.'"[17]

A story entitled "Jumping Monkey Hill" gives a pointed portrayal of the representational demands made on African writers. The heroine, Ujunwa, is attending a two-week writers' retreat at a posh South African estate, presided over by an elderly white man, Edward, who hits on the attractive women in the group. During their stay, each participant writes a story to present to the group. Edward lectures a Zimbabwean writer that her story isn't "authentic," as it isn't political enough: "The writing was certainly ambitious, but the story itself begged the question 'So what?' There was something terribly passé about it when one considered all the other things happening in Zimbabwe under the horrible Mugabe" (107). Asserting his privilege in the very act of denying it, he insists that he isn't speaking "as an Oxford-trained Africanist, but as one who was keen on the real Africa and not the imposing of Western ideas on African venues" (108). When Ujunwa reads her story of a banker crassly trying to seduce two women who need his business, Edward dismisses it as "implausible," declaring: "This is agenda writing, it isn't a real story of real people." Ujunwa retorts that it was taken directly from her life. She returns in tears to her cabin, and in the story's metafictional final sentence, "as she walked back to her cabin, she wondered whether this ending, in a story, would be considered plausible" (114).

Chinua Achebe wrote a glowing blurb for Adichie's novel *Half of a Yellow Sun*, calling her "a new writer endowed with the gift of ancient storytellers." In turn, in 2010 she wrote the introduction to the Everyman edition of his *African Trilogy*. Yet by then her writing had moved considerably beyond his orbit. In "Jumping Monkey Hill," two of the writers argue over his legacy: "The Zimbabwean said Achebe was boring and did nothing with style, and the Kenyan said that was a sacrilege and snatched at the Zimbabwean's wineglass, until she recanted, laughing, saying of course Achebe was sublime" (102).

The collection's final story, "The Headstrong Historian," subtly but firmly rewrites *Things Fall Apart*. Whereas the other stories are set in the present, this story begins with the protagonist, Nwamgba, recalling her life in an Igbo village in the late nineteenth century. Years later, she is remembering her deceased husband, Obierika, which is the name of Okonkwo's closest friend in Achebe's novel. This might seem a mere coincidence, but soon the connection is made direct. Unable to have a child, Nwamgba decided to find a second wife for her husband. Her best friend "promptly suggested, for Obierika's second wife, the young girl from the Okonkwo family; the girl had beautiful wide hips and was respectful, nothing like the young girls of today with their heads full of nonsense" (201).

Then Nwamgba succeeds in having a son, and Adichie revisits the major themes of *Things Fall Apart*, including the son's conversion to Christianity and his estrangement from his family. But unlike Okonkwo's hypermasculine world, Adichie's village features a strong Women's Council, which restrains Nwamgba's cousins from stealing her land after her husband's death. Eventually her son marries and has a daughter, whom Nwamgba regards as Obierika brought back to life; she names her Afamefuna, "My Name Will Not Be Lost" (214).

Years later, a dying Nwamgba is visited by Afamefuna, now going by her baptismal name, Grace. In a culminating rewriting of *Things Fall Apart*, Grace is carrying a British textbook with a chapter titled "The Pacification of the Primitive Tribes of Southern Nigeria" (215). Achebe's colonial history of the pacification of the "Lower Niger" is now nationalized to "Southern Nigeria," but otherwise it seems that little has changed in the European male discourse. Then in a flash-forward, we learn that Grace will go on to become a prize-winning professor of history. She'll travel to London and Paris, "sifting through moldy files in archives, reimagining the lives and smells of her grandmother's world, for the book she would write called *Pacifying with Bullets: A Reclaimed History of Southern Nigeria*" (217). A Nigerian woman's history replaces the neocolonial textbook, even as Adichie's story itself rewrites *Things Fall Apart*.

Then the story, and the collection, ends with a return to the present, leaving rewritings behind to show Grace beside her dying grandmother: "But on that day as she sat at her grandmother's bedside in the fading evening light, Grace was not contemplating the future. She simply held her grandmother's hand, the palm thickened from years of making pottery" (218). A human connection, and a woman's everyday artistry: a perfect anticipation of Adichie's own craft.

CHAPTER SEVEN

Israel/Palestine:
Strangers in a Strange Land

31. The Hebrew Bible

The issues of imperial conquest and colonial rule that we've explored in sub-Saharan Africa have deep histories farther north as well. Throughout the past four millennia, the region of Israel/Palestine has seen particularly fraught conflicts between—and among—local populations and a whole series of foreign powers. On my first trip to Jerusalem some years ago, I was taking a taxi to give a lecture up at Hebrew University on Mount Scopus, when we passed an anomalously vacant lot. When I asked the driver why such a large plot was standing empty, he replied: "Every meter of this land is covered in blood." No further explanation was offered, or apparently needed.

The bestselling book of all time, the Bible gives eloquent expression to the region's religious, cultural, and political life two and three millennia ago. It continues to offer us deep literary pleasure today, even though most of the biblical writers wouldn't have thought of themselves as writing "literature" at all. With the exception of a few texts such as the Book of Jonah, they certainly weren't in the business of writing fiction, and they composed poetry for liturgical or prophetic purposes, not as Egyptian-style "songs of excellent enjoyment" to be served up at banquets. Yet the Hebrew Bible grew out of a vibrant poetic and storytelling tradition. With some exceptions (one scholar has spoken of "the Death Valley of the Chronicler"),[1] the Bible's religious messages are often conveyed through eminently literary means.

The Hebrew Bible presents a transcendent vision of a single and all-powerful God, as merciful as he is just. He has embodied his covenant with his chosen people in a comprehensive ritual order, grounded in history and reinforced with psalms, prophetic poetry, and evocative storytelling. Yet unlike the epic productions of imperial powers, the Bible's stories and poetry are profoundly marked by the traumas of repeated invasion and the perennial threats of assimilation and the loss of cultural memory. These dangers reached a high point in 597 B.C.E., when the Babylonian king Nebuchadnezzar conquered Jerusalem and deported its leaders and many of the people into exile. The Babylonian exile inspired some of the greatest biblical writing, such as the haunting Psalm 137:

> By the waters of Babylon,
>   there we sat down and wept
>   when we remembered Zion.
> On the willows there
>   we hung up our pyres.
> For there our captors
>   required of us songs,
>   and our tormentors, mirth, saying,
> "Sing us one of the songs of Zion!"
> How shall we sing the Lord's song
>   in a foreign land?[2]

In that climactic line, *eik nashir et-shir-Adonai al admath nekhar?*, the term *nekhar*, "foreign," is aptly chosen for its Babylonian setting: it is cognate with Akkadian *nakarum*, which means "enemy" or "rebel."

The biblical writers were often caught, if I can put it this way, between Iraq and a soft place, the soft place being the seductive "fleshpots of Egypt." One of the masterpieces of biblical narrative is the story of Joseph in Genesis 37–50, and it shows the dangerous attraction that Egypt presented for the migrant laborers who periodically ventured down to find work in the fertile Nile Delta. As the story begins, Joseph's father has been showing favoritism toward him, and his jealous older brothers are about to kill him when they observe a caravan approaching, carrying spices to sell down in Egypt. These passing traders provide a safety valve for the family conflict: the brothers sell Joseph to the traders, who in turn sell him to the Egyptian official Potiphar.

Egypt was everything Israel was not: a polytheistic land of myriad temples and magical transformations, a wealthy and secure country, with long-established cultural traditions and with rigid social hierarchies. A foreign slave would ordinarily have no prospect of success in this environment, but God causes Joseph to prosper in everything he does, and Potiphar puts him in charge of his household. But then, filled with passion for Joseph, Potiphar's wife tries to seduce him. When he rejects her, she claims that he has tried to rape her, and she emphasizes his foreignness: "See," she tells her servants, "my husband has brought among us a Hebrew to mock us!" (Genesis 39:14). Her servants might really have more in common with Joseph than with their haughty mistress, but Potiphar's wife shrewdly invokes ethnic loyalty ("to mock *us*," "l'zahak ba*nu*") to override any solidarity among workers.

In this episode, Joseph isn't only thrust into a foreign land. He is caught up in a foreign story as well, much as a character who goes to Prague today will often have Kafkaesque experiences there. An Egyptian story, "The Tale of the Two Brothers," had previously featured a false accusation by a spurned wife.[3] The hero of the tale, Bata, is working for his older brother, Anubis, when Anubis's wife asks him to become her lover. Bata refuses, whereupon she tells her husband that he's tried to seduce her. The two stories develop this theme in very different ways. The Egyptian tale proceeds by a fairytale logic, complete with talking animals and the hero's transformation into a bull and then a pine tree. In the form of a splinter, he impregnates his sister-in-law, who has become the pharaoh's mistress, and he's reborn as the next pharaoh, whereupon he executes his sister-in-law-turned-surrogate-mother. By contrast, Joseph prospers by prudently managing the economy for the pharaoh, with no miraculous abilities beyond his God-given skill at interpreting dreams, and eventually he magnanimously forgives his brothers for having sold him into slavery.

Joseph's success has an ambiguous undercurrent. During the seven years of famine that follow the prosperous years when he stockpiled grain, Joseph distributes the grain to the starving Egyptians in exchange for their servitude to the pharaoh—in effect, visiting slavery upon the entire population. The immigrant can get the job done, but it's a bad business. His own descendants may not enjoy the benefits: no sooner has Joseph died than "there arose a new king over Egypt, who did not know Joseph" (Exodus 1:8), and he enslaves the entire population of Hebrew guest workers. God now provides a great leader, Moses, to lead the Israelites out of Egypt—a story that African American slaves would later look to for inspiration—but Moses barely lives to begin his tale. Having been saved from slaughter when his mother sets him adrift on the Nile, he is found and brought up by the pharaoh's daughter, but then he kills an overseer who is beating a Hebrew slave. He flees Egypt, but he isn't restored to his ancestral homeland, as we might expect; instead, he settles in an in-between space, the land of Midian on the Arabian Peninsula, where the locals think he's an Egyptian. There he marries a Midianite woman and has a son. He gives the child a resonant name: Gershon, derived from the term *ger*, "stranger, resident alien." "For he said, 'I have been a stranger in a strange land'" (Exodus 2:22, in the eloquent phrasing of the King James Version).

Moses is on the verge of permanent assimilation, until God appears to him in the form of a burning bush and enlists him to lead his people to freedom. God describes Israel as "a land flowing with milk and honey," but he somewhat ominously adds that it's also "the place of the Canaanites, the Hittites, the Amorites, the Perizzites, the Hivites, and the Jebusites" (Exodus 3:8). From

27. Israelites going into exile

the Bible's Joseph to Kafka's Joseph K., peripheral or minority characters have often found themselves to be strangers in a strange land even when they're at home.

For many of the Israelites, it wouldn't be home for long. The twelve Hebrew tribes became a united kingdom under Saul in around 1047 B.C.E., but following the death of Solomon in 930 the kingdom split into Israel to the north and the smaller kingdom of Judah in the south. In 750 B.C.E. the northern kingdom was overrun by the Assyrians, who deported a substantial portion of the ten tribes living there, resettling different groups all around Mesopotamia. In Figure 27 the exiles' miserable condition is underscored by the ribs showing through the flanks of their emaciated cattle.

It is this devastating loss that underlies the instructions in Exodus 28 for the elaborate garments that Aaron as High Priest is to wear when he comes before God, with gemstones on his shoulders engraved with the names of the twelve tribes, six names on each shoulder, "as stones of remembrance for the sons of Israel" (Exodus 28:12). He will also wear a breastplate, adorned with four rows of precious stones:

> A row of carnelian, chrysolite, and emerald shall be the first row; and the
> second row a turquoise, a sapphire, and a diamond; and the third row a
> jacinth, an agate, and an amethyst; and the fourth row a beryl, an onyx, and

a jasper; they shall be set in gold filigree. There shall be twelve stones with
their names according to the names of the sons of Israel; they shall be like
signets, each engraved with its name, for the twelve tribes . . . So Aaron
shall bear the names of the sons of Israel in the breastpiece of judgment upon
his heart, when he goes into the holy place, to bring them to continual
remembrance before the Lord. (Exodus 28:17–29)

Reflecting the intimate connection of ritual and poetry in the Hebrew Bible,
this passage is echoed in the climactic lines of the Song of Songs:

> Set me as a seal upon your heart,
> as a seal upon your arm;
> for love is strong as death,
> passion fierce as the grave.[4]

So the lovers affirm; but the Priestly writer who set the twelve jeweled names
as a seal upon Aaron's heart was writing two or three centuries after the
northern kingdom's destruction, and he knew that ten of those twelve tribes
had long ago vanished from the world. They live today in the Lord's memory,
and thanks to the Bible's poetry and prose, in ours as well.

32. The New Testament

The cultures of the ancient Near East were often in conflict, but they also had
much in common, including similar scribal cultures. Despite their differing
writing systems, overlapping literary traditions connected the Song of Songs
to Egyptian love poetry and the story of Noah to the Mesopotamian flood narratives from which it derives. As an index of an underlying Near Eastern identity, we might take the first-person pronoun "I," which is *ani* in Hebrew, *ana*
in Arabic, *anakum* in Akkadian, and *anek* in Egyptian. The Israelites managed
to hold their own throughout waves of Babylonian, Egyptian, Assyrian, and

Persian invasions, but a different kind of challenge had arisen by the time of Jesus's birth: the soft power of Hellenistic culture, reinforced by the military might of the expanding Roman Empire. By the second century B.C.E., Jews in Egypt needed the Bible translated into Greek, and by Jesus's time Greek was edging out Hebrew and Aramaic in the Roman province of Judea, at least among the upper classes.

The seductive power of Greco-Roman culture was brought home to me on a visit to Masada, the palace-fortress that Herod the Great built in the 30s B.C.E., perched high above the Dead Sea (Figure 28). Masada was besieged and overrun by Roman troops during the First Jewish-Roman War of 66–73 C.E., and in modern Israel it has become an emblem of resistance to foreign domination. But what most struck me there was Herod's calidarium, where steam would be piped in beneath the floor for the final stage of his bath. Here I was, on a sun-blasted mountaintop in one of the hottest places on earth, where a visiting tourist had died of heat stroke a few days before, and Herod needed a *sauna*? But of course he did; in his day, there was no place like Rome. The Romans loved to build forums and refreshing bath complexes in the most

28. The view from Masada

God-forsaken outposts, even including the distant, dank colony of Britain that Conrad evokes at the start of *Heart of Darkness*. You can still visit the Roman bath from which the resort city of Bath takes its name. Under the inexorable pressure of Greco-Roman culture, the literatures of Egypt, Babylonia, and many smaller cultures had vanished by the time of Jesus's birth. Their very writing systems were supplanted by the Greek and then Roman alphabet, and the Mediterranean had been knitted into the Roman *mare nostrum*.

Yet it was precisely this newly integrated world that enabled a reform movement within the local Judean community to go viral; merchant vessels and Roman triremes served as prime vectors of the viral spread, much as cruise ships and 747s do today. Even before they began traveling abroad, the apostles could spread the word about their faith in a newly globalized Jerusalem. As we're told in the book of Acts, "there were devout Jews from every nation under heaven living in Jerusalem," together with a growing number of gentiles. God had enabled Joseph to interpret the pharaoh's dreams in Egyptian, but at Pentecost he now gives the apostles the miraculous ability to be understood in every possible language:

> The crowd gathered and was bewildered, because each one heard them speaking in the native language of each. Amazed and astonished, they asked "Are not all these who are speaking Galileans? And how is it that we hear, each of us, in our own native language? Parthians, Medes, Elamites, and residents of Mesopotamia, Judea and Cappadocia, Pontus and Asia, Phrygia and Pamphylia, Egypt and the parts of Libya belonging to Cyrene, and visitors from Rome, both Jews and proselytes, Cretans and Arabs—in our own languages we hear them speaking about God's deeds of power."[5]

Even without the linguistic miracle of Pentecost, the New Testament's writers could address their entire known world through the medium of Greek. This opportunity presented an unprecedented literary challenge: How to tell a local story for a global audience? This is a fundamental issue for writers today, especially if they live in peripheral areas and can't assume that readers elsewhere will know anything about Turkish or Thai literature and history. The New Testament gives one of the earliest cases of peripheral writing intended for a wider world.

It is this changing audience that accounts for the progressive rewriting of Jesus's startling last words on the cross. The earliest of the gospels, perhaps written in around 50 C.E., Mark's gospel gives Jesus's utterance in Aramaic and then translates it: "At three o'clock Jesus cried out with a loud voice, 'Eloi, eloi, lema sabachthani?' which means, 'My God, my God, why have you forsaken me?'" (Mark 15:34, NRSV). Writing slightly later, Matthew follows Mark, though he changes "Eloi" to the Hebrew form, "Eli." Modern readers have often taken these words as a cry of existential despair, but the evangelists couldn't possibly have seen Jesus as doubting God's constant presence. Jesus has previously predicted his necessary death, and just before he is arrested in the Garden of Gethsemane, he is grief-stricken and agitated, but he asks of God only that "if it is possible, let this cup pass from me; yet not what I want but what you want" (Matthew 26:39). So what could Jesus's words on the cross really mean?

In recording Jesus's last words, Matthew and Mark expect their readers to recognize their source, for Jesus is quoting Psalm 22:

My God, my God, why have you forsaken me?
Why are you so far from helping me,
    from the words of my groaning?
O my God, I cry by day, but you do not answer;
    and by night, but find no rest. (22:1–2)

This psalm was traditionally interpreted as a prayer in which King David successfully sought God's protection when his son Absalom attempted to usurp the throne. Having voiced his anguish, the poet immediately evokes God's steadfast aid:

Yet you are holy,

 enthroned on the praises of Israel.

In you our ancestors trusted;

 they trusted, and you delivered them.

To you they cried, and were saved;

 in you they trusted, and were not put to shame.

(22:3–5)

As poems in the Near East were known by their first line, we may infer that Jesus was comforting himself in his agony by reciting the entire psalm. Just from the opening line, a Jewish audience would immediately understand the point, much as if someone today might say "A stitch in time..." knowing that the listener will reflexively supply "saves nine."

The psalm was helpful not only to Jesus but to Matthew and Mark as they sought to make sense, and an ordered narrative, out of "the scandal of the cross." Matthew in particular always wants to show how Jesus's life and teachings fulfill biblical prophecies, and he adds in the detail of the Roman soldiers casting lots for Jesus's clothing, an element taken directly from the same psalm ("they divide my clothes among themselves, / and for my clothing they cast lots," 22:18). Some manuscripts of the gospel actually quote these lines and say that the soldiers divided Jesus's clothing "in order that what had been spoken through the prophet might be fulfilled."[6]

Very well; but what about Luke's gospel? There Jesus's last words become far less emotionally fraught: "Father, into your hands I commit my spirit" (Luke 23:46). Yet rather than a repression of existential dread, this change reflects the young religion's expanding audience. Luke was writing some thirty years after Mark, and he frames his gospel as addressed to a Greek friend, "most excellent Theophilus" (lover of God). Luke has in view a mixed audience of Jews and gentiles, and he knows that his gentile readers won't get the reference to Psalm 22. So he quotes Jesus citing a *different* psalm, with a line that can be taken out of context without confusion:

In you, O Lord, I seek refuge;

   do not let me ever be put to shame;

   in your righteousness deliver me.

Incline your ear to me,

   rescue me speedily.

Be a rock of refuge for me,

   a strong fortress to save me.

You are indeed my rock and my fortress;

   for your name's sake lead me and guide me,

   take me out of the net that is hidden for me,

   for you are my refuge.

Into your hand I commit my spirit;

   You have redeemed me, O Lord, faithful God.

            (Psalm 31:1–5)

A couple of decades later, John's gospel doesn't look for a biblical reference at all, but simply has Jesus say: "It is completed" (John 19:30). (This is usually translated "It is finished," which may wrongly suggest that the jig is up; what Jesus says in Greek is "*Tetelestai*," signifying the reaching of a goal or *telos*.) John cites the Hebrew Bible only half as often as the earlier gospels do, and he frequently adds explanations for the foreign reader. His focus is on the significance for readers everywhere of Jesus's life and teaching.

Jesus only died once, but in the gospels his death was reborn in three different ways: first as a decisive intervention within Judaism, lastly in what we can call John's universal literature. In between these poles, Luke is writing a locally grounded work that is shaped so as to be read by different audiences at home and abroad—a solution that many world writers pursue today. The arc of Luke's narrative in Luke–Acts extends from Jesus in Nazareth to Paul in Rome. In the closing lines of the Acts of the Apostles he lives in Rome "for two whole years at his own expense" (Acts 28:30), boldly proclaiming Jesus's teachings to all comers, in the very heart of the world's greatest empire. Paul was a pivotal figure in the translation of Christianity into a world religion; for his part, writing for multiple audiences around the Mediterranean world, Luke composed what may well be the first narrative ever conceived as a work of world literature.

33. D. A. Mishani, *The Missing File*

In the opening scene of *The Missing File*, a weary detective, Avi Abraham, is visited at the end of the day by a woman who wants him to find her teenager, who hasn't come home from school. Avi assures her that the boy has probably just gone off to see a girlfriend or smoke some weed, and then bursts out: "Do you know why there are no detective novels in Hebrew?" He continues:

> Because we don't have crimes like that. We don't have serial killers; we don't
> have kidnappings; and there aren't many rapists out there attacking women
> on the streets. Here, when a crime is committed, it's usually the neighbor,
> the uncle, the grandfather, and there's no need for a complex investigation to
> find the criminal and clear up the mystery. There's simply no mystery here.[7]

Needless to say, Mishani will prove Avi wrong.

Avi's claim reflects the situation that Dror Mishani found when he was growing up in the 1980s. Like Chimamanda Adichie, he was a precocious reader, and again like her, the books he could find—at least in the detective genre to which he was drawn—were British imports. As he says in an essay entitled "The Mystery of the Hebrew Detective," he became a devotee of Conan Doyle at age eight, and by the time he was twelve, he'd read all the Agatha Christies available in his local public library. "I was standing in front of the library shelves that offered almost no other detective novels and asked myself: *And now what? Are there really no other detectives in the world for me to read?*"[8]

Mishani goes on to say that issues of ethnicity, class, and nationalism had suppressed the genre in Israel. Instead there were thrillers and spy novels, often tied to the Arab–Israeli conflict, where the real action was in the Mossad intelligence agency and the state security force, the Shin Bet. Ordinary domestic crimes were investigated by the local police forces, largely staffed by Mizrahis—Jews of Middle Eastern or North African descent—and their work wasn't seen as emblematic of the nation or even as involving dramatic conflict. Mishani's novels fill this gap, and the sly brilliance of his plotting, together with the emotional depth of his writing, have put his detective fictions on the world map. Like Donna Leon, he is participating in the most international of literary genres, and like her, he is also praised for conveying the flavor of his chosen locale, the gritty Tel Aviv suburb of Holon.

As we've seen with Luke's gospel, a work's meaning changes as it travels abroad. In Mishani's case, his work has become both more local *and* more international in the process, as we can see if we compare the current Hebrew version to the 2013 American edition (Figure 29). The starkly stylized cover of *Tik ne'edar* shows the teenager with his backpack—a detail that reflects a pun in Hebrew, as the word *"tik"* means "bag" or "file," and so it suggests both the boy's missing school bag (a key clue in the plot) and the case gone astray. Below the title, we're told that this is the first Avi Abraham investigation. The emphasis is on the mystery to be solved, with no specific local or international reference.

By contrast, the American edition is reframed for its international audience.

29. *Mishani in Hebrew and in English*

Dror Mishani himself has been renamed as a more British-style "D. A. Mishani," and the cover is adorned with a glowing blurb from HENNING MANKELL, INTERNATIONAL BESTSELLING AUTHOR OF THE KURT WALLANDER MYSTERY SERIES. Whereas the front cover emphasizes the book's international appeal, the back cover goes local. A description at the top situates the novel in a "quiet suburb of Tel Aviv," while a central blurb emphasizes that "the sense of place here is fascinating," and a final quote announces that "Readers of edgy mysteries set in unusual places will eagerly await his planned sequel."

I first became interested in Mishani when I was co-editing a collection on *Crime Fiction as World Literature* (2017), together with my European colleagues Louise Nilsson and Theo D'haen. We included an excellent contribution from Maayan Eitan, then a graduate student at the University of Michigan, who was skeptical of the claim that detective fictions really give any local reality beyond a veneer of local color. She gave the example of a passage from the Nordic Noir of Mishani's admirer Henning Mankell:

> The skies above the police station and the Ystad Hospital were almost
> pitch-black when Wallander left the building. It was past seven. He turned
> right at Kristianstadsvägen and right again onto Fridhemsgatan, getting
> swallowed up among the walkers. [...] He tried not to get caught up in their
> walking pace. Slower, slowly. It was a pleasant early-September evening.
> There wouldn't be many like this in the coming months.[9]

Eitan then revealed that she'd played a trick on us, as the passage is actually taken from Mishani's novel. All she had to do was to change a couple of names (the Holon Institute of Technology becoming Ystad Hospital, Fichman Street becoming Kristianstadsvägen), and she turned a pleasant Israeli May evening into a Scandinavian September.

Building on Eitan's shrewd observation, we can add that sometimes not even the names need to be changed. When Avi reflects on how his neighborhood has altered since he was a boy, the changes largely involve the new presence of international chains:

> The dunes between Neve Remez and Kiryat Sharet, the two grey
> neighborhoods he had lived in all his life, were almost gone—replaced by
> apartment towers, a public library, a design museum, and a shopping mall,
> glowing in the darkness like a space station on the moon. At the halfway
> mark to Kiryat Sharet, the bright neon signs of Zara, Office Depot, and Cup
> o' Joe beckoned to his left, and he thought about crossing the street and
> going into the mall. (11–12)

Yet local differences remain. Like the gospel writers' references to the Hebrew Bible, these will often loom larger for the local audience than for the foreign reader. The ethnic tensions between Mizrahi immigrants and Zionist "Sabras" of Israeli birth will be suggested to Mishani's countrymen by the very difference of their names, as the Mizrahis typically have Arabic-sounding names such as Sharabi and Mantsour. This difference can be seen in the patronizing way in which Avi is addressed by a Shin Bet officer: "'Uri from the service' had spoken to him like the owner of a restaurant would speak to his lowliest dishwasher, despite probably being his junior both in age and in rank" (89). Even so, the ethnic difference underlying Uri's obnoxious attitude probably won't be evident to a foreign reader.

Other local differences continue to have a strong impact, even in translation. Avi has comically awkward interactions with his distracted father and his nudgy Jewish mother. He must be the first detective in literature to get a call from his mom, while he's on a trip to Brussels for police work, hoping that he's properly bundled up against the rain. More somberly, the missing boy's mother turns out to be an abused wife, caught within the limited options offered to her in her environment: "She appeared lost. She wasn't used to making decisions—or insisting. 'I don't know if something happened to him,' she said. 'It's not like him to disappear like this' " (5). Later, as the situation worsens, "her whimpering was soft, stifled, fragmented, like that of a dog that has been left outside the house and is trying to get in" (48).

The Missing File is at once local and global, not in a fixed proportion but on more of a sliding scale, whose balance will be set differently by different readers. People attuned to the Israeli context will perceive more of that dimension, while other readers will enjoy Mishani's engagement with the world of crime fiction. My favorite intertextual moment is the opening scene in *A Possibility of Violence*, the second Avi Abraham novel. He is sitting on a park bench in Brussels, together with his Slovenian-Belgian girlfriend, Marianka, taking a break from reading "a detective novel by Boris Akunin,"[10] when suddenly they're accosted by a mentally disturbed woman. What Avi doesn't realize is that the situation he is thrust into is a variation on the opening scene of Boris Akunin's *The Winter Queen*, the first in his series featuring his Sherlockian hero Erast Petrovich Fandorin.

Avi has been thinking he's in the homeland of Agatha Christie's Belgian hero, Hercule Poirot, whom he believes regularly gets his cases wrong, but he fails to see that he's just been transported into Akunin's czarist Russia. But then, as we're told in the epigraph to *The Missing File*, taken—untranslated—from Diderot's *Jacques le fataliste*: *"Comment s'étaient-ils rencontrés? Par hasard, comme tout le monde"* ("How did they meet? By chance, like everyone"). They haven't met each other by chance, in fact, but by authorial design, as Mishani situates his Israeli detective squarely within the capacious frame of world literature.

34. Émile Habibi, *The Secret Life of Saeed the Pessoptimist*

While Dror Mishani's Mizrahi characters experience life in Israel as second-class citizens, the situation of Palestinians is considerably more fraught. This is true even for Palestinian Christians such as Habibi. Born in 1921 to an Arab

Christian family in Haifa, then under British rule, Émile Habibi (or Habiby) became a journalist in the 1940s, editing a leftist newspaper, *Al-Ittihad* (Unity). Both Arab and Jewish resistance to the British had been growing since the 1930s, but after the United Nations set up a partition plan in late 1947 an open civil war broke out, which led to the unilateral declaration of the establishment of the State of Israel on May 14, 1948. A coalition of Arab states invaded Israel the next day. They expected a decisive victory but were defeated in 1949 after more than a year of hard fighting. During this period, known in Arabic as the Nakba (the catastrophe), some 700,000 Palestinians went into exile.

In the ensuing three years an equivalent number of Jews migrated into the new state, and the Palestinians who remained in Israel came inexorably under Israeli rule. Habibi continued his journalism and heightened his political activity during this period. He co-founded the Israeli Communist Party, though he left it in 1991 when party members opposed Mikhail Gorbachev's reforms in the Soviet Union. He was sharply critical of Israeli policies toward Palestinians but supported the goal of peaceful coexistence in two states. He served in the Israeli Knesset for two decades, resigning in 1972 to devote himself to his writing, and published his masterpiece, *The Secret Life of Saeed the Pessoptimist*, in 1974. In the early 1990s he received literary prizes both from the Palestine Liberation Organization and from the State of Israel. In response to criticism of his accepting the Israeli prize, he wrote: "A dialogue of prizes is better than a dialogue of stones and bullets."

Like many postcolonial writers, Habibi combines local and European traditions. His antihero is a classic Arab trickster figure whose tale is framed in terms drawn from Voltaire's *Candide*. After the Arab–Israeli war of 1948–9, Saeed becomes an informer for the Israeli police against Palestinian Communists, hoping to be able to live in his hometown of Haifa and be reunited with his sweetheart, Yuaad, who has been forced out of Israel but whose name means "will return." Saeed ends up marrying another woman, with whom he has a son. A series of darkly comic misadventures culminates in the death of his son, who is killed after becoming a resistance fighter. Saeed becomes

convinced that he's been contacted by aliens and writes his story while confined in an insane asylum located in a former British prison. At the novel's end,
Saeed himself has disappeared; he may have died, or else he is hiding in ancient
catacombs beneath the city of Acre, or perhaps he's been spirited away to outer
space by his alien friends.

Saeed's family goes by the name of Pessoptimist, an appellation they've
richly earned. The family has a long lineage of marital infidelities and political
compromises; the wives have always been unfaithful, and the men work for the
Israeli government and for dictators around the Middle East. Saeed proudly
states that "the first Arab to be appointed by the government of Israel as head
of the Committee for the Distribution of Dandelion and Watercress in
Upper Galilee is from our family," having sold out for an absurdly trivial
reward. He is continuing to struggle, but not for justice or for some meaningful
promotion: he is seeking, "so far unsuccessfully, distribution rights for Lower
Galilee too."[11]

As an example of the family's pessoptimism, Saeed quotes his mother's response when one of his brothers is killed in an industrial accident. Unwittingly
echoing Voltaire's Pangloss, "she said hoarsely: 'It's best it happened like this
and not some other way!'" Her newly widowed daughter-in-law angrily asks
what could possibly have been worse, to which the mother calmly replies: "For
you to have run off during his life, my girl, to have run away with some other
man." Saeed dryly adds: "One should remember, of course, that my mother
knew our family history all too well." Soon the young widow does run off with
another man, who proves to be sterile. "When my mother heard that he was
so, she repeated her favorite saying, 'And why should we not praise God?'"
Saeed concludes: "So what are we then? Optimists or pessimists?" (13).

One chapter is devoted to "The Amazing Similarity between Candide and
Saeed." Criticized by his extraterrestrial friend for imitating Candide, Saeed
retorts: "Don't blame me for that. Blame our way of life that hasn't changed
since Voltaire's day, except that El Dorado has now come to exist on this
planet" (72)—a Panglossian assertion that fatuously echoes Zionist utopian-

ism. Habibi's satire leaves no one untouched. Voltaire saw himself as the voice and arbiter of reason, and Candide was an honorable innocent, but Saeed is at once naïve and corrupt. In 1948, as head of the collaborationist Palestinian Union of Workers, he filches property abandoned by fleeing Arabs, taking what's left after the homes have been pilfered by the Custodian of Abandoned Properties and by Haifa's newly installed Arab leadership. Then in 1956, after the Six-Day War, when Saeed sees destitute people selling their wedding dishes for a British pound per set, he pessoptimistically concludes: "from *gratis*, we had moved to one pound. Things are truly progressing!" (45).

Throughout the novel, we see how resistance and betrayal are intricately intertwined. The Palestinians who have been coopted into working for the State of Israel have become complicit in the Israeli program to "render a whole nation utterly and completely forgotten" (16). Habibi brings this theme home through telling details. Thus after the 1948 war, having commandeered a schoolroom, the occupying force uses the blackboards for Ping-Pong tables. Yet the State of Israel and the cooperating Palestinians aren't the only targets of Habibi's satire. Running through the novel is a searching critique of Arab elites around the Middle East, who have kept Palestinians in refugee camps and promoted popular anger against Israel as a way of deflecting attention from their own authoritarianism and greed. It is no wonder that Saeed's always compromised family, scattered among "all of the Arab countries not yet occupied," includes a captain in Syria, a major in Iraq, a lieutenant-colonel in Lebanon, and a relative "who has specialized in lighting the cigarettes of different kings" (9).

As we'll see when we come to *Candide*, Voltaire satirized religious dogmatism, but he soft-pedaled criticism of his own aristocratic class. By contrast, Habibi shows the investment in the status quo on the part of powerful Arabs and Israelis alike, and even as he enlists our ironic sympathy for his hapless hero, Saeed, he suggests that powerlessness as well as power can corrupt. Voltaire's heroine, Cunégonde, does what she has to do to survive, but she maintains her poise and a fundamental integrity throughout her checkered career;

Saeed's choices involve a far more troubling blend of cowardice and treachery. His son finally rebels against his passivity, and though he dies in the attempt, he points the way toward an ongoing resistance that is the only hope for ultimate success—a resistance that Habibi wants thoughtful Arabs and Jews alike to mount against the status quo. Saeed hopes that the situation can one day change, but only if the people find better alternatives than collaboration or bullets. They need to work together to build society on a new basis, something Saeed isn't about to attempt himself. At the story's end, sitting like a saintly ascetic upon a high pillar—apparently a television antenna—Saeed finds himself carried into the sky like a cloud. Far below, he sees his ancestors and his loved ones all gathered together. Looking up at him, his lost wife, Yuaad, declares: "When this cloud passes, the sun will shine once more!" (160).

35. Mahmoud Darwish, *The Butterfly's Burden*

I first encountered Mahmoud Darwish's poetry through the work of Edward Said. Among Said's many books, my personal favorite is *After the Last Sky* (1986), in which he evokes an exile's memories of home as he reflects on photographs of everyday Palestinian life by a French photographer. Said took his title from Darwish's poem "The Earth Is Closing on Us," in which the poet—then living in exile in Beirut—asks: "Where should we go after the last frontiers? / Where should the birds fly after the last sky?"[12] The Canadian artist Freda Guttman used these lines in 2008 in a resonant collage (Figure 30). There is a nice ambiguity in Guttman's use of the poem. The opening lines appear at the bottom, and if we read the images going upward from there, we see the progressive disappearance of the Palestinian refugees during the Nakba—the Catastrophe—of 1948. Yet in that direction, the three questioning lines are in the wrong order. They should be read from the top downward, and in that event the poetry brings the displaced Palestinians increasingly into focus.

Presence and absence are intertwined throughout Darwish's work, up

Where should we go after the last frontiers?

Where should the birds fly after the last sky?

Where should the plants sleep after the last breath of air?

The earth is closing in on us pushing us through the last passage, and we tear off our limbs to pass through.

30. Freda Guttman, The Earth
Is Closing on Us *(2008)*

through his late book *In the Presence of Absence* (*Fī Hadrat al-Ghiyāb*), published two years before his death in 2008. In that shifting collection of epigrams, prose poems, and vignettes, he recalls his many experiences of dislocation and exile. These began in 1948 when he was seven years old, when Israeli forces invaded his village and the family fled in the night toward Lebanon.

> We had no enemy at that time except light and sound. That night we had
> no ally but luck. The soft voice of fear reprimands you: Do not cough,
> boy, because coughing leads death to its destination! Do not light a match,
> father, because a glimpse of your little flame will attract a barrage of
> bullets . . . When a distant light appeared, you had to take the shape of a
> shrub or a tiny rock and hold your breath, lest the slandering light
> hear you.[13]

The family returned from Lebanon a year later, but the Israelis had destroyed their village, and so they settled in Acre, within the borders of the new State of Israel. As they'd been away, they were now in the oxymoronic category of "present-absentees," constantly having to justify their right to be back in their homeland. Darwish began publishing strongly political poetry in the 1960s, and he was repeatedly jailed until he went into exile, living in Moscow, Cairo, Beirut, Tunisia, and Paris. He returned in 1995 in order to work with his friend Émile Habibi on a film about Habibi's life and work, but he arrived only in time for Habibi's funeral. He divided his time thereafter between Amman, Jordan, and Ramallah, on the West Bank.

As fundamental as the Palestinian struggle was for Darwish, he developed his work in dialogue with world poetry, and his earliest commitment was to poetic language itself. In *In the Presence of Absence*, he addresses his childhood self: "You love poetry, and the rhythm spurred on by the letter *Nūn* takes you into a white night . . . No tribe has triumphed without a poet and no poet has triumphed unless defeated in love." He adds: "You will enter rooms you do not know as one tale begets another in Scheherazade's endless nights. You become part of a tale in a magical world that resembles nothing around you" (29). He feels that "words are beings. The game will so bewitch you that you become part of it." But he wonders: "How can words have enough space to embrace the world?" (31).

Darwish embraced the world in a cascade of poems collected in more than thirty volumes. There is no comprehensive collection of his poetry in English, though there is a good selection of poems from the 1980s and 1990s under the title *Unfortunately, It Was Paradise* (2013), and *The Butterfly's Burden* brings together three short volumes from 1998 to 2003. Appropriately, to gain a broad view of Darwish's output we have to piece together scattered publications from several countries, in books, journals, and newspapers. As Darwish says in "You'll Be Forgotten, As If You Never Were," a late poem in *The Butterfly's Burden*, "I am the king of echo. My only throne is the margin."[14]

Darwish's later poems often echo his earlier ones. *The Butterfly's Burden* takes its title from a 1998 poem in the collection, but it was originally a line in a poem from 1977. Darwish also often quotes his favorite poets, both past and present. His 2003 collection *Don't Apologize for What You've Done* (the third section of *The Butterfly's Burden*), features a dual epigraph, from the ninth-century Syrian poet Abu Tammam, "Neither you are you / nor home is home," and from the Spanish modernist Federico García Lorca, "And now, I am not I / and the house is not my house." Darwish describes these parallel verses as "a telepathy of minds, or a telepathy of destinies" (175).

Darwish's interchanges were particularly intense with his fellow Palestinians. In "Face Lost in the Wilderness," Fadwa Tuqan (1917–2003) expresses deep ambivalence about the dangerous pull of memory—of a lost country, or a lost lover, or both:

No! Don't ask me to remember. Love's memory
is dark, the dream clouded:
love is a lost phantom
in a wilderness night.

Friend, the night has slain the moon.

In the mirror of my heart you can find no shelter,

only my country's disfigured face.

her face, lovely and mutilated,

her precious face...[15]

In "Diary of a Palestinian Wound: Rubaiyat for Fadwa Tuqan," Darwish replies:

We're free not to remember because Carmel's within us

& on our eyelashes grows the grass of the Province of Galilee.

Don't say: I wish we were running to it like the river /

don't say this.

We exist in the flesh of our country & it in us.

. . .

Leave all this death to me O sister

Leave all this vagrancy.

Look! I'm braiding it into a star above its catastrophe.[16]

Darwish was also in dialogue with Edward Said, his friend for thirty years. In an essay entitled "Reflections on Exile," Said described exile as

the unhealable rift forced between a human being and a native place, between the self and its true home: its essential sadness can never be surmounted. And while it is true that literature and history contain heroic, romantic, glorious, even triumphant episodes in an exile's life, these are no more than efforts meant to overcome the crippling sorrow of estrangement. The achievements of exile are permanently undermined by the loss of something left behind forever.[17]

When Said died of leukemia at age sixty-seven in 2003, Darwish composed an elegy in which he underscored the pain but also the freedom of exile: "The outside world is exile, / exile is the world inside. / And what are you between the two? / . . . By traveling freely across cultures / those in search of the human essence / may find a space for all to sit."[18] There is a video of him reading the elegy in 2004—and his hands are as eloquent as his voice.[19]

Darwish entitled his elegy *Tibaq* ("Counterpoint"), recalling Said's "contrapuntal" approach to critical thinking, never satisfied with a single or static line of reasoning. The poem itself is contrapuntal, blending elegy and interview, as he and Said ask each other challenging questions. The poem describes Said as a heroic embodiment of intellectual resistance ("He was like the last epic hero / defending the right of Troy / to share the narrative") and also as someone enjoying the daily pleasures of life in New York and in an Ivy League university:

New York. Edward wakes up to
a lazy dawn. He plays
Mozart.
Runs round the university's tennis
court.
Thinks of the journey of ideas across
borders,
and over barriers. He reads the *New York Times*.
Writes out his furious comments. Curses an Orientalist
guiding the General to the weak point
inside the heart of an Oriental woman. He showers. Chooses
his elegant suit. Drinks
his white coffee. Shouts at the dawn:
Do not loiter.[20]

The poem ends:

Farewell,
farewell poetry of pain.[21]

In 2013 my son Peter was teaching in Jordan after graduating from college, and he gave me a present of a line from this poem (Figure 31), which he had a mosaic artist set in stone: "He thinks of the journey of ideas across borders." A perfect image of both Edward Said's and Mahmoud Darwish's lives and works—and of our own literary journey as well.

31. "He thinks of the journey of ideas across borders"

CHAPTER EIGHT

◦

Tehran–Shiraz: A Desertful of Roses

36. Marjane Satrapi, *Persepolis*

Until my wife, Lori, and I went to Iran, in 2011, I'd always thought of myself as a reasonably skeptical consumer of American media. As expected, there were carefully preserved murals with the "Death to America" slogans from the time of the Islamic Revolution, and there were many images of the Ayatollah Khomeini, in one case giving his blessing to a host of breeze-borne flowers representing the souls of martyrs in the war against Iraq. But we hadn't realized how comfortably the Iranian middle class has long blended Western and Middle Eastern cultures, and I'd unwittingly absorbed an assumption that "Shi'ite" means a particularly rigorous (even "fundamentalist") mode of Islam. So it was a surprise to find that many Iranians have a flexible mode of religious practice. They've determined, for example, that the five daily prayers can be performed in three groupings, more easily worked into the fabric of their day, and a deep religious belief isn't at all incompatible with an active engagement in contemporary world culture.

Even the Islamic Revolution itself has become infused with up-to-date brand messaging, as we found from a banner at the city airport in Tehran on our way down to Shiraz (Figure 32). Having made sure, as instructed, to

32. Branding the Islamic Revolution

associate the revolution with the Imam's name, we went on to have a nice day, and an excellent visit.

These complexities are brilliantly illustrated in Marjane Satrapi's bestselling *Persepolis*, first published in French in four volumes in 2000–2001, then in English translation in 2003–4 and in several more languages since then. In 2007 Satrapi wrote and directed a prize-winning animated film based on her book.[1] As Satrapi says in a preface to the book, since the revolution of 1979,

> this old and great civilization has been discussed mostly in connection with fundamentalism, fanaticism, and terrorism. As an Iranian who has lived more than half of my life in Iran, I know that this image is far from the truth. This is why writing *Persepolis* was so important to me. I believe that an entire nation should not be judged by the wrongdoings of a few extremists. I also don't want those Iranians who lost their lives in prisons defending freedom, who died in the war against Iraq, who suffered under various repressive regimes, or who were forced to leave their families and flee their homeland to be forgotten.
>
> One can forgive but one should never forget.[2]

Persepolis explores the ambiguous power of words and images, which can preserve memories that shouldn't be forgotten but can also distort or repress them. The book is at once an autobiography, a capsule history of the revolution and its aftermath, and a meditation on the cultural complexity of the contemporary world. Satrapi recounts the history of her secular family, who were opposed to the Shah's regime and then to the repressive Islamic state that replaced it. Amid the bombarding of Tehran during the Iran–Iraq War, Marjane's parents send her at age fourteen to school in Austria, where she struggles to fit in and gradually falls into heavy drug use and a period of homelessness. Returning home at age eighteen, she studies graphic design, has a brief and unsatisfying marriage, and finally leaves Iran forever four years later. In the book's final panel, Marjane bids farewell to her hopeful parents and her tearful grandmother. At the bottom of the panel, she says that "I only saw her again once, during the Iranian New Year in March 1995. She died January 4, 1996 . . . Freedom had a price . . ." (341).

Like Primo Levi and Paul Celan, Satrapi confronts the limits of language in the face of trauma, and in her case she probes the limits of visual as well as verbal representation. When a playmate is killed in a bombardment, young Marjane discovers her friend's arm—still wearing a favorite bracelet—protruding from the rubble of her building (Figure 33). We see Marjane's horrified reaction, and then the panel goes black.

Persepolis was the ceremonial capital of the Achaemenid Empire in the sixth to fourth centuries B.C.E., and is famous for its elegant relief sculptures. Generations of visitors have left their mark on the site. On my own visit there, I was startled to find a graffiti inscription reading "Stanley NEW YORK HERALD 1870." Here was Conrad's nemesis, Henry Morton Stanley, proudly advertising his employer, shortly before the *Herald* sent him to Africa on his epic quest to find Dr. Livingstone. Satrapi's evocation of ancient Persian culture in her title could be an essentializing gesture, but throughout the book she satirizes Iranian exceptionalism, and she mocks the efforts of political and religious leaders to cloak their self-interested policies in rhetorics of ancient glory

33. Marjane encounters death

or modern martyrdom alike. Her one representation of Persepolis satirizes Shah Reza Pahlavi's use of the site to his own greater glory in 1971, when he staged a massive party to celebrate the 2,500th anniversary of the site's establishment by Cyrus the Great (Figure 34).

Like many of Orhan Pamuk's characters, in *Persepolis* Marjane finds herself painfully caught between cultures. After she returns from Austria, she falls into a suicidal depression: "My calamity could be summarized in one sentence: I was nothing. I was a Westerner in Iran, an Iranian in the West. I had no identity. I didn't even know anymore why I was living" (272). Yet throughout her tribulations, she retains an indomitable rebellious streak. She also has a wry, self-mocking sense of humor that yields many comic moments in the book, leavening her tragic tale of ever-renewed wars and oppressions. When she visits a childhood friend who has returned severely disabled from the front in the Iran–Iraq War, their conversation falters until her friend tells a delightfully obscene joke. Their laughter restores their ability to communicate.

34. Persepolis in Persepolis

Marjane's resistance is inspired by her parents, her grandmother, and the memory of a beloved uncle executed by the Ayatollah's regime. When she was still a little girl, he'd told her the story of his years of imprisonment by the Shah's regime, enjoining her to remember everything: "Our family memory must not be lost. Even if it's not easy for you, even if you don't understand it all." Sitting cross-legged in her pajamas by his chair, she replies: "Don't worry, I'll never forget" (60). *Persepolis* is an extraordinary act of personal and cultural memory, though in its highly individual framing it certainly isn't (and doesn't claim to be) the whole story of Iranian history and culture. Almost without exception, for example, the Iranians we meet in the book are either idealistic leftists or repressive Islamists. A good complement to Satrapi's contemporary, secular quest for identity is the book we'll now turn to, Farid ud-Din Attar's twelfth-century *Conference of the Birds*, a work infused with Sufi mysticism that provides Attar with his own basis for a searching critique of his culture and its ideologies.

37. Farid ud-Din Attar, *The Conference of the Birds*

One of the greatest of all narratives of spiritual quest and fulfillment, Attar's masterpiece has affinities both with Dante's *Commedia* and with Boccaccio's *Decameron*, as it combines mystical allegory with down-to-earth storytelling. It also resembles the framed tales of *The Thousand and One Nights*, whose Persian original would have been created a couple of centuries before Attar composed his poem in the late twelfth century. Within the overall frame of the birds' quest, a series of historical anecdotes and tall tales blend instruction and entertainment. And like Dante a century after him, or Marjane Satrapi today, Attar composed his poem in the wake of imperial conquests and internal strife.

Shakespeare's Prospero famously said that "we are such stuff / as dreams are made on, and our little life / is rounded with a sleep."[3] Attar too presents our little life as an insubstantial dreamworld, but his own life was rounded with invasions. He was born in Nishapur, 400 miles east of Tehran. It had become a major city along the Silk Road running from China to the Levant, and it was a tempting prize for invaders both from the east and from the west. Nishapur was sacked by Oghuz Turks in 1154, when Attar was about nine years old, and he lost his life when Genghis Khan destroyed the city in 1221.

In an epilogue to the poem Attar speaks in his own name, or more precisely his pen name; "Attar" means a dealer in herbs, whether for medicine or perfume, appropriately for a work that both instructs and delights. He describes himself as a kind of internal exile from a failed social world:

I'm Attar, one who deals in drugs, but my
Own heart's as dark as any musky dye,
Grieving in solitude for people who
Lack salt and sense in everything they do.
I spread the cloth, and wet my crust of bread
With all the copious salty tears I shed;

It is my heart I cook, and I am blessed
From time to time when Gabriel is my guest,
And since an angel dines with me, how can
I break the bread of every foolish man?

Just in case the political implication isn't clear, he continues:

Thanks be to God, I say, I don't consort
With worthless dupes, or hang around a court;
Why pawn my heart like this? Why eulogize
Some idiotic fool as great and wise?
No tyrant feeds me, and I've never sold
The dedication of a book for gold.

Not unlike Dante being welcomed into the circle of poets in Limbo, he declares: "My predecessors welcome me, why then / Should I seek out self-centered, vapid men?"[4]

In the body of the poem, Attar mounts his critique of a politically and morally bankrupt society through the guise of a chaotic community of birds who seek a leader to bring some order to their lives. The one sensible bird in the group, the hoopoe, knows of such a spiritual guide, the mythical bird called the Simorgh, and he proposes seeking him out. Their journey will involve seven difficult stages, from the initial Valley of the Quest to the regions of Love, Insight, Detachment, Unity, Awe, Bewilderment, and finally Nothingness. "And there you are suspended, motionless," he tells them: "Till you are drawn—the impulse is not yours—/ A drop absorbed in seas that have no shores" (181).

The hoopoe's bird-brained friends enthusiastically agree to the plan, but then they begin to have their doubts. Attar wittily associates each speaker with a different rationale, tied to the bird's appearance, its habitat, its song, or its poetic associations. The nightingale can't bear to leave his roses and his lovers.

The duck simply loves waddling in streams and resists venturing into the desert, while the bejeweled partridge only cares for gems. The hawk is too tied to his status as a courtier: "I know court etiquette," he boasts, and asserts: "When I approach the king, my deference / Correctly keeps to the established rule." Ironically, the hawk is blinded by the very king he loves to serve: "My eyes are hooded and I cannot see, / But I perch proudly on my sovereign's wrist" (55).

The bulk of the poem develops the theme of the earthly attachments that keep the birds from embarking on their quest. The hoopoe responds to their ongoing worries and objections with various strategies—logic, moral teachings, and one tale after another. In the tale of "Shah Mahmud and the stoker at the public baths," a lowly bath attendant displays great hospitality to the shah but refuses promotion to the court. As he tells the shah, "If you weren't king you could be happy, sire; / I'm happy shoveling wood on this great fire—/ So I'm not less than you or more, you see . . . / I'm nothing next to you, your majesty" (160). Like many of the tales, this one works on two levels: in earthly terms, it shows a noble rejection of wealth and power, while on the spiritual level the shah can stand for God and the attendant for any earthling, humbly recognizing our insignificance before the divine.

The stoker's reply may indicate satisfaction with the status quo, but elsewhere burning wood suggests the suffering of those who give pleasure to the privileged:

A perfumed wood was burning, and its scent
Made someone sigh with somnolent content.
One said to him: "Your sigh means ecstasy;
Think of the wood, whose sigh means misery." (122)

Throughout the poem, it is Sufi dervishes who have renounced the world and its temptations. Ordinary people think they're crazy, but the Sufis are attuned to the emptiness of worldly success and the ultimate unity of all things. The divine radiance is so bright that our flickering selves will melt away like shadows in sunlight, and even the Prophet himself leads the way to the extinction of all selfhood. In Islamic tradition, Muhammad miraculously journeyed overnight from Mecca to Jerusalem and then ascended into heaven on the back of a winged beast, Boraq. In Attar's rendering, this physical ascent itself evaporates:

> First put aside the Self, and then prepare
> To mount Boraq and journey through the air;
> Drink down the cup of Nothingness; put on
> The cloak that signifies oblivion—
> Your stirrup is the void; absence must be
> The horse that bears you into vacancy.
> Destroy the body and adorn your sight
> With kohl of insubstantial, darkest night.
> First lose yourself, then lose this loss and then
> Withdraw from all that you have lost again. (221)

Finally the hoopoe cajoles the birds into setting out on their journey, which is described in just a single page: the real struggle isn't the journey itself but mustering the willpower to undertake it. A hundred thousand birds set out, but only thirty survive the arduous expedition. Finally they reach the Simorgh, whom they expect to be a magnificent otherworldly being, as he is portrayed in Persian miniatures (Figure 35).

Yet to their astonishment, this fabulously exotic creature only turns out to look like themselves: "They gazed, and dared at last to comprehend / They were the Simorgh and the journey's end" (234). The Simorgh explains that "I am a mirror set before your eyes, / And all who come before My splendour see / Themselves, their own unique reality" (235). He now reveals the pun that must have inspired the entire poem: in Persian *si morgh* would mean "thirty birds." He goes on to say that if forty or fifty of them had arrived, then they

35. Persian Simorgh

would have met with him in forty or fifty guises. They now assess "their lives, their actions, set out one by one" (234), and their souls are freed from all their past ambitions and misdeeds.

At the end of *In Search of Lost Time*, Proust describes his novel as an optical instrument through which his readers can look into themselves. In Attar's otherworldly earthly masterpiece, all history, all storytelling, the Holy Qur'an, and the poem we're reading become a hall of mirrors in which we see ourselves multiply, refracted, guided by the poet who cooks his own heart into verse.

38. *Faces of Love: Hafez and the Poets of Shiraz*

Poetry has traditionally been the most highly favored literary mode in Iran, as generally in the Middle East, and classical poetry continues to have an active life even today. Forty miles southwest of Persepolis, the city of Shiraz has long been a center of poetic production, and to this day, people love to stroll in the evening in the gardens surrounding the tomb of Shiraz's most famous poet, Hafez (1315–90). When Lori and I went on from Tehran to Shiraz, our host, Alireza Anushiravani of the University of Shiraz, took us there one evening, together with his daughter-in-law, a physician, who began reciting poems by Hafez that she knew by heart.

Hafez was one of the first Persian poets to become known in the West, and Goethe studied Persian in order to get at least a flavor of the originals. He then began writing poems to Hafez, eventually collected in his *West-Eastern Divan* (1819), using many of Hafez's images and his major theme of an elevated enjoyment of life's pleasures. Thus one poem, in which the poet runs his fingers through his lover's luxurious hair, concludes: "So hast du, Hafis, auch getan, / Wir fangen es von vornen an"[5]—"So, Hafiz, just as you did then, / We now begin to do again."

In creating a posthumous dialogue with his great predecessor—whom he addresses intimately as "du," not the formal "Sie"—Goethe was taking part across the centuries in the kind of playful poetic conversation that Persian poets loved to conduct. We get a good sense of this poetic environment in Dick Davis's collection *Faces of Love: Hafez and the Poets of Shiraz*, which includes a comprehensive introduction together with sparkling translations of poems by Hafez and two of his contemporaries: Jahan Malek Khatun—a major woman poet, unusually for the time—and Obayd-e Zakani, who is less profound than Hafez but exceptional in his frank eroticism.

These poetic rivals wrote under conditions of violent change. They came to prominence during the reign of a patron of the arts—and of Shiraz's vineyards—named Abu Es'haq, who ruled the region between 1343 and 1353. He was driven out by a warlord named Mobarez al-Din, who exiled the poets he didn't kill, forbade musical performances, and closed the city's many wine shops, which were popular gathering places for conversation, recitations, and

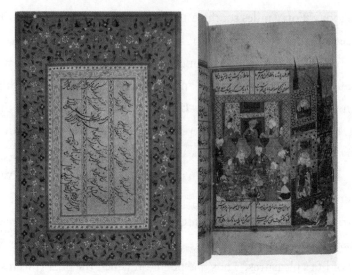

36. Hafez manuscript pages

flirting—or more—with handsome young wine servers. Five years later, Mobarez's son Shoja had his father blinded and imprisoned, and took the throne. The wine shops reopened, and the poets returned.

During his lifetime, Hafez became the most prominent poet in Persia, and ever since his day, his *divan* (collected poetry) has inspired innumerable illuminated manuscripts, featuring calligraphy as gorgeous as the scenes of poetic fellowship (Figure 36). All three of our poets speak of Shiraz as an earthly paradise. Thus Hafez: "A breeze that's scented with Shiraz's gardens / Is all the guard to guide you that you need."[6] Or again Jahan:

> Shiraz when spring is here—what pleasure equals this?
> With streams to sit by, wine to drink, and lips to kiss,
> With mingled sounds of drums and lutes and harps and flutes;
> Then, with a nice young lover near, Shiraz is bliss. (193)

During the period of banishment by Mobarez, Obayd mourned the loss of the city:

Where is Shiraz's wine, that burned our grief away?
And those brisk, pretty boys who served us, where are they?
Tomorrow if, in heaven, there is no wine or pleasure,
God's heaven will be hell, just like Shiraz today. (207)

The Shirazi poets valued shiraz-fueled companionship as highly as religious observance, even as a form of religious observance:

The ascetic longs to drink from Kosar's steam
    In paradise's shade,
And Hafez longs for wine; until, between
    The two, God's choice is made. (39)

We feel that Hafez expects God to approve his choice. For her part, Jahan is remarkably open in voicing her desires: "How envious our clothes were when we lay / Without them, clasped together, you and I!" (162).

The most popular form for these poets was the ghazal, a set of loosely connected couplets (sometimes translated as quatrains), often compared to pearls strung on a necklace:

Hafez, your poem's written now,
    The pearl you've pierced is poetry's;
Sing sweetly—heaven grants your verse
    The necklace of the Pleiades. (129)

Each couplet of a ghazal would end with the same word, the poem's leitmotif, with a rhyme leading up to it. This structure is well shown in Davis's translation from one of Jahan's poems:

Come here a moment, sit with me, don't sleep tonight,
Consider well my heart's unhappy plight, tonight;

And let your face's presence lighten me, and give
The loveliness of moonlight to the night, tonight.

Be kind now to this stranger, and don't imitate
Life as it leaves me in its headlong flight, tonight.

The poem ends:

If for a moment, I could see you in my dreams,
I'd know the sum of all this world's delight, tonight. (154)

Poets customarily name themselves at the end of their ghazal: here, as often, Jahan is punning on her own name, which means "world."

It's far from certain that Jahan actually had lovers, though according to tradition she had two husbands; rather than confessing to her adventures, she may have been showing her skill at playing with common tropes. Not everyone, though, was pleased to see a woman playing this game. A poem attributed to Obayd takes Jahan's poems literally, and insultingly plays on the meaning of her name:

My lord, the world's a faithless whore;
Aren't you ashamed of this whore's fame?
Go, seek some other cunt out—God
Himself can't make Jahan feel shame. (lxi)

In another of his poems, a woman's genitals become a patron of the arts:

Pussy remarked: "This prick's a masterpiece,
They've hung the balls beneath it very nicely;
From tip to toe, you'd say that it's as though
They'd followed my prerequisites precisely." (209)

Hafez and Jahan were never so crude, but they certainly had similar interests. We've seen Farid ud-Din Attar cooking his heart into verse, but Jahan has a different meal in mind:

> A picnic at the desert's edge, with witty friends,
> And tambourines, and harps, and lutes, is very sweet,
> And if my lover, for a moment, should drop by,
> I'll grill his liver with my body's fiery heat. (189)

Perhaps "his liver" stands in for a body part that Jahan is a little too discreet to specify.

Recalling that a name for God in the Qur'an is "the Friend," the Shirazi poets celebrate the moral virtues of deep friendship, and Hafez repeatedly mocks strict religionists who don't practice what they preach: "Although our preacher might not like to hear me mention it, / He'll never be a Moslem while he's such a hypocrite" (106). Shiraz had Jewish and Christian populations among the Muslim majority, and Hafez suggests that they too can reach God. "Everyone searches for the Friend," he says in one poem, "And love's in every house—the mosque / And synagogue are just the same" (34). Hafez finds in wine, and in love, the dissolution of self that Attar found in Sufism:

> Between the lover and the loved
>   There will be no divide,
> But you yourself, Hafez, must draw
>   The veil of Self aside. (111)

Or as he says in another poem's closing lines:

> No one has drawn aside the veil
>   of Thought as Hafez has

Or combed the curls of Speech
  as his sharp pen has, line by line. (41)

Combing the curls of speech by playing endlessly with their repertoire of themes and images—the nightingale, the rose, the overflowing wine and tears—the poets of Shiraz created a garden of poetry amid the desert of mortal life.

39. Ghalib, *A Desertful of Roses*

Born from the Arabic *qasida* or ode, the Persian ghazal spread farther east with the Mughal conquest of north India in the sixteenth century. Persian remained the prestigious literary language in the Mughal courts, and Ghalib, the greatest modern practitioner of the ghazal, wrote them both in Persian and in Urdu. Born in 1797, Mirza Asadullah Beg Khan was the descendant of Turkish aristocrats who had moved to India; by age eleven he was already showing precocious talent, and he soon began writing under the pen name Ghalib ("Victorious"). Modesty was never his prime characteristic. Though he was supported by powerful patrons, including the Mughal emperor Bahadur Shah, like Hafez he was skeptical of political power and of religious orthodoxy alike. Bahadur somewhat reluctantly appointed him as his court poet in Delhi, only after the death of his less talented poetry teacher.

During Ghalib's lifetime, people often weren't sure what to make either of his politics or of his religious views, which he expressed ambiguously or even in contradictory terms. Thus in one poem he declares: "I know that Heaven doesn't exist, but the idea / Is one of Ghalib's favorite fantasies."[7] In another poem, he asserts his piety and then immediately qualifies his belief: "I believe in one God only, and my religion is breaking rules: / When all sects go to pieces, they'll become part of the true religion" (114). Ghalib resisted pleas even from his fellow poets to write more readily understandable poems. As he says in one of his ghazals: "I have to write what's difficult, otherwise it is difficult to write" (76). In a letter to a friend he wrote, "I leave sentence upon sentence implied," and he defended himself with a quotation from Hafez: "But 'Every utterance has its time and every point has its place.' This difference is intuitively perceptible, not expressible in words."[8]

Even when they are recited, his verses can express silence—and his uncertainty as to whether the silence is within himself or in the world around him:

> Either the world is a spellbound city of the silent,
> Or I'm a stranger in the land of speech and hearing.[9]

Ghalib is a kind of Mughal modernist, "making it new" (as Ezra Pound would say) with the fragments of the tradition he draws on, first in his ghazals and then in his *divans* of collected poems: "Ghalib, I think we have caught sight of the road of oblivion. / For this is the binding string of the scattered pages of the world."[10] He uses many of the images that we've seen in Hafez and the other Shirazi poets; he cries tears of blood over his sorrows in love, and finds solace in poetry, companionship, and wine. Yet he is often uncertain of the meaning of classical tropes: "Her eyebrows do make a bow, but the rest is unclear. / What are her eyes? An arrow or something else?"[11] He also brings very modern elements into his repertoire:

> My fate with you, like a combination lock,
> Was written: at the moment we clicked, to part.[12]

Ghazals typically take the form of a loose sequence of couplets, often compared to a necklace string with pearls. Each couplet is usually linked to its neighbors less by any direct narrative or thematic progression than by a common set meter and rhyme. Or as Frances Pritchett and Owen Cornwall put it: "From the listeners' point of view, the ghazal is like a box of chocolates that are outwardly identical; only as you bite down on each one do you discover whether its heart is creamy, nutty, or full of some liqueur" (10). Within the set structure, the pleasure comes in seeing what the poet—or a group of poets composing a ghazal together—would do next. Traditionally, the second line of a couplet would have a fairly clear (though sometimes unexpected) relation to the first, but Ghalib loved to create deep and enticing ambiguities within his couplets. As a friend of his wrote, since Ghalib "avoided common principles as much as possible and didn't want to move on the broad thoroughfare, rather than wanting every verse to be widely understandable he preferred that inventiveness and un-heard-of-ness be found in his style of thought and his style of expression" (112). Appropriately, Adrienne Rich references Arthur Rimbaud's famously ungrammatical phrase "Je est un autre" in her translation of another of Ghalib's couplets:

> I is another, the rose no rose this year;
> without a meaning to perceive, what is perception?[13]

In one of his most beautiful ghazals, Ghalib identifies his poem with his own brokenness, in a complex dynamic with the woman who is said to have caused his unhappiness—and to have enabled him to compose his poem:

> I am neither the flower of music, nor the string of an instrument.
> I am the sound of my own breaking.

> You were meant to sit in the shade of your rippling hair;
> I was made to look further, into a blacker tangle.[14]

And as he says in another poem,

> I am in a place where even to me
> No news comes about myself.[15]

Ghalib's eloquent, ironic ghazals have reached a worldwide audience. Most recently, they have been disseminated on the internet in *A Desertful of Roses*, a remarkable website created by Columbia's Frances W. Pritchett.[16] As she says on a page "About this project," in 1999 she began working on a three-volume scholarly edition and commentary. But then came the attacks of 9/11, and she decided that the wider world needed to have access to this cosmopolitan Mughal poet. She has continued working on the site ever since, and it has evolved into an immense compendium. Ghalib's 234 Urdu ghazals can all be seen there, not only in the original Arabic-Persian script but also phonetically transcribed, both into the Roman alphabet and into the Hindi Devanagari script. Each ghazal is given a literal word-for-word translation, and links are provided to performances of many of them.

In a page entitled "About the ghazals," Pritchett says that translating Ghalib "in a serious literary way is a doomed mission" and "basically impossible," but she herself has been unable to resist this doomed mission; she and Owen Cornwall have recently brought out a valuable collection of Ghalib's *Selected Poems and Letters* (2017). On her website, Pritchett gives some fifty translations into English of two of his most famous ghazals, published over the course of the past hundred years. Many are fairly pedestrian, but the best translators achieve beautiful results, as can be seen from the very different renderings of the opening couplet of #111 by the poet-translators Adrienne Rich and W. S. Merwin. Rich renders the couplet as:

> Not all, only a few, return as the rose or the tulip;
> what faces there must be still veiled by the dust!

By contrast, Merwin expands each line into its own brief, unpunctuated stanza:

> Here and there in a rose or a tulip
>   a few of the faces

> only a few
>> but think of those that the dust
>>> keeps to itself

Pritchett doesn't provide poetic translations for the other ghazals, but her literal translations and commentaries make an ideal companion to reading whichever Ghalib collection one may choose to buy, including her own. Even without a printed volume at hand, you can lose yourself in *A Desertful of Roses* for hours at a time. Pritchett's website is infused with her love for Ghalib and his world, and instead of reaching a few hundred readers in print, it receives upward of 14,000 visits *per week*—a million views every sixteen months.

The broken mirrors of Ghalib's ghazals give us glimpses of what lies beyond our suffering, as he brings the entire world into his work, as Proust and the poet Stéphane Mallarmé in turn would aspire to do in France. As Ghalib says in the closing lines of one of his poems, characteristically speaking both to himself and to his reader, or to himself *as* his own reader:

> Think of it as an enchanted world with a treasury of meaning—
> Every word, Ghalib, that would come into my verse.[17]

40. Agha Shahid Ali, *Call Me Ishmael Tonight*

A leading practitioner of the ghazal has been the Kashmiri-American poet Agha Shahid Ali (1949–2001). Born in Srinagar, Ali went to Delhi for college and then moved to the USA in 1976, earning a PhD in English from Pennsylvania State University and an MFA from the University of Arizona. He went on to teach at a series of creative writing programs, and directed the MFA program at the University of Massachusetts at Amherst. Even given his Indian upbringing, the ghazal was a surprising choice for a contemporary poet in the United States. In his 1983 essay "Secular Criticism," Edward Said celebrates freely chosen modern "affiliations" against the unquestioned adherence to older "filiations."[18] In Said's terms, we might consider the ghazal as a classic instance of literary filiation, as it spread from Arabic to Persian and then Urdu under the aegis of successive cultural-political hegemonies, including the Mughal Empire. Yet Shahid Ali made an active affiliative choice to revive this classic form in English, pressing against the individualistic free-form verse that pervaded American creative writing programs at the time. He was not only a practitioner but also a promoter of the ghazal; his collection *Ravishing Disunities* brings together ghazals he'd solicited from a wide range of contemporary poets—often people who would otherwise have relegated set meter and rhyme to the dustbin of literary history.[19]

Shahid Ali was raised in a secular household, but his ghazals are haunted by the Qur'an as well as by the Persian and Arabic literary traditions, written in languages that were lost to him. Translators usually despair of conveying the sense of a ghazal while also preserving its monorhyme scheme, though as we've seen with the Shirazi poets, Dick Davis sometimes did succeed in producing couplets always leading to the same rhyme. Shahid Ali was composing directly in English and had no difficulty creating his rhyme schemes, but at times he foreswore rhyme for strategic effect. In a poem entitled "Arabic," Ali reflects on a language he couldn't speak:

The only language of loss left in the world is Arabic—
These words were said to me in a language not Arabic.

Ancestors, you've left me a plot in the family graveyard—
Why must I look, in your eyes, for prayers in Arabic?[20]

Here he gives us a deconstructed ghazal, lacking rhyme or even any set meter; it's as though his poem is translated from a lost original. It has lost the very language of loss.

The "absent presence" (as Darwish would have said) of Arabic and Persian pervades Ali's work, and he mobilizes them for current concerns. The long-running Kashmiri conflict features in many of his works, notably in his collections *The Half-inch Himalayas* (1987) and *The Country Without a Post Office* (1997). His final collection, *Call Me Ishmael Tonight* (2003), has many references to the first Gulf War and to the Israeli–Palestinian conflict. It confronts ultimate realities of war, faith, and mortality in personal as well as political terms: he completed the collection as he was dying at age fifty-two of a brain tumor.

If Arabic is now "the only language of loss left in the world," this is partly because of the resurgence of Hebrew in Israel. Long the lost language of diasporic Judaism, Hebrew is now once again a living language, and one with a hegemonic force, converting the Arabic around it into the medium in which Palestinians record their losses. Ali's loss of the language of the classically untranslatable Qur'an does not, however, entail an erasure of its sacred history, which still persists intermingled with the tropes of classical poetry. His poem "Arabic" continues:

Majnoon, his clothes ripped, still weeps for Laila.
O, this is the madness of the desert, his crazy Arabic.

Who listens to Ishmael? Even now he cries out:
Abraham, throw away your knives, recite a psalm in Arabic.

From exile Mahmoud Darwish writes to the world:
You'll all pass between the fleeting words of Arabic.

Ironically playing on the Hebrew meaning of "Ishmael," "God will hear," the poem rewrites the history it recalls, having Ishmael cry out against the violence represented by God's mysterious command to Abraham to sacrifice his brother Isaac. Ali then identifies his loss of Arabic with Darwish's long exile from his homeland.

The Qur'an still holds prophetic power in Ali's verse. In its second sūrah (chapter), the Qur'an ordains a severe fate for apostates; in "Arabic," this fate is now fulfilled by earthly violence, whether in bombs raining down on Iraq or in the murder of García Lorca during the Spanish Civil War:

> The Koran prophesied a fire of men and stones.
> Well, it's all now come true, as it was said in the Arabic.

> When Lorca died, they left the balcony open and saw:
> His *qasidas* braided, on the horizon, into knots of Arabic.

The losses extend to a Palestinian village destroyed in 1948 after the Zionist Stern Gang had massacred its inhabitants: "Where there were homes in Deir Yassein, you'll see dense forests—/ That village was razed. There's no sign of Arabic" (25). Amid all these losses, the poem closes by forging a poetic connection across languages and cultures, citing the great Israeli poet Yehuda Amichai:

> I too, O Amichai, saw the dresses of beautiful women,
> And everything else, just like you, in Death, Hebrew, and Arabic.

> They ask me to tell them what Shahid means—
> Listen: it means "The Beloved" in Persian, "witness" in Arabic.

Like Hafez and Ghalib, Shahid Ali undercuts any sharp distinction between sacred and secular histories, between political writing and aesthetic artistry, between classical and modern traditions, and in his case also between the Old World and the New. *Call Me Ishmael Tonight* takes its title from the collection's penultimate poem, "Tonight," whose closing lines merge Islamic traditions with the famous opening of Melville's *Moby Dick*:

> The hunt is over, and I hear the Call to Prayer
> fade into that of the wounded gazelle tonight.
>
> My rivals for your love—you've invited them all?
> This is mere insult, this is no farewell tonight.
>
> And I, Shahid, only am escaped to tell thee—
> God sobs in my arms. Call me Ishmael tonight. (83)

The collection ends with a moving poem, "Existed," that consists of just a single couplet:

> If you leave who will prove that my cry existed?
> Tell me what was I like before I existed. (84)

Brief though it is, this poem can be read in several ways. Just who are "you" and "I"? As in Ghalib or the Sufi poet Rumi, the addressee may be the Beloved, who could be God or a human lover. Perhaps only God can tell us what we were like before we existed, or else it is the lover in whom the poet discovers himself. But Shahid Ali may be addressing us, his readers; his cry will be forever lost if we forget him after we close his book. On the other hand, perhaps it's the reader speaking to the poet, urging him not to cease transmuting our cries into verse. But the dialogue between the poet and God, or his lover, or his reader, may equally be a dialogue between the poet and the poem itself. Here too, "you" and "I" can change places, as the poet asks his poetry not to abandon him, or, finally, as the poem begs the dying poet not to depart forever. The only way to read such a poem is to reread it, and to savor its multiple reflections in the poet's, or the poem's, or our own, "I."

If you leave who will prove that my cry existed?
Tell me what was I like before I existed.

37. Agha Shahid Ali

CHAPTER NINE

Calcutta / Kolkata: Rewriting Empire

41. Rudyard Kipling, *Kim*

Once a small trading village on India's east coast, Kalikata (or Calcutta as the British called it) became the base of the British East India Company and then the capital of the British Empire in India. In a reflection of changing identities, the city was renamed Kolkata in 2001. Even when the city was known under the British spelling and pronunciation, it was represented in very different ways by authors of different backgrounds. We begin with the radically divergent representations of India in the work of two Nobel laureates, Rudyard Kipling and Rabindranath Tagore. With all their differences, both see India as an entire world in itself, or rather as a variety of overlapping, interlocking, and disjointed worlds.

Kipling was born in 1865 in Bombay (itself now renamed Mumbai), where he was raised mostly by Hindi-speaking nannies before he was sent at age six to England for schooling. He returned to India at age sixteen and found work as a reporter for the *Civil and Military Gazette* in Lahore, where his father had become director of the city's museum. Kipling's editors were happy to run poems and stories by their young reporter when they had space to fill, and at the age of twenty-one he published his first collection of verse, *Departmental Ditties* (1886), followed two years later by *Plain Tales from the Hills* and no fewer than four more collections of short stories. He was writing for the people he was writing about. His early works feature local settings and slang that he expects his readers to recognize: they didn't need to be told that characters who have "tiffined at Peliti's" have had lunch at a posh hotel in the British summer capital of Simla.

Yet Kipling was already writing as both an insider and an outsider; after his return to India in 1881 he saw his boyhood haunts with an "England-returned" perspective. As his works caught on abroad, it was only a step farther for Kipling to translate his local knowledge for distant readers. In 1889, a year after *Plain Tales from the Hills* came out in Lahore and Calcutta, it was republished in New York and Edinburgh and in translation in Germany. Many more languages were soon to come, but thanks to the reach of English in and beyond the Empire, Kipling was becoming a global author even without translation. In 1890, *Plain Tales* appeared in multiple editions in India, England, and the USA, and his works began to do a brisk trade in Canada, South Africa, and Australia. Kipling was twenty-five.

Kipling may well be the first truly global author, in the sense of someone writing for a worldwide audience almost from the start of his career. He became adept at folding explanations and outright translations into his tales, particularly after he left India for good in 1889, living first in London, then in Vermont, then finally settling in England again. His novel *Kim* (1901) begins with a lively scene at the entrance to his father's museum, setting the stage both politically and linguistically for foreign readers:

> He sat, in defiance of municipal orders, astride the gun Zam-Zammah on her brick platform opposite the old Ajaib-Gher—the Wonder House, as the natives call the Lahore Museum. Who hold Zam-Zammah, that "*fire-breathing dragon,*" hold the Punjab; for the great green-bronze piece is always first of the conqueror's loot.
>
> There was some justification for Kim—he had kicked Lala Dinanath's boy off the trunnions—since the English held the Punjab and Kim was English.[1]

Within a few pages, Kipling goes on to give a number of Hindi terms (*jadoo, faquirs, ghi, parhari,* and more), sometimes translating them in parentheses, sometimes defining them in a paraphrase or shaping the context to suggest the meaning.

Throughout the novel, Kipling multiplies opportunities to explain local customs to us. Kim is alternately a knowledgeable insider, through whose eyes we can see India, and an Anglo-Irish outsider who needs things explained to him—and thus also to us. On the cusp of adolescence, he is both a child of his country and a neophyte in the adult world who has to be taught the ins and outs of political intrigue. For much of the book he accompanies an aged Tibetan lama, who is adept at explaining ancient Oriental ideas but is often clueless about Indian customs, which Kim can then explain.

Still more clueless are many of the Europeans who appear in the story, not only Englishmen but also rival French and Russian agents, all jockeying for power in "the Great Game" to control the subcontinent. The most interesting player of the game in Kipling's novel is Hurree Chunder Mookerjee, a "Babu" or Indian employee of the colonial government. Kipling had previously used the name in "What Happened," an anxiously jokey early poem about the danger of allowing natives to put on airs. "Hurree Chunder Mookerjee, pride of Bow Bazaar, / Owner of a native press, 'Barrishter-at-Lar,' " is granted the right to carry weapons, but then the practice spreads to less savory types:

But the Indian Government, always keen to please,
Also gave permission to horrid men like these—
Yar Mahommed Yusufzai, down to kill or steal,
Chimbu Singh from Bikaneer, Tantia the Bhil;

Killar Khan the Marri chief, Jowar Singh the Sikh,
Nubbee Baksh Punjabi Jat, Abdul Huq Rafiq—
He was a Wahabi; last, little Boh Hla-oo
Took advantage of the Act—took a Snider too.[2]

The Snider was the latest in precision riflery. Soon Mookerjee disappears, evidently murdered for his weapons. The poem concludes:

What became of Mookerjee? Ask Mahommed Yar
Prodding Siva's sacred bull down the Bow Bazar.
Speak to placid Nubbee Baksh—question land and sea—
Ask the Indian Congressmen—only don't ask me! (16)

As usual in his early work, Kipling assumes that his readers know the local landscape (here, Bow Bazar, a central Calcutta thoroughfare), and he shares his Anglo-Indian community's nervousness about the potential for new stirrings of the rebellion that had almost lost England control of India in the "Mutiny" of 1857. His interest in India's ethnic and cultural variety is here mobilized only to suggest that the country is too various, and the natives too untrustworthy, to be managed by the Hindu-dominated Indian National Congress, which had recently been established to give Indians a consultative voice in political affairs.

A decade and a half later, the Hurree Chunder Mookerjee of *Kim* is an altogether more complex character. If Kim serves as our ethnographic guide to Indian society, Hurree actually makes ethnographic observations at every opportunity, and his highest ambition is to become a Fellow of the British Royal Society. Given his subaltern colonial position, this dream is unrealistic, even absurd. Yet instead of mocking Hurree for his pretensions as he'd done in his earlier poem, Kipling makes this unlikely dream a bond between Hurree and the British spymaster Colonel Creighton. Creighton too sends essays to the Royal Society, for "deep in his heart also lay the ambition to write 'F.R.S.' after his name . . . So Creighton smiled, and thought the better of Hurree Babu, moved by the like desire" (147–8).

Hurree's ethnographical skill—like Kipling's reporter's eye—gives him insight into the manners and motives of Indians and Europeans alike, and he is adept at disguising his own motives from Europeans by playing the role of the hapless Oriental. In a key episode, he gets the better of a pair of foreign agents by pretending to be a drunken victim of British oppression: "He became thickly treasonous, and spoke in terms of sweeping indecency of a Government which had forced upon him a white man's education and neglected to supply him with a white man's salary. He babbled tales of oppression and wrong till the tears ran down his cheeks for the miseries of his land." He then staggers off, "singing love-songs of Lower Bengal" (the "lower" is a lovely touch), and collapses on a wet tree-trunk. The spies are completely taken in:

> "Decidedly this fellow is an original," said the taller of the two foreigners. "He is like the nightmare of a Viennese courier."
>
> "He represents in little India in transition—the monstrous hybridism of East and West," the Russian replied. "It is *we* who can deal with Orientals." (198–9)

Too often regarded simply as the poet of the "White Man's Burden," Kipling here stands firmly on the side of cultural hybridism, many decades before hybridity became a central element of Homi Bhabha's postcolonial theory. This hybridity appears monstrous only to the smug Russian agent who is falling victim to his own stereotypes.

Though they usually and justifiably reject his politics, a host of later Anglophone world writers are in Kipling's debt as they refine or subvert his strategies for melding many strands of English into a unique language that might best be called "Kiplingese." Kipling can be said to have invented India for many foreign readers, much as Oscar Wilde thought that Dickens and Turner had invented London. Six years after he published *Kim*, Kipling was awarded the Nobel Prize, whose citation praised him for "the power of observation, originality of imagination, virility of ideas and remarkable talent for narration which characterize the creations of this world-famous author."[3] Another six years later the Nobel was awarded to Rabindranath Tagore, who was no fan of Kipling's ideas, however virile they were. In *The Home and the World* he paints a radically different picture of his country, its people, and its needs.

42. Rabindranath Tagore, *The Home and the World*

In approaching Tagore's most famous novel, we need to appreciate the complexity of Tagore's understanding of his position both at home and in the world at large. He published the novel in 1916, just three years after he unexpectedly became the first Asian winner of the Nobel Prize for literature, but his novel is squarely directed toward social and political issues in India, and in Bengal in particular. His winning of the prize was a fluke. Annoyed with a poor English translation from Bengali of his philosophical poem cycle *Gitanjali*, he'd undertaken his own flowing, Whitmanesque translation:

> The same stream of life that runs through my veins night and day runs
>   through the world and dances in rhythmic measures.
> It is the same life that shoots in joy through the dust of the earth in
>   numberless blades of grass and breaks into tumultuous waves of leaves
>   and flowers.
> It is the same life that is rocked in the ocean-cradle of birth and of death,
>   in ebb and in flow.
> I feel my limbs are made glorious by the touch of this world of life. And
>   my pride is from the life-throb of ages dancing in my blood this moment.[4]

While visiting England in 1912, he showed the manuscript to Yeats, who wrote a glowing preface for the book, praising Tagore both as a poet and as a mystical seer. Though Tagore's translation hasn't aged well, readers at the time were charmed. When the prize was awarded to Tagore the following year, he was taken completely by surprise, and was annoyed by the fuss. If Kipling had made his name as the interpreter of India for the world, now Tagore was thrust into the role of a truly native informant. He became a world traveler, meeting with a host of writers, artists, and dignitaries on multiple trips abroad—everyone from Albert Einstein in the USA to his friend (and sometime lover) Victoria Ocampo, founder of the influential magazine *Sur* in Buenos Aires.

Tagore's first world-circling journey took place in 1916, a few months after he published *The Home and the World*. He visited Japan and then proceeded to the United States, addressing large audiences across the country before sailing to Europe and then home. In a *New York Times* interview, "A Talk with Sir Rabindranath Tagore," he was presented not only as the new voice of India, but as the embodiment of the Oriental mind in general. As the sub-headline announces: "A Bengali Poet, Nobel Prize Winner, Now in This Country, Gives His Poetic Creed and Explains Oriental Attitude Toward Literature."[5] The interviewer was Joyce Kilmer, a poet of some talent sadly known today only for his often parodied "I think that I shall never see / A poem lovely as a tree." Kilmer noted the similarity of Tagore's verses to Whitman's *Leaves of Grass*, and described him as looking like Whitman, "but with more delicacy." Tagore's delicately spiritual persona is highlighted in a sketch that my great-aunt Helen, then a young artist in New York, made of him during this trip (Figure 38).

38. *Helen Damrosch Tee-Van, portrait of Tagore (1916)*

The Home and the World was written on the threshold of Tagore's emergence as a global phenomenon. Its focus is on the advent of modernity in India and its profound effects—at once destructive and creative—on traditional life, both in public and in the domestic sphere. The novel stages debates among its three central characters: the aristocratic landowner Nikhil, his restless wife, Bimala, and the seductive political firebrand Sandip. Sandip enlists Bimala in the new cause of *Swadeshi*—the promotion of Indian manufacture and rejection of British-made goods, intended to loosen England's grip on the country and to build the economic basis for independence. He flatters Bimala as a goddess who can escape the monotony of household life and become the movement's figurehead, while Nikhil sees her slipping away but refuses to try to force her to stay within an Indian wife's traditional role.

Tagore's cautiously progressive Nikhil is often seen as a self-portrait, and Nikhil sometimes debates Sandip in terms drawn directly from Tagore's political essays, but it is Bimala whose consciousness is at the center of the story. She has to decide how to respond to Sandip's romantic and political seductions—whether to become his lover, and whether to venture from her home out into the world, or even from her women's quarters into the public rooms at the front of the mansion. In this sense, Bimala is equally a self-portrait of Tagore, loyal to her home that she knows needs to change, as she stands on the threshold of the wider world.

Tagore was then on the threshold of the *Swadeshi* movement. He had supported the movement at first, but he grew disillusioned with the growing violence of many of its partisans. He later became close friends with Gandhi and a champion of his non-violent independence movement, but in the 1910s he was sharply critical of a narrowing nationalism that favored the interests of Hindu landowners and manufacturers, to the ruin of Muslim traders whose livelihoods were being destroyed with the burning of their stocks of inexpensive British imports. Late in the novel, an angry Muslim mob attacks the estates of a wealthy Hindu landowner, and Sandip welcomes the opportunity to further the interests of his Hindu-based party. Nikhil objects to Sandip, "Why is it possible to use the Mussulmans thus, as tools against us? Is it not because we have fashioned them into such with our own intolerance?"[6] Tagore's novel was criticized for not supporting the decisive action needed to achieve independence, but it now looks prescient in diagnosing the dangers of an exclusionary nationalism that heightens Hindu / Muslim tensions to this day.

The Home and the World also portrays the personal struggles of Nikhil and Bimala to rethink the bond of marriage in a world of ambiguous new freedoms. All three of Tagore's protagonists describe themselves as split personalities, and the narrative itself is split: sections shift between the voices of Bimala, Nikhil, and Sandip, evidently in the form of their notes or diary entries, with no overall authorial consciousness. The novel thus anticipates modernist works such as Ryūnosuke Akutagawa's 1922 story "In a Budding Grove" (the primary basis for Kurosawa's film *Rashomon*), which is narrated by a series of speakers at a trial, or the multiple narrators of William Faulkner's *As I Lay Dying* (1930). Yet Tagore was first and foremost a poet, and poetry and songs appear throughout the text.

Beyond actual lines of verse, the characters' prose entries themselves are fundamentally lyrical. The book is often approached through comparisons to novelists such as Tolstoy or Tagore's Bengali predecessor Bankim Chandra Chatterjee, but it may be better to think of *The Home and the World* as a cross between the philosophical dialogues of the *Bhagavad Gita* and the dramatic monologues of Robert Browning. The book several times cites the *Gita* (which Sandip distorts for his own nefarious purposes), and at a critical moment Sandip quotes Browning's dramatic monologue "Cristina," which is spoken by a man in thrall to a powerful woman, as he is to Bimala. Surprisingly, it turns out that Sandip has tried translating Browning into Bengali. He tells Nikhil and Bimala that "I really did think at one time that I was on the verge of becoming a poet, but Providence was kind enough to save me from that disaster" (157). So even Sandip is a kind of self-portrait, at least of Tagore as he might have been if he'd become a politician instead of a poet.

These are literary contexts for reading the novel, but a quite different aspect stands out for me now, one that I wouldn't have noticed at another time: *The Home and the World* is a novel about infection. We've seen in *The Decameron* that Boccaccio linked the fever of love to the plague devastating Florence, and Tagore associates both political and romantic passion with imagery of disease. Sandip's henchmen spread lies "like flies carrying pestilential germs," and Bimala realizes that she has become "infected with their excitement" (106, 178). Like Covid-19, the virus is a foreign import. As Nikhil exclaims: "What a terrible epidemic of sin has been brought into our country from foreign lands" (166). Conversely, good impulses can go viral, and near the novel's end Sandip tells Nikhil that "the contagion of your company has turned me honest" (200)—at least to a degree. In Sandip's and Bimala's bodies, as in the body politic, different contagions are at war.

For Tagore, as in the Persian poetic tradition, it is poetry and song that can heal our divided souls. As he said in his *New York Times* interview, shortly before he sat for Aunt Helen to sketch his portrait: "The proper function of the poet is neither to direct nor to interpret his fellows, but to give expression to truth which has come to his life in fullness of music."

43. Salman Rushdie, *East, West*

The sectarian conflicts that Tagore dramatized in 1916 exploded upon India's independence in 1947, with the traumatic partition of the country into the Hindu-dominated Union of India and the Muslim Dominion of Pakistan (now further divided into Pakistan and Bangladesh). Amid waves of violence, over ten million people were displaced. Salman Rushdie was born into this time of conflict, whose long effects have marked much of his work. In his best-known novel, *Midnight's Children* (1981), he included his narrator-hero Saleem Sinai among one of 1,001 "midnight's children" born in the first hour of Indian independence on August 15, 1947 (he himself was actually born two months earlier). Saleem is born in Bombay to an impoverished Hindu single mother, but he is switched at birth with a child from a wealthy Muslim family. He grows up in the luxury that should have been enjoyed by his substitute, who becomes a street criminal and Saleem's nemesis.

Rushdie's sprawling novel plays on everything from *The Thousand and One Nights* and *A Passage to India* to Bollywood film, but here I'll focus on Rushdie's distillation of his themes in his brilliant short-story collection *East, West* (1994), which brings us fully into our present global era. Three stories under the heading "East" are set in India, three stories under the heading "West" are set in Europe, and then three stories under the heading "East, West" shift back and forth between continents. Throughout the collection, Rushdie slyly mixes realism and fantasy. A story in the "East" section, "The Prophet's Hair," tells what seems to be a completely fantastic tale: a vial containing hair from the beard of the Prophet Muhammad is stolen from the Hazratbal Shrine in Srinagar, causing a huge public disturbance and also leading to upheavals in the life of Hashim, a moneylender who acquires it. "As though, under the influence of the misappropriated relic, he had filled up with some spectral fluid,"[7] he suddenly becomes intensely religious, and he begins uncontrollably speaking harsh truths to his family, with fatal results. The only real beneficiary of the relic's presence is Hashim's blind wife, who miraculously recovers her sight.

This tale's magical realism is grounded in concrete realities. The vial of the Prophet's hair was in fact stolen from the Hazratbal Shrine, on December 26, 1963. There were mass protests all over the region, and a group called the Awami Action Committee was formed to recover the relic, which was located a few days later. This incident crystallized Kashmiri Muslims' sense of their culture being under siege by the Hindu majority. The Awami Action Committee gave rise to the Jammu and Kashmir National Liberation Front, which launched its armed struggle for an independent Kashmir.

The story's political subtext is doubled by a more personal one. Rushdie's 1988 novel, *The Satanic Verses*, had provoked demonstrations by Muslims deeply offended by the novel's irreverent depiction of the Prophet and his wives, and Iran's Ayatollah Khomeini issued a decree announcing a death sentence and promising a large reward to Rushdie's killer. Rushdie wrote *East,*

West while in hiding in England under police protection, and several of the stories obliquely reflect his situation. In "The Prophet's Hair," the money-lender Hashim is an avid collector of all sorts of odds and ends, much like Rushdie the novelist, from butterflies to samovars to bath toys. Hashim mistakenly thinks that he can treat the vial as an aesthetic object like any other: "Naturally, I don't want it for its religious value," he tells himself. "I'm a man of the world, of this world. I see it purely as a secular object of great rarity and blinding beauty" (44). He soon learns, to his and his family's cost, that he can't prize form over content, beauty over meaning. "The Prophet's Hair" is a double-edged scalpel, probing the author's self-centered secularism as well as the fundamentalists' self-righteous anger.

"Chekov and Zulu," the central story of *East, West*'s final section, inscribes duality in its very title. Yet the story doesn't treat of Russians and South Africans at all. Instead, the title characters are Indian employees of the British secret service—modern versions of Kipling's Hurree Babu—who like to imagine themselves as enacting roles from *Star Trek*. They have modified the name of the Japanese Mr. Sulu: "Zulu is a better name for what some might allege to be a wild man," Chekov says. "For a suspected savage. For a putative traitor" (153). When Zulu gets into a tight spot with a group of Sikh separatists he has infiltrated, he sends Chekov an urgent message: "*Beam me up*" (166).

Earlier, Zulu had disappeared while doing undercover work shortly after the assassination of Indira Gandhi in 1984 by one of her Sikh bodyguards. As the story opens, India House has sent Chekov to Zulu's house in suburban London to make an inquiry. Chekov's conversation with "Mrs. Zulu" is a comic masterpiece of Indian-English dialogue, but it also reveals a suspicion that her husband has been profiting from shady dealings with his fellow Sikhs:

"Fixed the place up damn fine, Mrs. Zulu, wah-wah. Tasteful decor, in spades, I must say. So much cut-glass! That bounder Zulu must be getting too much pay, more than yours truly, clever dog."

"No, how is possible? Acting Dipty's tankha must be far in excess of
Security Chief." (149)

The free intermixture of English and Hindi syntax and vocabulary plunges the
reader into the characters' bicultural life.

The two friends had adopted their nicknames as schoolboys, identifying
with *Star Trek*'s multinational crew: "Intrepid diplonauts. Our umpteen-year
mission to explore new worlds and new civilizations" (151). Yet the global landscape is never flat. Chekov and Zulu didn't become *Star Trek* devotees through
the original television series: "No TV to see it on, you see," Chekov recalls.
Unable to watch the show, they become fans by reading "a couple of cheap
paperback novelizations" (165). Significantly, they are attending the Doon
School, an elite British-style academy established in the waning years of the
Raj to train future Indian politicians and civil servants. As Rushdie's Indian
readers would know, the most famous graduates of the school were Indira
Gandhi's sons Sanjay and Rajiv.

In their adult lives, the two friends shuttle back and forth between England
and India, engaged in political work and espionage. By the story's end, Chekov
has been caught up in a repressive complicity between the British and Indian
governments, which are both using the threat of terrorism to stifle opposition,
and he dies in the explosion when a Tamil separatist assassinates Rajiv Gandhi.
In his last moments, Chekov thinks about the global spread of terror in import–
export terms:

> Because time had stopped, Chekov was able to make a number of private
> observations. "These Tamil revolutionists are not England-returned," he
> noted. "So, finally, we have learned to produce the goods at home, and no
> longer need to import. Bang goes that old dinner-party standby; so to
> speak." And, less dryly: "The tragedy is not how one dies," he thought. "It
> is how one has lived." (170)

By this point, Zulu—outraged at the Indian government's use of terror threats as an excuse to oppress Sikhs—has resigned from governmental service. He has settled in Bombay as head of a pair of private security companies, which he calls Zulu Shield and Zulu Spear, now directly honoring the Zulus in South Africa who had resisted the Dutch settlers and then fought against the British. Futuristic fantasy and imperial history—*Star Trek* and the Boer Trekkers— come together in Zulu's bicultural Bombay.

Like Kipling and Tagore before him, Rushdie writes both for a home audience and a global readership, but even the term "home" is ambiguous for him. In a reflective essay, "Imaginary Homelands," written in 1982 in the wake of the sudden success of *Midnight's Children*, Rushdie describes returning to Bombay after many years away, and then attempting in his novel to recreate his early years while knowing that his memories were fragmentary and uncertain. In a resonant pun, he says that "the Indian writer, looking back at India, does so through guilt-tinted spectacles." He adds that "our identity is at once plural and partial. Sometimes we feel that we straddle two cultures; at other times, that we fall between two stools." Yet he argues that such a double identity is fertile for a writer: "If literature is in part the business of finding new angles at which to enter reality, then once again our distance, our long geographical perspective, may provide us with such angles."[8]

44. Jamyang Norbu, *The Mandala of Sherlock Holmes*

In 1903, a decade after a Sherlock-weary Arthur Conan Doyle killed off his famous detective in "The Final Problem," he bowed to public demand and brought Sherlock back to life. In "The Adventure of the Empty House," Holmes astonishes Watson by reappearing in London. He explains that he hadn't in fact fallen into the Reichenbach Falls together with his nemesis, Professor Moriarty, but had fled Europe incognito in order to escape the revenge of Moriarty's henchmen: "I travelled for two years in Tibet, therefore, and amused myself by visiting Lhassa, and spending some days with the head lama."⁹ Nine decades later, the Tibetan activist and writer Jamyang Norbu decided to tell the story of that sojourn. He'd been writing essays for the exile community on the struggle for independence from China (a selection of his essays has been collected under the title *Shadow Tibet*), but he wanted to reach a broader audience, and so he turned to the global genre of the detective story.

In *The Mandala of Sherlock Holmes*, Sherlock solves a murder mystery in Bombay before journeying to Tibet, where he saves the life of the young Dalai Lama of his era. In the process, he becomes a strikingly otherworldly figure, even as Norbu employs Sherlock for very worldly ends. His novel was published in 1999 in India, where it won a prize, then in the USA in 2001 under the title *Sherlock Holmes: The Missing Years*. (The publisher evidently didn't think that American readers would be interested in mandalas, or perhaps know what they are.) The English edition, meanwhile, decided to have it both ways, titling the book *The Mandala of Sherlock Holmes: The Missing Years*; already in English, the book takes on new forms for different national markets—and even in different printings in the USA (Figure 39).

In addition to playing with Conan Doyle's tales, Norbu drew heavily on Kipling to create his evocation of British India; his characters, like Kipling's, enjoy "tiffining at Peliti's."¹⁰ Needing a narrator, Norbu filled Dr. Watson's shoes with *Kim*'s Hurree Chunder Mookerjee, making him the novel's dominant voice. In a preface, Norbu speaks of the puzzling Victorian terms that he encountered when first reading Conan Doyle: "For a boy from Tibet there

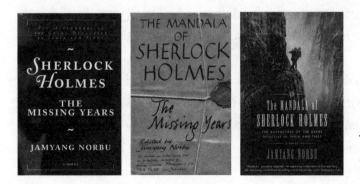

39. *Norbu in the USA, in the UK, and again in the USA*

were details in those stories that did at first cause some bewilderment. I went around for some time thinking that a 'gasogene' was a kind of primus stove and that a 'Penang lawyer' was, well, a lawyer from Penang—but these were trifling obstacles and never really got in the way of my fundamental appreciation of the stories" (x). But these phrases aren't mysterious only to Tibetan boys; I myself had to look up the meanings of "gasogene" (a seltzer-maker) and "Penang lawyer" (a cane). Norbu uses historical fiction to level the literary playing field: he can master Kipling's and Conan Doyle's fictional world, and its language, as fully as any contemporary English writer.

As in *Kim*, Norbu's Hurree works as a spy for the imperial secret service. He meets his match, however, when he is sent to sound out the motives of a mysterious Norwegian who has just arrived in Bombay—none other than Sherlock Holmes in disguise. Hurree tries a disguise of his own; he poses as a shipping company's guide, "Satyanarayan Satai, Failed Entrance, Allahabad University." Yet Holmes instantly discerns a contradictory fact of Hurree's past: "You have been in Afghanistan, I perceive." (A brilliant use, here, of Holmes's famous remark to Watson when they first meet in *A Study in Scarlet*.) Discomfited, Hurree bursts out in a kind of hyper-Babu-speak:

> Wha . . . ! Oh no, no sahib. I am most humble Hindu from Oudh, presently in remunerative and gainful employment in demi-official position of agent, *pro tem*, to respectable shipping firm. Afghanistan? Ha! Ha! Why sahib, land is wretched cold, devoid of essential facilities and civilised amenities, and natives all murdering savages—Musselmanns of worst sort—beyond redemption and majesty of British law. Why for I go to Afghanistan?

Holmes isn't fooled. " 'Why indeed?' said he, with a low chuckle that sounded rather sinister" (6). Sherlock is the first European Hurree has ever met who isn't blinded by Orientalist preconceptions: Sherlock actually sees him for who he is.

Norbu isn't just making fun of Mookerjee; instead, he builds on Kipling's portrayal of Hurree as a shrewd undercover operator, heightening Hurree's skills both as a spy and as an ethnographer. On the novel's title page, we learn that he has in fact become a Fellow of the Royal Society, as he'd fantasized in *Kim*, and a member of learned societies in Calcutta and in St. Petersburg. As the novel progresses, Hurree and Holmes learn a great deal from each other as they confront Tibet's encroaching Chinese enemies, and they part as the best of friends. *Kim*'s portrayal of the excitable, superstitious Hurree, loyal servant of Empire, makes uncomfortable reading for some of my friends in India, but the British Empire isn't Norbu's concern, and he mines Kipling in a mode of affectionate parody to bolster his attack on Chinese imperialism.

Norbu goes beyond Kipling by making Hurree a thoroughgoing rationalist; conversely, Holmes becomes a mystical seeker who uses his formidable powers of observation to pierce the veil of earthly illusion. As the novel progresses, we learn that Holmes's cocaine habit represents an attempt to blunt the emotional impact of his Buddhist awareness of the essence of life as suffering. Once he and Hurree reach Tibet, Holmes gets in touch with his inner bodhisattva. He gives up drugs and pays his respects to the gods, declaring that "from here on, science, logic and Mr. Herbert Spencer simply cease to exist. *Lha Gyalo!* [Victory to the gods!]" (138). In Tibet, Holmes and Hurree are attacked by Professor Moriarty, who is revealed as a reincarnated lama. Holmes in turn proves to be the reincarnation of "the renowned Gangsar *trulku*, former abbot of the White Garuda Monastery, one of the greatest adepts of the occult sciences" (242). In a dramatic confrontation, Moriarty and Holmes battle to the death using their spiritual powers. Moriarty is defeated, and his Chinese patrons' quest to control Tibet is stymied, at least for the remainder of the pre-Communist era.

In bringing Sherlock Holmes into the realm of what can be called Tibetan world literature, Jamyang Norbu has done more than reinvent the great detective for his political purposes; he has also revealed a spiritual dimension already encoded in the original tales but rarely seen by Western readers. Thus in one story, Holmes asks Watson: "What object is served by this circle of misery and violence and fear? It must tend to some end, or else our universe is ruled by chance, which is unthinkable. But what end? There is the great, perennial problem to which human reason is as far from an answer as ever."[11]

Grounded in Norbu's creative rereading of Kipling and Conan Doyle, *The Mandala of Sherlock Holmes* blends genre fiction and political advocacy in a mode of metafictional play, in which Tibetan Buddhism is shown to be a moral resource for the whole world, transcending greed and the quest for domination, in an ideal blend of religion and science, ancient and modern, East and West together. The book has been translated into many languages, including French, German, Hungarian, Spanish, and Vietnamese. In a further twist of the book's global life, it was reissued in 2003 in the United States under its original title, *The Mandala of Sherlock Holmes*, the third cover shown in Figure 39. Yet this new edition doesn't involve some recovered Tibetan authenticity, seconded by an image of a mandala or a temple such as several of the novel's translations use. Instead, the American reissue is geared for a postmodern audience. The image is a detail from a painting by an American artist, Mark Tansey, entitled *Derrida Queries de Man*, which shows the great deconstructionists in the guise of Holmes and Moriarty wrestling on the path above the Reichenbach Falls. The towering cliffs around them are formed not of stone but of text.

Like the novels of Donna Leon and D. A. Mishani, *The Mandala of Sherlock Holmes* testifies to the power of crime fiction to reach a worldwide audience, at once entertaining and educating its far-flung readers. The novel embodies Norbu's hope, expressed in an essay in *Shadow Tibet*, that literature can succeed where more direct political action fails:

> somehow, Lu Xun's writings have outlived the propaganda and ideology
> of his old nemesis, the Kuomintang, and will no doubt continue to be read
> and admired long after the disappearance of the Chinese Communist Party
> and its hacks and apologists. Good literature not only seems to be able to

outlast tyranny, but further seems to have a regenerative effect on devastated political and psychological wastelands left behind by the likes of Hitler, Stalin or Mao.

So, Nietzsche was wrong and the apostle John right. "In the beginning was the word..."[12]

45. Jhumpa Lahiri, *Interpreter of Maladies*

The globalization of Indian literature by exiles and emigres such as Rushdie or Norbu reaches a further stage in the work of the children of immigrants. They look back from a generational remove at their parents' homeland, which can still have an ongoing presence in their lives in a very different country. Jhumpa Lahiri gives moving expression to these concerns in her Pulitzer Prize-winning collection *Interpreter of Maladies* (1999). She was born in London in 1967, after her parents had emigrated from India to England, but when she was two years old the family moved to Rhode Island, where her father had found a job as a college librarian. Earlier generations of immigrants often had little contact with their homelands, but Lahiri's mother wanted her to feel connected to her extended family in India. They made frequent trips to Bengal while she was growing up, so her experience was one of ongoing connection, but at a distance.

Like Rushdie's *East, West*, Lahiri's *Interpreter of Maladies* consists of nine stories, some set in India and the rest in America; tellingly, the proportion has shifted, with only three of the nine taking place in India. Her characters are typically settled permanently in the United States, often the children of immigrants rather than immigrants themselves. Yet their lives remain tentative, unsettled to a significant degree. The opening story, "A Temporary Matter," concerns a young married couple, Shoba and her husband, Shukumar. Having grown up in Arizona and in New Hampshire respectively, they met in Cambridge, Massachusetts, at a recital by a group of Bengali poets, where they bonded over their difficulty in following the poets' literary Bengali.

Lahiri paints Shoba's and Shukumar's bicultural life through sharply observed details such as the mixture of Indian spices and Italian pasta in their pantry. Lahiri had earned a PhD in Renaissance drama at Boston University, and the story reads almost like a one-act play, set on the domestic stage of the couple's apartment, as they struggle to deal with their grief over the loss of their first child, stillborn several months earlier. Their unexpressed feelings well up during several candlelit evenings when the neighborhood's electricity is out—the "temporary matter" of the story's title, though at the story's end, it appears that their marriage may only be temporary too.

The title story, "Interpreter of Maladies," features a young couple from New Jersey, Raj and Mina Das, and their very American third-generation kids: Tina, Ronny, and Bobby. On holiday in India, the family is visiting the massive Sun Temple at Konarak, renowned for its erotic carvings of intricately intertwined lovers (Figure 40). They are led by a guide, Mr. Kapasi (no first name is given), who gives tours to supplement his income from his job at a doctor's office. There he uses his multilingual abilities to serve as an "interpreter of maladies," translating between the doctor and his many patients who speak

40. Sun Temple, Konarak

Gujarati, which the doctor doesn't know. As the tour progresses, we see Mr. Kapasi's discomfort with the bored Raj and the attractive but self-centered Mina as they fail to discipline their whiny kids, who even address their parents by their first names. The tourists barely glance at the temple's intricate sculptures; Raj calls them "cool,"[13] while Mina calls them "neat"—"Mr. Kapasi was not certain exactly what the word suggested, but he had a feeling it was a favorable response" (59). Yet as he points out details to Mina, he starts to see the sculptures freshly: "Though Mr. Kapasi had been to the temple countless times, it occurred to him, as he, too, gazed at the topless women, that he had never seen his own wife fully naked" (58).

Raj goes off with the kids and Kapasi finds himself alone with Mina; he feels a sudden intimacy and imagines forming a friendship by mail. Unexpectedly, Mina makes a confession to him, perhaps moved by the sight of the passionate figures they're examining: Bobby isn't her husband's son but was the product of a one-night stand that she'd had with a Punjabi friend of his. Kapasi senses that Mina wants him to interpret her marital malady, and he imagines mediating if she decides to break the news to Raj. Yet when he tries to probe her feelings, his effort backfires.

> He decided to begin with the most obvious question, to get to the heart of the matter, and so he asked, "Is it really pain you feel, Mrs. Das, or is it guilt?"
>
> She turned to him and glared, mustard oil thick on her frosty pink lips. She opened her mouth to say something, but as she glared at Mr. Kapasi some certain knowledge seemed to pass before her eyes, and she stopped. It crushed him; he knew at that moment that he was not even important enough to be properly insulted. (66)

The epistolary connection that Kapasi has envisioned will never come to pass.

Most of the stories in *Interpreter of Maladies* concern second-generation characters, but in the closing story, "The Third and Final Continent," Lahiri gives a fictionalized account of her parents' immigrant experience. The story is narrated by a young Bengali who has emigrated from Calcutta to London for university, and has moved to Cambridge, Massachusetts, to work as a librarian at MIT. As in the opening story, his adjustment to America is connected with food and domesticity: "at the time I had yet to consume any beef. Even the simple chore of buying milk was new to me; in London we'd had bottles delivered each morning to our door" (175).

His parents had arranged a marriage for him, and before moving to the United States he'd flown home for the wedding. As the story opens, he is nervously anticipating the arrival of his wife, Mala, with whom he hasn't yet had marital relations. He had been renting a room in the home of an aged lady, Mrs. Croft, but in preparation for Mala's arrival he has moved to a small apartment, where she awkwardly begins to settle in. Their initial weeks are strained, and he finds himself unable to have any real feelings for her. It seems that the marriage may fail, until he takes her to visit Mrs. Croft, who declares Mala to be "a perfect lady!" (195). Her old-fashioned phrase is a function of her advanced age; she is over a hundred years old. Rather than finding Mala incongruous in contemporary America, Mrs. Croft can connect with her in terms of her own youth, perhaps sensing the lingering echoes of the British Raj in Mala's dress and bearing. The narrator says that "I like to think of that moment in Mrs. Croft's parlor as the moment when the distance between Mala and me began to lessen" (196).

Interpreter of Maladies can be thought of as a response to Rushdie's *East, West*, even a critique of it. Magical realism is replaced by domestic realism, conveyed with understated eloquence rather than Bollywood exuberance. A recurrent subject of discussion between the narrator and Mrs. Croft is the first American moon landing, which has recently taken place: "The astronauts had landed on the shores of the Sea of Tranquility, I had read, traveling farther than anyone in the history of civilization" (179). Instead of *Star Trek*'s "intrepid diplonauts" confronting alien beings on imaginary planets, we hear about real-life astronauts on the actual moon. This epochal voyage is counterpointed against that of the narrator and his wife: "Like me, Mala had traveled far from home, not knowing where she was going, or what she would find, for no reason other than to be my wife" (195).

At the story's end, the couple has a son at Harvard. "Whenever he is discouraged, I tell him that if I can survive on three continents, then there is no obstacle he cannot conquer. While the astronauts, heroes forever, spent mere hours on the moon, I have remained in this new world for nearly thirty years" (197–8). Spectacular assassinations, magical relics, and verbal pyrotechnics aren't needed to unveil the tensions and opportunities to be explored in the global village of Cambridge, Massachusetts. As Lahiri's narrator says in the final words of the story, and of the book: "there are times I am bewildered by each mile I have traveled, each meal I have eaten, each person I have known, each room in which I have slept. As ordinary as it all appears, there are times when it is beyond my imagination" (198).

CHAPTER TEN

Shanghai–Beijing: Journeys to the West

46. Wu Cheng'en, *Journey to the West*

Moving eastward from India to China, we begin with a novel that moves westward from China to India. *Journey to the West* is based on an actual journey by a seventh-century monk named Xuanzang, who spent seventeen years traveling and studying in Central Asia and India. He finally returned to China in 645 with a trove of more than 600 Buddhist treatises, and he spent the rest of his life working with a team of colleagues to translate the Sanskrit originals and to write commentaries on them. Master Xuanzang's emperor asked him to write down the story of his epochal journey, and nearly a millennium later, his *Great Tang Records of the Western Regions* became the basis for one of the "Four Classics" of traditional Chinese fiction.

Published anonymously in 1592, *Journey to the West* is usually attributed to Wu Cheng'en, a minor official in the Ming Dynasty. In Wu's account, Master Xuanzang is called Tripitaka, or "Three Baskets," referring to three categories of Buddhist texts he brought home. He travels with four fanciful companions provided for him by Guanyin, the Goddess of Mercy: a reformed river ogre, a humanized pig, a dragon-turned-horse, and most importantly a loquacious and unruly monkey, Sun Wukong or "Monkey Awakened to Emptiness." Together, they become a sort of Fellowship of the Sutras. In the course of a hundred chapters, they surmount eighty-one dangers and ordeals, from wild animals to bandits to demons, before finally reaching their goal in India, where they receive the gift of scriptures from the Buddha himself.

The historical Xuanzang was a pilgrim who ventured to India despite an imperial ban on foreign travel, but Wu Cheng'en adds a Confucian emphasis. He makes Tripitaka a faithful servant of his emperor, who commissions him to seek out the scriptures, and the opening and closing chapters frame the tale within sixteenth-century concerns over imperial governance and the growth of bureaucracy. Further, the eighty-one adventures that occupy the bulk of the narrative feature alchemical practices and magical transformations common to popular Daoism. Whereas Xuanzang was devoted to textual analysis and philosophical debate, Wu's narrative reflects a Daoist understanding of the world as fundamentally a mental construct, with meaning best grasped through wordless meditation. At one point, Tripitaka and Sun Wukong are arguing over the meaning of a key Sanskrit text, the *Heart Sutra*: " 'Ape-head!' snapped Tripitaka. 'How dare you say that I don't know its interpretation! Do you?' " Sun Wukong insists that he does, but then falls silent. When the pig and the ogre mock him as too ignorant to respond, Tripitaka reproves them. "Stop this claptrap!" he says; "Wukong made his interpretation in a speechless language. That's true interpretation."[1]

According to the novel, the Buddha has observed that in China, "they are greedy, lustful, murderous and quarrelsome. I wonder whether a knowledge of the True Scriptures would not cause some improvement in them?" And so he inspires China's emperor to send a pilgrim to receive his "three baskets" of scriptures. "One contains the Vinaya, which speaks of Heaven, one contains the Sastras, which tell of Earth, one contains the Sutras, which save the damned. The whole is divided into thirty-five divisions, written on 15,144 rolls. These are the path to perfection, the only gate to virtue" (1:78).

A basic question for any reader of *Journey to the West* is the relation between this religious cosmology and the social and political geographies of the human world. The two major translators of the story into English, Arthur Waley and

Anthony Yu, have taken very different approaches. Anthony Yu's four-volume translation gives the work entire, including its 745 reflective poems, and in a hundred-page introduction he details the religious and philosophical background for understanding the book as an allegory of spiritual self-cultivation. Thus Sun Wukong embodies the Buddhist concept of "the monkey of the mind," whose restless striving must be calmed and enlightened.

By contrast, in his 1943 translation Arthur Waley created a modern novel out of the original (as he'd earlier done with *The Tale of Genji*, which we'll look at in our next chapter). He suppressed almost all of the poems and he radically abridged the text, focusing on the exploits of the anarchic Sun Wukong; he even titled his version *Monkey*. As given by Waley, the first seven chapters of the novel detail Sun Wukong's magical origins (he's born from a stone) and portray his nearly successful attempt to invade and rule heaven, aided by his vast alchemical powers and his ability to split himself into an entire monkey army. The heavenly Jade Emperor tries to buy him off with a minor post, but the monkey isn't satisfied. As the celestial bureaucracy tries to bring him in line, Sun Wukong sounds like a powerful warlord testing the limits of an earthly emperor. "What crime is there that you have not committed?" the Jade Emperor's outraged minions reproach him. "You have piled up sin upon sin; do you not realize what you have done?" "Quite true," he calmly replies, "all quite true. What are you going to do about it?"[2]

Bureaucracy even rules the underworld. When Sun Wukong is hauled away to the Land of Darkness, he challenges the clerks of the King of Death to find him in their records, but he doesn't fit any of their categories: "The official dived into a side room and came out with five or six ledgers, divided into ten files, and began going through them one by one—Bald Insects, Furry Insects, Winged Insects, Scaly Insects . . . He gave up in despair and tried Monkeys. But the Monkey King, having human characteristics, was not there." Finally Sun Wukong locates himself in a miscellaneous category: "Parentage: natural product. Description: Stone Monkey" (39–40). His entry shows a life span of 342 years, but Sun Wukong asserts that he's become immortal, and he boldly crosses out his name and those of his monkey henchmen; the underworld bureaucrats are too terrified to oppose him.

Mysticism and realpolitik rub shoulders throughout the narrative. At the climax of the story Tripitaka and his companions finally reach the long-sought Holy Mountain in India. There the Buddha graciously orders two assistants to make an ample selection of scrolls "for these priests to take back to the East, to be a boon there forever" (284). All should be well, but Tripitaka neglects to bribe the assistants, and they get their revenge by packing up a hefty but deceptive bundle of scrolls. On the way home, the pilgrims make a shocking discovery: the scrolls are all blank. Weeping, Tripitaka exclaims that he can't possibly bring back empty scrolls to his emperor. They rush back to the Holy Mountain—only to have a smiling Buddha reply that he knew all along what would happen. He reveals that the assistants had done the right thing despite themselves, for "these blank texts are actually true, wordless scriptures, and they are just as good as those with words." He concedes, though, that "the creatures in your Land of the East are so foolish and unenlightened that I have no choice but to impart to you now the texts with words" (Yu trans., 4:354). Language and perception here reach their limit, as in Attar's *Conference of the Birds*, where the road to enlightenment runs through the regions of Bewilderment and Nothingness.

Whether in Arthur Waley's simian-centered abridgement or in Anthony Yu's sprawling hundred-chapter version, *Journey to the West* is a tour de force, a great work both of world literature and of *other*worldly literature. We might get a similar effect in European literature if we could combine Dante's hundred-canto *Divine Comedy* with *Don Quixote*, another extended narrative of comic misadventures, which similarly centers on an idealistic master and his earthy companion. Cervantes published the first volume of *Quixote* in 1605, just a few years after Wu Cheng'en's masterpiece appeared in 1592. These two great writers couldn't have known of each other, but their heroes, Quixote and Tripitaka, and their sidekicks, Sancho Panza and Sun Wukong, could walk a long way together "nel mezzo del cammin di nostra vita," as Dante would say: in the middle of our life's road.

47. Lu Xun, *The Real Story of Ah-Q and Other Stories*

Whereas Wu Cheng'en dramatized Master Xuanzang's "journey to the west," one of modern Chinese literature's dominant figures, Lu Xun, found his direction in life by a journey to the east, in his case to Japan, where he began medical studies in 1904. He changed course after a professor proudly showed his class an image from the Russo-Japanese War (1904–5), in which a Japanese soldier was about to behead a Chinese spy in Japanese-occupied Manchuria, as a crowd of Chinese looked passively on. Shocked by the applause of the students around him, Lu Xun decided to abandon medicine for literature. As he wrote in the preface to his first collection of stories, *Outcry*: "However rude a nation was in physical health, if its people were intellectually feeble, they would never become anything other than cannon fodder or gawping spectators, their loss to the world through illness no cause for regret. The first task was to change their spirit; and literature and the arts, I decided at the time, were the best means to this end."[3]

Lu Xun had little interest in building on the Confucian traditions that he and many reformists felt needed to be swept away, and for inspiration he turned to world literature. In Tokyo in 1907, he and his brother Zhou Zuoren planned to publish a magazine, *Xinsheng* ("New Life"), concentrating on translations of Western literature; the very name of their journal evokes Dante's *Vita Nuova*. But the magazine's expected contributors and backers dropped out, and it never saw the light of day. As Lu Xun ironically remarks in the preface to *Outcry*, "our *New Life* ended in stillbirth" (17).

Despite this failure, the brothers worked extensively on magazines once they returned to China. Most notably, they became closely involved with *New Youth*, the most important magazine of China's "New Culture" movement. It was first published in 1915 in the French Concession of Shanghai, under the

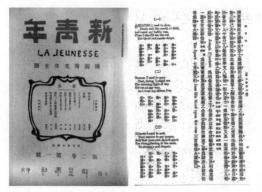

41. New Youth *magazine*

dual title *Qīngnián / La Jeunesse*. The French title was dropped the following year, and the Chinese title was changed to *Xīn Qīngnián*, "New
Youth," highlighting the journal's modernizing emphasis. The editors introduced new literary forms such as the Western-style short story, and they
sought to elevate the vernacular language of common people in place of the
stylized classical Chinese used for elite literary writing. They published new
poetry and fiction and translated everything from "La Marseillaise" to Oscar
Wilde, freely interspersing both Chinese characters and the Roman alphabet
(Figure 41).

The magazine's interplay of Chinese and Western scripts figures at the beginning of Lu Xun's most famous work, *The Real Story of Ah-Q* (1921–2).
In a preface to his novella, Lu Xun claims that Ah-Q must have had a
proper Chinese name such as "Quei," now lost to history. "As Confucius
says, 'If a name is not right, the words will not ring true,'" he declares,
"but I have no idea what Ah-Q's surname was" (79–80). He consults a
scholar, who blames *New Youth*'s advocacy of the Roman alphabet, "which had
brought the national essence into such terminal decline that no one could
fix even on the spelling of Ah-Quei." This leaves Lu Xun no choice "but
to transcribe the mysterious Quei into the English alphabet, abbreviating it
for convenience's sake, to Q: Ah-Q. Which compromise reduces me to
the level of those reprobates in charge of *New Youth*." He adds that "the

only thing that consoles me is the fact that the character 'Ah' is absolutely correct" (82–83).

Ah-Q stumbles through life as revolutionary changes sweep his village. As in Tagore's *The Home and the World*, the revolutionaries and local officials work together to serve their own interests. At the end of the story, Ah-Q is executed for a robbery he didn't commit; the magistrate needs someone to blame. A kind of Chinese Candide, Ah-Q takes his own death in stride: "He did not, in truth, feel too badly about things . . . veering between fear, calm and the dawning sense that in the rich tapestry of life, a man is destined sometimes to have his head cut off" (120, 122).

Lu Xun first explored the fine line between revolution and reaction, sanity and madness, in "A Madman's Diary" (1918). Loosely based on Gogol's "Diary of a Madman," Lu Xun's tale shocked and inspired readers with its sharp social satire, its disjointed form, and its use of vernacular prose, which demonstrated that a work of high literary value could be written in the vernacular. A running theme is people's resistance to breaking with the past. Lu Xun's madman believes that his fellow villagers intend to kill him and eat him, and he feels that they began to turn on him when "twenty years ago, I stamped on the Records of the Past, and it has been my enemy ever since" (22).

The story opens with a preface in sober classical Chinese, infused with modern terminology that Lu Xun had absorbed during his medical studies. If we read it closely, though, the preface unsettles the seeming clarity of the objective case study of a "persecution complex" that "may be of use to medical research." The narrator begins by telling us of his discovery of the diary:

At school I had been close friends with two brothers whose names I will omit to mention here. As the years went by after we graduated, however, we gradually lost touch. Not long ago, I happened to hear that one of them had been seriously ill and, while on a visit home, I broke my journey to call on them. I found only one of them at home, who told me it was his younger brother who had been afflicted. Thanking me for my concern, he informed me that his brother had long since made a full recovery and had left home to wait for an appropriate official post to fall vacant. Smiling broadly, he showed me two volumes of a diary his brother had written at the time. (21)

This all sounds fine, but why has Lu Xun given his madman a brother, and why does he say that he isn't telling us their names? The key phrase here may be "I found only one of them at home, *who told me* it was his younger brother who had been afflicted." Does the narrator even know which brother is which? Can we really be sure we're meeting the sane brother and not the madman himself? Just what kind of broad smile is the unnamed brother giving as he hands over the diary?

If the narrator may be meeting the madman, what has become of the older brother? The diary ends with its famous final entry: "Are there children who have not yet eaten human flesh? Save the children..." (31). Possibly the madman came to his senses after writing these despairing words, passed his rigorous exams, and is now a fine, upstanding citizen. Yet the alternative is equally possible: certain that his brother was about to murder and eat him, he made the first strike. Visiting the house, our sober-minded narrator thinks that he lives in a world of science and rationality, but he himself may be about to become dessert.

In his preface to *Outcry*, Lu Xun says that he wrote the story in response to a friend's request for a contribution to *New Youth*. At first he resisted: "This is what I replied: 'Imagine an iron house: without windows or doors, utterly indestructible, and full of sound sleepers—all about to suffocate to death. Let them die in their sleep, and they will feel nothing. Is it right to cry out, to rouse the light sleepers among them, causing them inconsolable agony before they die?'" His friend replies: "But even if we succeed in waking only the few, there is still hope—hope that the iron house may one day be destroyed." Lu Xun gives in: "He was right: however hard I tried, I couldn't quite obliterate my own sense of hope" (19). He remained troubled that his pessimism would only discourage his readers: "I didn't want to infect younger generations—dreaming the glorious dreams that I too had dreamed when I was young—with the loneliness that came to torment me" (20). Lu Xun shifted from medical studies to literature in hopes of curing the souls of his countrymen, but now he feared that his stories would spread the very disease they were meant to cure. Yet the "Madman's Diary" that resulted from Lu Xun's internal civil war between pessimism and hope inaugurated a literary revolution. As we'll see in our next selection, a generation later Eileen Chang would carry his vernacular revolution further in a China caught up in a new era of global war.

48. Eileen Chang, *Love in a Fallen City*

One of the most important modern Chinese writers, Eileen Chang (1920–95)—also known as Zhang Ailing—is also one of Chinese literature's most worldly figures. She was born in China's most international city, Shanghai, with its British, French, and American settlements dating back to the mid-nineteenth century. Her mother was educated partly in England and went skiing in the Alps despite having had her feet bound as a child; she later divorced her unfaithful, opium-addicted husband. Chang learned English at an Anglican school in Shanghai. She became devoted to British fiction (H. G. Wells and Somerset Maugham were favorite authors), but she was equally drawn to *The Story of the Stone* and other classic Chinese novels. She was offered a full scholarship by the University of London in 1939, but the upheavals of the Second Sino-Japanese War prevented her from pursuing her studies in England; she went instead to study English in Hong Kong, later returning to Shanghai, where she established herself as a prominent writer while still in her mid-twenties (Figure 42).

She married a literary man, Hu Lancheng, who collaborated with the Chinese puppet government installed by the Japanese; the marriage dissolved after a few years, as a result of his multiple infidelities. The overlaying of sexual and political betrayal wasn't only a literary theme for Chang, and after moving to the United States in 1955 she spent years writing and

42. Eileen Chang in Hong Kong

revising a partly autobiographical novella, *Lust, Caution*, which the Tai-wanese film maker Ang Lee made into an intense (and sexually explicit) movie in 2007.

Early on, Eileen Chang developed a keen eye for the complexities of life in a Shanghai poised—or caught—between tradition and modernity, waning patriarchy and nascent feminism, Asian and European cultures. Her stories of the early 1940s were written under Japanese occupation and avoid making open political statements, but the wartime setting is always in the background. In one story, "Sealed Off," a man and a woman form an instant but ephemeral bond while they're stuck on a tram when soldiers have sealed off a street for an unknown reason. The man is bringing home some steamed spinach buns, wrapped in a Western-style newspaper:

A piece of newspaper had stuck to a bun, and gravely he peeled it away; the ink had transferred to the bun, and the writing was in reverse, as in a mirror. He pored over the words till he could make them out: "Obituaries . . . Positions Wanted . . . Stock Market Developments . . . Now Playing . . ."—all normal, useful expressions, though funny, somehow, seen on a bun.[4]

Nearby, a medical student is making a diagram of the human body, which a fellow passenger mistakes for "this cubism, this impressionism, that's so popular these days." Another onlooker, seeing that the student has carefully labeled each bone and muscle, asserts: "That's the influence of Chinese painting. Nowadays a bit of writing is often added to Western art too—clearly a case of 'Eastern ways spreading westward'" (242).

Wu Cuiyuan, the young woman whom the bun-reading businessman meets on the tram, wouldn't make such a mistake. She has majored in English and is now teaching at her alma mater—"A girl in her twenties teaching at a university! It set a new record for women's professional achievement" (241). Though she's proud of her success, Cuiyuan feels dislocated and lonely, thinking of herself as someone who is lost in translation, even multiple translations: "Life was like the Bible, translated from Hebrew to Greek, from Greek to Latin, from Latin to English, from English to Mandarin Chinese. When Cuiyuan read it, she translated the Mandarin into Shanghainese. Some things did not come through" (241). Rebelling against her prim, repressive family, Cuiyuan half agrees to a sudden proposition by the businessman to become his mistress, but as the tram starts up again the man retreats into his shell and the flirtation leads nowhere. As Cuiyuan reflects at the story's end, "everything that had happened while the city was sealed off was a nonoccurrence. The whole city of Shanghai had dozed off and dreamed an unreasonable dream" (251).

Wartime politics are openly translated into sexual politics in several of Chang's major stories. In her novella *Love in a Fallen City* (1943), an impoverished young woman, Bai Liusu, engages in an extended series of skirmishes with a wealthy playboy, Fan Liuyuan. Then he takes Liusu to Hong Kong, booking them adjacent rooms in the lavish (and aptly named) Repulse Bay Hotel. Even then, he holds off on making an obvious move, evidently wanting her to surrender to him without his having to make any commitments. Liusu fears that "he would suddenly drop the pretense and launch a surprise attack. But day after day he remained a gentleman; it was like facing a great enemy who stood perfectly still" (144–5). Yet she holds her own, and she can run circles around him in their verbal jousting. At one point, when Liuyuan claims to value honesty above all, Liusu gives him a sidelong glance, and replies, "Your idea of the perfect woman is someone who is pure and high-minded but still ready to flirt . . . You want me to be good in front of others, but bad when I'm with you." Liuyuan replies that he doesn't understand, whereupon Liusu reverses herself: "You want me to be bad to others, but good only to you." Baffled, Liuyuan complains,

> "Now you've turned it around again! You're just making me more confused."
> He was silent for a while, then said: "What you're saying isn't so."
> Liusu laughed. "Ah, so now you understand." (135)

Finally they become lovers, but Liuyuan still won't commit himself, though he rents a house for her in the Hong Kong hills. The date is December 7, 1941; unbeknownst to them, the Japanese are attacking Pearl Harbor. The very next day, the Japanese begin bombing Hong Kong prior to invading the city, causing massive destruction. "Then, at night, in that dead city . . . there was only a stream of empty air, a bridge of emptiness that crossed into the dark, into the void of voids. Here, everything had ended." Yet this shocking turn of events ends up bringing Liuyuan and Liusu together; in a more melancholy version of Wu Cheng'en's Sun Wukong, they too are "awakened to emptiness." Chang says that "they looked and saw each other, saw each other entirely. It was a mere moment of deep understanding, but it was enough to keep them happy together"—adding, with characteristic irony, "for a decade or so" (164).

Eileen Chang perfected the use of vernacular that Lu Xun had pioneered, though she was less confident in literature's ability to "save the children" and inspire a generation of New Youth. As Liusu worries that her youth is passing by, she reflects:

> Don't worry, in another few years you'll be old, and anyway youth isn't
> worth much here. They've got youth everywhere—children born one after

another, with their bright new eyes, their tender new mouths, their quick new wits. Time grinds on, year after year, and the eyes grow dull, the minds grow dull, and then another round of children is born. The older ones are sucked into that obscure haze of crimson and gold, and the tiny flecks of glinting gold are the frightened eyes of their predecessors. (161)

At the story's end, Liusu lights a pan of incense, not to honor her ancestors or give thanks for her survival but to repel mosquitos, and the narrator concludes: "Hong Kong's defeat had brought Liusu victory. But in this unreasonable world, who can distinguish cause from effect?" Or we might ask, following Émile Habibi's Saeed the Pessoptimist: Who can distinguish optimism from pessimism? In this world of warring empires, families, and sexes, Liusu is a self-possessed survivor: "Liusu didn't feel there was anything subtle about her place in history. She stood up, smiling, and kicked the pan of mosquito-repellent incense under the table." Voltaire's Cunégonde would appreciate that smile, as would the heroines of the great Ming Dynasty novels. As the narrator comments, "Those legendary beauties who felled cities and kingdoms were probably all like that" (167).

49. Mo Yan, *Life and Death Are Wearing Me Out*

Born to a peasant family, Guan Moye was eleven years old when the Cultural Revolution was launched in 1966. He left school to work for a decade in the fields and in a factory before joining the army. There he began to write, taking the pen name Mo Yan ("He can't speak"), ironically heeding his father's warnings not to speak his mind outside the home. Having been raised largely on Chinese socialist realism, he began to read more widely. He developed a strong interest in the works of Lu Xun and in the classical vernacular narratives, including *Journey to the West*, and he began to become acquainted with Western novelists as well. In his Nobel Prize lecture in 2012, he said that in the course of creating my literary domain, Northeast Gaomi Township, I was greatly inspired by the American novelist William Faulkner and the Colombian Gabriel García Márquez. I had not read either of them extensively, but was encouraged by the bold, unrestrained way they created new territory in writing, and learned from them that a writer must have a place that belongs to him alone . . . a few pages were sufficient for me to comprehend what they were doing and how they were doing it, which led to my understanding of what I should do and how I should do it.[5]

His 2006 novel, *Life and Death Are Wearing Me Out*, builds on all these sources and more, as it weaves an epic tale of Chinese history from 1950 to 2000.

The story proceeds from the Agricultural Cooperative Movement of the 1950s through the Cultural Revolution, the death of Mao Zedong, and the advent of China's global prosperity. Much of the novel is narrated by Ximen Nao, whose story begins on January 1, 1950, as he tells us in the novel's opening sentence (shades of Salman Rushdie's *Midnight's Children*, with its 1,001 children born at the moment of India's independence in 1947). A prosperous, apolitical landowner, Ximen Nao is shot when the Communists come to power in his town. He is outraged at his unjustified murder, and when his spirit descends to the underworld court of Lord Yama, he insists on being sent back to earth. Lord Yama reluctantly agrees, but on returning to his village, Ximen Nao is shocked to find that he's been reborn as a donkey, and he grows up in service to his own former farmhand Lan Lian. As the narrative proceeds, Ximen Nao repeatedly dies and is reborn as an ox, then as a pig, a dog, and a monkey, before finally achieving rebirth as a human baby, born at midnight as "fireworks lit up the sky of Gaomi County's new century, the first of a new millennium."[6]

We won't be mistaken if Ximen Nao's animal reincarnations remind us of Tripitaka's companions in *Journey to the West*. In the first chapter, as Ximen

Nao is being escorted to his village to be reborn, "we encountered a group of men on stilts who were reenacting the travels of the Tang monk Tripitaka on his way to fetch Buddhist scriptures. His disciples, Monkey and Pigsy, were both villagers I knew" (8). Ximen Nao believes that Lord Yama is failing to see the justice of his cause and is perversely sentencing him to one animal rebirth after another, but he finally learns that Yama has always been planning his ultimate salvation, much as Tripitaka discovers that the blank scriptures are the best ones. Ximen Nao has to be reborn in animal form until he has finally purged himself of hatred; only then can he become Millennium Baby, and the story can truly begin at the novel's end.

As he cycles through the decades, Ximen Nao experiences the injustices and repressions that accompany the Great Leap Forward and the Cultural Revolution, which he observes with a naïve wonder reminiscent of Lu Xun's Ah-Q. But instead of being executed just once, in his animal incarnations he is eaten by starving villagers, then burned alive in a riot, then drowned, then he loyally commits suicide together with Lan Lian, and lastly he is shot by a jealous husband. As for Lan Lian, he is a stubborn individualist, the only farmer in the village who refuses to join the collective farming enterprise. He manages to hold on for years, aided by Ximen Nao in several of his incarnations, before he finally commits suicide. In the process, we come to see the reality behind the Party's rhetoric of glorious progress (Figure 43).

A second narrator is Lan Lian's son, Lan Jeifang. His mother had been a concubine of Ximen Nao, but shortly after his murder she married Lan Lian. Lan Jeifang becomes part of the village power structure, in marked contrast to Ximen Nao and to the novel's third authorial figure, Mo Yan himself, who appears in a satiric light, mocked by everyone he knows. "Mo Yan had deviant talents," Ximen Nao remarks: "At the time, no one paid the kid any attention. He was almost unbelievably ugly and carried on in the most peculiar ways. Given to saying crazy things that had people scratching their heads, he was to some an annoyance and to others a pariah. Even members of his family called

43. "The Tractor-ploughing Squadron" (1965)

him a moron" (248). Yet the villagers are wary of him, since "Mo Yan would be bound to write about them sooner or later. Every resident of Ximen Village will find himself in one of Mo Yan's notorious books" (250). Here we seem to have a version of James Joyce's ambition to recreate Dublin in *Ulysses*, and there is also an echo of *Finnegans Wake*, with its caustic descriptions of Joyce's stand-in, the disreputable Shem the Penman. Ximen Nao ends the novel by declaring: "My story begins on January 1, 1950" (540), thus returning us to his opening sentence, as Joyce had done in *Finnegans Wake*, which was being translated into Chinese at the time Mo Yan was writing his novel.

Yet Mo Yan's cyclicality is more Buddhist than postmodernist, and the cycle of five rebirths is overlaid on the decades of China's post-1949 history. As Ximen Nao remarks in the middle of the novel,

Some time later, when I was reborn as a dog, a friend of mine, an experienced, knowledgeable, and wise German shepherd assigned to guard a city government guesthouse, concluded: People in the 1950s were innocent, in the 1960s they were fanatics, in the 1970s they were afraid of their own shadows, in the 1980s they carefully weighed people's words and actions, and in the 1990s they were simply evil. I'm sorry, I keep getting ahead of myself. It's a trick Mo Yan uses all the time, and I foolishly let it affect the way I talk. (266)

Not that people's innocence in the 1950s prevented disaster. As Ximen Nao's murderer calmly explains to him, "I am obliged to eliminate you. This is not personal hatred, it's class hatred" (47). On a broader scale, ambitious five-year plans for collectivization led to mass starvation. The novel includes a chapter in which the villagers lose their crops after being diverted to work at harvest time smelting iron. By the end of the novel, prosperity—and BMWs—have come to the village. Plans are afoot "to turn Ximen Village into a resort with a Cultural Revolution theme" (421), complete with a golf course, an amusement park, and a casino. The farmers whose fields will be requisitioned for this sprawling complex will work as actors reenacting the village's history for the visiting tourists.

Mo Yan's remarkable novel treads a fine line on the edge of unacceptable criticism of the system, shielded in part by his use of animal narrators who don't understand (or who "don't understand") politics. He has been criticized for not supporting dissident writers, but he has chosen to offer satiric critiques of the system from within. Like Lu Xun and Eileen Chang, he dramatizes the challenges of surviving amid shifting political currents in chaotic times, and his novel makes a plea for an end to hatred and for openness to different perspectives—an openness exemplified by his use of multiple narrators and proliferating intertexts, both Chinese and foreign. As Ximen Nao remarks, on finding himself reborn for a third time, "here I was, a pig not even a year old, young and sprightly, enjoying life. Being reborn over and over may wear a guy out, but it has its advantages" (237).

50. Bei Dao, *The Rose of Time*

Like a real-life version of Mo Yan's hero, Bei Dao has undergone multiple re-incarnations in a single lifetime. Born in 1949, Zhao Zhenkai had a bourgeois childhood in Beijing, then became a Red Guard revolutionary, followed by disillusionment leading to early prominence as a dissident poet, when he began writing under the pen name Bei Dao ("North Island," suggesting a certain independence or isolation). He then spent years in exile in a series of countries, and in his fifties he returned to China with a professorship in Hong Kong. Even then his transformations hadn't ended, as a stroke left him unable to speak for four years; he reinvented himself as a visual artist, before finally recovering and becoming a poet again. Life and death may have worn out Ximen Nao, but not Bei Dao.

In his first phase as a writer, Bei Dao became part of a group of young poets who were seeking to revitalize poetry, carrying on in new ways the vernacular revolution inaugurated in the 1910s and 1920s by Lu Xun and his associates in the New Culture movement. Bei Dao was inspired by Western poets, not to imitate them (as he was sometimes accused of doing) but seeking to "make it new" within Chinese poetry itself, writing irregular free verse marked by surprising juxtapositions and shifts in register. Members of the cultural establishment in Beijing had their doubts about these sometimes obscure experiments, dubbing the group "the Misty Poets," but they weren't seen as dangerously political poets, unless in their very insistence on not writing political poetry.

As debates over democratization heightened in the mid-1970s, Bei Dao began writing poems expressing his disillusionment with the Cultural Revolution and the stifling of democratic impulses. His 1976 poem "The Answer" became a rallying cry among pro-democracy protestors. It is filled with "misty" ambiguities and seeming non-sequiturs:

The Ice Age is over now,

Why is there ice everywhere?

The Cape of Good Hope has been discovered,

Why do a thousand sails contest the Dead Sea?[7]

What was a good cultural bureaucrat—or indeed a good populist revolutionary—to make of such lines? Like Ghalib, Bei Dao apparently found it difficult to write poetry that wasn't difficult. Verses like these seem less like European free verse than some of the more ironic couplets of Hafez or Ghalib that double in on themselves. Yet everyone could see Bei Dao's challenge to the imperative to subscribe to party doctrine, even though he expressed his unbelief in oblique terms:

I don't believe the sky is blue;

I don't believe in thunder's echoes;

I don't believe that dreams are false;

I don't believe that death has no revenge. (7)

No specific death is specified, but Bei Dao's readers might well think of the millions who had died in the famines brought on during the period of collectivization, or the death of dissidents in police custody. These lines would have had a more personal valence for Bei Dao himself: his aunt had committed suicide in 1968 after she'd been investigated as a bourgeois counter-revolutionary.

"The Answer" was one of the texts that pro-democracy activists posted on the "Democracy Wall" where dissident ideas were briefly allowed to be displayed in the winter of 1978–9. Yet Bei Dao doubted that poetry could change the world. His poem "The Art of Poetry" begins:

in the great house to which I belong

only a table remains, surrounded

by boundless marshland
the moon shines on me from different corners
the skeleton's fragile dream still stands
in the distance, like an undismantled scaffold
and there are muddy footprints on the blank paper (49)

We may no longer be locked inside Lu Xun's iron house, but this house is sur-rounded by a wasteland, and the only paper we have is a blank page that's been trodden underfoot by muddy footprints—unless those footprints *are* the text we read?

Bei Dao was becoming known abroad and made his first foreign trips in the early 1980s, but he wasn't optimistic that world poetry would provide any great refuge, still less make any substantial impact back home. As he wrote in a poem entitled "Language,"

many languages
fly around the world
the production of languages
can neither increase nor decrease
mankind's silent suffering[8]

Soon, however, he was forced to begin flying around the world himself; he and several other "Misty Poets" were exiled in 1989, following the crushing of the protests in Tiananmen Square. For seventeen years he lived in Europe and in the United States, and many of his poems deal with exile. As he wrote in "Road Song," "at the end of an endless trip / night turns all the keys of gold / but no door opens for you." In these lines "you" may be the poet, but then the referent may change to China itself: "I walk straight toward you / as you open the fan of history / that's folded in an isolated song." The poem ends: "sunset seals the empire / the earth's book turns the page of this moment."[9]

Exile meant manifold losses, including the collapse of his marriage, but it also brought extensive contact with poets worldwide. He traveled to Palestine in 2002 at the request of Mahmoud Darwish, in a delegation for the International Parliament of Writers; the delegation included the Nobel laureates Wole Soyinka and José Saramago. In his essay collection *Blue House* (2000), Bei Dao gives affectionate portraits of several of his poet friends, including Allen Ginsberg, Octavio Paz, and Gary Snyder ("Gary has a face that is hard to forget: deep lines that are essentially all vertical").[10] In a poem dedicated to the Swedish poet Tomas Tranströmer, he praises his friend in terms that could also apply to himself: "dancing with headless angels / you kept your balance."[11]

In 2001 Bei Dao returned briefly to China to see his gravely ill father. As he wrote during that visit, in a poem entitled "Black Map," "I've come home— the way back / longer than the wrong road / long as a life / . . . my father's life-spark small as a pea / I am his echo."[12] There is a video of Bei Dao in New York in 2011 giving eloquent readings of poems from *The Rose of Time*, with his translator Eliot Weinberger reading the translations. They begin with "Black Map," and end with the collection's title poem, "The Rose of Time."[13]

Bei Dao was allowed to return permanently to China in 2006. He settled in Hong Kong as a professor at Hong Kong University, and he remarried and had a son. His life seemed finally to have settled down, but in 2012 he suffered a stroke and for four years he had severe difficulty forming sentences. He turned to painting, but found that he had trouble tracing steady lines, and so he began using thousands of dots of ink on paper, creating haunting calligraphic land- scapes (Figure 44). As he has written in an essay titled "The Ink Point's Rev- elations," in these paintings "everything is created within and by these points: attachment, separation, mutation, flow." He adds that "the medium of writing is in fact quite close to ink points, and at times they are difficult to distinguish from each other. In a sense, ink points are always lurking behind writing, present yet nameless."[14]

Like his art, Bei Dao's poems display what the poet Michael Palmer has called "a poetry of complex enfoldings and crossings, of sudden juxtapositions and fractures, of pattern in a dance with randomness."[15] His wide-ranging

44. Bei Dao, Moment *(2013)*

collection of old and new poems, *The Rose of Time*, ends with its title poem, which I'll give here entire. If its four-line stanzas were set as couplets, we'd readily recognize this as a ghazal, in the tradition of Shahid Ali's reworking of Hafez and Ghalib, as we see Bei Dao's life, like his poetry and his visual art, emerging in disappearance:

> when the watchman falls asleep
> you turn back with the storm
> to grow old embracing is
> the rose of time.

> when bird roads define the sky
> you look behind at the sunset
> to emerge in disappearance is
> the rose of time.

> when the knife is bent in water
> you cross the bridge stepping on flute-songs

to cry in the conspiracy is
the rose of time.

when a pen draws the horizon
you're awakened by a gong from the East
to bloom in the echoes is
the rose of time.

in the mirror there is always this moment
this moment leads to the door of rebirth
the door opens to the sea
the rose of time. (281)

CHAPTER ELEVEN

Tokyo–Kyoto: The West of the East

51. Higuchi Ichiyō, *In the Shade of Spring Leaves*

Born in Tokyo in 1872 to a family of modest means, Higuchi Ichiyō received an excellent classical education before her father's fortunes and health declined; he died when she was seventeen. She had shown a precocious talent for composing poetry in classical style and she determined to become a writer, replacing her given name, Natsuko, with the poetic pen name of Ichiyō, "One Leaf." She had no way to earn a living as a poet, however, and after her father's death she and her mother and sister were living a hand-to-mouth existence as seamstresses on the edge of Tokyo's red-light district (Figure 45). She turned to fiction at age twenty and began publishing a series of increasingly brilliant short stories in new magazines such as *Miyako no Hana* (Flower of the Capital), which an early observer described as "a journal for light literature."[1]

Her fame grew rapidly in the tragically few years before she died of tuberculosis in 1896 at age twenty-four. By then, she was recognized as the leading woman writer of her generation. Here I'll focus on my favorite of her stories, "Separate Ways," one of several in Robert Lyons Danly's collection *In the Shade of Spring Leaves* that show close attention to the lives of women and of adolescents—the "new youth" of Japan, struggling to find their way in times of rapid and unsettling change.

45. Low-ranking geishas on display, Tokyo, 1890s

The flowering of publications such as *Miyako no Hana* was a result of technological innovations. Japan had a long tradition of woodblock printing, but imported Western printing presses provided the impetus for new outreach to a broad audience. Thus the Dai Nippon Printing Company was founded in 1876 in order to fulfill "the founders' passionate desire to help raise the level of people's knowledge and culture through letterpress printing," as the company's website declares.[2] A host of newspapers and periodicals sprang up, providing crucial commercial outlets for writers such as Higuchi Ichiyō who didn't come from privileged backgrounds and who could gain income and an audience through the new modes of print.

Higuchi Ichiyō was primarily in dialogue with Japanese writers, from Murasaki Shikibu in the Heian era and Ihara Saikaku in the seventeenth century up to her own times, and yet from the outset her work was read in light of world literature as well as Japanese traditions. This is clearly shown in an enthusiastic review of her novella *Child's Play* by the writer Mori Ōgai in 1896. "What is extraordinary about *Child's Play*," he wrote, "is that the characters are not those beastlike creatures one so often encounters in Ibsen or Zola, whose techniques the so-called naturalists have tried imitating to the utmost. They are real, human individuals that we laugh and cry with." He concluded: "I do not hesitate to confer on Ichiyō the title of a true poet."[3] Ōgai had spent several formative years in Germany, and he was at the forefront of developing Westernized fiction, but it is notable that in praising *Child's Play* he conferred on Ichiyō "the title of a true poet," not "a true novelist." Poetry remained at the top of the Japanese genre hierarchy, and he saw in Ichiyō a rare talent for dealing with concrete realities in poetic prose.

As Mori Ōgai's review shows, Ibsen was in the air. Ichiyō's heartbreaking story "Separate Ways," written that same year, develops themes also advanced in works such as Ibsen's play *A Doll's House*. Like his Nora, Ichiyō's heroine, Okyō, is making her way as best she can in a world of rigid and unequal gender and class relations. She has been trying to get by as a seamstress, but she has decided to give up her struggle for independence and go off into a loveless arrangement as a kept woman. Again like Nora, Okyō is observed by an uncomprehending man (here, a young orphan, Kichizo) who can't understand how she could sink to such depths of depravity. The story presents a small but transformative moment, comparable to a Joycean "epiphany," in which Kichizo realizes the weakness of the pseudo-familial bonds he has established with his employers and with Okyō. We never learn anything definite about Okyō's lover—or keeper—but romance has been reduced to a commercial transaction. Kichizo thus comes to a realization of the corruption of adult sexuality, not unlike the young heroine of Henry James's novel *What Maisie Knew*, which was first serialized a year later in an American "little magazine," *The Chap-Book*.

Ichiyō presents a world that is at once paralyzed and in radical flux. This condition is epitomized in Kichizo's status. He is an orphan with no known relatives, and Okyō has become his sole point of reference in an ephemeral world. At the story's end he loses that one security. "How pointless everything turns out," he says sadly. "What a life! People are friendly, and then they disappear. It's always the ones I like" (294). There will be no sudden happy ending, or even a moving love suicide such as would have taken place in a popular melodrama, and there are no stirring Ibsen-style speeches to inspire social change. The closest thing to a moral conclusion—"The boy was unyielding in his notion of integrity" (293)—is almost a throw-away line, and it's hard to say whether we should admire Kichizo's strict morality or regret his rigidity. The story ends with a bleak final exchange with Okyō, who says:

> "It's not the sort of thing anybody wants to do. But it's been decided. You can't change things."
> He stared at her with tears in his eyes.
> "Take your hands off me, Okyō." (295)

The tragedy of "Separate Ways" is that there is no grand tragedy to play out. Nor are the resources of popular romance available to save the day. Kichizo had been a homeless street performer until a kindly old woman invited him into her home. Yet his "Granny," as he calls her, was no fairy godmother; she exploited him to work as a virtual slave in her umbrella shop. Even she has died two years before the story takes place, and the shop has new owners who barely tolerate him. Kichizo seeks an alternative family tie in Okyō: "you seem almost like a sister to me," he tells her, and asks: "Are you sure you never had a younger brother?" (289). Okyō, however, is an only child, and she too has no family to support her in life. Unable to assent to Kichizo's fantasy of a family tie, she hopes for some miraculous resolution for him. As she asks: "Don't you have some kind of proof of your identity? A charm with your name on it, for instance? There must be something you have" (290). In a popular tale or puppet play, such a charm would reveal Kichizo's (preferably noble) origins, and he could be restored to his lost family. But he and Okyō are living in the wrong era.

Really, they are living in the *wrong genre*. Their story isn't an entertaining tale with a happy ending of the sort that Okyō might read in a typical issue of

Flower of the Capital, nor is it one of the popular plays that Kichizo used to act out on the street. Okyō and Kichizo are living in the modern world of nineteenth-century realism—even the modernist world of the *fin de siècle*, moving away from the direct statements and moral certainties that are still quite visible in Ibsen. Robert Lyons Danly has written of Ichiyō's "allusive and elliptical style" (324), and this is a quality that Western writers were experimenting with at the same time. Three years after Ichiyō wrote her story, the nameless narrator of *Heart of Darkness* tells his listeners that the meaning of Marlow's inconclusive tale "was not inside like a kernel but outside, enveloping the tale which brought it out only as a glow brings out a haze."[4] The same can be said of Ichiyō's major stories.

When she succeeded in selling her first story, Ichiyō recorded in her diary the drama of returning home to announce: "Look, mother, I received 10 yen today for my first installment in *Miyako no Hana*!" Her sister declared, "You are now a professional writer," and added: "Who knows? You may become so famous that someday your face will be the one appearing on a Japanese banknote!" Ichiyō laughed and told her sister not to get carried away—"A woman's face on a note in Japan?"[5] In an act of true poetic justice, since 2004 Ichiyō has been featured on the ¥5,000 banknote. She is the third woman ever to be so honored, after an empress and her own favorite writer, Murasaki Shikibu, to whom we now turn.

52. Murasaki Shikibu, *The Tale of Genji*

Murasaki Shikibu was not only Higuchi Ichiyō's greatest predecessor as a Japanese woman writer, but she too was a poet turned writer of fiction. Murasaki's masterpiece challenges us today on many levels, beginning with the nearly 800 poems interspersed through her book's fifty-four chapters. Arthur Waley, who first translated *Genji* into English in the 1920s, excised most of the poetry and turned the surviving lyrics into prose, making the *Genji* look more like a European novel, or we might say a kind of sophisticated fairytale for grownups. His approach is well shown by the epigraph that he chose for the title page of his translation, not from any Japanese source but from the tale of Cinderella by Charles Perrault, whom he quotes in French: *"Est-ce vous, mon prince? lui di-telle. Vous vous êtes bien fait attendre!"* ("Is it you, my prince?" she said to him. "You've certainly taken your time!").[6] Here Cinderella's Handsome Prince is overlaid on Murasaki's "Shining Prince" Genji, in a quotation that empha-sizes the heroine's cool self-possession, expressed with quite un-Japanese directness.

There have been three complete English translations since Waley's time, by Edward Seidensticker in 1976 (the translation I'll cite here), Royall Tyler in 2001, and Dennis Washburn in 2016. All three have given full weight to Mu-rasaki's poetry. The predominance of poetic values in premodern Japan had major consequences for her practice as a writer of prose. Her story is built around poetic moments, and she had fairly little interest in such staples of modern fiction as character development or a plot with clear beginning, middle, and end. Her lead characters, Genji and his child-bride, Murasaki— from whom Murasaki Shikibu took her own pen name—die two thirds of the way through the book, which then starts up again with a new set of characters in the next generation. There has been speculation that the later chapters may have been written by someone else, but most accounts favor a single author revisiting her themes on a deeper level. The story reaches a tentative stopping-point in its fifty-fourth chapter, but it doesn't end in any way that readers of Western novels would expect. Murasaki may have intended to carry the story farther one day, but it doesn't appear that a climactic "novelistic" ending was ever an integral part of her plan.

Murasaki presents her characters as well as the action in poetic terms. They are usually identified not by name but by shifting series of epithets, often de-rived from lines in poems they quote or write. "Murasaki" isn't a proper name at all but a plant bearing lavender flowers, used along with wisteria in several poems associated with Genji's many love affairs. Indeed, "Murasaki" first ap-pears as the epithet for Genji's first love, his father's consort Fujitsubo. The epithet is only later transferred to her niece, the tale's principal heroine. The very name "Genji" merely means "bearer of the name" (of Minamoto), a surname bestowed on him as an illegitimate child by his emperor father. Genji, in short, is *a* genji, a son who is recognized but excluded from the imperial family. As vividly as Murasaki develops her major characters, they continue to suggest general qualities as they play out recurrent patterns that emerge in generation after generation, in a narrative unfolding of poetic moments of fellowship, longing, rivalry, and reverie.

Murasaki was writing in, and revolutionizing, a genre known as monogatari, extended prose narratives typically set in the past and dealing with romance. Monogatari had to compete not only with poetry at the top of the genre hierarchy but also with history in between poetry and prose fiction. In addition, Japanese writers were overshadowed by the greater prestige of their Chinese counterparts. Like Latin in medieval Europe, Chinese was studied and written by upper-class men, and women weren't expected to learn Chinese, much less to develop literary ability in it. Vernacular monogatari became popular among women, but like "chick lit" today, these works were regarded as light entertainment of dubious moral worth. Rebutting such views, Murasaki includes an explicit defense of her work within the tale itself. In the twenty-fifth chapter, "Fireflies," we learn that the women in Genji's household are amusing themselves during the spring rainy season by reading illustrated romances. Genji happens by the room of a young ward of his, Tamakazura, "the most avid reader of all." Looking around her room,

> Genji could not help noticing the clutter of pictures and manuscripts. "What a nuisance this all is," he said one day. "Women seem to have been born to be cheerfully deceived. They know perfectly well that in all these old stories there is scarcely a shred of truth, and yet they are captured and made sport of by the whole range of trivialities and go on scribbling them down, quite unaware that in these warm rains their hair is all dank and knotted."

Yet no sooner has he delivered this genially sexist judgment than he qualifies it, adding that "amid all the fabrication I must admit that I do find real emotions and plausible chains of events." Shifting ground once again, he undercuts this compliment with a renewed attack on the tales' truthfulness: "I think that these yarns must come from people much practiced in lying." In reply, Tamakazura pushes away her inkstone—has she been starting to write a tale herself?—and gives as good as she gets: "I can see," she retorts, "that that would be the view of someone much given to lying himself."[7]

A flirtatious discussion follows, counterpointing the truth-giving lies of fiction with the seductions of Genji's cheating heart. Genji ends up allowing that "I should imagine that it is in real life as in fiction. We are all human and we all have our ways." He agrees that even his young daughter can be exposed to the tales, and then spends "a great deal of time selecting romances he thought suitable"—no doubt enjoying them in the process—"and ordered them copied and illustrated" (1:439). This single scene tells us as much about the literary milieu within and against which Murasaki was writing as we might learn from an entire treatise on the art of fiction.

Both Genji and the women in his life try to negotiate the possibilities of life in a patriarchal court society, where walls are made of paper and everyone is always seen—and gossiped about—by others (Figure 46). A good source to contextualize Murasaki's portrayal of court life is *The Pillow Book*, the diary of her contemporary Sei Shōnagon. Here she describes the behavior of a good lover:

> A good lover will behave as elegantly at dawn as at any other time. He drags himself out of bed with a look of dismay on his face. The lady urges him on: "Come, my friend, it's getting light. You don't want anyone to find you here." He gives a deep sigh, as if to say that it is agony to leave. Once up, he does not instantly pull on his trousers. Instead he comes close to the lady and whispers whatever was left unsaid during the night. Presently he raises the lattice, and the two lovers stand together by the side door while he tells her

46. Voyeuristic Genji

how he dreads the coming day, which will keep them apart; then he slips away. The lady watches him go, and this moment of parting will remain among her most charming memories. Indeed, one's attachment to a man depends largely on the elegance of his leave-taking.[8]

For all its emphasis on human passion and natural beauty, Murasaki's narrative is infused with a Buddhist sense of the transience of all earthly pleasures, from lovemaking to political success, from music under a full moon to exchanges of poems with an attractive stranger glimpsed through windblown curtains. After Murasaki dies, Genji reads over her old letters:

Though a great many years had passed, the ink was as fresh as if it had been set down yesterday. They seemed meant to last a thousand years. But they had been for him, and he was finished with them. He asked two or three women who were among his closest confidantes to see to destroying them. The handwriting of the dead always has the power to move us, and these were not ordinary letters. He was blinded by the tears that fell to mingle with the ink until he was unable to make out what was written . . . Seeking to control a flow of tears that must seem hopelessly exaggerated, Genji glanced at one of the more affectionate notes and wrote in the margin:

"I gather sea grasses no more, nor look upon them.
Now they are smoke, to join her in distant heavens." (2:733–4)

After a thousand exchanges of poem-letters with the love of his life, Genji can't help writing once more to her, but no answering poem will ever come back to him.

As Murasaki lay dying, the empress had come to visit her. "Gazing at the two of them, each somehow more beautiful than the other, Genji wished that he might have them a thousand years just as they were; but of course time runs against these wishes. That is the great, sad truth" (2:717). Time runs against these wishes in life, but not in art. Murasaki composed her great novel from around the year 1000 to her death in 1012; a thousand years later, Genji's entire world has utterly vanished, but *The Tale of Genji* lives on.

53. Matsuo Bashō, *The Narrow Road to the Deep North*

Together with Murasaki Shikibu, Matsuo Bashō (1644–94) is the most prominent premodern Japanese writer in world literature. Starting in the late nineteenth century, readers around the world were struck by the contemplative beauty of his haiku, and Ezra Pound and the European Imagists were strongly influenced by poems such as his famous haiku on a frog in a pond:

an ancient pond
a frog jumps in—
the splash of water[9]

47. The silent waterfall

Bashō practiced self-forgetting through close observation of creatures such as frogs or fish, both in verse and in art. On a landscape painted by a friend, Bashō added a haiku; the poem and the painting together silently depict the thundering of a massive waterfall (Figure 47). Yet in that very poem, the "forgotten" self implicitly sees itself reflected in the scene:

Quietly, quietly,
yellow mountain roses fall—
sound of the rapids[10]

The silent roses, falling into the rapids that sweep them over the waterfall, become an image of the ephemerality of life.

Bashō has often been seen as a solitary hermit, relaxing outside his hut beneath the banana tree (*bashō*) from which he took his pen name. Yet this view misses Bashō's sociality and his deep engagement with collaborative poetic composition (*renga*), which he preferred to his haiku. Many of his haiku themselves were inspired by meetings with people he encountered on his journeys around Japan, which he recorded in a series of poetic travelogues, *haibun*—a term that he coined. His journeys had more to do with a deep restlessness than with contemplative withdrawal. As he says in the opening of *The Narrow Road to the Deep North*: "The gods seem to have possessed my soul and turned it inside out, and roadside images seemed to invite me from every corner, so that it was impossible for me to stay idle at home."[11]

Like *The Tale of Genji*, Bashō's travelogues create a compelling mixture of poetry and prose, as he leaves the comforts of Edo (today's Tokyo) in order to reconnect to nature and revitalize his poetry. He is also testing the limits of his endurance, laying his life on the line as he explores the world's ephemeral beauties. Mortality is a constant concern in Bashō's travel accounts. He imagines himself done in by bandits or by sheer exhaustion, and he is traveling through fleeting time as well as space, as in *The Narrow Road*'s famous opening:

> Days and months are travellers of eternity. So are the years that pass by. Those who steer a boat across the sea, or drive a horse over the earth till they succumb to the weight of years, spend every minute of their lives travelling. There are a great number of ancients, too, who died on the road. I myself have been tempted for a long time by the cloud-moving wind—filled with a strong desire to wander. (97)

Another of his travel accounts, *The Records of a Weather-Exposed Skeleton*, begins with a haiku that asserts his positive desire to die on the road:

> Determined to fall a weather-exposed skeleton
> I cannot help the sore wind
> blowing through my heart. (51)

Here Bashō's weak heart, unable to keep out the autumn wind, resembles a bamboo flute, conveying the wind's melancholy melody.

Bashō's very personal poetry is often socially generated. His travelogues reflect a search for serenity amid a troubled, unstable society, which he constantly encounters even as he seeks to leave it behind. Most strikingly, as he sets out on the journey recorded in *The Records of a Weather-Exposed Skeleton*, he comes upon an abandoned child: "As I was plodding along the River Fuji, I saw a small child, hardly three years of age, crying pitifully on the bank, obviously abandoned by his parents. They must have thought this child was unable to ride through the stormy waters of life which run as wild as the rapid river itself, and that he was doomed to have a life even shorter than that of the morning dew." He wonders:

> How is it indeed that this child has been reduced to this state of utter misery?
> Is it because of his mother who ignored him, or because of his father who
> abandoned him? Alas, it seems to me that this child's undeserved suffering
> has been caused by something far greater and more massive—by what one
> might call the irresistible will of heaven. If it is so, child, you must raise your
> voice to heaven, and I must pass on, leaving you behind. (52)

It may seem that Bashō is responding to this heartbreaking encounter by retreating into otherworldly disengagement. On a closer look, though, we can see the complexity of Bashō's reaction. First, he processes the raw scene through a comparison to nature: "The child looked to me as fragile as the flowers of bush-clover that scatter at the slightest stir of the autumn wind." Next, his poetic perception breeds a practical response: the sight "was so pitiful that I gave him what little food I had with me." Then comes the third response—a haiku:

> The ancient poet who pitied monkeys for their cries,
> what would he say, if he saw
> this child crying in the autumn wind? (52)

Interestingly, the form of the haiku itself seems to be under stress here: in place of the usual 5-7-5 syllable count, this haiku has an irregular count of 7-7-5. As he often does elsewhere, Bashō counterpoints his experience against a prior poetic response, in this case a travel poem written 900 years earlier by the Chinese poet Li Bai. Rather than rendering a judgment on the scene, he wonders what "the ancient poet" would say if he could see the child. This question at once connects Bashō to the older tradition and outdoes it, both through his engagement with the suffering caused by poverty and through the heightened realism of the surrounding prose description.

Yet Bashō hasn't made his haiku out of his initial response, in which he compared the child to the fragile flowers of the bush-clover. That would have been a perfectly good basis for a haiku, but evidently it wasn't enough. What Bashō is experiencing, after all, is a profoundly *unpoetic* moment, a scene that would rarely if ever have been recorded by a classical Chinese poet or by Bashō's Japanese predecessors. Rather than retreat into versifying about clover blossoms, Bashō stops to give the child all his food, and his slender supplies implicitly connect him to the impoverished child. Only then does he compose the poem in which he poses the unanswered—and perhaps unanswerable—question of what Li Bai would have written if he'd ever tackled so unpoetic a subject.

The process of poetic creation doesn't take place in solitude but in an ever-widening circle: older poets inspire Bashō's journey. A good example of Bashō's creative process can be seen after he passes through the Shirakawa Gate that marks the entry into the northern region. As he reports,

> I called on the Poet Tōkyū at the post town of Sukagawa, and spent a few
> days at his house. He asked me how I had fared at the gate of Shirakawa. I
> had to tell him that my body and spirit were tired from the pain of the long
> journey; my heart was overwhelmed by the landscape. The thoughts of the
> distant past tore through me, and I couldn't think straight. It was deplorable,
> however, to have passed the gate of Shirakawa without producing a single
> verse, so I wrote:

Beginnings of poetry—
rice-planting songs
of the Deep North

Bashō's poem is a deeply personal response to the landscape, but it is mediated through a web of social relations. It is his host's friendly inquiry that spurs him to overcome his weariness and to gather his scattered thoughts into a poem, and this poem in turn sets off a round of *renga*: "Using this poem as a starting piece, before we knew it we made three sequences of linked verse."[12] What is more, Bashō isn't simply responding to the sight of the Shirakawa Gate, or to the sound of women singing folksongs while they plant their rice. As he says, he was preoccupied with "thoughts of the distant past" while he stood at the barrier, and throughout his journals his thoughts often center on earlier poets and their responses to the same or similar scenes. As Haruo Shirane has written: "The Shinakawa Barrier here exists almost entirely in the traveler's imagination, as a circle of poetic associations."[13]

Long a uniquely Japanese poetic form, the haiku has become a worldwide genre, thanks in no small measure to Bashō. Today the Haiku Society of America (http://www.hsa-haiku.org) publishes a lively journal, *Frogpond*. Bashō has even figured in an episode of *The Simpsons*, in which the recent American Poet Laureate Robert Pinsky (voicing himself in cartoon form) reads a haiku in praise of Bashō. This delights a rowdy bunch of Bashō fans in the audience, who have his name painted in red on their chests. They even have the correct macron on the letter ō. An aptly ephemeral immortality for Bashō today: fifteen pixels of fame.

54. Yukio Mishima, *The Sea of Fertility*

One of Japan's greatest, and strangest, writers, Yukio Mishima had a meteoric career as a novelist, playwright, poet, actor, and film maker, producing some three dozen novels and fifty plays before he committed ritual suicide in 1970 at age forty-five. A right-wing nationalist, he had built up a private militia, and he wanted to inspire his countrymen to return the Japanese emperor to true political power, as a counterweight to Japan's growing Westernization. Despairing of the direction of his culture, and hating to grow old, he made an appointment with the commandant of the Tokyo headquarters of the Japanese Self-Defense forces. He and a group of four followers barricaded the door and tied the commandant to his chair, and then Mishima delivered a speech to soldiers in the courtyard below, urging them to join him in staging a coup d'état. When—as he'd expected—his audience reacted with jeers, he went back inside and disemboweled himself, having instructed his followers to complete the task by beheading him.

Earlier that day, he'd written the final sentence of his magnum opus, the tetralogy of *Spring Snow*, *Runaway Horses*, *The Temple of Dawn*, and *The Decay of the Angel*, with the ironic overall title *The Sea of Fertility*, named after a region on the moon. Spanning the years from 1912 into the near future of 1975, the tetralogy follows the career of Kiyoaki Matsugae, who dies at the end of the first volume and then is reborn three times, first as a nationalistic extremist, then as a Thai princess, Ying Chan, and finally as a manipulative orphan—a Higuchi Ichiyō adolescent gone wrong. *The Sea of Fertility* offers a cornucopia of strategies for interweaving a premodern Asian past and a global modernity. While working on the series, Mishima traveled to India as well as Thailand, and he discussed problems of rural development with Indira Gandhi in addition to visiting temples and burning-ghats. Equally, he drew extensively on fictional models, both Japanese and Western, including two of his key intertexts: the works of Murasaki Shikibu and Marcel Proust.

In *Spring Snow*, Mishima satirizes both the old and the new orders of Japanese life through a pointed rewriting of *The Tale of Genji*. The heritage of the Heian period is embodied in the passive, decaying aristocracy of the Ayakura family of the book's heroine, Satoko, while the Westernizing post-Meiji era is satirized in the figure of Kiyoaki's father, the crass Marquis Matsugae. Mishima was fatally invested in the fantasy of reviving some version of a glorious pre-Meiji past, but his portrayal of the Ayakuras indicates that no direct recourse to past tradition is really possible. Instead, Mishima conducts a complex triangulation between ancient Asia and modern European culture.

Mishima's antihero, Kiyoaki, is a Prince Genji with no purpose in life, and he actually first makes love with Satoko behind a Genji screen—most likely an old six-panel screen adorned with images from Murasaki's novel. Yet Kiyoaki can't bring himself to feel anything for Satoko, until he has an elaborate moment of recollection. He keeps putting off proposing marriage, but then learns that she has become engaged to a son of the Emperor. Instead of being crushed by this news, Kiyoaki is filled with an obscure satisfaction. He picks up a scroll that he and Satoko had used as children for writing poetry exercises, and he has a sudden recollection of the chrysanthemum cookies that he'd be given when they'd play a Heian board game:

> Each piece of the Empress's confection, the prize for winning at *sugoroku*, had been molded in the form of the imperial crest. Whenever his small teeth had bitten into a crimson chrysanthemum, the color of its petals had intensified before melting away, and at the touch of his tongue, the delicately etched lines of a cool white chrysanthemum had blurred and dissolved into a sweet liquid. Everything came back to him—the dark rooms of the Ayakura mansion, the court screens brought from Kyoto with their pattern of autumn flowers, the solemn stillness of the nights, Satoko's mouth opening in a slight yawn half-hidden behind her sweep of black hair—everything came back just as he had experienced it then, in all its lonely elegance. But he realized that he was now slowly admitting one idea that he had never dared entertain before.
>
> Something sounded within Kiyoaki like a trumpet call: *I love Satoko.*[14]

As the chrysanthemum cookie dissolves on Kiyoaki's tongue, it becomes a version of Proust's famous madeleine, which Proust had already described in

Japanese terms, comparing it to origami that blossom when placed in a bowl of water, so that "the whole of Combray and its surroundings, taking shape and solidity, sprang into being, town and gardens alike, from my cup of tea."[15]

The chrysanthemum cookie does more than evoke memories of Kiyoaki's lost childhood: it gives him access to a new universe of Proustian desire. He realizes that he finally desires Satoko precisely because she has become unavailable, much as we see in Swann's tortured love affair with Odette, or Marcel's with Albertine. Under the force of his cookie-induced recovery of time past, Kiyoaki finds that "his sexual impulses, so diffident until now, had been lacking just such a powerful impulse. It had taken so much time and effort to find his role in life" (179). He seeks out Satoko, and begins a clandestine and ultimately fatal love affair with her.

But the result is no simple imitation of Proust; for Mishima, that wouldn't be any better than the fatuous Westernization of Kiyoaki's vulgar father. Instead, Proust serves as a conduit to bring the story back to Murasaki Shikibu's world, but in a new and modernist way. Throughout *Spring Snow* Kiyoaki has mysterious dreams, but instead of revealing a lost or repressed past, as they would in Proust or in Freud, these dreams foreshadow Kiyoaki's *future* reincarnations, depicted in the ensuing volumes of the series. What his dreams reveal, though he—and we—can't yet know this, can be called remembrances of things future.

Over the decades Kiyoaki and his reincarnations are observed by his close friend Shigekuni Honda. It is Honda who finally discerns the pattern of rebirth, and also its ultimate meaninglessness, following the inconclusive death of Kiyoaki's final avatar in *The Decay of the Angel*. Honda then makes a pilgrimage to see Satoko, who is now eighty-three years old and a nun, only to find that she claims to have no memory at all of her epochal early love affair. "Did you really know a person called Kiyoaki?" she asks Honda. "And can you say definitely that the two of us have met before?" This most Proustian of Japanese novels hasn't brought Honda to a triumphant "time regained," but instead to "a place that had no memories, nothing."[16] Or so Honda reflects in the novel's final lines, as "the noontide sun of summer flowed over the still garden." These are the words that Mishima wrote on November 25, 1970, the date given on the final page—the day he went out to commit his spectacular suicide.

Though Honda feels that he has come to a place of "no memories, nothing," we could also say that this long Proustian detour has brought us to a quite specific literary locale, the novelistic equivalent of the "poetic places" that Bashō loved to visit. Where the novel has brought us, in fact, is to *The Tale of Genji*. Satoko's proclaimed failure to recall her love affair with Kiyoaki closely mirrors the ending—or non-ending—of Murasaki's great monogatari, whose final heroine, Ukifune, flees entrapment by two unwelcome suitors, Genji's supposed son, Kaoru, and grandson, Niou. Taking refuge in a Buddhist convent, she claims amnesia so as to conceal her identity, and she insists on shaving her hair and becoming a nun.

Murasaki's unfinished narrative breaks off with Kaoru scheming to get Ukifune back, and we can't know whether she'll succeed in escaping from the world, but Mishima gives Satoko the success in renunciation that Ukifune may never achieve. "Memory is like a phantom mirror," Satoko tells Honda. "It sometimes shows things too distant to be seen, and sometimes it shows them as if they were here." Taken aback, Honda stammers,

> "But if there was no Kiyoaki from the beginning . . . there was no Ying Chan, and who knows, perhaps there has been no I."
> For the first time there was strength in her eyes.
> "That too is as it is in each heart." (246)

Taking Buddhism in an existentialist and even nihilistic direction, Mishima has used Proust to reincarnate the Heian world on new terms, and at the same time he uses Murasaki to deconstruct Proust. This double process frees Mishima from imitative dependence on either tradition, even as he draws deeply upon both of them. It is the *incommensurability* of ancient and modern eras, Asian and European traditions, that fuels Mishima's most ambitious contribution to world literature.

55. James Merrill, "Prose of Departure"

Our visit to Japan concludes with a remarkable contemporary use of Bashō's *haibun* genre: a poetic travelogue entitled "Prose of Departure" (1986) by the American poet James Merrill. Merrill was one of the most creative poets of his generation, winner of the Pulitzer Prize, the Bollingen Prize for Poetry, and the National Book Award. He was playful and ironic, and he loved to make use of traditional forms such as the sonnet and villanelle. In his twenty-page "Prose of Departure," he weaves his narrative around a suite of haiku. Appropriately, Merrill's *haibun* recounts a journey to Japan. It takes the form of a series of episodes, typically a page or two in length, which frame one or two haiku of his own composition, building on Bashō's emphasis on the body as site of ephemeral beauty and spiritual reflection.

In the opening lines of *Records of a Travel-Worn Satchel*, Bashō had emphasized the decaying body as the site of his poetic spirit: "In this mortal frame of mine which is made of a hundred bones and nine orifices there is something, and this something is called a wind-swept spirit for lack of a better name, for it is much like a thin drapery that is torn and swept away at the slightest stir of the wind. This something in me took to writing poetry years ago."[17] Merrill in turn wrote "Prose of Departure" in the shadow of the AIDS crisis of the 1980s. Many of his friends were dying, and he himself was ill, though he doesn't indicate this directly. His opening vignette evokes, and ironizes, Bashō's theme of life as a voyage. He and his lover are about to depart for a trip to Japan when they receive a call from their close friend Paul, who is undergoing cancer treatment at Minnesota's Mayo Clinic. Merrill describes the clinic as "vast and complex as an ocean liner," mostly occupied by aging couples.

Paul, though, was by himself, was perhaps not even "sailing." Waiting to hear over his own system the stern voice calling *Visitors ashore!* he would have begun to feel that, aside from the far too young and noncommittal crew, bona-fide passengers only were expected to circulate there, all in the same boat, their common dread kept under wraps, yet each of them visibly

> at sea. Yes, yes, these
> old folks grown unpresuming,
> almost Japanese,
>
> had embarked too soon
> —Bon voyage! Write!—upon their
> final honeymoon.[18]

Merrill's own verse here is "almost Japanese," even using a "cutting word" as haiku often do, here marked with a dash: "Write!"

Merrill and his lover go off to Japan, though they feel guilty for not staying to help Paul, not unlike Bashō regretfully leaving behind the crying child at the start of *Records of a Weather-Exposed Skeleton*. The next vignette shows the travelers going to a modern poetic place: the Aoyama cemetery in Tokyo. There, they seek the grave not of an ancient poet but of a modern gay novelist, none other than Mishima: "Yukio Mishima is buried down one of its paths bordered by cherry trees in full, amazing bloom" (54). They fail to find the grave, and instead encounter living people picnicking among the graves, "a few ghostly parties" in the dusk, listening to transistor radios.

The third vignette brings them to "Donald's Neighborhood" (55). This is the film scholar Donald Richie, an American expatriate who had been living in Japan since 1947. Richie often served as host and guide for foreign visitors; he had hosted Marguerite Yourcenar (another devotee of Mishima) on her visit to Japan not long before. "Prose of Departure" is dedicated to him, and so it can be seen as an extended parting poem sequence, if we take "departure" to mean the departure from Japan as well as the initial departure from the United States to Japan.

Again as in Bashō, the journey is also about taking leave from life. Merrill's dying friend "Paul" is based on David Kalstone, an authority on Renaissance and contemporary poetry, including a study that featured Merrill as one of five leading American poets. Kalstone died of AIDS-related illness in June 1986; Merrill published "Prose of Departure" in the *New York Review of Books* that December. Yet Merrill's biographer Langdon Hammer reports that Kalstone was never treated at the Mayo Clinic. Instead, Merrill is recalling his own time there, which he combined with Kalstone's experiences to create the composite figure of "Paul." As Hammer says, Merrill's Japanese journey "involves, as for Bashō, a giving up of self."[19]

When they visit Donald Richie's Tokyo apartment, Merrill and his companion find that he is both an aesthete and an ascetic: "Two midget rooms, utilitarian alcoves, no trace of clutter. What he has is what you see, and includes the resolve to get rid of things already absorbed. Books, records. His lovers he keeps, but as friends—friends take up no space. He now paints at night" (55). In the next vignette, Merrill describes retreating from his worries by composing haiku:

Halfway around the globe from Paul the worst keeps dawning on us . . . I need a form of conscious evasion, that at best permits odd moments when the subject

> looking elsewhere strays
> into a local muse's
> number-benumbed gaze

—fixed there, ticking off syllables, until she blinks and the wave breaks . . . If every trip is an incarnation in miniature, let this be the one in which to arrange myself like flowers. Aim at composure like the target a Zen archer sees through shut eyes. (57)

Richie escorts his guests down to Kyoto and Osaka, where they attend a bunraku puppet performance, which features a love suicide. The heroine is beheaded after she refuses to renounce her love, and her head is sent in a box across the river that separates her from her beloved; he commits suicide upon receiving it. In a haiku, Merrill anticipates Paul's death and envisions taking a boat to dispose of his ashes:

> (Into the Sound, Paul,
> we'd empty your own box, just
> as black, just as small.) (67)

A subtle play on words links the physical and the poetic: Merrill and his lover will distribute Paul's ashes in Long Island Sound, but also into the silent sound of the haiku that commemorates the emptying of the box of ashes.

Like Bashō's travelogues, "Prose of Departure" is set in the present time of Merrill's journey but was actually written (or at least completed) after his return. David Kalstone's death is invoked elsewhere in *The Inner Room*, the collection in which "Prose of Departure" appeared in 1988. The next-to-last poem in the book, "Farewell Performance," gives the scene of scattering the ashes, now described after the fact rather than in anticipation. As his lover Peter grasped a buoy to hold the boat steady, Merrill submerged the box of Paul's ashes, "freeing / all it contained" (93). *The Inner Room* ends with a short poem in which a drop of water is "translated" by a freezing wind into a "six-pointed Mandarin"—that is, into a snowflake. It soon melts, becoming a gingko leaf and then lead turning to gold by a playful transposition of letters, from "lead" to "load" to "goad" to "gold" (95).

In Merrill as in Bashō, a constant theme is the presence of the past, the focus for memory and desire, all mediated through writing in the face of death. In *The Inner Room* directly before "Prose of Departure" there is a villanelle entitled "Dead Center," which indeed is placed at the center of the collection. It begins:

Upon reflection, as I dip my pen
Tonight, forth ripple messages in code.
In Now's black waters burn the stars of Then.

The poet's reflections take him back in time:

Or else I'm back at Grandmother's. I'm ten,
Dust hides my parents' roadster from the road
Which dips—*into* reflection, with my pen.

"Dead Center" ends with someone struggling for breath—perhaps David /
Paul in intensive care, or Merrill himself—before it stages a haunting return
to its beginning:

Breath after breath, harsh O's of oxygen—
Never deciphered, what do they forebode?
In Now's black waters burn the stars. Ah then

48. *James Merrill, 1973*

Leap, Memory, supreme equestrienne,
Through hoops of fire, circuits you overload!
Beyond reflection, as I dip my pen
In Now's black waters, burn the stars of Then. (50)

Memory leaps into the past, in a dynamic echo of Vladimir Nabokov's *Speak, Memory*. The villanelle concludes with the same line that ended the opening stanza, but with one small, crucial change: the addition of a comma, which turns a declarative statement into a poetic imperative. In just this way, premodern Japanese literature lives on, long after the dissolution of Bashō's fragile body and of his entire world, providing an inspiration and a challenge to poet and reader alike:

In Now's black waters, *burn* the stars of Then.

*49. James Merrill,
early 1990s*

CHAPTER TWELVE

Brazil–Colombia:
Utopias, Dystopias, Heterotopias

56. Thomas More, *Utopia*

Though Phileas Fogg sailed from Japan to San Francisco, our itinerary continues to expand on his, and so we proceed to South America, now in the fictionalized tracks of one of the earliest European explorers, Amerigo Vespucci. After exploring the coast of Brazil between 1499 and 1502, Vespucci (or someone using his name) published an account boldly entitled *Mundus Novus*. The title announced that what Columbus had stumbled upon a decade earlier wasn't the coast of Asia after all, but an altogether "New World," and in 1507, the map-maker Martin Waldseemüller named the entire landmass "America" in Vespucci's honor. The map of the world, and the map of world literature, would forever change.

According to the young English lawyer Thomas More, Vespucci's crew-member Raphael Hythlodaeus went ashore in Brazil and then headed inland. Eventually he reached the Pacific coast, where he found a unique society living on an island named Utopia. By 1515 he was back home in Antwerp, where he described his discoveries to a group of friends, including More, who was visiting from England. *Utopia* (1516) represents a new kind of world literature, as it is the first major work to reflect the dizzying expansion of the globe in More's day. Europeans now had to find their place in a world whose true dimensions had been unknown to their parents. In the popular imagination, explorers like Vespucci were opening up virgin lands where an aging "old world" could be rejuvenated by encountering the new one. In Jan van der Straet's *Vespucci Awakening America* (Figure 50), armed with religion and science (his cross and sextant), Vespucci accosts a willing Brazilian maiden, whom he is about to free from the company of the cannibals who are roasting an enemy's leg in the background.

Building on the early dreams of the New World, More's *Utopia* gave the adjective "utopian" to the world, and it spawned an entire genre of utopian fiction, from the sensual paradise of Charles Fourier's *Le nouveau monde amoureux* (1816), a land of sexual equality, polygamy, and even "omnigamy," to the socialist William Morris's *News from Nowhere* (1890), to the darkly *dys*topian vision of Margaret Atwood's *The Handmaid's Tale* and *The Testaments*. It remains an open question whether More was serious in proposing a society of equality, communal property, and religious freedom. Utopia means

50. *Theodore Galle, after Jan van der Straet,*
Vespucci Awakening America *(c. 1600)*

"No-place" in Greek, and the name of More's supposed informant, Hythlo-daeus, means "Nonsense-monger." No less a reader than C. S. Lewis proposed that we should only regard *Utopia* as a playful work of fantasy. It may be better, though, to think of Utopia as what the philosopher Michel Foucault called a *heterotopia*: a world within the world, a place of otherness that can expose the tensions of a society in crisis.

More created Utopia as a radical cure for society's ills. Much of the book is devoted to imagining solutions to the problems of conspicuous consumption by the nobility—the one-percenters of More's day—and grinding poverty among the peasants who supported them. So in Utopia, everyone has to work, but only six hours a day, and everyone takes a turn at farming. Freed from want and from overwork, the Utopians live for pleasure—rational pleasures, but pleasures all the same. Entire neighborhoods get together in large dining halls, enjoying plentiful meals and good conversation. The Utopians love learning, and they turn out to have a natural aptitude for Greek, which their own alphabet resembles. Music is popular in Utopia, as it was in More's house-hold; married twice, he taught both of his wives to play instruments. Marriage in Utopia is more than a practical economic decision; prospective spouses are allowed to see each other naked, to be sure that physical attraction will under-gird the marriage.

Both "No-place" and a very good place (*eu-topos* in Greek), Utopia is a paradise on earth, governed by elected magistrates, in a democratized version of Plato's philosopher kings. Yet this New World society is no New Age com-mune; fixed hierarchies provide order and give everyone a sense of their pur-pose and place in life. Children obey their parents, wives obey their husbands, and sons follow their father's profession, as More himself had done. The least desirable jobs are done by slaves. Some of them are condemned criminals, while other slaves—in a startling imperial fantasy—are *volunteers*, who have come to the island for a better life than they've had on the mainland.

Yet there seem to be snakes in paradise. What were those criminals up to, before they were caught and enslaved? Some were no doubt motivated by garden-variety greed, but running through More's account is an undercurrent of another concern: that sectarian factions could arise and tear the island nation apart. England had only recently emerged from the drawn-out Wars of the Roses that ended with the establishment of the Tudor dynasty by Henry VII, an avaricious and unpopular monarch. His son Henry VIII, who had succeeded him at age seventeen in 1509, was a more promising figure—fluent in four languages, a good musician, and a lover of books and ideas—but it remained to be seen whether the young king could hold the kingdom together. This task would be all the more challenging amid the stirrings of religious controversy on the Continent. Protestantism was a natural outgrowth of Renaissance humanism's emphasis on free inquiry and personal integrity, but to papal loyalists such as More, the multiplying Protestant sects were chaotic breeding grounds for heresy and civil war. Above all, the Utopians reject fanaticism. One of Hythlodaeus's companions, who starts promoting Christianity "with more enthusiasm than good sense," is arrested and sent into exile, "on a charge not of religious contempt but of creating public disorder."[1]

As they preside over Utopia's banquet halls, the magistrates make sure that every single person is constantly in view, oddly foreshadowing Orwell's dystopian *1984*, where Big Brother is always watching you. Throughout Utopia, the magistrates have eliminated opportunities for private gatherings, conspiracies, and plots: there are severe restrictions on movement between towns, taverns are banned, and there is no truly private time or space anywhere on the island. And despite More's claims that the Utopians are delighted to live in the best of all possible polities, and his emphasis that "everyone should be free to follow the religion of their choice" (109), he gives a chilling reason for banishing atheists, or anyone else (Jews, most likely) who would disbelieve in life after death. "Anyone who denies this they regard as a renegade to humanity, since he's reduced the aspiring nature of his own soul to the level of an animal carcass. Even less will they admit him as a citizen since, unless he's checked by fear, he'll have no regard for their laws or customs" (110). No one, the Utopians say, would restrain their desires and live moral lives unless they feared punishment after death. Utopia's rational, convivial, communal society is ultimately ruled by fear.

More's own fears were realized in the years following *Utopia*'s publication, when his friend and patron Henry VIII broke with Rome and established the Church of England, partly in order to divorce Catherine of Aragon and marry his mistress Anne Boleyn, but also to cement his power by redistributing Church lands to his favorite nobles. Horrified, More resigned his post as Lord Chancellor and tried to stay away from the court. He went so far as to commission a tombstone for himself in his parish church, with a long inscription asserting that he'd retired to spend his declining years in study and prayer after loyal service to his beloved monarch. This forward-looking tombstone didn't fool anybody: More had refused to attend Anne Boleyn's coronation or to affirm Henry's status as head of the Church of England, and he was far too prominent to be allowed to retreat into silence. He was arrested and repeatedly interrogated; when his questioners couldn't trap him in treasonous statements, he was convicted on the basis of false testimony.

Utopia was farther from England than ever. Despite twenty years' service to the King, More was beheaded in July 1535. Unlike the Utopians, More had no fear of what awaited him after death, and he even joked with his executioner as he approached the scaffold ("I pray you, Mr. Lieutenant, see me safe up; and for my coming down, let me shift for myself").[2] More's tombstone had a message for the King's spies to see, but the inscription ended on a more private note, invoking the women who were to be buried beside him: his wife, Joan, who had died at age twenty-three after bearing him four children, and his second wife, Alice, whom he had married within a month of Joan's death. Though Jesus had declared that there would be no marriage in heaven, More hoped otherwise, as he reveals in a final paragraph that the utopian libertarian Fourier would have approved:

Here lieth Jone the wellbeloved wife of me Thomas More, who have appointed this tomb for Alis my wife and me also; the one being coupled with me in matrimony, in my youth brought me forth three daughters & one son, the other hath been so good to my children (which is a rare praise in a stepdame) as scant any could be better to her own. The one so lived with me, & the other now so liveth, that it is doutfull whether this or the other were dearer unto me. Oh how well could we three have lived joined together in matrimony, if fortune and religion wolde have suffered it. But I beseech our Lord that this tombe and heaven may join us together. So deathe shall give us, that thing that life could not.[3]

Together with Alice and Joan, in death More could finally reach the shores of Utopia.

57. Voltaire, *Candide, or Optimism*

Thomas More composed *Utopia* at the very beginning of Europe's encounter with the Western Hemisphere, but by the time Voltaire wrote *Candide* in 1759, the Americas were firmly under Europe's sway, and the "Old" and "New" worlds were becoming deeply intertwined. Like More, Voltaire was primarily interested in South America as a setting for a critique of his own culture, but his Brazilian scenes could now be based on a far more extensive and realistic literature of exploration and settlement.

Following in Raphael Hythlodaeus's footsteps, Voltaire's endlessly optimistic young Candide and his more pragmatic beloved Cunégonde venture to Brazil, decamping from Lisbon after Candide rashly murders Portugal's Grand Inquisitor and a Jewish moneylender who have been enjoying Cunégonde's favors on alternate days. Candide hopes for a better world than a corrupt and war-torn Europe, but in Buenos Aires Cunégonde is propositioned by the governor and Candide is pursued for the Grand Inquisitor's murder. He flees into the interior, accompanied by a mixed-race servant, Cacambo. Voltaire had never been to South America, but he could flesh out his descriptions with details picked up from the literature of exploration, as with the description of an aviary: "Candide was immediately led into a leafy nook surrounded by a handsome colonnade of green and gold marble and trellises amid which sported parrots, birds of paradise, hummingbirds, guinea fowl, and all the rarest species of birds."[4]

In Brazil Candide encounters noble savages who seem to have stepped out of the pages of Michel de Montaigne's essay "Of Cannibals" (1580). Montaigne had met a group of Brazilian Tupinambá in Rouen; in his essay, he portrays the cannibals as horrified by the inequality they find in European society, and he comes to see their ritual consumption of their enemies as more honorable than European armies' indiscriminate brutality. The indigenous inhabitants also assist Voltaire in undercutting Christian pieties. When Candide and Cacambo escape from a group of Jesuit pursuers by donning Jesuit disguise, they are caught by a band of cannibals, who prepare to eat them. Candide protests their violation of Christian ethics, but this argument gets him nowhere. Cacambo mollifies them by revealing that they too are enemies of the Jesuits, who fully deserve to be eaten: " 'Gentlemen,' said Cacambo, 'you have a mind to eat a Jesuit today? An excellent idea . . . Though we Europeans don't exercise our right to eat our neighbors, the reason is simply that we find it easy to get a good meal elsewhere' " (35). The cannibals rejoice at the discovery of these anti-Jesuit allies and let them free.

Traveling farther into the interior, they come upon El Dorado. The myth of El Dorado had inspired a series of real-life expeditions, most famously by Sir Walter Raleigh, who ventured from Guiana down the Orinoco River in search of this golden city, where jewels were strewn on the streets. In a seventeenth-century Dutch map of the Amazon that I inherited from my artist-explorer Aunt Helen, the interested traveler can locate El Dorado on the northwest border of the vast (though, sadly, nonexistent) Lake Parime (Figure 51).

When Candide and Cacambo reach El Dorado, they encounter children playing with the requisite jewels on the streets. Like More's Utopia, this primitive but noble city-state has no need for lawyers, courts, or elaborate religious

51. Amazon map showing El Dorado (1647)

establishments. The absence of such institutions was commonly remarked on by European visitors, sometimes with admiration but often to justify their programs of conquest and conversion, as we've seen in Conrad and Achebe. In 1570, a Portuguese chronicler claimed that the Brazilian natives possessed "neither faith, nor law, nor king" (in Portuguese, *fé*, *lei*, and *rei*) because they couldn't pronounce the letters F, L, and R.[5] This was *probably* a joke.

El Dorado does have a king, but he opposes tyranny, and his witticisms surprise Candide because they're actually funny. In a nod to the classical myth of Amazonian warriors, the king's guard is composed of twenty powerful (but still elegant) women. Amid the common tropes of primitive virtue, what is most distinctive about Voltaire's utopia is that El Dorado is a *techno*-paradise. Engineering is more highly developed than in Europe, and Candide admires "the palace of sciences, in which he saw a gallery two thousand paces long, entirely filled with mathematical and physical instruments" (42). If More's Utopia was a humanist paradise, Voltaire's is an Enlightenment ideal. Yet Candide soon decides to leave: "If we stay here, we shall be just like everybody else," he says. He proposes taking away some sheep loads of gold and jewels, so that "we shall be richer than all the kings put together" (42). Almost as an afterthought, he adds that he'll surely be able to get Cunégonde back once he's the richest man in the world.

El Dorado's engineers rig up an elaborate system to get them up over the cliffs that secure El Dorado from the outside world, and they head off northwards. The next place they come to is Surinam, in a tip of Voltaire's plumed hat to Aphra Behn's *Oroonoko* (1688), which gives a tragic account of an abortive slave revolt there. In Surinam, Candide and Cacambo encounter a severely injured Negro slave, who soberly explains: "If we catch a finger in the sugar mill where we work, they cut off our hand; if we try to run away, they cut off our leg: I have undergone both these experiences. This is the price of the sugar you eat in Europe" (44) (Figure 52).

A common theme in early travel accounts is the European explorer's surprise at finding someone in a distant land who knows his language, a moment

52. *"The price of sugar"*

of linguistic connection that makes it possible to communicate with the locals and get assistance. Voltaire gives a parodic version of such scenes when Candide and Cunégonde, still in Europe, meet an old woman (daughter of a pope and a princess) who has suffered a life of misadventures. Abducted by Moroccan pirates, she is among people whose language she can't speak, and matters get worse when the pirates are attacked by rivals who try to steal their plunder and their captives. She faints after seeing her mother raped and dismembered, then recovers consciousness only to find that a fellow Italian prisoner, a castrato, is now trying to rape her, "groaning and saying under his breath: '*O che sciagura d'essere senza coglioni!*'" ("Oh, what a misfortune to have no testicles," 24). Far from being outraged, the old woman says that she was "amazed and delighted to hear my native tongue."

It is especially the women in Voltaire's tale who possess an adaptability that allows them to survive all the misadventures that befall them. When Candide murders the Grand Inquisitor and the moneylender, Cunégonde is upset: "How shall we live? what shall we do? where shall I find other inquisitors and Jews?" (20). Later, when Candide has to flee Buenos Aires, he worries how Cunégonde will manage. "She'll become what she can," Cacambo replies; "women can always find something to do with themselves" (29). He proposes going to Paraguay, where (in another Voltairean irony) Candide can make his fortune by training troops in the latest European military techniques.

Voltaire uses his worldly setting to destabilize his readers' self-satisfaction with their own social arrangements as representing "the best of all possible worlds," but he isn't a radical relativist, nor is he interested in other cultures for their own sake. Candide, Cunégonde, and their companions discover that human nature is largely the same everywhere, though this isn't a happy discovery. All in all, Cacambo tells Candide in Brazil, "You see that this hemisphere is no better than the other" (36). There's no Utopia, apparently, in Utopia.

Returning to Europe, Candide asks an old philosopher, Martin, whether "men have always massacred one another as they do today? That they have always been liars, traitors, ingrates, thieves, weaklings, sneaks, cowards, back-biters, gluttons, drunkards, misers, climbers, killers, calumniators, fanatics, hypocrites, and fools?" Martin asks him whether hawks have always eaten pigeons. Candide replies: "Of course," whereupon Martin retorts: "if hawks have always had the same character, why do you suppose that men have changed?" (50).

Finally reunited, Candide and Cunégonde settle in the liminal space of Turkey, deciding simply to tend to their own lives. In the tale's famous conclusion, "Il faut cultiver notre jardin." As with Dante's *Commedia* beginning in the middle of our life's path, this is a social rather than an individualistic imperative: "We must cultivate *our* garden" (81). Their Brazilian sojourn has given Candide and Cunégonde a philosophical awareness of a universal humanity, coupled with a chastening of European fantasies of innate superiority. If the wider world doesn't offer lasting opportunities for fame, fortune, or conquest, it does offer endless possibilities for adventures and ways to reinvent ourselves. As Cacambo tells Candide: "If you don't get your rights in one world, you will find them in another. And isn't it pleasant to see new things and do new things?" (29–30).

58. Joaquim Maria Machado de Assis, *Posthumous Memoirs of Brás Cubas*

Not everyone who came to Brazil found it so pleasant to see and do new things. Nearly five million slaves were transported to Brazil from Africa from the sixteenth century until 1888, when Brazil finally became the last country in the Western Hemisphere to abolish slavery. After centuries of intermarriage—as well as rape and concubinage—nearly half the population was classified as mulattos (people of mixed European and African parentage), in addition to other racial mixtures. A social hierarchy gradually developed, based not on race but on skin color, and lighter-skinned mulattos had greater possibilities for social mobility than those with darker skins.

Machado de Assis (often known simply as "Machado") was such a person, but even so, it could hardly have been predicted that the son of a mulatto house painter and a laundress from the Azores would emerge as the most important Brazilian writer of the century and would become President of the Brazilian Academy of Letters. His mother died when he was ten years old, and his father moved from Rio de Janeiro to São Cristovão, a provincial city in the northeast, where he remarried. Machado's stepmother managed to get him into classes in a girls' school, where she worked making candles, but he only had a few years of formal education in all. As an adolescent, he became friendly with a mulatto printer who also put out a local newspaper, which published Machado's first poem when he was fifteen years old. By age nineteen he was scraping by as a typesetter, proofreader, and part-time journalist; often he could only afford to eat one meal a day. Yet he had a passion for learning and a deep ambition to

53. Machado de Assis in youth and middle age

become a writer. A baker friend taught him French at night, and a local politician taught him English (he would later teach himself German and Greek); journalists and writers he met encouraged his writing. By age twenty-five, we already see Machado as a self-confident young gentleman—at least in the photographer's studio (Figure 53, left).

In reality, success came slowly. Afflicted with stuttering and periodic bouts of epilepsy, Machado wrote constantly after work, first as a journalist and then in minor government posts. Two early volumes of poetry were poorly received, and he wrote plays he couldn't get produced. Finally he turned to writing novels. Imbued with the Romanticism of the day, they were popular successes but critical failures. He had succeeded in embarking on a happy marriage, despite the disapproval of his in-laws, who weren't happy to have a mulatto son-in-law, but the couple never had children, and by the time he was forty years old, Machado seemed destined to be forgotten after a marginal literary career. His very whiskers were turning into a mask or a shield.

It was then that he threw Romanticism to the winds and wrote *Memórias Póstumas de Brás Cubas* (1881). The French statesman and novelist Chateaubriand had arranged for his *Mémoires d'Outre-Tombe* to be published after his death in 1848, but Brás Cubas goes him one better, actually *writing* his memoir beyond the grave. The *Memórias Póstumas* was the first of several ambitious and innovative novels, and by the late 1880s Machado was recognized as Brazil's leading novelist. In 1896 he became a founding member of the Brazilian Academy of Letters, serving as its president until his death in 1908, and after his funeral, a crowd of admirers carried his coffin from the doors of the Academy. He had traveled an extraordinary distance from his birthplace a mile or two away.

Machado had no real expectation of success with this unconventional fiction, which looks back to the satiric playfulness of *Tristram Shandy* over a century earlier, and at the same time foreshadows much later metatextual experiments such as Orhan Pamuk's *My Name Is Red*, which similarly begins with its narrator's death. In a preface, Brás Cubas wonders whether his memoir will find any sympathetic readers at all, and he dedicates his book to his first (and perhaps only) reader, or we might say, his first consumer:

TO THE WORM

THAT

FIRST GNAWED AT THE COLD FLESH

OF MY CADAVER

I DEDICATE

AS A FOND REMEMBRANCE

THESE

POSTHUMOUS MEMOIRS[6]

Here we already see the book's distinctive mode of dark humor.

In view of Machado's struggle to establish himself socially and artistically, it is surely no coincidence that in a prefatory note Brás describes his book as the product of an awkward mixed marriage, virtually a literary mulatto: "This is, it's true, a diffuse work, in which I, Brás Cubas, if I have adopted the free form of a Sterne or a Xavier de Maistre, may have added a few grumbles of pessimism. That may well be. The work of a deceased man, I wrote it with the pen of mirth and the ink of melancholy, and it is not difficult to predict what may come of such a union" (3). After I decided to include Machado's novel in this book, it was with a shock of recognition that I returned to it and read these words, which evoke both *Tristram Shandy* and de Maistre's *Voyage autour de ma chambre*—two of the primary inspirations for this eighty-book voyage. Machado even describes his novel *as* a voyage. In a preface to the fourth edition, he observes that de Maistre traveled around his room, and Sterne traveled in foreign lands (in his *Sentimental Journey through France and Italy*). "Of Brás Cubas," he concludes, "one might perhaps say that he traveled around life itself" (xliii).

The book's ending further connects it to the present project. After a series of romantic misadventures and social disappointments, Brás finally reaches the point of settling down with a lovely young woman, Dona Eulália (nicknamed Nhã-loló), only to lose her to an epidemic. In Shandyesque fashion, her death is prefaced by a one-paragraph chapter, "An Interlude":

What lies between life and death? A short bridge. Nevertheless, if I were not to compose this chapter, the reader would suffer a grave shock, one quite inimical to the effect of the book. To jump from a portrait to an epitaph may be altogether real and ordinary; the reader, however, only seeks refuge in a book to escape from life. This is not to say that this reflection is my own; I will say that there is a measure of truth in it, and that, at the least, the form of it is picturesque. And I repeat: it is not my own. (240)

The next chapter consists solely of Dona Eulália's epitaph:

HERE LIES

DONA EULÁLIA DAMASCENA DE BRITO

DEAD

AT NINETEEN YEARS OF AGE

PRAY FOR HER! (241)

The chapter that follows begins: "The epitaph says it all. Better than narrating to you Nhã-loló's illness, her death, the despair of the family, the funeral. You are hereby informed that she died; and I will add that it was on the occasion of the first outbreak of yellow fever." Brás takes the epidemic less as a tragedy than as an annoyance. He says that "I was somewhat hurt by the blindness of the epidemic, which, in killing left and right, also carried off a young lady who was to be my wife; I could not understand the need for the epidemic, much less for that particular death" (242). And now he processes this loss by recourse to another eighteenth-century model, which we ourselves have just encountered: Voltaire's *Candide*.

Throughout the novel, a foil for Brás Cubas is a self-seeking philosopher, Quincas Borba, who will steal your watch while he preaches the virtues of Humanitism, a kind of absurd amalgam of Buddhism, Nietzsche, and social Darwinism. Just before the epidemic strikes, Borba unveils a massive treatise in which he argues that pain is an illusion, and warfare and famine are mere diversions from monotony. Mankind's goal is dominion over the earth, "which was invented solely for his recreation, along with the stars, breezes, dates, and rhubarb. Pangloss, he told me as he closed the book, was not as foolish as Voltaire made him out to be" (231). Upon Dona Eulália's death, Quincas Borba assures Brás

> that epidemics were useful for the species, albeit disastrous for a certain
> number of individuals; he had me observe that, as horrendous as the
> spectacle was, there was a considerable advantage: the survival of the
> greatest number. He even asked me if, amidst the general mourning, I didn't
> feel some secret delight in having escaped the clutches of the plague; but this
> question was so senseless that it was left unanswered. (242)

At least Borba doesn't claim that the epidemic can be stopped in the best of all possible Brazils by injecting bleach.

A morally compromised Candide, Brás Cubas dissects the contradictions of a patriarchal, slave-owning society devoted to progress and human self-realization. He ends his memoir expressing relief that he never had children, so he hasn't added to the sum total of human misery. Yet we can see him today as a literary stepfather to Lu Xun's Ah-Q and Habibi's Saeed the Pessoptimist. In his "free form" novel as in his life, Machado de Assis made his way, like some Yosemite free climber, up the cracks and fault lines of Brazilian society. He left us an incomparable map of a distinctly un-utopian Brazil in the melancholy comedy of his deceased yet immortal hero's journey around life.

59. Clarice Lispector, *Family Ties*

Clarice Lispector's rise to fame as one of Brazil's most iconic modern writers was perhaps even more improbable than that of Machado de Assis. To begin with, she wasn't even Brazilian. Born in 1920 in Ukraine as Chaya Pincha-sovna Lispector, she was brought to Brazil as an infant when her parents fled a pogrom during which her mother was raped and contracted syphilis, from which she died when her daughter was nine years old. Her father ended up as a street vendor in Recife in northeast Brazil, then they moved to Rio de Janeiro when she was a teenager. He encouraged her to pursue the literary career he'd been unable to have; he died shortly after she published her first story, at age nineteen.

Lispector managed to go to law school, but she never wished to practice law. Like Machado, she found work as a journalist and worked on her fiction. She became famous at age twenty-three with her prize-winning first novel, *Near to the Wild Heart* (*Perto do Coração Selvagem*, 1943)—the title taken from a phrase in Joyce's *A Portrait of the Artist as a Young Man*—which employed intense interior monologue not seen before in Brazilian literature. By then she'd married a fellow law student who was embarking on a diplomatic career, and starting in 1944 they lived abroad, with postings in Europe and the United States. Increasingly dissatisfied with the life of a diplomat's wife, Lispector ended the marriage in 1959 and returned to Rio with her two young sons. The next year, she published her remarkable short-story collection, *Family Ties* (*Laços de Família*).

Her publisher included a prefatory note saying that "we feel delighted to be able to present to the reading public Clarice Lispector's return to Brazilian let-ters."[7] She had in fact been steadily publishing in Brazil while abroad, but now she was returning to the fold. From then on, Lispector became increasingly identified with Rio de Janeiro, and her readers in turn have closely identified with her, often by her first name. Today you can take a tour of "the Rio of

Clarice," and take a selfie with her statue overlooking the beach at Copacabana
(Figure 54). In a sign of Lispector's international prominence, Google featured
her on their homepage doodle on what would have been her ninety-eighth
birthday in 2018, just a year and a half after they'd accorded the same honor to
Machado de Assis.

With her foreign roots and her many years abroad, Lispector is among the
most worldly of local writers, even when her stories are set in precisely rendered domestic spaces. Her great forebear Kafka, for example, hovers in the
background of her uncanny five-part tale "The Fifth Story," published in her
collection *The Foreign Legion* (1964), which followed *Family Ties*. (Both collections are included in the comprehensive *Complete Stories*, published by her
biographer Benjamin Moser in 2015; the translations by Katrina Dodson won
a PEN translation award.) In "The Fifth Story," Kafka's Gregor Samsa is reincarnated in an entire army of cockroaches that invade the narrator's apartment, marching up the drainpipes at night. The narrator debates with herself
how to tell the story of her Kurtz-like attempts to exterminate the tiny brutes,
which she murders with a plaster mix that they ingest and that solidifies inside
them. As the story begins: "This story could be called 'The Statues.' Another

54. Lispector at the beach

possible name is 'The Murder.' And also 'How to Kill Cockroaches.' So I will tell at least three stories, all true because they don't contradict each other. Though a single story, they would be a thousand and one, were I given a thousand and one nights."[8]

Our murderous Scheherazade comes into the kitchen the morning after she has set out her poisonous recipe, finding "dozens of statues scattered, rigid." She realizes that "I am the first witness of daybreak in Pompeii." In other versions (or retakes) of the story, she becomes Saint Peter denying Jesus, a sorceress, and then a demonic divinity: "from my cold, human height I look at the destruction of a world" (310–11). In the story's closing words, we are finally given—and refused—the fifth story promised by the title: "The fifth story is called 'Leibniz and the Transcendence of Love in Polynesia.' It begins like this: I was complaining about cockroaches" (312).

Leibniz was the philosopher against whom Voltaire wrote *Candide*. Brazil became Voltaire's ultimate *reductio ad absurdum* for Leibniz's *Theodicy*, which justified God's creation of the best of all possible worlds, but now for Lispector the reality of life in Rio forces a displacement of utopian fantasy to Polynesia. The story folds in on itself, returning to the first story, which begins with the narrator complaining to her neighbor about the cockroaches. We're caught in a Borgesian Möbius strip, not in the Library of Babel but within everyday life.

In one of *Family Ties'* key stories, "Happy Birthday," an aging matriarch sits at her dining table on her eighty-ninth birthday, sourly contemplating her quarrelsome brood of children, grandchildren, and great-grandchildren as she waits to be served her cake. Her descendants are caught between cultures they're unable to assimilate. With the room decorated with balloons that say "Feliz Aniversário" on one side and "Happy Birthday" on the other, they try singing "Happy Birthday" to her, but "since they hadn't coordinated ahead of time, some sang in Portuguese and others in English. Then they tried to correct it: and the ones who'd been singing in English switched to Portuguese, and the ones who'd been singing in Portuguese switched to singing very softly in English" (155). The grandmother is disgusted with her pitiful offspring, whom she judges incapable of initiative or joy, and she wonders, "how could someone as strong as she have given birth to those dimwitted beings, with their slack arms and anxious faces?" She only makes an exception for her seven-year-old grandson, Rodrigo, "the only one who was the flesh of her heart, Rodrigo, with that tough little face, virile and tousled" (157). In a shocking moment, she expresses her scorn for the others by spitting on the floor.

Among the squabbling siblings and spouses, one character is filled with passionate intensity: young Rodrigo's mother, Cordélia. Amid the swirl of the party, she seems strangely anxious for some response from her mother-in-law, hoping against hope to hear the words "You must know. You must know. That life is short. That life is short." But to no avail: "Cordélia stared at her in terror. And, for the very last time, she never repeated it—while Rodrigo, the birthday girl's grandson, tugged at Cordélia's hand, tugged at the hand of that guilty, bewildered and desperate mother who once more looked back imploring old age to give one more sign that a woman should, in a heartrending impulse, fi-nally cling to her last chance and live." In *Ulysses*, Joyce's hero, Stephen Deda-lus, is a would-be Hamlet; here, Lispector rewrites *King Lear*, reversing genders as well as generations. Now, it isn't Cordelia who refuses to say the loving words demanded by the aged Lear; instead, it is the matriarch, "her hand clenched on the tablecloth as though grasping a scepter" (161), who re-mains silent in the face of her daughter-in-law's need.

But why is Cordélia so guilty, bewildered, and desperate? We're never told, but as in Lu Xun's "Diary of a Madman," there is evidence that we can piece together. Perhaps the grandmother is speaking more truly than she realizes when she lashes out at her family: "The devil take you, you pack of sissies, cuckolds and whores!" (159). Perhaps Rodrigo, the one "virile" member of the entire family, isn't her son's child after all. The guilty Cordélia may be thinking of finally running away with the boy's father, or perhaps with a new lover, in a heartrending impulse to cling to her last chance and live.

Interestingly, the story's excellent translator, Katrina Dodson, hasn't seen this submerged story, and as a result she mistranslates a crucial sentence. She has the mute grandmother "telling the unhappy daughter-in-law she irremediably loved perhaps for the last time" that life is short. But in the Portuguese, it isn't that Cordélia is the one whom the grandmother irremediably loves, which would be "quem sem remédio amava." The actual wording speaks of the unhappy daughter-in-law *who* ("que") was loving for the last time.[9]

Clarice Lispector was the most clear-eyed of observers and the most precise of writers, intimately connected to Rio de Janeiro and yet strangely distant at the same time. As the Brazilian poet Lêdo Ivo has written: "The foreignness of her prose is one of the most overwhelming facts of our literary history, and, even, of the history of our language."[10] Whether in Portuguese or in translation, her works offer us a series of enigmatic epiphanies, for us to translate as best we can into our own troubled lives.

60. Gabriel García Márquez, *One Hundred Years of Solitude*

The most famous novel ever to come out of Latin America, *Cien años de soledad* (1967) provides an apt transition from South America to Mexico—all the more as García Márquez wrote his great novel in Mexico City, where he'd settled in 1961. We can notionally reach his fictional Macondo by crossing the Orinoco where it forms the border between Brazil and Colombia, though the country is never named in the novel; the hundred-year saga of Macondo's rise and fall, focused on seven generations of the Buendía family, recapitulates the entire history of Latin America's exploration, nation building, political turmoil, and its uneasy entry into modern times.

García Márquez often acknowledged his debt to William Faulkner's chronicles of Yoknapatawpha County, but Macondo is equally descended from older accounts of El Dorado and New World utopias. García Márquez made this lineage clear in his Nobel Prize lecture, "The Solitude of Latin America" (1982). He says that fantastic elements appear regularly in the sober accounts of early explorers, and he adds that "Eldorado, our so avidly sought and illusory land, appeared on numerous maps for many a long year, shifting its place and form to suit the fantasy of cartographers." He allows that the region's long history has been far more dystopian than utopian, but he ends with a stirring call for writers to envision new and better utopias:

> On a day like today, my master William Faulkner said, "I decline to accept the end of man." I would fall unworthy of standing in this place that was his, if I were not fully aware that the colossal tragedy he refused to recognize thirty-two years ago is now, for the first time since the beginning of humanity, nothing more than a simple scientific possibility. Faced with this awesome reality that must have seemed a mere utopia through all of human time, we, the inventors of tales, who will believe anything, feel entitled to believe that it is not yet too late to engage in the creation of the opposite utopia. A new and sweeping utopia of life, where no one will be able to decide for others how they die, where love will prove true and happiness be possible, and where the races condemned to one hundred years of solitude will have, at last and forever, a second opportunity on earth.[11]

Like Voltaire's El Dorado, Macondo is cut off from the outside world by an almost impassable mountain range. The city's founder, José Arcadio Buendía, makes his way over the mountains with a motley group of followers in search of an outlet to the sea; they settle down when they find their further progress blocked by swamps. Less a utopia than an ambiguous heterotopia, Macondo becomes a precarious space of freedom from control by the distant and corrupt national government, and a place where seemingly impossible events are daily occurrences.

One Hundred Years of Solitude shares with Machado de Assis's *Posthumous Memoirs of Brás Cubas* a darkly ironic view of Latin American politics and of human relations, but where Machado looked back to Voltaire and Sterne in constructing the "free form" of his novel, García Márquez drew on writers of his own times. Macondo can be thought of as Faulkner's world seen through Kafka's eyes and then refracted in one of Jorge Luis Borges's uncanny mirrors. García Márquez decided to become a writer, in fact, when a college friend gave him a copy of Borges's translation of Kafka's *Metamorphosis*:

> The first line almost knocked me off the bed. I was so surprised. The first line reads, "As Gregor Samsa awoke that morning from uneasy dreams, he found himself transformed in his bed into a gigantic insect..." When I read the line I thought to myself that I didn't know anyone was allowed to write things like that. If I had known, I would have started writing a long time ago. So I immediately started writing short stories.[12]

Like Kafka, García Márquez matter-of-factly narrates outlandish events. Visiting gypsies float past on their flying carpets, people's ghosts regularly return to their homes, and a character dies after her hundred and forty-fifth birthday. In one of the novel's signature surreal moments, the radiantly gorgeous Remedios the Beauty ascends into the sky one day while folding sheets, "waving good-bye in the midst of the flapping sheets that rose up with her, abandoning with her the environment of beetles and dahlias and passing through the air with her as four o'clock in the afternoon came to an end, and they were lost forever with her in the upper atmosphere where not even the highest-flying birds of memory could reach her." Though "outsiders" suspect that the story is a cover for something more disreputable (has she run off with a lover?), the family accepts her ascension as a sign of divine grace. Remedios's sister-in-law Fernanda is envious of her achievement, but her greatest regret is purely practical: "for a long time she kept on praying to God to send her back her sheets."[13]

One Hundred Years of Solitude portrays everyday life in a mode of exuberant excess. The story's occasional "magical" elements are actually less prominent than the heightening of realistic events. Colonel Aureliano Buendía doesn't just raise a rebellion against the central government; he starts thirty-two civil wars, all failures, and in the end his allies in the Liberal Party abandon him after they're bought off with positions in the Conservative-dominated government. During his years of rebellion he doesn't just father an illegitimate child or two; he has no fewer than seventeen illegitimate sons around the country, all of them named Aureliano. When a period of heavy rain begins, it doesn't last a week, or even the biblical forty days and nights, but goes on for an exaggeratedly precise period of "four years, eleven months, and two days" (315). But we shouldn't be surprised by this endless downpour, as we've already experienced a deluge of Buendías, from the founder José Aureliano to his sons Aureliano and José Arcadio, to their sons Aureliano José and Arcadio, and then Arcadio's sons José Arcadio Segundo and Aureliano Segundo, then *his* son José Arcadio, and in the sixth generation Aureliano Babilonia, who is both the cousin and the father of a short-lived final Aureliano.

By flooding his pages with a plethora of similarly named characters, and further complicating his narrative with frequent flashbacks and flash-forwards, García Márquez challenges us to remember people and details that we've seen dozens or even hundreds of pages before. His novel is a vast memory palace, but it's made out of shifting halls of mirrors, and as the novel progresses the entire building starts to fall apart. Individual and collective memories alike are always under threat, whether from illness, old age, political repression, or the sheer ephemerality of human existence.

Like Boccaccio's *Decameron* and Tagore's *The Home and the World*, García Márquez's novel is partly a plague narrative (a theme he returned to two decades later in *Love in the Time of Cholera*). Characteristically, the plagues are not one but many. The gypsy Melquíades "was a fugitive from all the plagues and catastrophes that had ever lashed mankind. He had suffered pellagra in Persia, scurvy in the Malaysian archipelago, leprosy in Alexandria, beriberi in Japan, bubonic plague in Madagascar, an earthquake in Sicily, and a disastrous shipwreck in the Strait of Magellan" (5)—around the world in eighty plagues, we could say. Macondo is soon gripped by a plague of insomnia, and people start forgetting the names of things. Aureliano Buendía briefly solves this problem by attaching labels to things, but soon people can't remember what the words stand for. Throughout the novel, the Buendías are afflicted by "the pox of solitude" (395), which isolates them from each other, though it can also inspire uncontrollable incestuous passion; as in Boccaccio and Tagore, people are plagued by love.

At the heart of the book is a traumatic event that occurred in Colombia in 1928, when government troops massacred a thousand or more banana planta-tion workers who were striking in hopes of gaining adequate working condi-tions from the American-based United Fruit Company. In the novel, the government spirits the bodies away by train and insists that no massacre ever took place, and before long people forget that they've had friends and relatives who have disappeared. By the novel's end, the few remaining Buendías are un-known to their townsfolk, who don't even remember that their founding family ever existed. Then a vast wind erases Macondo from the world, just when Au-reliano Babilonia finishes deciphering a manuscript written in Sanskrit by Melquíades that foretold the entire story, up to and including the moment when he decodes the last page and the hurricane arrives.

Amid the shifting currents of political turmoil and family conflict, it is often the women who hold the Buendía household together. Long after the death of the original José Arcadio, his indomitable wife (and cousin) Úrsula presides over the lives of her children, grandchildren, great-grandchildren, and great-great-grandchildren. As she passes her hundredth year, like Clarice Lispector's matriarch she broods over her children's degenerate offspring. Upon her death, late in the novel, the house "fell into a neglect from which it could not be rescued even by a will as resolute and vigorous as that of Amaranta Úrsula," her great-great-granddaughter (345). Like Voltaire's Cunégonde, these women are consummate survivors, and at the end, as in *Candide*, Amaranta Úrsula tends her garden as best she can. On taking charge of the decaying house, she brings rosebushes back to life and plants ferns, oregano, and begonias in pots on the porch. Abandoned by her husband, who heads off to develop enterprises in the Belgian Congo (shades of Conrad's Kurtz), Amaranta Úrsula takes as a lover her nephew Aureliano Babilonia, who has been worshipping her from afar.

> In that Macondo forgotten even by the birds, where the dust and the heat had become so strong that it was difficult to breathe, secluded by solitude and love and by the solitude of love in a house where it was almost impossible to sleep because of the noise of the red ants, Aureliano and Amaranta Úrsula were the only happy beings, and the most happy on the face of the earth . . . when they saw themselves alone in the house they succumbed to the delirium of lovers who were making up for lost time. (404–5)

Marcel Proust thought of *In Search of Lost Time* as an optical instrument with which we can look inside ourselves as we follow his hero's quest to recover his long-lost memories. Bringing the world, and the world's literature, into the pages of his own epic novel, García Márquez has constructed an optical instrument through which we look outward beyond ourselves and recover an entire culture's memory.

CHAPTER THIRTEEN

·

Mexico–Guatemala: The Pope's Blowgun

61. *Cantares Mexicanos: Songs of the A\<tecs*

We now head northward to Mexico and Guatemala, where literature has long played a key role in the preservation of cultural memory, both for people of European descent and for the indigenous communities that continue to have a major presence in both countries. Some nine million people speak one of the indigenous languages, chiefly Nahuatl or one of twenty-one Mayan languages, often with many Spanish words mixed in. Religiously and culturally as well, Mexico and Guatemala are home to complex interweavings. Thirty years ago, I bought a striking mask in an outdoor market on the edge of Mexico City. It portrays a woman who could be a Hollywood starlet, but for her horns, adorned with ribbons in the colors of the four sacred directions (Figure 55). When I asked the seller who she was, he replied: "Esa es La Malinche"— Hernán Cortés's Mayan interpreter and lover; their son, Martín, was one of the first mestizos born in the hemisphere. In native representations, her skin is often given a pink hue to signify the passion that led her to betray her people; in this case, the artist has gone so far as to make her a blue-eyed *gringa*.

Having subdued the Aztec Empire over the course of 1519–21, in 1525 Cortés sent an embassy to Pope Clement VII in Rome. With Clement's support, he could advance the spiritual conquest of colonial "Nueva España" and

55. Malinche mask (c. 1980)

solidify his political position back in Madrid. To pique the pope's interest, Cortés sent gifts of ornate native feather work, together with several Aztec nobles, regal representatives of twenty million souls ripe for conversion to the True Faith. Unfortunately for Cortés, His Holiness—bastard son of Giuliano de' Medici—wasn't impressed by feathers. Clement was consumed with power struggles in Italy, and he had little time for exotic visitors from the other side of the world. One of these unwelcome guests, though, was a poet who composed a sardonic record of the encounter in Nahuatl:

> Friends, willow men, behold the pope,
> who's representing God, who speaks for him.
> The pope is on God's mat and seat and speaks for him.
> Who is this reclining on a golden chair? Look! It's the pope.
> He has his turquoise blowgun and he's shooting in the world.
> It seems it's true, he has his cross and golden staff, and these are
>   shining in the world.
> I grieve in Rome and see him in the flesh, and he's San Pedro, San Pablo!
> It seems that from the four directions they've been captured:

you've made them enter the golden refuge, and it's shining.

It seems the pope's home lies painted in golden butterflies. It's beaming.[1]

The pope probably wasn't sitting on a mat and shooting darts from a turquoise blowgun, but this was a way to convey his power to the audience back home. The poet goes on to sum up the true interests of the heir of Saint Peter and Saint Paul: "He's said: What do I need? Gold! Everybody bow down! Call out to Tiox in excelsis!" (341). Here three languages rub shoulders in four words: wedged in between the Nahuatl *tlamataque* ("call out to") and the Latin *in excelsis*, the seemingly foreign figure of Tiox is none other than the Spaniard's God, the poet's approximation of "Dios." World literature is often the product of worlds in collision.

Some 150 Nahuatl poems survive from the sixteenth century, and they give us unique access to the thought world of the Aztecs and their (often reluctant) allies, helping us to understand a culture that seemed utterly foreign to the Spanish invaders. Late in life, Cortés's soldier Bernal Díaz del Castillo recalled that "when we saw all those cities and villages built in the water and other great towns on dry land . . . some of our soldiers asked whether it was not all a dream. It is not too surprising therefore that I here write in this vein. It was all so wonderful that I do not know how to describe this first glimpse of things never heard of, seen, or dreamed of before."[2] As Calderón de la Barca would later put it in his best-known play, *La vida es sueño*: "Life is a dream."

The polytheistic, cannibalistic Aztecs were radically different in many respects from their astonished visitors, but their poets too often spoke of life as a dream:

So it has been said by Tochihuitzin,
so it has been said by Coyolchiuqui:
We come here only to sleep, we come here only to dream;
it is not true, it is not true that we come to live on earth.[3]

A delicate aestheticism pervades many poems, imbued with a sense of the transience of life:

> Have we arrived, have we sprung up on earth in vain?
> Shall I perish like the flowers?
> Will my fame eventually fade away,
> will my renown be nothing on earth?
> At least flowers, at least songs![4]

The Aztecs had something else in common with their European counterparts: they were enthusiastic imperialists, expanding their empire by conquest, shifting alliances, and brutal suppressions of revolt. These activities too were celebrated by their poets, who seem to have vied with each other to create ever more striking images to link beauty and terror: "Jaguar flowers are opening, / knife-death flowers are becoming delicious upon the field" (Bierhorst trans., 213). Warfare even becomes a grotesque kind of girls' picnic: "Get up, sisters, and let's go! Let's go look for flowers . . . Here they are! Here! Blaze flowers, shield flowers! Desirable, pleasurable war flowers!" (385).

The Aztecs' delicate, violent world turned upside down with the Spanish conquest. Language and writing were as important instruments of conquest as rifles and armor, as can be seen in the *Lienzo de Tlaxcala*, a sixteenth-century painting that shows Hernán Cortés accepting the Aztec rulers' surrender (Figure 56). The Tlaxcalan painting shows a lordly Cortés, somewhat implausibly adorned with a feathered crown, with La Malinche behind him as translator, accepting the defeat of the Tlaxcalans' bitter enemies, the Mexica (commonly known today as the Aztecs). Standing behind her is Jerónimo de Aguilar, holding an eagle to signify his name. Aguilar was a Spanish friar who'd been shipwrecked on the Yucatán coast several years before; he'd stayed and started a family, and had learned Mayan. La Malinche was fluent in Nahuatl as well as Mayan and could translate the Aztecs' statements into Mayan for Jerónimo, who could convey them to Cortés in Spanish. From the

56. Vignette from the Lienzo de Tlaxcala *(c. 1550, redrawn)*

beginning, communication in the New World was a complicated affair, and writing played its own often ambiguous part. The painting's caption reads (or should read) "Yc poliuhque mexiica" ("Here the Mexica surrendered"). The native artist has almost got the Roman alphabet right, though he's written the first "u" of "poliuhque" upside down, looking like an "n."

It soon became clear to the Tlaxcalans just how much they'd lost with their victory over Moctezuma. Between the hardships of forced labor and the drastic effects of smallpox, by the century's end Mexico's native population had been reduced by some ninety percent. The poets who survived the Conquest could no longer celebrate their leaders' victories or the aesthetic pleasures bought with imperial wealth. Instead, poetry became a means of resistance. One poem affirms the power of song to strengthen the Aztec leaders even when the Spanish tortured them in hopes of finding hidden stashes of gold: "Yet peacefully were Motelchiuh and Tlacotzin taken away. They fortified themselves with song in Acachinanco when they went to be delivered to the fire in Coyohuacan" (153).

Though the Spaniards burned almost all the native books they could find, oral traditions were harder to extirpate. And for all the destruction caused by the conquest, the Spaniards brought with them a powerful technology—the Roman alphabet—that would prove to be critical for the survival of the early court poetry that we can still read today. Seeking to better understand the natives he was trying to convert, a sixteenth-century priest named Bernardino de Sahagún compiled a bilingual ethnographic encyclopedia, the multivolume *Historia general de las cosas de la Nueva España*. In addition, disturbed by the persistence of native songs and dances, he composed an entire volume of psalms in Nahuatl. In a preface to his *Psalmodia Christiana*, he notes that the natives were faithfully attending Mass, "but in other places—in most places—they persist in going back to singing their old canticles in their houses or their palaces (a circumstance that arouses a good deal of suspicion as to the sincerity of their Christian faith)."[5] He tried to win the natives over with psalms written in familiar terms: Jesus is implanted as a quetzal feather in Mary's womb, and local songbirds such as troupials and trogons celebrate his birth. The volume was soon banned, however, by Church authorities who didn't want to give even that much ground to local traditions, and it was forgotten for centuries.

The only lasting result of Sahagún's counter-poetic endeavor was a rich trove of native poems that he apparently compiled as a database for his own compositions. These are preserved in two manuscripts known today as the *Romances de los señores de la Nueva España* (Ballads of the Lords of New Spain) and the *Cantares Mexicanos*. There is an excellent bilingual edition of the *Cantares* by John Bierhorst, and a selection from both manuscripts can be found in Miguel León-Portilla and Earl Shorris's anthology, *In the Language of Kings*. In these poems, we can see the Aztecs' world from within, and we can envision Moctezuma not as an enigmatic and defeated figure, but as a poet in his own right, preserving his lost world in his immortal songs: "Moctezuma, you creature of heaven, you sing in Mexico, in Tenochtitlan. / Here where eagle multitudes were ruined, your bracelet house stands shining—/ there in the home of Tiox our father . . . / and in that place these nobles gain renown and honor, / bells are scattered, dust and lords grow golden."[6]

With their intense awareness of the brevity of life, and their faith in the transcendent power of poetry, the Aztec court poets would surely appreciate the poetic irony that their songs survive today precisely as a result of Sahagún's attempt to stamp them out.

62. *Popol Vuh: The Mayan Book of the Dawn of Life*

Like the Aztecs, the Maya in Yucatán, Chiapas, and what is now Guatemala had developed an elaborate hieroglyphic writing system, used for inscriptions and for thousands of books on treated deerskin or bark. In the years following the Conquest, the Spanish seized and burned almost every native book they could find, considering them as portraying demons. Only a handful remain today. We owe the survival of the most important Mayan text, the *Popol Vuh*, or "Council Book," to the fact that an author or authors in the town of Quiché in highland Guatemala made a version of its hieroglyphic text in the new Roman alphabet sometime in the early 1550s, three decades after Guatemala was subdued by Cortés's brutal lieutenant Pedro de Alvarado. As Martin Puchner has said: "In order to preserve their own literature, they would have to give up their own precious writing system and use the weapons of the enemy."[7] The authors are cagey about whether the hieroglyphic Mayan version is hidden away or has been destroyed; if it did still exist, it was subsequently lost.

In 1701, a priest named Francisco Ximénez, living in the Quiché territory, happened to see the Romanized Quiché version of *Popol Vuh*, and he made a transcription with a Spanish translation in parallel columns. Long forgotten, Ximénez's text received two translations in Europe in the mid-nineteenth century, and it's had several English translations since then. In particular, in 1985 Dennis Tedlock made a beautiful "foreignizing" translation to convey a sense of the original style, as in the opening account of creation: "This is the account, here it is: Now it still ripples, now it still murmurs, ripples, it still sighs, still

hums, and it is empty under the sky. Here follow the first words, the first eloquence."[8] In 2007 Allen Christenson published another translation, less poetic
but very clear and with hundreds of explanatory notes.[9] Both he and Tedlock
worked in consultation with Mayan shamans, who had never seen the text but
who were still employing many concepts and practices it describes.

The *Popol Vuh* is at once a work of myth and a work of history. It tells the
story of how the sea and sky gods joined together to create land, plants, and
living creatures on the earth, and stars, planets, and suns in the sky. The gods
make four attempts at creating humans: one results in monkeys, who can't pray
or speak; one results in mud creatures who dissolve; one results in wooden
people who don't pray and are destroyed by the gods. At the end of the book,
the gods succeed on their fourth attempt, when they make men out of maize.
Before that final creation, the body of the book recounts the adventures of a
series of divine heroes on earth and in the underworld, Xibalba. (As with Nahuatl, in the Spanish-derived orthography of the time, the X is pronounced "sh.")

Much of the story concerns the exploits of two pairs of divine twins, whose
adventures on earth and in the underworld make the world a safer place for humanity. The story moves back and forth across time and space, as the older
twins and then their offspring outwit a series of evil figures such as Seven
Macaw and his sons, Earthquake, and a crocodile-like monster named Zi-
pacna. In the end, the younger twins, Hunahpu and Xbalanque, use trickery
and exceptional skill at the sacred Mayan ball game to defeat the underworld's
rulers, One Death and Seven Death. Mayan temple complexes always included
courts for this game, held between pairs of warriors, which would end with the
ritual sacrifice of the defeated player. At the end of the game, Xbalanque
shocks the underworld audience by sacrificing Hunahpu and then magically
bringing him back to life. The underworld gods are thrilled by this performance and ask to be slain in turn; the twins do so, but then they refuse to re-
store them to life until the Xibalbans agree to moderate their behavior. They
will have to accept incense and animal offerings rather than always requiring
human sacrifices, and they'll only have power over evildoers. Now the book

details the creation of the first eight humans from maize—an Adam and Eve for each of the four sacred directions.

The *Popol Vuh* has often been taken as a timeless mythic narrative, yet even though it was written down only thirty years after the Conquest, it is already in dialogue with the biblical traditions that were being transmitted to the writers along with the alphabet. From the start, the authors allude to their present setting: "Here we shall inscribe, we shall implant the Ancient Word, the potential and source for everything done in the citadel of Quiché, in the nation of Quiché people . . . We shall write about this now amid the preaching of God, in Christendom now" (Tedlock trans., 71). The imported Roman alphabet enables the authors to give a new and probably much fuller version of their hieroglyphic "Council Book," which they claim to have lost ("there is no longer a place to see it"), but which they appear to be consulting as they retell their stories: "There is the original book and ancient writing, but he who reads and ponders it hides his face" (71).

The hieroglyphic version seems to have been basically an aid to divination, charting the movements of the sun, moon, and planets, with brief notes on the divine activities that were thought to underlie the astral order. So the alphabetic *Popol Vuh* is a much fuller literary work than its hieroglyphic predecessor would have been. At the same time, it is deeply marked by its authors' fear for the loss of cultural memory threatened by the invasion that has brought the alphabet to them "in Christendom now." The second half of the *Popol Vuh* centers on the migration of the Quiché ancestors from Tulan in eastern Yucatán to their new home in Guatemala. As they head westward, they bewail the loss of their homeland, which they describe as a linguistic loss: " 'Alas! We left our language behind. How did we do it? We're lost! Where were we deceived? We had only one language when we came to Tulan, and we had only one place of emergence and origin. We haven't done well,' said all the tribes beneath the trees and bushes" (173). A later expedition retrieves their sacred writings, and with these they can establish themselves in their new land.

The ancestral journey isn't only shaped by indigenous cultural memories but also builds on biblical themes. Thus the Quiché ancestors reach their new homeland by parting the waters of the Caribbean: "it isn't clear how they crossed over the sea. They crossed over as if there were no sea. They just crossed over on some stones, stones piled up in the sand. And they gave it a name: Rock Rows, Furrowed Sands was their name for the place where they crossed through the midst of the sea. Where the waters divided, they crossed over" (177). This account combines two distinct modes of crossing the sea, on a rock bridge or by the parting of the waters. Quite likely, the rock bridge was the original means, as reflected in the name "Rock Rows," while the second method has been adapted from the story of Moses parting the Red Sea.

This identification of a biblical source might seem a little far-fetched, except that we find a direct reference to this very piece of biblical history in a related text, the *Title of the Lords of Totonicapán*. This work was written in 1554, quite possibly by the same person or people who wrote the alphabetic *Popol Vuh*. In this text, the native nobility of Totonicapán record their history so as to justify continuing to hold title to their lands, in the face of Spanish efforts to take them over. When they'd encountered the massive temple pyramids of Meso-america, the conquistadores couldn't believe that mere natives could ever have created such remarkable constructions. The major Mayan cities and temple complexes had been abandoned by around the year 900, evidently as a result of warfare, overpopulation, and resulting environmental degradation. Seeing these traces of an ancient culture, the Spaniards were reminded of the pyra-mids of Egypt, and they speculated that the natives were the lost tribes of Israel—a persisting idea that in the nineteenth century became part of Mormon belief. Figure 57 shows a pair of the Mayan temples at Palenque, in Chiapas in southern Mexico, which is perhaps the most numinous site I've ever seen anywhere.

The lords of Totonicapán were evidently aware of the Spaniards' theory, which they turn to their advantage. This is how they describe the crossing of the Caribbean from Tulan, under the guidance of their culture hero Balam-Quitzé: "When they arrived at the edge of the sea, Balam-Quitzé touched it

57. Temples at Palenque

with his staff and at once a path opened, which then closed up again, for thus the great God wished it to be done, because they were sons of Abraham and Jacob."[10] Taking a page from their oppressors' sacred book, the lords of Totonicapán assert that the title to their land was given them by the Spaniards' own God. The *Popol Vuh* is both the greatest compilation of pre-Conquest Mayan tales and also one of the most resolute responses to the challenge of the Conquest itself.

63. Sor Juana Inés de la Cruz, *Selected Works*

In our pandemic times we're sensitized to epidemic themes, from Boccaccio's *Decameron* to the literal or metaphoric plagues in Tagore and García Márquez. Sor Juana, though, is the first of our authors (and we'll hope the only one) actually to die in an epidemic. Plague swept through Mexico in 1695, when she was about forty-seven years old; she died after tending her sisters at her convent. By then, she'd had a literary career three decades long. Collections of her poetry had gone through multiple editions, and soon after her death a final collection was published in Madrid. There the famous author is described as "the Mexican Phoenix," the "Tenth Muse"—heir to the classical nine goddesses—and the "American Poetess."[11] She'd already started composing poetry as an eight-year-old, and she soon became proficient in Latin, and later learned Nahuatl. In addition, she had a great interest in science, including chemistry, astronomy, and optics. In her autobiographical "Response to Sor Filotea," she says that even when her prioress tried forbidding her to read secular books, she continually made observations and deductions, including while cooking. "I say that if Aristotle had cooked, he would have written a great deal more."[12]

Colonial Nueva España was administered on behalf of the Spanish king by a series of viceroys, and at age sixteen the young Juana Ramírez de Asbaje became a lady-in-waiting at the viceregal court, a position that can be compared to Murasaki Shikibu's in Heian Japan. She became close to a series of viceroys and their wives, who soon realized her prodigious talents. Already her early poetry shows an impressive blend of classical learning and sharp, satiric observation of the world around her, as we can see in this epigram:

You say, Leonor, for beauty
you should be given the palm;
the one for virgin is better,
and this your face guarantees. (23)

Juana had been born out of wedlock, and in another epigram she counters "a proud man" who had slighted her birth: "Your mother was more merciful / for she made you heir of many, / so that among them all, you can / take the one who suits you best" (24).

More seriously, she wrote hundreds of widely admired sonnets and "décimas" (poems in ten-line stanzas) on love and on events at court. Several of the love poems are addressed to women; there is no way to know whether she was actually in love or was simply participating in the largely male Petrarchan tradition (she even gives one of her frequent addressees the poetic name

"Laura"). In either case, these poems often play a delicate game of confession and concealment:

> I adore Lisi but do not pretend
> that Lisi will return my token of love,
> for if I deem her beauty within reach,
> I offend both her honor and my mind.
> To intend nothing is all my intention. (39)

Upon the early death of "Laura," she writes: "let my forlorn lyre die, where you inspired / echoes that mournfully cry out for you, / and let even these ill-favored strokes become / the black tears of my melancholy pen" (41).

Juana loved her life at court, but lacking family resources she had only two respectable choices in life: to marry, or to enter a convent. In her "Response to Sor Filotea," she says that "considering the total antipathy I had toward matrimony," the convent was the most honorable decision she could make. She took the veil at age nineteen, despite her fear of routines that "would limit the freedom of my studies, or the noise of a community that would interfere with the tranquil silence of my books" (97). She did at least get a cell of her own, and she amassed a library of several thousand volumes and a collection of scientific instruments. No contemporary portrait of her survives, but a retrospective portrait from 1750 well reflects her character and setting (Figure 58).

She continued her prolific output, including many hymns in praise of the Virgin Mary. She became sought after to write plays for performance on feast days, and to compose "villancicos," songs to be performed with accompanying dances (a native form, the *tocotín*). Carrying on the syncretistic practice pioneered by Bernardino de Sahagún a century earlier, she composed some entire poems in Nahuatl, while several of her villancicos mix Nahuatl into the surrounding Spanish. One "Tocotín mestizo de Español y Mejicano" is introduced by an Aztec singer, who declares:

58. Miguel Cabrera,
Sor Juana Inés de la
Cruz *(1750)*

Los Padres bendito	The blessed Fathers
tiene un Redentor	have a Redeemer;
amo nic neltoca	in vain is faith
quimati no Dios.	without knowledge of God.
Sólo Dios *Piltzintli*	Only God the Son
del Cielo bajó,	came down from Heaven,
y nuestro *tlatlácol*	and our sins
nos lo perdonó.	he forgave us.[13]

In one of her plays, *The Divine Narcissus*, she allegorically presents the life of Jesus through the death and rebirth of the classical figure of Narcissus. This classical-Christian syncretism is introduced by a *loa* (prefatory scene) which stages a Christian-Mexica syncretism of its own. An Aztec nobleman ("Occidente") and his wife ("America") learn that the rain god Tlaloc, whom they venerate as the *Dios de las Semillas* (God of the Seeds), is none other than Jesus

Christ. Strikingly, within the *loa* a narrow-minded critic named "Zeal" questions the propriety of writing a play that will portray Christ through the story of Narcissus. To this criticism, the right-thinking figure of Religion replies,

> Do you mean you have never seen
> a thing created in one place
> that is of use in another?
> Moreover, writing it was not
> only a whim or mere caprice
> but an act of due obedience
> striving for the impossible. (80–1)

As Sor Juana's fame grew, so did objections to the propriety of her writings, and in 1691 the Bishop of Puebla—writing under the pen name of Sor Filotea ("Lover of God")—published a letter sternly admonishing his "sister" to confine herself to religious books and subjects. Pretending not to know the actual identity of her critic, Sor Juana wrote her extraordinary "Response of the Poet to the Very Eminent Sor Filotea de la Cruz," in which she describes her God-given attachment to learning, which neither she herself nor anyone else has managed to repress. As for earthly vanity, she asserts that she was annoyed by the fame her writing had brought, all the more because "among the flowers of these same acclamations more serpents than I can count of rivalries and persecutions have arisen and awakened" (103). With impeccable logic and using examples from the Bible, the Church Fathers, and classical philosophy, she asserts the right of women to knowledge of all kinds. In a rhetorical move that can hardly have pleased the bishop, she even compares herself to Christ: "it is not enough in the world for a wise brain to be ridiculed, it must also be wounded and mistreated: a head that is a treasury of wisdom should not expect any crown other than one of thorns" (106).

Sor Juana may have won the battle, but she lost the war. In 1694, after a series of polemics exchanged between her supporters and detractors, she was ordered to sell her books and her scientific instruments and to recommit herself to her religious vows. This she did, in a declaration signed with her own blood. A year later, the plague took her to meet the Virgin and her Son, from whom Sor Juana could expect a warmer reception than she'd received from the Bishop of Puebla. Yet she left behind the most wide-ranging body of writing ever created by an intellectual of her century in the Americas. We can end with some lines from her longest and most ambitious poem, known as "The Dream" (or "First Dream"; she may have intended to write sequels). In her dream, her soul rises from her bed and soars into the empyrean, seeking to comprehend the universe. The heart of the poem is a heartfelt evocation of the joy of learning, as her soul "ascends / the high rungs, devoting herself first to one / then another faculty,"

> until immaterially she looks upon
> the honorable summit,
> the sweet conclusion of her arduous zeal
> (bitterly sown, a fruit pleasing to the taste,
> even her long fatigue a small price to pay)
> and with valiant foot she treads
> the soaring pinnacle of that lofty brow. (58)

Yet her finite mind can never truly comprehend what only God can know, nor can she stay forever in her dream. Gradually she wakes, and two centuries before Proust's Marcel she compares her vision to the fleeting projections of a magic lantern. The phantom images flee, she says, "their form changed to evanescent smoke," "as a magic lantern represents / diverse feigned and painted figures on a white / wall, assisted no less by shadow than by / light: maintaining in tremulous reflections / the distance mandated by / a learned perspective" (64). Then in the final lines, the sun comes up:

> while the fair golden mane of the Sun lit our
> hemisphere, with just light and distributive

order, gave all things visible their colors,

restoring to the external senses their

function, the world illuminated with more

certain light, and I, awake. (65–6)

64. Miguel Ángel Asturias, *The President*

The vibrant indigenous cultures of Mexico and Guatemala have had a major impact on the literature written by Creole writers (those of European descent). In the case of Guatemala's Nobel laureate and diplomat Miguel Ángel Asturias, the road to Mayan culture went through Paris. Born in Guatemala City in 1899, he'd been fascinated as a child by myths and legends told to him by his indigenous nanny, and as a high school student he drafted a story that became the germ of his breakthrough novel. His father, a judge, had lost his job after he issued a ruling that displeased the country's dictator, Manuel Estrada Cabrera, who became the model for Asturias's paranoid, authoritarian "Señor Presidente."

Asturias participated in an uprising against Estrada Cabrera in 1920 and co-founded a progressive political party. He received a law degree in 1923, winning a prize for a thesis on Indian problems, then went to Europe for further study. His twin interests in Mayan culture and in contemporary politics crystallized in Paris. There he studied ethnography at the Sorbonne under Georges Raynaud, a specialist in Mayan religion, whom he helped in preparing a French translation of the *Popol Vuh*; he then made his own Spanish translation from the French. At the same time, he became friends with André Breton and his surrealist circle. He wrote a series of stories on Mayan life that became his first book, *Leyendas de Guatemala* (1930); in a preface to the French translation, the poet Paul Valéry praised the stories as "dream-poems."[14] Often considered a precursor to Latin American magical realism, the stories also reflect Asturias's life in bohemian Montparnasse, which he described as "un mundo mágico."[15]

Estrada Cabrera was forced out of power in 1920, but he was succeeded by a shifting set of equally authoritarian rulers, and Asturias's student years turned into a decade of exile in Paris. He completed *El Señor Presidente* in 1932 and hoped to publish it on his return to Guatemala the following year, but it was forbidden publication on the order of Jorge Ubico, who'd come to power in 1931 and rightly considered that the novel would reflect badly on his own regime. It was finally published in 1946 during the term of Juan José Areválo, Guatemala's first democratically elected president. Three years later, Asturias published another major work, *Hombres de maíz* (*Men of Maize*), whose title recalls the final creation of humanity in the *Popol Vuh*.

The President focuses on urban creoles, rather than rural Maya, but native elements intrude amid the surrealist-inflected depiction of life under the thumb, or the boot, of the unnamed President. As the novel opens, a group of beggars are heading for the night to their city's cathedral. "With nothing in common but their destitution, they mustered to sleep together in the Porch of Our Lord"[16]—in Spanish, "el Portal del Señor," setting up the ironic parallel to the godlike, demonic Señor Presidente. As they approach, the cathedral's bells summon people to evening prayer, in lines reminiscent of the musical opening of the "Sirens" chapter in Joyce's *Ulysses*, which Asturias greatly admired: "Alumbra, lumbre de alumbre, Luzbel de piedralumbre! Como zumbido de oídos persistía el rumor de las campanas a la oración, maldoblestar de la luz en la sombra, de la sombra en la luz. ¡Alumbra, lumbre de alumbre, Luzbel de piedralumbre, sobre la podredumbre! ¡Alumbra, lumbre de alumbre, sobre la podredumbre, Luzbel de piedralumbre!" (In Frances Partridge's translation: "Boom, bloom, alum-bright, Lucifer of alunite!...")[17]

The beggars include a legless blind man called the Mosquito and "a degenerate mulatto known as the Widower," as well as "an idiot" nicknamed Pelele ("the Dummy," or "the Zany" in Partridge's translation). When a passing colonel amuses himself by insulting the Zany's deceased mother, the enraged beggar murders him, then flees. This impulsive moment of violence sets in motion a series of tragedies, as the President tries to determine which of his enemies must have murdered his colonel; the search becomes a witch hunt that he and his craftiest henchmen can use to destroy their rivals.

Asturias's antihero, known as Miguel Cara de Ángel ("Angel Face"), is a lawyer and presidential adviser who becomes ensnared in the search for the culprit. "As beautiful and wicked as Satan" (37), Miguel Angel Face is a negative image of his creator, a Miguel Ángel who has joined the regime, thinking he can moderate the President's worst excesses while making a comfortable life for himself. In the course of alerting a retired general that the President has decided to arrest him, Angel Face becomes involved with the general's daughter, Camila; with the President's nominal blessing, they marry, and Camila becomes pregnant. By then, though, the President has been persuaded that Angel Face was in cahoots with the retired general, who has fled the country and is preparing an invasion.

Asturias's Joycean tale turns increasingly Kafkaesque. As one of the President's henchmen, the Judge Advocate, tells a well-meaning assistant, "When will you understand that you mustn't encourage people to hope? In my house the first thing everyone, down to the cat, has to learn is that there are never grounds for hope of any description for anyone" (234). As the net tightens around Angel Face, he dreams of seeing a funeral procession for Camila amid a storm, replete with surreal images that could have been painted by Salvador Dalí:

> A horse's ribs serve as a violin for the raging hurricane. He sees Camila's funeral passing by. Her eyes are swimming in foam from the bridles of the river of black carriages . . . the Dead Sea must have eyes!
>
> Her green eyes! . . . Behind the funeral procession an ossuary full of children's thighbones is singing: "Moon, moon, take your prune and throw the stone in the lagoon!" Hip-bones with eyes like buttonholes . . . Why does daily life have to go on? . . . Why does the tram go on running? . . . Why doesn't everyone die? (180)

At its climax, the dream gives a modern version of the *Popol Vuh*'s trickster twins Hunahpu and Xbalanque playing with their heads as they outwit the underworld gods: "The men in red trousers are having a game with their heads . . . The men in red trousers take off their heads and throw them in the air, but do not catch them when they fall. The skulls smash on the ground in front of the two rows of motionless figures with their arms tied behind their backs." Waking, Angel Face thinks, "What a horrible nightmare! Thank heaven reality was quite different" (182).

He's wrong, of course, though he does manage a brief idyll with Camila following their marriage, when they escape for a while into the countryside. Bathing with her in a stream, "he could feel Camila's body through her thin blouse as one feels the smooth, silky, moist grains of maize through the young leaf" (237–8). But then they return to the capital, and the President orders Angel Face to go to Washington as his ambassador, to counter the lies being told there about his regime. Angel Face fears a set-up and tries to refuse the assignment, but the President insists.

About to leave the President's office, Angel Face "began to be aware of the pulsation of an underground clock marking the fatal passage of time." He has a vision of "a little man with a face like a dried fruit; his tongue protruded between his cheeks, there were thorns on his forehead, he had no ears, and wore round his navel a woolen cord from which hung warriors' heads and calabash leaves" (259). This proves to be Tohil, the Giver of Fire, issuing a demand for human sacrifice. "After this inexplicable vision, Angel Face said goodbye to the President" (260). As he unconsciously realizes, his fate is sealed, in a manner that the President engineers with heartbreaking cruelty. Camila, though, gives birth to a son, whom she names Miguel. "Little Miguel grew up in the country and became a countryman. Camila never again set foot in the city" (277).

Asturias's extraordinary synthesis of European surrealism and Mayan myth gave an uncanny power to the first major work in what became an entire genre of the Latin American dictator novel. Together with *Hombres de maíz* and a trilogy on the exploitation of Indians on banana plantations, *El Señor*

59. Mayan Asturias

Presidente led to the award of the Nobel Prize in 1967. By then, Asturias had become the Guatemalan ambassador to France, and while he spent his final years in Madrid, he is buried (together with Marcel Proust, and not far from Gertrude Stein) in Paris's Père-Lachaise cemetery. The headstone features a portrait of Asturias, carved in the style of a Mayan relief (Figure 59). Having brought surrealism to Guatemala at the start of his career, in death Asturias brought Guatemala to Père-Lachaise.

65. Rosario Castellanos, *The Book of Lamentations*

A pioneer of women's writing in Mexico, Rosario Castellanos (1925–74) was a prolific poet as well as a novelist, and she published the first feminist essays ever written in Mexico. Raised on the border of Guatemala in Chiapas, where the majority of the population are Maya, like Asturias she developed a deep and abiding interest in indigenous culture. From childhood she was intent on making a career as a writer—an improbable endeavor in mid-century Mexico for a young woman of a modest background. Orphaned at age seventeen, she managed to complete university and then found work with the National Indigenous Institute, writing educational puppet plays to be performed on market days in Chiapas. All the while, she pursued her writing, including journalism on indigenous and women's issues. As her countrywoman Elena Poniatowska has said, "Before her no other woman except Sor Juana . . . truly committed herself to her vocation."[18]

Castellanos's feminist awareness began early. One of her first memories was of an aunt telling her mother that she'd had a vision that one of her sister's two children would die young. Horrified, her mother cried out: "Not the boy!" Castellanos felt isolated throughout her life, and she later wrote that even her parents' deaths seemed natural to her: "Abandoned to the resources of my imagination during adolescence, it seemed logical to me that I would suddenly be left utterly orphaned." She goes on to say that "for company, I virtually never had need of another's physical presence" (x). Like Sor Juana, she found her true companions in books, though she did marry in her mid-thirties and had a son; the marriage itself didn't last.

Her family had been well off during her childhood, but in the late 1930s the president Lázaro Cárdenas instituted a program of land reform and peasant emancipation that stripped away most of the family's holdings, after which they moved to Mexico City. Castellanos returned to the era of this wrenching change in *The Book of Lamentations* (1962). It deals directly with the land reform, but not at all sympathetically to the townspeople, who do everything they can to keep their coffee and cocoa plantations out of the hands of the Tzotzil Maya who work as virtual slaves on their own ancestral lands.

The action of the novel takes place in and around a city modeled on San Cristóbal de las Casas. With its cobblestone streets and wrought-iron balconies, San Cristóbal has been designated a "Pueblo Mágico" by the government. Outside the magical city, however, large stretches of the impoverished countryside are controlled by the Zapatista Army of National Liberation, led by the charismatic, enigmatic Subcomandante Marcos. *The Book of Lamentations* draws on the earlier history of nineteenth-century peasant rebellions as well as the renewed unrest of the 1930s. The prosperous ladinos of Spanish descent who control the city are unabashedly racist toward their Indian servants and the peasants in the countryside. The novel begins with the rape of a Tzotzil girl (she may be fourteen, though she doesn't know her age) by a wealthy ladino, Leonardo Cifuentes, who "has a taste for Indian girls" (12). Like the colonel's murder at the start of *El Señor Presidente*, this act of violence has far-reaching consequences. It produces a boy, Domingo, whose death provides the novel's shocking climax, in an uncanny merger of Christian self-sacrifice and Mayan human sacrifice. This is an uneasy, self-cancelling syncretism, presented with a decidedly unmagical realism.

The townspeople are deeply suspicious of "foreigners"—meaning anyone from outside Chiapas—who might try to change the order of things. Two idealistic young men learn this lesson to their sorrow. The newly ordained Padre Manuel attempts to instill real faith, and actual morality, in his flock. After receiving mounting complaints from his irritated parishioners, Manuel's bishop exiles him to a punitive rural posting. On the secular side of the scale, a civil engineer, Fernando Ulloa, moves into town with his wife, sent from the capital to survey the region's lands prior to the planned redistribution. The result is disastrous for Ulloa himself and for the natives, who are stirred up to try to seize their land directly, only to be viciously put down by the ladinos. Once again a plague narrative comes into play—this time not in fact but as a cover story. In the aftermath of the suppressed rebellion, when the Governor of Chiapas visits in order to learn what has transpired, he is alarmed to find "towns, even towns of some prominence, abandoned as if a plague had struck them." His local representative replies: "They were decimated by epidemics, señor Gobernador. But we're not the ones who should be accused of that—it's the filth they wallow in" (350).

Whereas Asturias's *El Señor Presidente* focuses largely on the men involved in their political conflicts, Castellanos gives greater weight to the women who are caught up in the tumult, from the abused Tzotzil girl to the procuress who has provided her to Leonardo Cifuentes, to Cifuentes's emotionally cold wife, to their daughter, Idolina. In a heightened version of Castellanos's own isolation and estrangement from her family, Idolina confines herself to bed for years, pretending to be lame. Amid all the gossip and sniping among the city's women, moments of solidarity occasionally emerge: Idolina is lovingly tended by her Tzotzil nurse, Teresa, and she is finally cajoled out of her pretended paralysis by Fernando Ulloa's wife, Julia, who sees through Idolina's manipulative efforts to stay the center of attention even as she holds her family at bay.

At the heart of the story is the complex character of an indigenous healer, Catalina Díaz Puiljá, who becomes convinced that she has discovered a cluster of Mayan divinities hidden in a cave in the form of sacred stones. People begin to flock to her cave, awed by prophecies she utters after falling into a trance. In the process, Catalina gains power not only over her fellow villagers, but even over the stone figures in her cave: "She had established herself as their equal . . . Yes, they did look into the entrails of time and if they squeezed the world between their fingers they could lay it to waste. But without Catalina, through whom they had manifested themselves, without her to serve as their interpreter, what would they be reduced to? Invisibility and muteness once more" (251).

Meanwhile, Julia Ulloa has failed to make friends among the women of the town, who regard her as vulgar and lower in status than themselves. Increasingly bored and restless, she becomes Cifuentes's mistress, following an extended flirtation that fails even to make her husband jealous ("Fernando made Leonardo's bed for him, she concluded malevolently," 191). But as Fernando remarks when his assistant hints that something is going on,

> I can't take her out because I'm always away and there isn't much to do in Ciudad Real anyway. You can't go to the movies more than twice a week, when the program changes. And even then you have to resign yourself to watching a movie that dates from the year one and doesn't interest you in the least and you can't even tell what it's about because the film keeps breaking and the sound doesn't work very well. And the people in the balcony take their discomfort out on the rest by spitting on the orchestra seats and shouting crass comments. (174–5)

The Book of Lamentations searchingly portrays the limited opportunities available to women of all classes in their patriarchal, provincial society, coupled with a satiric take on the men's ability to stifle reform while clothing themselves in the high-minded defense of tradition. In its major third dimension, the novel shows the continually frustrated efforts of the Tzotzil population to ease their oppression, or even to make ends meet. In its epic sweep and its exceptionally varied cast of characters, *The Book of Lamentations* is one of the most eloquent of all portrayals of Mexico's multidimensional reality.

As the English version's title suggests, the novel has a tone of lamentation, though the Spanish title, *Oficio de tinieblas*, is more specific: the "Office of Darkness" (*Tenebrae* in Latin) is an evening service during Holy Week, commemorating Jesus's death and burial on Good Friday. Castellanos follows her Catholic title with an epigraph from a very different religious source, the *Popol Vuh*:

> Whereas your glory is no longer great;
> whereas your might exists no more
> —and though without much right to veneration—
> your blood will prevail a while…
>
> All the children of dawn, the dawn's offspring,
> will not belong to your people;
> only the chatterboxes will yield themselves to you.
>
> People of Harm, of War, of Misery,
> you who did the wrong,
> weep for it. (xvii)

CHAPTER FOURTEEN

The Antilles and Beyond:
Fragments of Epic Memory

66. Derek Walcott, *Omeros*

We now move to "The Antilles, fragments of epic memory," as Derek Walcott titled his Nobel Prize lecture in 1992, and to islands beyond the Caribbean. Islands often produce a distinctive mode of writing, rooted in the writers' sense of being at once isolated and insulated from the wider world—two terms that both derive from Latin *insula*. Writers such as Walcott, James Joyce, and Jean Rhys, who all grew up on colonized islands, can feel the need to invent a language suited to their island's modest material circumstances, intense localism, and distance from the metropolitan centers of politics, history, and culture. Island-based writers often orient themselves in the world with reference to other islands, near or far. In this chapter, we'll proceed from Walcott to two of his inspirations, Joyce and Rhys, and then to Margaret Atwood's feminist rewriting of Joyce's rewriting of Homer, and finally to Judith Schalansky's mapping of remote islands around the world.

Born in 1930 in the small city of Castries on Saint Lucia, Walcott was only a year old when his father died, leaving his mother to raise him and his two siblings on her income as a seamstress and schoolteacher. Of mixed African,

English, and Dutch heritage, Walcott was raised within the island's small Methodist community. The Methodist school provided an English-oriented education on an island where 95 percent of the population speak Antillean Creole, derived from French and African languages. In his Nobel lecture, Walcott describes his upbringing not in terms of deprivation but of opportunity:

> There is a force of exultation, a celebration of luck, when a writer finds
> himself a witness to the early morning of a culture that is defining itself,
> branch by branch, leaf by leaf, in that self-defining dawn, which is why,
> especially at the edge of the sea, it is good to make a ritual of the sunrise.
> Then the noun, the "Antilles" ripples like brightening water, and the sounds
> of leaves, palm fronds, and birds are the sounds of a fresh dialect, the native
> tongue. The personal vocabulary, the individual melody whose metre is
> one's biography, joins in that sound, with any luck, and the body moves like
> a walking, a waking island.[1]

Walcott was as determined, and as precocious, as Machado de Assis and Sor Juana before him. He published his first poem in a local newspaper at age fourteen, and four years later he persuaded his mother to scrape together the cost of printing his first volume of poetry. It began with a prophetic poem, "Prelude," which already announces his ambition to become a world writer:

> I, with legs crossed along the daylight, watch
> The variegated fists of clouds that gather over
> The uncouth features of this, my prone island.
>
> Meanwhile the steamers which divide horizons prove
> Us lost;
> Found only
> In tourist booklets, behind ardent binoculars;

Found in the blue reflection of eyes
That have known cities and think us here happy.

Cruise ships were starting to invade the Caribbean islands. Watching the blue-eyed tourists watching him, the eighteen-year-old Walcott reflects that his verse "must not be made public / Until I have learnt to suffer / In accurate iambics."[2] Those lines are particularly elegant, as they are precisely *not* written in accurate iambics.

Despite warning himself against prematurely coming before the public, Walcott sent the slender volume to *Caribbean Quarterly*, a new journal based in Trinidad. The editors printed one of his poems, "The Yellow Cemetery," an elliptical, allusive description of a visit to his father's grave. They added a page-long "Note for the Reader of the Poem," which began by acknowledging that "readers who are unfamiliar with the more recent developments in English verse may find this poem difficult." Yet they clearly were pleased to showcase a young Afro-Caribbean poet able to write verse as challenging and up to date as anyone in London or New York. After outlining the poem's themes and techniques, they conclude that a careful reader will find that "his sympathy will have been engaged, his knowledge of human nature deepened," and "he will feel in touch with another West Indian of the highest integrity and sensibility."[3] High praise for a teenager from a small island! Walcott's international career was launched.

Already in "Prelude" we can see Walcott's abiding themes: his "prone" island's invasion by foreign powers, here tourists on cruise ships; the ambiguous afterlife of the classical heritage (the tourists "have known cities," as Homer describes Odysseus); and his struggle with his poetic vocation and language. The poem also evokes *The Divine Comedy*, which begins "in the middle of our life's path," where Dante's way is impeded by a leopard that symbolizes lust. In his concluding lines, Walcott reflects: "In the middle of the journey through my life, / O how I came upon you, my / Reluctant leopard of the slow eyes" (3–4).

In a poem entitled "Origins," Walcott writes that he seeks a new language

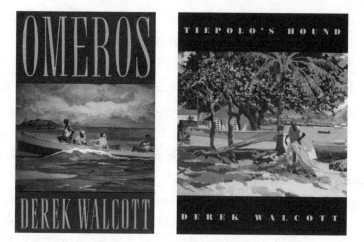

60. Walcott covers

for his island and for himself: "With hard teeth breaking the bitter almonds of consonants, / Shaping new labials to the curve of the wave" (14). Like his father, Walcott was a talented painter, and his watercolors adorn the covers of his books (Figure 60). He once remarked that "watercolor's an extremely difficult medium in the tropics. It's more or less a temperate medium . . . The incredible blue that is there in the tropics is almost impossible to get—the *heat* of that blue—in watercolor." He recalls meeting a German tourist who declared that "he couldn't paint there because it was too *green*."[4] In "Islands" (1962), he says that he sought to write

> Verse crisp as sand, clear as sunlight,
> Cold as the curled wave, ordinary
> As a tumbler of island water.[5]

No one, of course, can invent a poetry *ex nihilo*, and in a 1986 interview Walcott declared that:

> What we were deprived of was also our privilege. There was a great joy in
> making a world that so far, up to then, had been undefined . . . My

generation of West Indian writers has felt such a powerful elation at having the privilege of writing about places and people for the first time and, simultaneously, having behind them the tradition of knowing how well it can be done—by a Defoe, a Dickens, a Richardson.[6]

It's notable that he mentions three novelists, not any poets; writers are rarely as confined by genre as we may think when we describe someone as "a poet" or "a novelist."

In his poem "Volcano" (1976), Walcott meditates on his youthful experience of reading two other novelists, Conrad and Joyce, then pauses to wonder whether Joyce died in Zurich or Trieste. He decides that it doesn't matter: Joyce's death has become a legend, as is "the strong rumour that Conrad is dead / and that *Victory* is ironic"[7]—a reference to Conrad's 1915 novel, *Victory: An Island Tale*. Here Walcott plays on the trope of the peripheral colonial who only belatedly receives news from the metropole. He then punningly links himself to a pair of off-sea oil rigs, installed by some multinational corporation to extract resources from the seabed:

On the edge of the night-horizon
from this beach house on the cliffs
there are now, till dawn,
two glares from the miles-out-
at-sea derricks; they are like
the glow of the cigar
and the glow of the volcano
at *Victory*'s end.[8]

He feels tempted to give up and devote himself to becoming his great predecessors' ideal reader, but instead of abandoning writing, he makes a moving poem out of this very conflict.

Walcott didn't need to leave the Caribbean to become a world writer. He first established himself as a poet and playwright in Trinidad, and in his Nobel Prize speech he describes Trinidad, with its mixed African, Asian, and European heritage, as a microcosm of the world, "its humane variety more exciting than Joyce's Dublin." He was awarded the Nobel two years after he published *Omeros*, which is set on his native island but with excursions out into the humane variety of the wider world, from Africa to Europe to North America. The book's title evokes Homer not as an ancient classic but as a living figure. Walcott appears as a recurrent presence in the poem, and a Greek girlfriend in Boston tells him that Homer's name is pronounced "Omeros" in modern Greek. As Walcott voices the name, he immediately translates it into Creole:

and *O* was the conch-shell's invocation, *mer* was
both mother and sea in our Antillean patois,
os, a grey bone, and the white surf as it crashes

and spreads its sibilant collar on a lace shore.
Omeros was the crunch of dry leaves, and the washes
that echoed from a cave-mouth when the tide has ebbed.[9]

In his hybrid poem-novel, Walcott counterpoints the Antilles both against the Greek archipelago and against Joyce's Ireland. His leading characters, fishermen named Hector and Achille, fight for the affection of a beautiful waitress, Helen, whose name has an ironic local significance: having been traded back and forth multiple times between France and England, Saint Lucia became known in the nineteenth century as "the Helen of the West Indies." Their struggles are observed by a pair of Irish emigres, Major Plunkett and his wife, Maud, who have moved to the island in retirement. Later in the novel, Walcott visits Dublin, where he is shown around by James Joyce himself.

On a trip home from Boston he encounters the ghost of his father, who gives him his poetic vocation, in a scene reminiscent of Aeneas' underworld meeting with his father in the *Aeneid*. His father takes him down to the Castries harbor, and shows him a vision from his youth, when he would see indentured women, "those Helens from an earlier time," their gait "made beautiful by balance," carrying hundred-pound bags of coal up onto steamships. Linking physical and poetic "feet," he instructs his son:

> Kneel to your load, then balance your staggering feet
> and walk up that coal ladder as they do in time,
> one bare foot after the next in ancestral rhyme.

"Your duty," he concludes, "is the chance you now have, to give those feet a voice" (75–6).

67. James Joyce, *Ulysses*

Derek Walcott based the romantic conflict of *Omeros* on the *Iliad*, but he embodied the *Odyssey* in his Irish protagonists the Plunketts. Major Plunkett is "that khaki Ulysses" (263), while his wife, Penelope-like, spends years stitching an immense quilt. She embroiders it with images of birds, "making its blind birds sing" (88) (here Walcott puns on Homer as the blind bard). In a melancholy reversal, Maud's quilt doesn't end up covering her father-in-law's coffin but her own, as a ghostly projection of Walcott discovers. ("I was both there and not there, attending / the funeral of a character I'd created," 266). Now he recognizes that "there was a changing shadow of Telemachus in me, / in his absent war, and an empire's guilt / stitched in the one pattern of Maud's fabulous quilt" (263).

Plunkett may be a khaki Ulysses, but that isn't the name of Homer's Greek hero; Ulysses is the Latinized figure who appears in Virgil and in Dante, and who becomes Leopold Bloom in Joyce's *Ulysses*. Molly Bloom is an unfaithful Penelope, and Joyce's alter ego, Stephen Dedalus, takes the place of Telemachus. In identifying with Telemachus, Walcott is associating himself with Joyce's version of his own youthful self. Appropriately in terms of Maud's avian quilt, in *Ulysses* Stephen sees himself as an Icarus whose flight has failed, bringing him reluctantly home to roost: "Fabulous artificer. The hawklike man. You flew. Whereto? Newhaven–Dieppe, steerage passenger. Paris and back. Lapwing. Icarus. *Pater, ait.* Seabedabbled, fallen, weltering. Lapwing you are. Lapwing be."[10]

Late in *Omeros* Walcott visits Ireland, and there he seeks out "our age's Omeros, undimmed Master / and true tenor of the place" (200). He hums an Irish melody that Maud used to play on the piano, and then he suddenly has a vision of Joyce standing with "the Dead," leading them in song as Maud plays a pub piano. He sees Joyce as a "one-eyed Ulysses," "watching the mail-packet / butting past the Head, its wake glittering like keys" (201). Here Walcott takes us from *Dubliners'* final story to *Finnegans Wake*, now with the half-blind Joyce himself as Ulysses, returning from the dead to the island he never visited in the final three decades of his life.

Having fled Ireland together with Nora Barnacle in 1904, Joyce washed up in Trieste, teaching English as a second language. In 1907 he gave a public lecture on "Irlanda, Isola dei Santi e dei Savi" (Ireland, Island of Saints and Sages). There he asserted that the Irish language derived from Phoenician, brought northward by "the originators of trade and navigation."[11] Emphasizing the antiquity of Irish culture, Joyce declared that "the Irish nation's insistence on developing its own culture by itself is not so much the demand of a young nation that wants to make good in the European concert as the demand of a very old nation to renew under new forms the glories of a past civilization" (165). Yet what distinguishes Irish civilization for Joyce is its ethnic hybridity: "Do we not see that in Ireland the Danes, the Firbolgs, the Milesians from Spain, the Norman invaders, and the Anglo-Saxon settlers have united to form a new entity, one might say under the influence of a local deity?" Looking forward to Ireland's eventual independence from England (and, he hopes, from Roman Catholicism), Joyce returns in closing to the Greek world, asking, "Is this country destined to resume its ancient position as the Hellas of the north some day?" (171).

In the opening pages of *Ulysses*, Stephen Dedalus's obnoxious roommate Buck Mulligan remarks on his "absurd name, an ancient Greek!" (3). Looking out over Dublin Bay, he parodically translates the Victorian lyricism of Algernon Swinburne into Homeric epithets: "God! he said quietly. Isn't the sea what Algy calls it: a great sweet mother? The snotgreen sea. The scrotumtightening sea. *Epi oinopa ponton.* Ah, Dedalus, the Greeks! I must teach you. You must read them in the original. *Thalatta! Thalatta!* She is our great sweet mother" (4–5). Mulligan doesn't realize, though, that "the original" isn't a single language at all, but a congeries of dialects: the "wine-dark sea" would be *thalassa* in Homer's Ionic dialect, not *thalatta* as in Xenophon's Attic Greek. Joyce's Greece, like his Ireland or Walcott's Antilles, is a hybrid culture.

Insular communities are often deeply suspicious of outsiders, as we've seen in Rosario Castellanos's Chiapas. Both Leopold and Molly Bloom are in some sense "from away," as people say on Mount Desert Island in Maine, where I was born—a term that can apply there equally to people from Bangor or from Berlin. Though he's a born Dubliner, Bloom is the son of a Jewish immigrant from Hungary, while Molly grew up on Gibraltar, daughter of an Irish father and a mother of Spanish (and perhaps Jewish or Moorish) descent. Ignoring or resisting such hybridity, most of Joyce's Dubliners cling to an artificial image of their island's ethnic purity. In the second chapter, the schoolmaster Mr. Deasy declares that Ireland "has the honour of being the only country which never persecuted the jews"—for the simple reason that "she never let them in" (30). Leopold Bloom is the embodiment of the ethnic variety that Mr. Deasy can't see, but even Bloom is a hybrid individual. Though everyone thinks of him as a Jew, as he himself does, we first see him frying pork kidneys for breakfast, and we later learn that only his father was Jewish, not his mother, and so he wouldn't be Jewish under Jewish law. On top of that, he's actually been baptized. His Judaism isn't even skin-deep, as he's never been circumcised.

In his Trieste lecture, Joyce emphasized Ireland's ancient Celtic civilization, but he noted that it had been overwhelmed by centuries of invasions, from the

Norse to the English. The Irish language is almost as dead in Joyce's Dublin as Arawak is on Walcott's Saint Lucia. A visiting English ethnographer, staying with Stephen and Mulligan in their Martello tower, confidently addresses an old milkwoman in Irish, only to find that she thinks he's speaking French. "I'm ashamed I don't speak the language myself," she confesses when he sets her straight; "I'm told it's a grand language by them that knows" (13). With Gaelic lost outside Ireland's rural west, Joyce's Dubliners are caught between the stiff foreignness of British English and the liveliness of their demotic brogue. It is a mark of their outsider status that neither Bloom nor Stephen speaks in Irish English, though Stephen (and Joyce in turn) will precisely record the dialogue of their Irish characters, much as Walcott uses a creolized English to represent his characters' Antillean Creole, even as he writes his own brand of highly literary English.

Again like Walcott, Joyce seeks to reinvent English for his own purposes. He began by writing *Dubliners* in "a style of scrupulous meanness," as he told his publisher,[12] using "meanness" in the sense of "penury," as though he couldn't afford an extra adjective in his sentences. By the time of *Ulysses*, he was moving into a far more expansive—at times hallucinatory—language, which reaches its fullest embodiment in *Finnegans Wake*. There his authorial stand-in, Shem the Penman, has sold his linguistic birthright for a banquet of "once current puns, quashed quotatoes," and "messes of mottage."[13] A puzzled voice asks, "are we speachin d'anglas landage or are you sprakin sea Djoytsch?" (485). Ireland is both: a land that is at sea.

Amid all his linguistic exuberance, Joyce returns in key moments to an island language of elemental simplicity, most famously in Molly's words that end *Ulysses*, "and yes I said yes I will Yes" (644). To these words of one syllable I'd add another, the word "We," which appears twice in the book as a one-word paragraph. In the seventh chapter, Bloom is in the office of the newspaper for which he sells advertisements, trying to arrange for an advertiser to be given a blurb. He's used to being ignored or pushed aside, but the copyeditor agrees: "if he wants a par, Red Murray said earnestly, a pen behind his ear, we can do him one" (97). Joyce gives Bloom's unspoken reaction, set off as a paragraph of its own:

We.

A hundred pages later, Stephen learns that his sisters have pawned most of his books while he was away in Paris. "We had to," his sister Dilly says, as their father is drinking up everything he earns. Stephen thinks in anguish that they are both being pulled down by their sinking family:

> She will drown me with her, eyes and hair. Lank coils of seaweed hair
> around me, my heart, my soul. Salt green death.
> We.
> Agenbite of inwit. Inwit's agenbite.
> Misery! Misery! (200)

These two appearances of "We" link Stephen's and Bloom's innermost thoughts, but to opposite effect: whereas Bloom is grateful to be included for once in the plural pronoun, Stephen feels trapped, pulled down by his drowning sister. These two single-syllable paragraphs stand out, we might say, like lonely islands amid the billowing waves of Djoytsch.

68. Jean Rhys, *Wide Sargasso Sea*

While *Ulysses* provided Derek Walcott's ultimate inspiration for rewriting a classic work, in Jean Rhys he had a model closer to home. In a 1981 poem, "Jean Rhys," he gives a rare tribute to a woman in his mostly male personal pantheon. There he meditates on a photograph from her early days on the island of Dominica, two islands north of Saint Lucia, where she'd been born in 1890. In the image's sepia tones, he sees the figures "all looking coloured / from the distance of a century," with Rhys seeming like "some malarial angel."

61. Jean Rhys, young and old

Pondering the silent image, he imagines that "the cement grindstone of the afternoon / turns slowly, sharpening her senses, / the bay below is green as calalu, stewing Sargasso." At the poem's end, she stares at a candle, "her right hand married to *Jane Eyre*, / foreseeing that her own white wedding dress / will be white paper."[14]

By the time she came to rewrite *Jane Eyre* in the 1960s, Rhys had actually been married three times, never happily. She was living in obscurity in a village in southwest England, "a dull spot," she once said, "which even drink can't enliven much."[15] She hadn't published a book since 1939. Like Marguerite Duras, she was returning late in life to her adolescence in a vanished colonial world. An iconic early photograph of Rhys even looks a good deal like the young Duras, but once she was rediscovered after publishing *Wide Sargasso Sea* at age seventy-six, her portraits could illustrate Duras's description at the start of *The Lover* of her "ravaged" face (Figure 61).

As we learn from her memoir *Smile Please*,[16] Rhys recreated her early years on Dominica in *Wide Sargasso Sea*, but she did so very differently than Duras's *autoportrait* or her own early novels and stories, published in the 1920s and 1930s, when she was a rootless woman drifting around Paris and London and writing about rootless women drifting around Paris and London. Instead, she translated her experience into the untold story of *Jane Eyre*'s Bertha Antoinetta Mason, the Creole wife whom Charlotte Brontë's antihero, Mr. Rochester, has brought back from Jamaica. Hired as a governess for his daughter, young Jane Eyre is troubled by outcries from "the mad-woman in the attic." Rochester tells her that these come from a mentally disturbed servant, Grace Poole, who in actual fact is tending Bertha. Desperately in love with Jane, Rochester is on the point of consummating a bigamous marriage when Bertha's identity is revealed. Jane leaves the household, she thinks forever, but a year later she passes by the estate and can't resist looking in. She is shocked to find it in ruins, and she learns that not long after her departure Bertha had set the house on fire, killing herself and blinding Rochester. The story reaches a muted happy ending when Jane meets the blinded and crippled Rochester and is reconciled to him. As she famously tells us in the opening words of the final chapter: "Reader, I married him."[17]

Inventing the story of Bertha's Caribbean life, Rhys layered her own experience onto that of her heroine, now named Antoinette Cosway. Halfway through the novel, as their relationship deteriorates, her husband suddenly starts calling her "Bertha"—she is going to be transposed not only into another country but into someone else's novel. Even Antoinette / Bertha's change of name has a personal resonance for her author. Born Ella Gwendolyn Rees Williams, she changed her name several times before settling on the pen name of Jean Rhys on the advice of Ford Madox Ford, with whom she was having a—typically unhappy—love affair in 1925. As for Rochester, he is never named in the novel, partly because Rhys wanted her book to be able to stand on its own, but perhaps also because he really has no clear identity. His father and uncle have cooked up the plan for a financially advantageous marriage to the fatherless but propertied Jamaican girl, but he deeply resents being bundled off to the colonies in this way. Slavery has recently been abolished on the island, but both he and Antoinette are effectively being bought and sold by their relatives.

The novel's first and last sections are narrated by Antoinette, first in Jamaica and then when she's imprisoned in the attic in the "cardboard world" she's been taken to.[18] But the middle section is primarily told in Rochester's voice, in a tour de force of pitiless but not unsympathetic dissection of a man on the verge of a nervous breakdown. Yet Jamaica is in many ways the central protagonist of *Wide Sargasso Sea*. Both its landscape and its complex racial composition fuel the failing attempts of Antoinette and her new husband to build a connection, or even to achieve some minimal mutual understanding. The freeing of the slaves has severely affected the fortunes of the island's planters. Antoinette says that their garden "was large and beautiful as that garden in the Bible—the tree of life grew there. But it had gone wild. The paths were overgrown and a smell of dead flowers mixed with the fresh living smell. Underneath the tree ferns, tall as forest tree ferns, the light was green. Orchids flourished out of reach or for some reason not to be touched" (19). She feels safe in this decaying Eden, but her husband is put off by the "extreme green" of a landscape he finds "not only wild but menacing" (69). Wandering away from the house's grounds, he recalls, "I stepped over a fallen log swarming with white ants. How can I discover truth I thought and that thought led me nowhere . . . Here were the ruins of a stone house and round the ruins rose trees that had grown to an incredible height. At the back of the ruins a wild orange tree covered with fruit, the leaves a dark green" (104).

This is the Caribbean of intense colors that Walcott loved to portray in his paintings, but even the tropical sunsets are too much for Rochester. As he prepares to leave Jamaica, forcing Antoinette to come with him, he reflects:

> I hated the mountains and the hills, the rivers and the rain. I hated the sunsets of whatever colour, I hated its beauty and its magic and the secret I would never know. I hated its indifference and the cruelty which was part of its loveliness. Above all I hated her. For she belonged to the magic and the loveliness. She had left me thirsty and all my life would be thirst and longing for what I had lost before I found it. (172)

The secret that he will never know has multiple layers: the secret life of the island, the psyches of its people, and above all, the truth or falsity of rumors of hereditary madness in Antoinette's family and of her early sexual relations with a mixed-race cousin. These claims have been made in a poisoned-pen letter sent to him by Antoinette's half-brother—if he *is* her half-brother—Daniel Cosway. As Daniel says of Amélie, a serving girl who can vouch for his claims, "She knows, and she knows me. She belongs to this island" (99).

The increasingly distraught young Englishman knows that he doesn't belong to the island, but it isn't so clear that Antoinette does either. For Afro-Caribbeans like Daniel and Amélie, the European Creoles are all "from away," even after generations on the island. After Amélie mutters something "in patois" that Rochester can't understand, Antoinette tells him, "It was a song about a white cockroach. That's me. That's what they call all of us who were here before their own people in Africa sold them to the slave traders . . . . So between you I often wonder who I am and where is my country and where do I belong and why was I ever born at all" (102).

As in Castellanos's *Book of Lamentations*, a native healer tries to help the situation. At Antoinette's urgent request, the obeah woman Christophine prepares an aphrodisiac for Rochester, but the attempt backfires, as the potion makes him sick, and he feels more manipulated than ever. As he reflects, "She need not have done what she did to me. I will always swear that she need not have done it" (137).

The Sargasso Sea of Rhys's title is created by a confluence of ocean currents, where large patches of sargassum seaweed grow and where it was said that ships could be trapped, unable to escape. In the early 1930s, my great-aunt Helen served as a scientific illustrator on a research expedition off the coast of Bermuda conducted by the prominent naturalist William Beebe. Their trip included studying aquatic life in the Sargasso Sea, and the book he wrote on the trip, *Nonsuch: Land of Water*, includes an illustration by her of a fish concealing itself in a length of sargassum (Figure 62). Beebe comments that "there is no doubt but that the first weed was torn by storms from the rocks and reefs of the West Indies, and swept by wind and currents out into the great dead center of two and a half million square miles over which it is scattered today."[19]

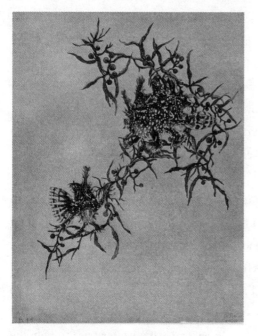

*62. Helen Damrosch
Tee-Van,*
Sargassum Fish
among its
floating weed

It is significant that the Sargasso Sea isn't in the Caribbean but out in the North Atlantic. If Rhys had chosen a Dickensian title, she could have called her novel *A Tale of Two Islands*, as both Antoinette and Rochester are caught in the vortex between Jamaica and England. When Antoinette describes England as "a cold, dark dream," an annoyed Rochester replies, "that is precisely how your beautiful island seems to me, quite unreal and like a dream" (80). But as Christophine asks Antoinette, "England . . . You think there is such a place?" (111). Rhys's novel connects the most imperial of islands with its Caribbean other, in a disenchanted version of More's Utopia, the good place and no-place, inextricably intertwined.

69. Margaret Atwood, *The Penelopiad*

While Joyce and Walcott shifted *The Odyssey* to Dublin and to Saint Lucia, Margaret Atwood set her *Penelopiad* in Odysseus's own Ithaca. Like *Wide Sargasso Sea*, the story is retold in two voices; Penelope's sardonic, self-justifying account of her life is punctured by songs sung by "The Chorus Line." These are the ghosts of the twelve serving maids whom Odysseus and Telemachus string together and hang at the climax of the epic after slaughtering Penelope's unwelcome suitors, with whom the maids have been sleeping. Whereas Jean Rhys counterpointed Antoinette's lush Jamaica against her confined afterlife in a cold and dark England, Atwood sets her speakers directly in the underworld. There, Penelope and her maids tell their tales, and they confront or avoid the ghostly cast of characters with whom they're eternally housed in Hades.

Early on, Atwood begins by comically deconstructing the pleasures of the afterlife:

> There are of course the fields of asphodel. You can walk around in them if you want. It's brighter there, and a certain amount of vapid dancing goes on, though the region sounds better than it is—*the fields of asphodel* has a poetic lilt to it. But just consider. Asphodel, asphodel, asphodel . . . I would have preferred the odd hyacinth, at least, and would a sprinkling of crocuses have been too much to expect? Though we never get spring here, or any other seasons. You do have to wonder who designed the place.[20]

Paradise, it turns out, is no paradise.

Still less is Ithaca, "a goat-strewn rock" (31). Penelope had grown up in a wealthy court on the mainland before being married off to Odysseus at age fifteen. Her sea voyage to Ithaca was "long and frightening, and also nauseating" (55), and on arrival she discovers that indeed "Ithaca was no paradise. It was often windy, and frequently rainy and cold. The nobles were a shabby lot compared with those I was used to, and the palace, although sufficient, was not what you would consider large." Yet she's happy (at first) with her new husband, and "in time I got more used to the place" (57, 59).

Published in 2005, *The Penelopiad* was the first novella in an ambitious Scottish series, *The Myths*, for which prominent writers are invited to recreate an ancient story "in a contemporary and memorable way." Other books in the series include retellings of the life of Jesus by Philip Pullman, the story of Samson by Israel's David Grossman, and the myth of the goddess Inanna by our author Olga Tokarczuk. By setting her tale in the eternal afterlife, Atwood is able to interweave antiquity and the modern world. Penelope is aware of new developments on earth ("I was very interested in the invention of the light bulb," 19) and she speaks in an entirely contemporary voice. Her mother-in-law, she says, "would freeze the balls off Helios" (61).

Atwood reworks Homer in a variety of contemporary modes, including a trial transcript and a lecture by an anthropologist who analyzes the solar symbolism of the twelve maids. (Here we can see an echo of the academic conference that concludes her 1985 dystopian novel *The Handmaid's Tale*.) Like Joyce's Buck Mulligan, Penelope employs decidedly un-epic similes: at her marriage, she says, "I was handed over to Odysseus, like a package of meat . . . A sort of gilded blood pudding." She adds, with characteristic Atwoodian irony: "But perhaps that is too crude a simile for you. Let me add that meat was highly valued among us—the aristocracy ate lots of it, meat, meat, meat, and all they ever did was roast it; ours was not an age of haute cuisine" (39).

The Penelopiad blends confessional memoir with elements of chick lit, particularly in the rivalry between plain Penelope and her seductive, narcissistic cousin Helen, whom Penelope describes as "poison on legs" (79). Helen specializes in bitchy put-downs: "I think Odysseus would make a very suitable husband for our little duckie . . . She can help him look after his goats. She and Odysseus are two of a kind. They both have such short legs." Humiliated in front of her sniggering maids, Penelope says that "I was crushed. I had not thought my legs were quite that short" (33–4).

The novel's emotional center is the series of interventions by the Chorus Line of murdered maids. In an afterword, Atwood describes the Chorus as "a tribute to the use of such choruses in Greek drama" (198), but here too she is blending ancient and contemporary modes. In calling the maids "The Chorus

Line," she is alluding to the Broadway musical that ran for fifteen years from 1975, becoming a major motion picture in 1985. In *A Chorus Line*, seventeen eager young performers have to show off their skills before a demanding director, as they compete to be chosen for a chorus line of eight singer/dancers. Unwittingly, an announcer brought out the Homeric parallel when the cast of the musical performed for the Tony Awards in 1976. In dramatic tones, he declared that whether actors are seasoned performers or just starting out, "all of them are stage-struck, and they have to come to New York to try to make the grade on Broadway. It's been going on a long time, this odyssey, and it's still going on now!"[21]

After writing *The Penelopiad*, Atwood actually created a stage version, which premiered in 2007 at the National Arts Centre in Ottawa and at Stratford-upon-Avon with the Royal Shakespeare Company. Both in the novel and in the play, Atwood gives a significantly darker turn to her chorus line than was seen in the Broadway "odyssey." As the serving maids sing in their opening number,

> we are the maids
> the ones you killed
> the ones you failed
>
> we danced in air
> our bare feet twitched
> it was not fair (5)

They haunt Odysseus in Hades, and he repeatedly escapes from them back into the upper world, where he's been reborn as everything from a French general to a Borneo headhunter to a film star to an advertising man (a nod, perhaps, to Leopold Bloom?). But as Penelope tells us: "It's always ended badly, with a suicide or an accident or a death in battle or an assassination, and then he's back here again" (190).

The maids haunt Odysseus but they shun Penelope, though she keeps trying to regain their friendship. As the story unfolds, it seems that it was Penelope who inadvertently engineered their downfall, as she encouraged them to sleep with her suitors as a way of getting intelligence on their plans. And there's a darker possibility as well. Penelope knew that the maids were spreading rumors that she hadn't been so very faithful to the absent Odysseus all those years; she may have set them up for slaughter before they could share this information with him.

Penelope's unspoken hostility to her maids is hinted at early on, when they obscenely make fun of her impending marriage to Odysseus on isolated Ithaca, suggesting that she may wake up to find herself in bed with some of his livestock: "A big strong ram! I bet our young duck would like that! She'd be bleating soon enough!" Penelope says that "I was mortified. I didn't understand the coarser kinds of jokes, not yet, so I didn't know exactly why they were laughing, though I understood that their laughter was at my expense. But I had no way of making them stop" (32). When Odysseus returns to Ithaca, she finally finds a way.

The chorus of maids gets the last word in *The Penelopiad*. The final chapter is entitled "We're Walking Behind You, A Love Song," in which they call out to Odysseus, "Yoo hoo! Mr. Nobody! Mr. Nameless! Mr. Master of Illusion! Mr. Sleight of Hand, grandson of thieves and liars! We're here too, the ones without names." They have numbers instead of names: "Twelve of us. Twelve moon-shaped bums, twelve yummy mouths, twenty-four feather-pillow tits, and best of all, twenty-four twitching feet" (191). Their prose "love song" concludes: "We're here to serve you right. We'll never leave you, we'll stick to you like your shadow, soft and relentless as glue. Pretty maids all in a row" (193). Then comes a closing "Envoi," which begins:

we had no voice
we had no name
we had no choice

we had one face

one face the same (195)

In *Omeros*, the ghost of Walcott's father shows him the vision of the indentured serving women toiling up the steamship ramps with massive bags of coal, and he tells his son that his duty "is the chance you now have, to give those feet a voice." In *The Penelopiad*, after three millennia of silencing, Margaret Atwood gives the maids' twitching feet their voice.

70. Judith Schalansky, *Atlas of Remote Islands*

As we've seen, island-based writers have often drawn connections with islands elsewhere, imaginatively crossing vast spans of time and space. Judith Schalansky's *Atlas of Remote Islands* (2009) goes so far as to draw an entire atlas of distant islands, giving each of them a short description—really, a prose poem—on the facing page. Each entry is headed with a timeline and a set of distances to other far-away places, together with a thumbnail hemispheric map to show the island's location. Schalansky meticulously drew each island to the same scale of 1:125,000, and as a result some islands crowd the margins of her oversized pages, while others are lost in a sea of blue.

Both in its overall project and in the predominant melancholy of its descriptions, the *Atlas* has a good deal in common with Italo Calvino's *Invisible Cities*, though in place of invisible cities Schalansky gives us unvisited islands. As her subtitle announces, these are *Fifty Islands I Have Never Set Foot On and Never Will*. In a preface, Schalansky says that "miniature worlds are created on these small continents,"[22] and her prose poems are miniature epics, typically based in some document that she has uncovered in her library in Berlin and then imbued with a poet-novelist's vision.

Her preface is entitled "Paradise is an island. So is hell" (6). She writes about the double nature of distant islands, which people have often thought of as "the perfect place for utopian experiments" (here we can think of More's

Utopia itself) and as "paradise on earth" (14). As she says, "Revolutions break out on ships, and utopias are lived on islands. It is comforting to think that there must be something more than the here and now" (48). Yet once they've made landfall, explorers have often found these Edens to be barren and inhospitable. Schalansky is drawn to such islands and the stories that unfold on them, though she does occasionally evoke the Edenic side of the island experience. For the South Pacific island of Pukapuka, she describes an American settler, Robert Dean Frisbie, sitting on the veranda of his small store:

> Suddenly a neighbor runs up to him, completely naked, wet from bathing, her hair plastered to her golden skin. She is out of breath, and her breasts rise and fall as she hurriedly asks for a bottle of something. Frisbie quickly passes her what she wants, and as she disappears into the dusk he stares after her for a long time, strangely moved. Although he has lived here for years now, he has still not got used to the nudity. In this respect, he is still the boy from Cleveland who could never have imagined the freedom here.

As Schalansky dryly ends her account: "In these matters, Pukapuka certainly has the edge over Cleveland, Robert Dean Frisbie thinks, as he puts out his verandah light" (88).

Here Schalansky is building on a published source, probably Frisbie's *The Book of Puka-Puka: A Lone Trader on a South Sea Atoll* (1929). He and his wife, Ngatokorua, had five children; their daughter Florence was the first Polynesian woman to become a writer. Written in a mixture of Pukapukan, Rarotongan, and English, then translated by her father, her first book tells the story of her family's life in the South Seas. It was published by Macmillan in 1948, when she was fifteen; still going strong nearly seventy years later, she published a second edition in 2016. In her book, she describes writing her first stories with a palm-frond stylus on sheaves of beach cabbage leaves, and she refers with amusement to the distress that native nudity caused in a Protestant missionary during his infrequent visits; she says that "he'd have had us dressed

63. *Miss Ulysses and her book*

like Eskimos in midwinter if he had had his way."[23] Figure 63 shows the proud
father with the budding author.

Remarkably for our Odyssean theme in this chapter, her book is entitled
Miss Ulysses from Puka-Puka. "When I think of the past," she writes, "I often
think of myself as a sort of Miss Ulysses, wandering from island to island in
the Aegean sea, and this because the two books of Homer have meant so much
to me. I find myself explaining things by some story in Homer" (164). Like
Derek Walcott after her, she finds her own Calypso, Lotus Eaters, and Sirens
on her South Sea atolls. You really can't make this stuff up, and Schalansky
didn't. Not that Schalansky mentions *Miss Ulysses*, or even her father's book,
but her quirky, suggestive commentary can tempt you to explore an island
beyond whatever inlet or episode she chooses to showcase.

A good example is Pitcairn Island, where the sailors of HMS *Bounty* settled
in 1790 after they'd mutinied and had set Captain Bligh adrift in a small boat.
Schalansky begins by describing the island's protective isolation ("There is no
better hiding place than this island, far off the trading routes and marked in the
wrong position on admiralty charts," 102), and the thumbnail sketch of its

102 *Pacific Ocean*

25° 3′ S
130° 6′ W **Pitcairn Island** (United Kingdom)

PITKERN *Pitkern Ailen*
4.5 km² | 48 inhabitants

480 km
----/----/→ Gambier Islands

1,000 *2,000* *2,130 km*
----/----/----/----/----/----/----/----/→ Tahiti

1,000 *2,070 km*
----/----/----/----/----/----/→ Easter Island (100)

January 1790: settled by the Bounty mutineers   1856: resettlement on Norfolk Island
1500   1600   1700   1800   1900   2000
----/----/----/----/----/----/----/----/----/----/----/----/----/----/----/----/----/

2 July 1767: discovered by Robert Pitcairn   2002–5: rape trial

64. Pitcairn Island timeline

location shows Pitcairn as a tiny dot in the middle of a world of water, with earth's continents barely visible around the fringes of the Pacific (Figure 64).

Yet instead of telling us much about the early settlement, Schalansky veers off into describing Marlon Brando's visit for the filming of *Mutiny on the Bounty*. Her account concludes: "The glittering curtains swish together and the most expensive film of all time comes to an end. But the island's story is far from its end" (102). It takes a sharp-eyed reader to discern just what this unfinished story may be, but if you look closely at the timeline for Pitcairn, you'll see a surprising final item: "*2002–5: rape trial*."

Schalansky says nothing about this trial, at which many of the island's men were convicted of raping underage girls. Their defense was that as descendants of mutineers, they weren't subject to British law, and they'd always considered that twelve was the age of consent. The jury assembled from New Zealand wasn't persuaded, partly because some of the victims were even younger; one was five years old. Schalansky alludes to this story in her introduction, but she has left it out of her entry on the island, keeping just the single trace on the timeline. *Atlas of Remote Islands* thus hints at explorations we can continue beyond its pages, and the very incompleteness of Schalansky's descriptions suits her world of islands, fragments of land that engender fragmentary tales.

In her preface, she says that "there is no untouched garden of Eden lying at the edges of this never-ending globe. Instead, human beings traveling far and wide have turned into the very monsters they chased off the maps." But she adds:

> It is, however, the most terrible events that have the greatest potential to tell a story, and islands make the perfect setting for them. The absurdity of reality is lost on the large land masses, but here on the islands, it is writ large. An island offers a stage: everything that happens on it is practically forced to turn into a story, into a chamber piece in the middle of nowhere, into the stuff of literature. What is unique about these tales is that fact and fiction can no longer be separated: fact is fictionalized and fiction is turned into fact. (19–20)

This transformation is well illustrated with Robinson Crusoe Island, located off the coast of Chile. Between 1704 and 1708, a Scottish buccaneer named Alexander Selkirk was stranded on the island then called *Isla Más a Tierra* ("closer to land," to distinguish it from a neighbor farther out). He published an account of his adventures, which Daniel Defoe used as the basis for his pioneering novel *Robinson Crusoe*. As Schalansky says, "The pirate Selkirk becomes the plantation owner Crusoe who constantly struggles with a restless desire to travel to distant lands, but as soon as he achieves this, yearns for his homeland" (74). Now the island has been renamed, not in honor of Selkirk but of Defoe's fictional version of him.

Defoe's novel spawned an entire genre of "Robinsons," most famously Johann Weiss's *Der schweizerische Robinson* (*The Swiss Family Robinson*, 1812), whose hero isn't even named Robinson; instead, he is *the Swiss* Robinson. The name continues to grace more than one island. Some years ago, I gave a talk on Derek Walcott at a conference on African diasporas held on Guadeloupe. Four miles down the coast from Pointe-à-Pitre is the little Îlet du Gosier. As the online *Caribbean Journal* says, the Îlet du Gosier offers "an island oasis in Guadeloupe," an escape from "the mainland" of Guadeloupe.[24] Every island, it seems, needs a desert island of its own.

The islet is a popular destination for devotees of its bar, "Ti' Robinson" (Little Robinson), whose name can appeal both to Anglophone readers of *Robinson Crusoe* and to European admirers of Weiss's Swiss Robinsons, as well as to locals who may just go for the rum. As one Tripadvisor reviewer says, in Creole, Ti' Robinson offers: "Wepas twès bon, alcool au bon degwé. Cadwe magnifiqwe, twès bon accueil. Twanquille donc no stwess. Nous wecommandons."[25]

Most relevant of all for our present purposes is Schalansky's account of Possession Island: "In 1962, the French name their first mission to the northernmost massif after the greatest engineer of fantasy their country has ever produced. Today, a precipitous mountain range on the island of Possession and a crater on the far side of the moon—both just the kind of places that he might have traveled to on his extraordinary journeys—bear the name of Jules Verne." She warns that "Jules Verne's mysterious island is far away, somewhere in the Pacific Ocean, and this is a most inhospitable place for any aspiring Robinson Crusoes" (58). But then again, Schalansky has taken us there without ever leaving Berlin—*Around the World in Fifty Islands*, so to say. She clearly feels a special affinity for Verne, whose novels she describes as "daydreams for everyday use, atlases for those who stay at home." No better way to travel, at least just now. No stwess.

CHAPTER FIFTEEN

Bar Harbor:
The World on a Desert Island

71. Robert McCloskey, *One Morning in Maine*

Though I was born on Maine's Mount Desert Island, it's been quite a while since it actually was a desert island. Wabenaki Indians had been living on the island for at least 6,000 years by the time the French explorer Samuel de Champlain came through in 1604 and gave the island its present name. Even he wasn't thinking of desert islands; he was struck by the treeless granite summits of the island's taller mountains, and named it "l'Île des Monts Déserts"—the island of bare mountains. Like Walcott's Saint Lucia, our region went back and forth between the British and French empires and their languages, until the English definitively integrated Maine into "New England" in 1763. In a further transformation of the name, in what Walcott would call our local patois "Mount Desert" is pronounced "dessert," a perfectly fitting name to a child's ears.

Maine was gradually settled in the eighteenth century by fishermen and small farmers, often people of few words. Over the years, most of the writing about the region has been by people "from away," from Henry David Thoreau (*The Maine Woods*, 1864) to the novelist Richard Russo and the environmentalists Helen and Scott Nearing. (Our best-known native Maine author,

Stephen King, began publishing only in the late 1960s.) Starting in the late nineteenth century, Mount Desert Island became a magnet for "rusticators," well-off denizens of Boston, New York, and Philadelphia who would flee their sweltering cities in summer and come up by steamship, first renting rooms from locals and then building increasingly elaborate shingle-style "cottages."

Among the rusticators at the turn of the century were my great-grandfather Frank Damrosch and his conductor brother, Walter. They could spend the summer months on Mount Desert while the New York musical scene was on pause and there weren't any classes at the conservatory that Frank had founded, the Institute for Musical Art (known today as Juilliard). My father in turn cherished memories of summers at "Grandpapa's house" in Seal Harbor, and when he and my mother decided to return to the United States after a dozen years in the Philippines, they settled on the island, in the first of a series of Maine parishes. Though we moved to Manhattan just after my tenth birthday, Mount Desert Island had become deeply imprinted on me by then, and now I too return with my family, atavistically, every summer.

A few months before I was born, Robert McCloskey published *One Morning in Maine* (1952), a book that my mother read to me before I could read it myself. In our Anglophile household, most of the children's books were by English authors, from Beatrix Potter to Kenneth Grahame and A. A. Milne, but in *One Morning in Maine* I could see my own environment, rendered in a kind of idealized realism. Born in Ohio in 1914, McCloskey had come to New York, where he became an illustrator and soon began writing and illustrating his own books. *One Morning in Maine* and its prize-winning predecessor *Blueberries for Sal* were set in and around the McCloskeys' summer home, a six-acre island off the shore of Little Deer Isle, some fifteen miles from Bar Harbor as the seagull flies. An intensely private man, McCloskey clearly needed an island even smaller and more deserted than Little Deer Isle (winter population: 300, though more in summer), and so they became the sole residents of Scott Island.

In *One Morning in Maine*, McCloskey sets out in a dinghy with his daughters, Sal and her toddler sister, Jane, to go shopping in the village of South Brooksville overlooking Buck's Harbor. In McCloskey's evocative drawings, the village is a miniature world with everything needed for life. We see the harbor, the church, and a grocery store and a garage, owned by two Condon brothers. Sal's adventure with her father and sister is almost derailed, however, when she brushes her teeth in the morning and discovers a loose tooth (Figure 65). "She wiggled it with her tongue, then she wiggled it with her finger. 'Oh, dear!' thought Sal. 'This *cannot* be true!'"[1]

Her parents reassure her that she can still go, and she can save the tooth when it falls out and make a secret wish. First she and her father go down to the shore of their island to gather clams, but there her tooth falls out and gets lost in the mud. Ever resourceful, Sal finds a feather and decides that she can make her wish on that. As they prepare to set out for Buck's Harbor, her father discovers that his outboard motor won't start, so he has to row them across the bay. Now his errands include lugging the engine up to the shop, where the

when she started to brush her teeth something felt *very strange!* One of her teeth felt loose! She wiggled it with her tongue, then she wiggled it with her finger.

"Oh, dear!" thought Sal. "This *cannot* be true!"

Standing on the stool, she looked in the mirror and wiggled her tooth again. Sure enough, it was loose! You could even *see* it wiggle.

65. *Sal's loose tooth*

relevant Mr. Condon replaces a spark plug. Then in the grocery store Sal is offered an ice-cream cone, which providentially fulfills her secret wish. The trio head back home across the bay, looking forward to lunch.

Not much of a story, you may say, but as millions of kids (and their parents) were finding, McCloskey had a pitch-perfect ear for everyday conversation, and a keen eye for portraying his family and their surroundings. The book shows both Sal and her dad overcoming unexpected obstacles, and it dramatizes Sal's dawning sense of herself as someone ready to take charge of her world. The distressingly lost tooth now becomes a sign of an approaching maturity. At the story's end, when her little sister begs for a second ice-cream cone, Sal admonishes her: " 'Silly!' exclaimed Sal. 'Our wishes are all used up.' Then she remembered that she was growing up, and just like a grownup she said, 'Besides, Jane, two ice-cream cones would ruin your appetite. When we get home we're going to have CLAM CHOWDER FOR LUNCH!' " (63–4).

Literature always gives us the pleasure of imaginatively transforming ourselves, and I could identify with a feisty girl like Sal as easily as with Christopher Robin or Peter Rabbit. There was a special fascination in following a story set so close to home, comparable to Chimamanda Adichie's pleasure when she finally found Nigerian stories to supplement the British imports that she too had always been given. The magic of McCloskey's book was inseparable from his illustrations, which could repay hours of study. The rambunctious toddler Jane is constantly exploring her world, scrambling up on a pair of tires, studying the used spark plug she's been given. A cat glares at her from under a bench, then on the next page it runs away; it peeks out at her on a third page, and finally watches regretfully as she leaves the store.

McCloskey renders his scenes with great precision, but there are intriguing shifts in perspective from one page to the next, and sometimes objects have mysteriously morphed or moved. What's become of a nut and bolt we've just seen on the Condon garage floor? Why is a crate now made with three rows of boards rather than four? Other elements complete the story: on one page,

66. Buck's Harbor

we see the box for the new spark plug, tossed onto the floor by Mr. Condon, while on the facing page Sal hands the old one to Jane. So compelling are the images that as recently as the early 2000s the latest Mr. Condon would give used spark plugs to visiting lovers of the book; as he told a reporter, "They'd go off happy with that."[2]

McCloskey subtly directs our gaze through an Impressionistic variability in outlines and shading. In his closing scene (Figure 66), his three characters are sharply outlined in their dinghy (here as elsewhere, McCloskey enjoyed presenting himself in rump perspective), while off to the left the shading becomes lighter, the lines less defined. Up on the dock, a figure is sketched in an almost Japanese calligraphic style, as he gazes down in the pose of an M. C. Escher figure.

The atavism that caused me to be born on the island where my father had spent his happiest summers extends to books, especially children's books. It's no coincidence that the books I was first exposed to were mostly ones that my parents, and often my grandparents, had once enjoyed, from *Peter Rabbit* to *The Wind in the Willows*. *One Morning in Maine* had only just been published when I was born, but the copy I'm using now was given by friends in Maine to our oldest daughter, Diana, as a present for her first birthday. Several years later, the first literary allusion she ever made was to this very book. Then about Sal's age, she could read it for herself, but she still enjoyed hearing me read it to her little sister and brother. One morning in Brooklyn, she looked into the bathroom mirror to examine a loose tooth. "Oh dear! *thought Sal*," she exclaimed with a sly smile, dropping her voice on "thought Sal," mimicking the way I'd read the passage. She didn't need to complete the thought ("This *cannot* be true!"), since she knew that her tooth was truly coming out. But she could identify with McCloskey's adventurous heroine, ready to take on Buck's Harbor and the entire world beyond.

72. Sarah Orne Jewett, *The Country of the Pointed Firs*

The traditional life of coastal Maine has never been more movingly portrayed than in the stories of Sarah Orne Jewett. Born in 1849 in the town of South Berwick in southern Maine, Jewett was a precocious and prolific writer. She published her first story in the *Atlantic Monthly* at age nineteen, and she produced a steady stream of stories and novels until a carriage accident in 1902 largely ended her writing career. During the 1880s and 1890s she became one of her generation's leading regional writers, part of a movement that sought to convey the flavor of life beyond the New York and Boston metropolitan areas that had long dominated American letters. She lived throughout her adult life with a sister in South Berwick, though she made regular trips down to Boston. There she became close friends with Boston's literati, including Henry James, who called her a "fellow craftsman and a woman of genius and courage."[3]

For many years, she had an intimate friendship (known as "a Boston marriage") with another writer, Annie Adams Fields, whose husband's publishing house, Ticknor and Fields, was one of America's leading literary publishers. After Fields's husband died in 1881, the women spent summers together in South Berwick and wintered in Boston, and several times traveled to Europe. They are shown in Figure 67 (at a discreet social distance) in Fields's

67. Fields and Jewett at home in Boston

capacious drawing room, where they regularly entertained writers, artists, and actors.

Jewett's best-known work, *The Country of the Pointed Firs* (1896), was written from the perspective of a summer visitor. This device gave her a special basis for describing Maine life for her readers, to whom her characters were almost as foreign as those in Kipling's India tales. Kipling, in fact, was another admirer of her work, though we may wonder what Jewett thought of a letter in which he praised her stories as possessing "more virility" than most stories by men, since, as he explained to her, "virility is power and poise, not noise."[4]

Jewett's first-person narrator is a writer who rents a room in the fictional town of Dunnet Landing. In 1994, when the Library of America published a volume devoted to Jewett, a reviewer noted that Dunnet Landing is "an imaginary town that will be recognizable to anyone who has been to the Acadia National Park or Mount Desert Island area."[5] The narrator has come there in order to work on her writing in peace and quiet. Unfortunately, the house has one fault, "its complete lack of seclusion" (3). Her talkative landlady, Mrs. Todd, is an herbalist with many customers who trust her more than the town's male doctor. In need of more solitude—in effect, an islet of her own in Dunnet

Landing—the narrator rents the village's one-room schoolhouse, which is unoccupied during the summer months, for fifty cents per week. There she ponders and records the stories she hears from Mrs. Todd and her neighbors concerning their lives and those on the outlying islands.

Rereading *The Country of the Pointed Firs* soon after Judith Schalansky's postmodern *Atlas of Remote Islands*, I was surprised to see how much the two books have in common, across the distance of more than a century. Jewett's book doesn't have a plot beyond the frame tale of the narrator's arrival and then her departure at summer's end. The nineteen stories within this frame are loosely connected, but they're short and often inconclusive, not unlike Schalansky's meditations on her remote islands. Jewett portrays plainspoken people in a hardscrabble landscape, an environment that challenges her writerly ambitions as well as her characters' lives. Describing a woman's decision to live alone on isolated Shell-Heap Island, Mrs. Todd declares: "There can't be much of it that the salt spray don't fly over in storms. No, 'tis a dreadful small place to make a world of" (66).

The sparse landscape of Shell-Heap Island nevertheless provides everything the recluse needs to make a world of, including (as on the McCloskeys' little island) "a sheltered cove on the south side, with mud-flats across one end of it at low water where there's excellent clams." There's also a cabin that her father had built: "He used to stay out there days to a time, and anchor a little sloop he had, and dig clams to fill it, and sail up to Portland. They said the dealers always gave him an extra price, the clams were so noted" (66). Here we see the precision of Jewett's rendering of Mrs. Todd's report. Gertrude Stein might think that a clam is a clam is a clam, but Mrs. Todd emphasizes their unusual quality, and the practical benefit that they fetch a good price. Further, though an outsider would think of Portland as down the coast from the Mount Desert region to the northeast, the woman's father sails "up to Portland" because he has to tack upwind against the prevailing winds, which is why coastal Maine is called "Down East."

Jewett returned to Dunnet Landing in several later stories. In "William's Wedding," she speaks of the challenge of writing about characters who often leave so much unsaid. Her narrator has tired of "the hurry of life in a large town, the constant putting aside of preference to yield to a most unsatisfactory activity," and so she has returned to Dunnet Landing for a second summer. "The coast still had a wintry look," she reports; "it was far on in May, but all the shore looked cold and sterile" (218). She returns to lodge with Mrs. Todd, but "I had an odd feeling of strangeness," like a hermit crab "in a cold new shell," and she says that "I felt as if I had after all lost my hold of that quiet life" (222). Slowly she gets glimpses of the events that have transpired during the fall and winter, including the unexpected marriage of Mrs. Todd's painfully shy brother William, an island dweller whose fiancée is on the mainland, but she rarely gets the full story. Now she addresses the reader directly, perhaps responding to reviewers who had complained of the lack of drama in *The Country of the Pointed Firs*:

> It is difficult to report the great events of New England: expression is so slight, and those few words which escape us in moments of deep feeling look but meager on the printed page. One has to assume too much of the dramatic fervor as one reads; but as I came out of my room at breakfast-time I met Mrs. Todd face to face, and when she said to me, "This weather'll bring William in after her; 'tis their happy day!" I felt something take possession of me which ought to communicate itself to the least sympathetic reader of this cold page. It is written for those who have a Dunnet Landing of their own: who either kindly share this with the writer, or possess another. (223)

Over the course of the summer of *The Country of the Pointed Firs*, the narrator had pieced together the hinted story of Mrs. Todd's own romantic life. Disappointed in love, she made a match with a more available local boy, but he drowned in a storm not long after their marriage; his ship's foundering could be seen from the shore. Taking the narrator to gather some medicinal penny-royal flowers, Mrs. Todd suddenly reveals her long-buried feelings:

> " 'Twas but a dream with us," Mrs. Todd said. "I knew it when he was gone.
> I knew it"—and she whispered as if she were at confession—"I knew it
> afore he started to go to sea. My heart was gone out of my keepin' before I
> ever saw Nathan; but he loved me well, and he made me real happy, and he
> died before he ever knew what he'd had to know if we'd lived long together.
> 'Tis very strange about love . . . But this pennyr'yal always reminded me, as
> I'd sit and gather it and hear him talkin'—it always would remind me
> of—the other one." (49)

That's as much drama—or trauma—as we're ever shown, but it's enough for the narrator, and for the reader Jewett is writing for.

By summer's end, the narrator reflects: "Once I had not even known where to go for a walk; now there were many delightful things to be done and done again, as if I were in London," but finally she has to "return to the world in which I feared to find myself a foreigner" (127). Home may no longer be home. Not wanting to see her leave, Mrs. Todd makes a point of heading off to gather herbs, and our narrator last sees her form in the distance, "with something about it that was strangely self-possessed and mysterious," stooping to pick something; "it might have been her favorite pennyroyal" (129). Then the narrator loses sight of her and goes down to board the little coastal steamer that takes her away.

Earlier, after Mrs. Todd concluded her account of her lost love and her brief marriage, the narrator says, "She looked away from me, and presently rose and went on by herself. There was something lonely and solitary about her great determined shape. She might have been Antigone alone on the Theban plain . . . An absolute, archaic grief possessed this countrywoman" (49). While Florence Frisbie saw herself as Miss Ulysses as she sailed the South Seas, Sarah Orne Jewett became the Sophocles of her North Atlantic archipelago.

73. Marguerite Yourcenar, *Memoirs of Hadrian*

Like Sarah Orne Jewett's fictional narrator, and like Robert McCloskey in fact, Marguerite Yourcenar came to the Mount Desert area as a summer resident, but she'd moved permanently to the island by the time she completed her most famous novel, *Mémoires d'Hadrien*. Published in France in 1951, it came out in English in 1954 in the translation lovingly prepared by her longtime companion, Grace Frick. Their home in Northeast Harbor, "Petite Plaisance," is now a museum, where their thousands of books carry a bookplate showing their hands sharing a book. *Memoirs of Hadrian* was an international bestseller, and it made Yourcenar one of the leading French writers of her generation.

In 1980, she became the first woman ever elected to the Académie Française in that distinguished body's 350-year history. She was an exceptional choice in more than one respect, as she'd moved to the United States forty years before, and she actually became an American citizen in 1947. She'd had success in avant-garde circles in the 1930s with a series of early novels but felt confined within the Parisian literary milieu. Her choice to settle in the United States, she later said, "is not that of America against France. It translates a taste for a world stripped of all borders."[6]

Like Jean Rhys's *Wide Sargasso Sea*, Yourcenar's novel was born after a long period of silence. In an afterword, she describes her state of mind during the 1940s, in a one-line paragraph: "The lapse into despair of a writer who does not write."[7] But in 1948 she received a trunk of old papers left behind in France when she departed on the eve of World War II, and she discovered a few pages beginning "Mon cher Marc." She wondered who she'd been writing to, then remembered that this was the opening of the long-contemplated work that she'd abandoned in 1938. As she says in her afterword, "From that moment there was no question but that this book must be taken up again, whatever the cost" (326).

It was her very distance from Paris that now enabled Yourcenar to translate

68. Yourcenar at home in "Petite Plaisance"

her European experience into the still more distant world of late antiquity. Describing her research for the novel, she says: "One has to go into the most remote corners of a subject in order to discover the simplest things, and things of most general literary interest" (338). Mount Desert Island was a similarly "remote corner" of the world, and her life with Grace Frick was one of resolute simplicity, lived not in some palatial shingle-style "cottage" but in the equivalent of a French country farmhouse (Figure 68).

Memoirs of Hadrian is a remarkable exercise of imaginative sympathy, written in the voice of the Roman emperor. Mortally ill, Hadrian is writing his memoirs to assess his life and give guidance for his successor, the future philosopher-king Marcus Aurelius. Yourcenar undertook intensive research into second-century Rome, but her visionary recreation of antiquity is also shaped by the European crisis of world war. As she says in her afterword, she'd originally been drawn to Hadrian as a poet, but after the war she saw the centrality of his success in holding his fractious empire together. The dislocation caused by the war, she adds, "was essential, perhaps, in order to force me into trying to bridge not only the distance which separated me from Hadrian, but, above all, the distance which separated me from my true self" (325).

Hadrian's meditative solitude reflects the bounded space of Mount Desert Island. Two pages into the novel, he speaks of his approaching death: "Like a traveler sailing the Archipelago who sees the luminous mists lift toward evening, and little by little makes out the shore, I begin to discern the profile of my death" (5). In her afterword, Yourcenar describes the day on which she completed the book:

> On the 26th of December, 1950, on an evening of freezing cold and in the almost polar silence of Mount Desert Island, off the Atlantic shore, I was striving to live again through the smothering heat of a day in July, in the year 138 in Baiae, to feel the weight of a sheet on weary, heavy limbs, and to catch the barely perceptible sound of that tideless sea as from time to time it reached a man whose whole attention was concentrated upon other murmurs, those of his approaching death. I tried to go as far as the last sip of water, the last spasm of pain, the last image in his mind. Now the emperor had but to die. (342)

There is an element of self-dramatizing fiction in this image of an almost polar island "off the Atlantic shore," which makes her adoptive home sound like one of Judith Schalansky's more inhospitable Arctic wastelands. The island is actually connected to the mainland by a short bridge, and it has several thousand year-round residents in its half a dozen towns; but there certainly is a deep, contemplative stillness to a Maine winter.

On trips off-island, Yourcenar and Frick traveled widely in the United States, whose expansive breadth Yourcenar praised. "If I were you I would start by hitchhiking to San Antonio or San Francisco," she wrote to one friend; "it takes time to get to know this great country, at once so spread out and so secret."[8] Deeply if selectively interested in American culture, she collected

African American spirituals in the South and translated them under the title *Fleuve profond, sombre rivière* (1964). Yourcenar's American experiences enriched her meditations on Hadrian's far-flung empire and informed her hero's bemused tolerance of minority populations such as the Jews in Roman Judea. Hadrian speaks of "my love of things foreign; I liked to deal with the barbarians" (47). She even has him describe learning Greek in terms of New World travel: "I was still a child when for the first time I tried to trace on my tablets those characters of an unknown alphabet: here was a new world and the beginning of my great travels" (35).

In her afterword Yourcenar wrote of the intense pleasure of resuming her long-abandoned novel during a train trip out to New Mexico:

> Closed inside my compartment as if in a cubicle of some Egyptian tomb, I worked late into the night between New York and Chicago; then all the next day, in the restaurant of a Chicago station where I awaited a train blocked by storms and snow; then again until dawn, alone in the observation car of a Santa Fé Limited, surrounded by black spurs of the Colorado mountains, and by the eternal pattern of the stars. Thus were written at a single impulsion the passages on food, love, sleep, and the knowledge of men. I can hardly recall a day spent with more ardor, or more lucid nights. (328)

Translating herself into ancient Rome, Yourcenar could also translate her sexuality into the novel's central love story, Hadrian's passionate attachment to his beloved Antinous, who has committed suicide in Egypt. The American edition of the *Memoirs* includes several images of statues that Hadrian erected in his honor; these images silently comment on the emotions that the always reserved Hadrian only hints at: "we were not wise, neither the boy nor I" (173). Antinous had dreaded growing old, and Hadrian realizes that "he must have promised himself long ago to die at the first sign of decline, or even before" (184). Here Yourcenar almost seems to anticipate Yukio Mishima's suicide two decades later. She herself must have been struck by this parallel, as she wrote a book-length meditation on his life and death, *Mishima, ou la vision du vide* (1980).

In *À la recherche du temps perdu*, Proust says that a novel is like a cemetery filled with people from the author's life, with the names no longer legible. Yourcenar adapts Proust's image when Hadrian speaks of Antinous's death: "The memory of most men is an abandoned cemetery where lie, unsung and unhonored, the dead whom they have ceased to cherish" (209). Refusing to allow Antinous to share this fate, Hadrian set up shrines to him around the empire and founded an entire Egyptian city, Antinoöpolis, in his honor. Yourcenar's novel in turn immortalizes Hadrian and Antinous by name, and through Antinous we may glimpse the beloved whom Yourcenar names in her afterword only as "G..." and as "G.F." She says that she would have dedicated the book to her, "were there not a kind of impropriety in putting a personal inscription at the opening of a work where, precisely, I was trying to efface the personal" (342).

She then devotes a moving paragraph to "G.F." and ends by describing her as "someone who leaves us ideally free, but who nevertheless obliges us to be fully what we are. *Hospes Comesque*" (343). These last words come from a poem by Hadrian that serves as the book's epigraph, in which the emperor describes his gentle and drifting soul as his body's "guest and companion." A quarter century later, Yourcenar had this very phrase inscribed in stone, just below Grace Frick's name (Figure 69). A visitor to Mount Desert Island can find this stone next to the one prepared a few years afterward for Yourcenar herself, beneath a pair of intertwined birch trees in the Brookside Cemetery in Somesville, a couple of miles from where I am writing these pages.

In the opening of *Swann's Way*, Marcel recalls his vanished childhood:

Never again will such moments be possible for me. But of late I have been increasingly able to catch, if I listen attentively, the sound of the sobs which I had the strength to control in my father's presence, and which broke out only when I found myself alone with Mamma. In reality their echo has never

69. Grace Frick, "Guest and companion"

ceased; and it is only because life is now growing more and more quiet round about me that I hear them anew, like those convent bells which are so effectively drowned during the day by the noises of the street that one would suppose them to have stopped, until they ring out again through the silent evening air.[9]

Setting the stage for her magnificent recreation of a vanished past—of ancient Rome, of prewar Paris—from the vantage point of her new American life, Marguerite Yourcenar made her own version of Proust's cork-lined study amid the "almost polar silence" of Mount Desert Island, l'Île des Monts Déserts.

74. Hugh Lofting, *The Voyages of Doctor Dolittle*

During my Bar Harbor years, my chief portal to the wider world was the Jesup Memorial Library, just across Mount Desert Street from the rectory where we lived. I became friends with the librarian, Miss Staples—who somewhat puzzlingly became Mrs. Staples after marrying a gentleman of the same name—and by the time I was nine years old I was carrying home an armful of books on a weekly basis. None more deeply captured my imagination than Hugh Lofting's dozen Doctor Dolittle novels.

Based in the town of Puddleby-on-the-Marsh, the good doctor seems quintessentially English, but his creator had emigrated to the United States at an even younger age than Marguerite Yourcenar. He'd been born in 1886 in a town to the west of London, to Catholic parents of Irish heritage. He studied engineering and then worked as a civil engineer in Canada, Africa, and Cuba, before moving to New York in 1912 to start a career as a journalist. Then came World War I, and in 1916 he returned to England to enlist in the Irish Guards regiment. While serving as a lieutenant in Flanders and France, he wanted to find something suitable to write to his young children in New York. Seeing how poorly wounded horses were treated at the Front, he began to imagine how helpful it would be if a veterinarian could talk to his patients, and Doctor Dolittle was born. After the war, Lofting and his family moved to Connecticut, where he expanded his letters into a book. *The Story of Doctor Dolittle* was published in New York in 1920 and was an immediate success; two years later, it was published in England as well, now with a glowing preface by the British novelist Hugh Walpole, who praised it as the first real children's classic since *Alice in Wonderland*.

John Dolittle is a family physician whose practice takes a new direction after his talking parrot Polynesia explains to him that animal languages are largely nonverbal. As an example, she says that dogs "nearly always use their noses for asking questions," and explains that the way his dog is twitching his nose means "Can't you see that it has stopped raining?" Lofting tells us that "after a while, with the parrot's help, the Doctor got to learn the language of the animals so well that he could talk to them himself and understand everything they said. Then he gave up being a people's doctor altogether."[10] No further explanation is offered, and the book's young readers were happy to follow the adventures that unfolded from this unlikely premise.

Lofting endowed his hero not only with preternatural linguistic abilities but with his own restlessness. Dolittle typically spends half the year in far-flung locales, often seeking to learn the language of another animal or fish or insect. In the process, he is regularly thrust into exciting adventures involving shipwrecks, pirates, tribal warfare, and lost civilizations. Dolittle has a unique method of deciding on a destination: he simply opens an atlas at random, closes his eyes, and jabs a page with a pencil. He then goes wherever the pencil decrees, with the sole caveat that he never goes somewhere he's already been—a rule that often requires making several stabs with the pencil.

At nearly 400 pages, *The Voyages of Doctor Dolittle* (1922) contains myriad adventures, illustrated with Lofting's lively line drawings. The voyages culminate in a war on Spidermonkey Island—a floating island—in which Dolittle leads the forces of Popsipetel in defeating the malevolent Bag-jagderags. The grateful Popsipetelans make him their ruler, under the name King Jong Thinkalot, and they enshrine him in their pictographic histories, as we can see in the book's frontispiece (Figure 70).

The story is narrated by Tommy Stubbins, who serves as an admiring Watson to Dolittle's Holmes. Writing as an old man, Tommy is recalling his adventures as a nine-year-old, when he became the doctor's apprentice. Reading the book myself at age eight or nine, I appreciated seeing the story through Tommy's eyes, but the real pleasure was to be found in the doctor's matter-of-fact interactions with his extensive household. These include the housekeeper Dab-Dab the duck, eternally annoyed at mud getting tracked into the house, the know-it-all parrot Polynesia (who has seen it all in her hundred and eighty-three years), and the winsome pig Gub-Gub. In *Doctor Dolittle's Post Office*, Gub-Gub becomes jealous of the doctor's extensive correspondence; wishing he had a penpal of his own, he starts sending himself anonymous letters. The others learn the truth when it turns out that the "letters" consist of banana peels; Gub-Gub has been sending himself correspondence he can really enjoy.

Rereading the book after these many years, there are aspects that haven't held up so well. One of the doctor's companions is an African prince, Bumpo,

70. *Frontispiece to* The Voyages of Doctor Dolittle *(1922)*

who is taking a break from his studies at Oxford. Bumpo enjoys reading Cicero but thinks that Cicero's son is on his college's crew team. He wears elegantly tailored suits but insists on going barefoot ("I threw the shoes over a wall as soon as I got out of the quadrilateral this morning"),[11] and he speaks a kind of Africanized Kiplingese that must have seemed more amusing in 1922 than it does today. The current editions of the series have actually been revised, with the agreement of Lofting's son, to remove certain epithets and illustrations, as well as some entire scenes set in Africa.

Then there is the ambiguous nature of *The Voyages'* primary adventure, an expedition in search of a great Native American naturalist, Long Arrow, with whom Dolittle is eager to exchange ideas. Dolittle finally locates him on Spidermonkey Island, in a scene reminiscent of Stanley presuming that he's found Doctor Livingstone. Long Arrow and Bumpo join Dolittle to defend the Popsipetel kingdom against the Bag-jagderags, and their success becomes a subject of song:

> Oh, strong was the Red-skin, fierce was the Black,
> Bag-jagderags trembled and tried to turn back.
> But 'twas of the White Man they shouted, "Beware!
> He throws men in handfuls, straight up in the air!" (281)

Lofting's story straddles the borderline between imperial fantasy and outright parody. The grateful Popsipetelans insist on crowning Dolittle their king, and he's too polite to refuse. He brings peace and order to the island, but he chafes against the disruption to his scientific work. He'd prefer to go off to learn the language of shellfish, and the ornate crown impedes his hunting of butterflies—which he catches not to kill but for conversation. At the book's end Dolittle, Tommy, and their animal crew hitch a ride home to England inside a giant sea snail, leaving the Popsipetelans to their own devices.

What are we to make of this imperial adventure? Lofting had returned from the Great War a confirmed pacifist, and with his Irish Catholic roots he was probably never a great admirer of the British Empire—a factor, perhaps, in his emigration. During Dolittle's reign he democratizes the island society, after engineering a peace treaty with the Bag-jagderags; "unlike most peaces," Tommy remarks, the treaty "was, and is, strictly kept—even to this day" (281). *The Voyages of Doctor Dolittle* advocates harmonious cohabitation among races and among species, though not every young reader will have gleaned that pacific lesson from Dolittle's adventures in the South Pacific.

For my part, the book's fascination centered on its extravagant multilingualism, a dimension that extends to modes of writing. At a key moment Long Arrow communicates to Dolittle via pictographs inscribed on the back of a beetle, an episode commemorated in the book's frontispiece. Lofting's illustration of the war against the Bag-jagderags (Figure 71) struck me less for the forcefulness of the warriors (comically including the pudgy doctor) than for the Mayan-inspired profiles and pictographs.

Even now, I am still basically following in the footsteps of Lofting's restless multilingualist, though I've never managed to acquire his fluency in the languages of horses, eagles, and giant snails. Dolittle never knew where the pencil stabbing his atlas would take him, but then again, authors never know where their books will take their readers.

The Terrible Three
From an Indian rock-engraving found on Hawks'-Head Mountain, Spidermonkey Island

71. Dolittle at war

75. E. B. White, *Stuart Little*

In 1952, the same year that Robert McCloskey published *One Morning in Maine*, E. B. White published *Charlotte's Web*, the bestselling American children's book of all time. The two works were as close in space as in time. White had been inspired by a spider spinning her web in the barn of his farmhouse in North Brooklin, Maine, just across Blue Hill Bay from Mount Desert Island and only a few miles from the McCloskeys. He too was dividing his time between summers in Maine and winters in New York, where he'd been a *New Yorker* contributor since its founding in 1925. In 1977, he wrote that for many years "I thrashed back and forth between Maine and New York for reasons that seemed compelling at the time." Now settled permanently in Maine, "I have finally come to rest."[12]

White published many humorous pieces in *The New Yorker*, as well as books such as *Is Sex Necessary?* (a parody of advice manuals that he wrote together with James Thurber), but he became famous for his children's books. Like Hugh Lofting, he built his tales around talking animals. In the case of Charlotte, she is a writer as well. She saves her friend Wilbur the pig from slaughter by weaving messages into her web such as "Terrific," "Humble," and "Some Pig." This seeming miracle makes Wilbur a tourist attraction, saving his life to the delight of his young friend Fern, daughter of the farmer who has been raising Wilbur for food.

White's previous children's book, *Stuart Little* (1945), had special significance for me when I first found myself faced with an uncertain future. A few weeks before my tenth birthday, my father accepted a call to a parish in Manhattan, and with typical impatience he decided to make the move in April, just after Easter but still in the midst of the school year. What was this new life going to be like? When my beloved librarian Mrs. (née Miss) Staples assured me that there would also be libraries in New York, I objected, "But they won't know I'm Davy"—a reply that became the basis for an editorial in the *Bar*

Harbor Times extolling the virtues of small-town life. Feeling like a church mouse about to be thrust into an immense city—Manhattan alone had a population larger than the entire state of Maine—I found it comforting to read about an endlessly resourceful little mouse-person as he makes his way in the metropolis.

New Yorkers always like to think of their city, and themselves, as larger than life; White's inspiration was to dramatize this quality through the eyes of a hero who is much *smaller* than life. "The truth of the matter was, the baby looked very much like a mouse in every way. He was only about two inches high; and he had a mouse's sharp nose, a mouse's tail, a mouse's whiskers, and the pleasant, shy manner of a mouse."[13] White himself was famously shy, often avoiding unfamiliar visitors by escaping down a fire escape outside his office at *The New Yorker*, but in Stuart he created a far more suave and self-confident self, as we see in Garth Williams's portrait (Figure 72).

Though Stuart's parents and brother are rather nonplussed by his size and appearance, they quickly adapt. His mother sews him several sets of clothes, including a tiny sailor suit, and his father makes him a cozy bed out of four clothes pins and a cigarette box. Meanwhile young Stuart rapidly masters the large world around him. He wields a miniature mallet to turn on a faucet for

*72. Stuart Little,
mouse about town*

his morning ablutions; on a morning walk, "full of the joy of life and the fear of dogs" (26), he climbs a fire hydrant like a sailor on a ship's rigging, using his tiny spyglass to keep a lookout for danger.

My identification with Stuart only increased once we moved to New York, where we lived just a couple of blocks from a pond in Central Park that had been created for people to sail their model boats, as I did myself. This pond is the setting for Stuart's most dramatic adventure, when he signs on as helmsman of a model yacht, the *Lillian B. Womrath*, and races against a boat belonging to "a fat, sulky boy of twelve," who doesn't know a squall from a squib or a jib from a jibe, and who wears "a blue serge suit and a white necktie stained with orange juice" (36–7). The boy's sloppy attire contrasts unfavorably with the always dapper Stuart, who wins the race even after the boats become entangled in a soggy paper bag amid a sudden squall.

Soon after this triumph, the book takes on a more melancholy tone. Stuart becomes fast friends with Margalo, a little bird who joins the family, until she realizes that the family cat intends to eat her, and one night she flies away. Heartbroken, Stuart heads north in a tiny model car to look for her. Various comic incidents take place en route, as when he becomes a substitute schoolteacher for a day. He prepares for the job by changing into "a pepper-and-salt jacket, old striped trousers, a Windsor tie, and spectacles" (86), then heads into the classroom. "Seizing a coat lapel in either hand, to make himself look like a professor" (89)—a technique I can recommend—he briefly quizzes the students on their subjects, then leads them in a free-form discussion on what matters in life; the answers include a note of music, ice cream with chocolate sauce, and "a shaft of sunlight at the end of a dark afternoon" (92). He issues decrees against swiping things and against being mean, and then dismisses the delighted children.

Resuming his journey, Stuart asks everyone he meets whether they've seen Margalo ("brown, with a streak of yellow on her bosom"), but he admits that "I rather expect that from now on I shall be traveling north until the end of my days" (128–9). In the book's final illustration, we have to look closely to see his tiny car, pressing onward amid the rolling landscape (Figure 73).

73. Traveling north

In a preface to a collection of American humor, published four years before *Stuart Little*, White noted that humorists have often been described as "clowns with a breaking heart." He continued:

> It would be more accurate, I think, to say that there is a deep vein of melancholy running through everyone's life and that the humorist, perhaps more sensible of it than some others, compensates for it actively and positively. Humorists fatten on trouble. They have always made trouble pay. They struggle along with a good will and endure pain cheerfully, knowing how well it will serve them in the sweet by and by.[14]

Stuart's final encounter is with a telephone repairman, who remarks that a person could do worse than to head north to the end of their days. He says that "following a broken telephone line north, I have come upon some wonderful places," including swamps where "turtles wait on logs but not for anything in particular," and "orchards so old they have forgotten where the farmhouse is" (129). He cautions Stuart that these locales "are a long way from here—don't forget that. And a person who is looking for something doesn't travel very fast." Stuart agrees, and in the book's final lines he gets back on the road. "As he peered ahead into the great land that stretched before him, the way seemed long. But the sky was bright, and he somehow felt he was headed in the right direction" (131). Fortified by Stuart's stoic optimism, I could think of my unknown southward destination the same way.

CHAPTER SIXTEEN

New York: Migrant Metropolis

76. Madeleine L'Engle, *A Wrinkle in Time*

In Maine I'd begun to experience the wider world through books, but soon after we moved to New York I encountered my first professional writer: a parishioner of my father's named Mrs. Franklin but better known by her pen name, Madeleine L'Engle. She had published *A Wrinkle in Time* a few months before our arrival and was giving copies to friends' children; she was pleased when I told her I'd liked it so much that I'd read it twice. A further connection developed when my brother Tom and I started going to an Episcopalian parochial school where her kids also went, and she periodically taught us creative writing.

Born in New York, Madeleine L'Engle Camp was a shy and awkward girl who struggled both socially and academically, baffling her sophisticated, accomplished parents (her mother a pianist, her father a foreign correspondent). Her early experiences fed directly into her portrayal of her heroine, Meg Murry, who perseveres despite her intense self-doubt. The stellar success of *A Wrinkle in Time*, which won the 1963 Newbery Award and has been a perennial bestseller in the U.S. since then, came after a full decade of failure. L'Engle had published three autobiographical novels while still in her twenties, all featuring awkward girls who don't fit in with their family or at school. The first of these had done well, but its successors sold poorly, and L'Engle began receiving rejection after rejection. On her fortieth birthday in 1958, receiving yet another rejection, she resolved to give up writing altogether. But then she realized that as soon as she'd made her decision, she'd begun planning a story about just such a choice. She returned to her desk and decided to write a novel that would bring together all of her interests, however eccentric and unsellable the combination might be.

Her new manuscript seemed fated to fail even more resoundingly than the ones she'd been writing during the previous decade. The novel features elements that had never been combined: science fiction (space travel through "tessering"), outright fantasy (embodied in the three angelic witches, Mrs. Whatsit, Mrs. Who, and Mrs. Which), and young-adult realism: Meg has to deal with mean girls at her school, and she feels a dawning love for the popular athlete Calvin O'Keefe, whom she's sure is far out of her league. Add to all this a sharp critique of mass culture and a deeply Christian theology, and you've got a seriously unmarketable manuscript. It was turned down by thirty publishing houses before she finally showed it to the publisher John Farrar, who was a fellow parishioner at the aptly named Church of the Resurrection, and her career was reborn.

After receiving the Newbery Award, L'Engle wrote an essay for the *New York Times Book Review* in which she discussed the value of fantasy in writing for young people. "It's often possible to make demands of a child that couldn't be made of an adult," she observes;

> a child will often understand scientific concepts that would baffle an adult. This is because he can understand with a leap of the imagination that is denied the grown-up who has acquired the little knowledge that is a dangerous thing . . . The child will come to it with an open mind, whereas many adults come closed to an open book. This is one reason so many writers turn to fantasy (which children claim as their own) when they have something important and difficult to say.[1]

This is well shown by a diagram in the book when Mrs. Whatsit explains the concept of the tesseract by asking Meg, Calvin, and Meg's brother, Charles Wallace, to imagine an ant trying to move across a skirt held between Mrs. Who's hands; if she then brings her hands together, the ant can jump immediately from one hand to the other (Figure 74). Five-year-old Charles Wallace intuitively understands, but Meg doesn't get it, and sighs, "I guess I *am* a moron." Mrs. Whatsit replies: "That is because you think of space only in three dimensions. We travel in the fifth dimension. This is something you can understand, Meg. Don't be afraid to try."[2] The diagram illustrates the result, but it really doesn't tell us anything about the underlying science. L'Engle trusted her young readers to embrace the concept without needing to understand the process, much as Hugh Lofting could tell us in a single sentence that "after a while, with the parrot's help, the Doctor got to learn the language of the animals," or as J. R. R. Tolkien could evoke the numinous powers of magic rings as self-evident truths within the world of Middle-earth.

Aided by the three witches, the youngsters venture into outer space to rescue Meg and Charles Wallace's father, a physicist who'd been experimenting with tessering and has become trapped on the evil planet Camazotz. From there the disembodied, throbbing brain of "IT" spreads darkness throughout

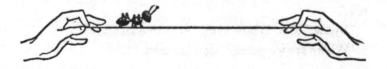

74. Mrs. Whatsit illustrates tessering

the universe, valiantly opposed by the forces of light. Life is strictly regimented on Camazotz: every father heads off to work at the same time, while outside their identical houses every kid plays jump-rope or bounces a ball in the same rhythm. I T succeeds in commandeering Charles Wallace's mind, and he explains to Meg that "on Camazotz individuals have been done away with. Camazotz is O N E mind. It's I T. And that's why everybody's so happy and efficient" (142).

In a used copy of the novel that I once picked up for L'Engle to inscribe for my daughter Eva (the store being out of new copies), I found extensive annotations by a closely engaged reader, but she wrote an angry comment to these lines: "O K this is pretty clear now: 'I T' = socialism/communism. Fuck you Mad L'Engle." This is surely too limited a view. Camazotz is better compared to the dystopias of Aldous Huxley's *Brave New World* and George Orwell's *1984*, which satirize capitalist as well as communist mass culture and groupthink. The Camazotz suburb resembles other American critiques of what Herbert Marcuse called *One-Dimensional Man* in 1964. Even Robert McCloskey had portrayed a similar town in his *Homer Price* (1945), where the people of Centerburg lose their way in a subdivision of identical prefabricated houses.

L'Engle's Christianity has proven more challenging for some readers. Fundamentalists have boycotted and even banned the book for featuring witches, perhaps not seeing how fully Mrs. Who, Mrs. Which, and Mrs. Whatsit form a feminized version of the Trinity; Mrs. Whatsit is even called "the comforter." Some committed sectarians have also objected to L'Engle's Christian universalism. She held that everyone who fights for the forces of light against darkness is a spiritual leader, and in a key passage in the book these figures include not only Jesus and Saint Francis, but also Shakespeare, Beethoven, Madame Curie, Einstein, and even Gandhi and the Buddha (89).

The novel's political critique and its religious penumbra are all grounded in Meg's relationship with her family, in particular her charismatic but vanished father and her preternaturally wise, though probably autistic, little brother

Charles Wallace. L'Engle gave him the first names of her father and her father-in-law, and she dedicated the novel to both of them. Her father's lungs had been damaged by mustard gas during World War I, and throughout her youth he struggled with his health; he died when she was in college. In *A Wrinkle in Time* Meg has to come to terms with the fact that even when she's finally found her father, he can't make everything right. As she realizes when the forces of I T seem triumphant: "Her father had not saved her" (170). Indeed, he's hardly even a grown-up; as he says to Calvin, "we know nothing . . . We're children playing with dynamite. In our mad rush we've plunged into this before—" (168). He's interrupted before he completes the sentence, which might have concluded "before we knew what we were doing," but he could also have meant "before now." The children playing with dynamite may suggest the mad rush into world war and then the nuclear arms race, which had almost gotten the world blown up during the Cuban missile crisis the year before L'Engle published her novel.

In the end it is Meg who saves the day, boldly venturing alone back to Camazotz to rescue Charles Wallace from I T's clutches. Mrs. Whatsit hints that only she has the ability to get through to her baby brother, and after resisting ("*I* can't go!" Meg cried. "I can't! You know I can't!," 195), she finally accepts the task—a decision parallel to Frodo's decision to take the One Ring to the Mountain of Doom in Mordor in *The Lord of the Rings*. Counterintuitively, what enables Meg to succeed in her quest aren't her virtues so much as her faults, which Mrs. Whatsit said at the outset that she'd need. "What were her greatest faults?" Meg asks herself. "Anger, impatience, stubbornness. Yes, it was to her faults that she turned to save herself now" (159). Displaying an equal stubbornness of her own, not quelled by ten full years of rejections, Madeleine L'Engle blended fantasy, science, and Christianity to come to terms with her lonely, awkward childhood and to bring her vanished father back to life.

77. Saul Steinberg, *The Labyrinth*

Perhaps no writer or artist in the postwar decades more fully embodied New York's life than Saul Steinberg. He's best known for his iconic *New Yorker* cover, "View of the World from 9th Avenue," which shows New Jersey as a thin strip beyond the Hudson. A handful of cities appear in the radically compressed distance out west, and on the horizon we glimpse China, Japan, and Siberia. But this is only one of dozens of representations of the city in his work. He was fascinated with New York's chaotic vibrancy, and some of his most vivid drawings evoke the city's street life, as in his portrait of Greenwich Village's Bleecker Street for a *New Yorker* cover (Figure 75).

I include Steinberg in this project because he was as much a writer as a visual artist. As he wrote in the catalogue for a major retrospective at the Whitney Museum: "The artist (and my idea of the artist, poet, painter, composer, etc. is *the novelist*) investigates all the other lives in order to understand the world and possibly himself before returning to his own, often for a short and dull time only." He adds, ironically: "It accounts for the delayed (even retarded) nature of the artist."[3]

Steinberg was born in 1914 in the Jewish minority of a city in southeast Romania, and grew up in Bucharest, where his father was a printer and bookbinder, and a manufacturer of decorated cardboard boxes (the decorations became a favorite source for his son's later art). Steinberg studied philosophy and literature at the University of Bucharest, then in 1933 moved to Milan, where he studied architecture and began drawing cartoons for a local humor newspaper. He fled fascist Italy in 1941, barely managing to get to the United States via Santo Domingo. He'd already begun publishing drawings in leading American magazines, and after serving in the Navy he became closely associated with *The New Yorker*, for which he drew dozens of covers and produced a plethora of drawings.

The black ink line provided a natural form for him, and he was fascinated

75. Saul Steinberg, Bleecker Street *(1970), ink, pencil, colored pencil, and crayon on paper, 29 ⅜ x 22 ⅜ in. Private collection. Drawing for* The New Yorker *cover, January 16, 1971.*

by the ways in which a line could endlessly transform itself. His first collection of drawings, based in part on his military service, was punningly titled *All in Line* (1945). As he said in the Whitney catalogue, "I am among the few who continue to draw after childhood is ended, continuing and perfecting childhood drawing—without the traditional interruption of academic training. The continuous line of my drawing dates from childhood and is probably a way of writing from my illiterate days" (235). *The Labyrinth* begins with a seven-page spread adapted from a 33-foot-long drawing that was enlarged for application to a wall of the "Children's Labyrinth" at the Milan Triennial exhibition in 1954, in which a straight line generates a vertiginous series of *trompe l'oeils*, from a Venetian canal to a clothesline to a railroad bridge and then a New York street, the Egyptian desert, and on and on.

New York became Steinberg's lifelong home base, but it was also the place from which he set off on journeys around the world, chronicled in his various collections. He never lost a sense of himself as an immigrant—one of his collections is titled *The Passport*—and fake documents, rubber stamps, and incomprehensible officialese figure in many of his drawings. He always returned to his adoptive city with renewed vigor and keen observation. In one of his drawings of New York's streets, he comically embodies the sudden shift from Park Avenue wealth to the poverty of East Harlem above 96th Street, where railroad tracks emerge into view (Figure 76). The little girls on the left look almost identical, but with witty precision Steinberg has fattened up 96th Street, as it's a double-width two-way street.

I met Steinberg in 1968, several years after he'd published *The Labyrinth*. I'd been drawing elaborate mazes for some time when I met him through the good offices of my ninth-grade English teacher, Maggie Staats. I'd given her a maze which she showed to Steinberg, whom she knew from *The New Yorker*, where she'd worked before becoming a teacher. He suggested trading drawings, so I made him a labyrinth and he gave me a drawing of a stately beauty queen, her sash labeled "North Dakota"; over her head, a bubble shows her

76. Saul Steinberg, Untitled *(1968), ink on paper, 14 ½ x 23 in.*
Beinecke Rare Books and Manuscript Library, Yale University.
Originally published in The New Yorker, *December 7, 1968.*

dreaming of her state's capital, Bismarck. When Maggie Staats took me to see him, I experienced several instances of his love of self-invention. He showed us a volume of Picasso's etchings, in which he'd written a glowing message to himself in French, supposedly from Picasso. He'd then left the book on a coffee table where a visiting interviewer would see it, and he was delighted when the published article spoke of Picasso's admiration for Steinberg's work—"Which is true," he made a point of telling us. He also described showing the playwright Eugène Ionesco around New York; they pretended that Ionesco knew no English and needed Steinberg to translate for him.

Two of my favorite Steinberg images serve as the endpapers to *The Labyrinth*. The opening endpaper (Figure 77) is a brilliant satire of America's self-image in the Eisenhower era, with unshackled Prosperity atop the pyramid, flanked by Santa Claus and Sigmund Freud, and below them a whole series of antinomies (Art & Industry, Vice & Virtue, Labor & Leisure), all reconciled in one comic way or another. At the monument's base, the Pursuit of Happiness bites its own tails, and Uncle Sam and Uncle Tom exchange congratulatory greetings.

77. Saul Steinberg, Prosperity (The Pursuit of
Happiness) *(1958–9), pencil, colored pencil, ink, and
crayon on paper, 22 ½ x 15 in. Karikatur Museum,
Krems. Drawing for* The New Yorker *cover,
January 19, 1959, used as opening endpaper
to* The Labyrinth *(1960).*

In the book's closing endpaper (Figure 78), America sets sail for its
dreamed-of future, on a sea where "Truth" is eaten by "Myth" and "Why" by
a pragmatic "How" with shark-like teeth. Democrats and Republicans appear
as rival baseball teams, while a Native American is ironically used to sym-
bolize freedom, an academic represents Business, and a Freemason represents
Order. Above them all, the empyrean features Marx, Freud, Joyce, the
American eagle—and Jules Verne. (In another version of this painting, the
ship is actually named the "Jules Verne.")[4] Steinberg's fondness for Verne is
eminently appropriate, as his drawings take us around New York and around
the world, and collectively they create one of the great American novels of
their time.

78. Saul Steinberg, Ship of State *(1959), pencil, colored pencil, ink, and crayon on paper, 22 ½ x 15 in. Drawing for* The New Yorker *cover, September 17, 1960, used as closing endpaper to* The Labyrinth *(1960).*

78. James Baldwin, *Notes of a Native Son*

A city as vast as New York can never be encompassed by any single perspective. The city has doubled in size since O. Henry published his collection *The Four Million* (1908); his title was a pointed response to a journalist who'd claimed that there were only 400 New Yorkers worth knowing in society. ("If you go outside that number," he'd declared, "you strike people who are either not at ease in a ballroom or else make other people not at ease.")[5] None of those 400 would have lived in Harlem. In discussing Saul Steinberg, I've noted the precision with which he portrayed the double-width 96th Street, but he didn't show the fact that girls living north of that dividing line would have been Latina or Black. For that New York, we'd have to turn to other writers, such as Piri Thomas, whose memoir *Down These Mean Streets* (1967) gave a complex view of East Harlem from the perspective of a "dark" child of Puerto Rican immigrants. His lighter-skinned neighbors looked down on him, and his own parents were in denial of the African strand in their ancestry.

No writer of the time gave more lucid and searching portrayals of this New York than James Baldwin. As a preacher's kid, I read with special interest the title essay of *Notes of a Native Son*, which describes Baldwin's difficult relationship with his father, a Baptist preacher in Harlem. Baldwin was just thirty-one when he published this essay collection in 1955; by the time I bought my copy in 1968 it was already included in Bantam's series of "Modern Classics." The title essay opens with a dramatic scene of personal loss and social chaos:

> On the 29th of July, in 1943, my father died. On the same day, a few hours later, his last child was born. Over a month before this, while all our energies were concentrated on waiting for these events, there had been, in Detroit, one of the bloodiest race riots of the century. A few hours after my father's funeral, while he lay in state in the undertaker's chapel, a race riot broke out in Harlem. On the morning of the 3rd of August, we drove my father to the graveyard through a wilderness of smashed plate glass.[6]

As if this weren't enough to deal with, he adds: "The day of my father's funeral had also been my nineteenth birthday." As he later dryly remarks: "When planning a birthday celebration one naturally does not expect that it will be up against competition from a funeral" (86–7).

Baldwin had been estranged from his father for several years by then. He was living in Greenwich Village, trying to establish himself as a writer and moving in artistic circles; Marlon Brando, then an aspiring actor, was a roommate and became a longtime friend. As for his father, Baldwin describes him as "certainly the most bitter man I have ever met; yet it must be said that there was something else in him, buried in him, which lent him his tremendous power and, even, a rather crushing charm" (72). As the essay proceeds,

Baldwin probes the roots of his father's bitterness, and he describes his own nearly disastrous outbreak at a restaurant in New Jersey, where he is told by an apologetic waitress that "we don't serve Negroes here" (80). He'd just been fired from a job at a factory, most of whose workers were from the South, and where he'd struggled against a stark racism that he hadn't encountered in Manhattan. Suddenly filled with rage, he hurls a water pitcher at the waitress and then flees, barely escaping a quickly forming mob intent on vengeance. That night, he says, "I could not get over two facts, both equally difficult for the imagination to grasp, and one was that I could have been murdered. But the other was that I had been ready to commit murder. I saw nothing very clearly, but I did see this: that my life, my *real* life, was in danger, and not from anything other people might do but from the hatred I carried in my own heart" (81). Like much of Baldwin's work, the essay dissects the factors that breed hatred in the hearts of the victims of injustice, and he argues that such hatred is far more destructive for the victims than for the objects of their hatred, the privileged individuals and institutions that won't be affected by the shattering of plate glass on ghetto storefronts.

A further factor in Baldwin's dissociation from his family, and from much of American culture, was the fact that in his teens he realized that he was gay. Like Gertrude Stein and Djuna Barnes before him, he moved to Paris seeking a freer environment, at age twenty-four, and he ended up settling permanently in France. Though Baldwin is often read in a purely American context, new perspectives emerge when we look at him as a writer of world literature— someone coming to a sense of himself as a writer while living as an American abroad (Figure 79). *Notes of a Native Son* concludes with four essays set in France. The first of these, "Encounter on the Seine: Black Meets Brown," develops the ambivalence of his dual identity as a Black man and as an American. In Paris, he is condescended to by sympathetic French people "who consider that all Negroes arrive from America, trumpet-laden and twinkle-toed, bearing scars so unutterably painful that all of the glories of the French Republic may not suffice to heal them" (101). He also meets Francophone African

79. Baldwin in Paris

students, and he comes to realize how different he is from them: "They face each other, the Negro and the African, over a gulf of three hundred years" (103). Gradually he finds in his alienation and rootlessness the essence of an Americanness he hadn't realized in himself until he moved to Paris.

In the essay's conclusion, he writes that one day the American expatriates will return home, and he predicts: "What time will bring Americans is at last their own identity. It is on this dangerous voyage and in the same boat that the American Negro will make peace with himself and with the voiceless many thousands gone before him" (104). Baldwin himself periodically returned to the United States, but never permanently. In 1961, he told an interviewer in New York that "I never intended to come back to this country," but he'd concluded that "I am an American writer. My subject is my country. I had to come back to check my impressions, and, as it turned out, to be stung again, to look at it again, bear it again, and to be reconciled to it again. Now, I imagine, I will have to spend the rest of my life as a kind of transatlantic commuter."[7] He and his partner, Bernard Hassell, eventually settled in southern France, where he entertained his many friends among artists, musicians, and writers; Miles

Davis and Nina Simone regularly came to stay, as did Marguerite Yourcenar, who translated his play *The Amen Corner.*

It was in France that Baldwin wrote his stories, novels, and plays, often revisiting his American experience from a distance comparable to Yourcenar's move in the opposite direction. As he wrote in a preface to *Notes of a Native Son*, for a creative writer "to go beneath the surface, to tap the source" of social turmoil, "it is absolutely necessary that he establish between himself and these affairs a distance which will allow, at least, for clarity, so that before he can look forward in any meaningful sense, he must first be allowed to take a long look back" (3–4).

In his often-anthologized story "Sonny's Blues,"[8] we can see the productive duality—or triangulation—of Baldwin's African-American-French writing. Jazz and blues had long been immensely popular in Paris. In a notable expression of this love, Jean-Paul Sartre used a jazz recording to bring a final, tentative peace to Roquentin, the tormented hero of his 1938 novel, *Nausea*:

> Now there is this song on the saxophone. And I am ashamed. A glorious
> little suffering has just been born, an exemplary suffering. Four notes on the
> saxophone. They come and they go, they seem to say: You must be like us,
> suffer in rhythm. All right! . . . I feel something brush against me lightly and
> I dare not move because I am afraid it will go away. Something I didn't
> know any more: a sort of joy. The Negress sings. Can you justify your
> existence then? Just a little?[9]

Baldwin's story moves, like Sartre's, toward an existential redemption through music, which fosters a reconciliation between the composer-pianist Sonny and his straightlaced brother. But Baldwin goes far beyond Sartre in setting Sonny's blues in its complex African American and New York context.

Baldwin's continuing importance was underscored in 2016 by Raoul Peck's excellent documentary, *I Am Not Your Negro*, and his work seems even more timely now than in 2016. I'd always remembered the shattered glass in the opening of "Notes of a Native Son," but I'd forgotten the riot's cause. After his father's funeral, while Baldwin was downtown "desperately celebrating my birthday," he says (91), a Negro soldier got into a fight in a Harlem hotel with a white policeman over a Negro girl (a prostitute, Baldwin indicates) whom they were both interested in. The fight ended with the policeman shooting the soldier, and the news, amplified with rumors and misstatements, sparked the riot. Written with an exceptional clarity grounded in a reflective distance from the American scene, Baldwin's 1955 essay speaks directly to reports that appear almost daily in American newspapers today.

79. Saul Bellow, *Henderson the Rain King*

Like Paris, New York has long been a mecca for writers. Since so much of American publishing is located in the city, even writers based elsewhere regularly come into town, and it was on one of his visits that I met Saul Bellow in 1969, seven years before he received the Nobel Prize. Bellow's reputation faded somewhat in his later years, partly because his cultural views shifted into conservatism (a marked change from his Trotskyite youth), and partly because his mode of existentialist realism was overtaken by the postmodernism of writers like Thomas Pynchon and the magical realism of Gabriel García Márquez. But he was at the height of his fame in the 1960s, and his influence went well beyond literary circles. In 1967 Joni Mitchell was reading *Henderson the Rain King* on an airplane, and she was struck by Henderson's reflection while he flies to Africa: "I dreamed down at the clouds, and thought that when I was a kid I had dreamed up at them, and having dreamed at the clouds from both sides as no other generation of men has done, one should be able to accept his death very easily."[10] This passage inspired Mitchell's most famous song, "Both Sides, Now," in which clouds' illusions shade over to the illusions of life and love. Decades before Beyoncé sampled Chimamanda Adichie, Joni Mitchell was sampling Saul Bellow.

Bellow's visit to New York had something to do with publishers or publicists, but it had a romantic purpose as well, as he was staying with Maggie Staats, whom he was asking to become the fourth Mrs. Bellow (out of an eventual total of five). They did get engaged for a while, until she thought better of the idea. But she showed him a little journal I'd been keeping, and she had me come to meet him one Saturday morning. I'd titled my journal "David Pepys at the World," in honor of Samuel Pepys's great *Diary*, and Bellow recommended reading more widely in the period. It was thanks to him—as well as to my brother Leo, just beginning his career in eighteenth-century studies—that I came to read Fielding, Defoe, Richardson, and Smollett. With unnecessary generosity, Bellow wrote me a kind note about my journal, "warning" that I might perhaps become a writer.

The writer John Podhoretz has described Bellow as someone who "inhaled books and ideas the way the rest of us breathe air."[11] He'd grown up reading Dostoevsky, Flaubert, and many other great nineteenth-century writers, and he was drawn as well to the early modern picaresque tradition and to the epistolary novels of the eighteenth century. So it was no coincidence that he pointed me toward Smollett, who wouldn't have been on everyone's reading list, but whose *Expedition of Humphry Clinker* is one of the great experiments in multivoiced epistolary writing. Five years before I met him, Bellow had won the National Book Award and reached the bestseller lists with *Herzog*, much of which takes the form of rambling letters written by his querulous, idea-besotted hero to a wide range of imagined recipients. They're imagined because Herzog never actually sends these missives to his old friends, former lovers, and ex-wives, and he couldn't in any event have sent the ones addressed to figures such as Nietzsche and God.

The closest model for Bellow's previous novel, *Henderson the Rain King* (1959), is another eighteenth-century work: *Candide*. East Africa takes the place of Voltaire's imaginary Brazil as the locale where the hero can encounter a radically non-Western culture, engage in discussions with a local philosopher king, and gradually come to terms with his own world. Henderson's principal involvement is with an isolated tribe called the Wariri. In a direct evocation of Voltaire's El Dorado, the Wariri territory is hidden from the outside world by mountains, and its King Dahfu even has a retinue of "female soldiers or amazons" (141). Like Voltaire, Bellow had never been to his exotic other-world, but he could base his scenes on more than travelers' tales. He'd studied anthropology at Northwestern and the University of Wisconsin, and his novel is grounded in anthropologists' accounts. Many of the tribal customs in *Henderson*, and some actual passages, are taken from *The Cattle Complex in East Africa* (1926) by Melville Herskovits, under whom Bellow had written his senior thesis.

Bellow is thought of as the quintessential Chicago novelist, but he was living in New York when he wrote *Henderson*. His hero, Eugene Henderson, has somewhat bizarrely started a pig farm on his estate in Connecticut outside New York City, where he goes to get his violin repaired on 57th Street "from an old Hungarian fellow named Haponyi" (30)—Bellow's New York was a city of immigrants like himself. Henderson even maps the city onto his own body: "My face is like some sort of terminal; it's like Grand Central, I mean— the big horse nose and the wide mouth that opens into the nostrils, and eyes like tunnels" (54). When he bolts to Africa in search of himself, he continues to orient himself through New York reference points. Thus King Dahfu's voice has a humming undertone that "reminded me of that power station on 16th Street in New York on a hot night" (208).

The best explanation Henderson can give for his sudden flight is that "there was a disturbance in my heart, a voice that spoke there and said, *I want! I want! I want!* It happened every afternoon" (29). In Africa, Henderson spends time with a peaceful tribe, the Arnewi, before moving on to the warlike Wariri. Such a pairing of opposite tribal mentalities was a staple of the discourse of figures such as Henry Morton Stanley, who undertook to pacify the warriors and exploit the peaceful tribes, and it has to be said that Bellow's novel continues to rely on some of the old imperialist tropes that Chinua Achebe found so offensive in Conrad's *Heart of Darkness*. Yet Henderson fails spectacularly at imperial mastery. In the chapters on his time among the Arnewi, the novel turns into the last of our project's plague narratives. The cattle are dying for lack of water, as there's been an extended drought and the huge cistern in which the village stores up water has been rendered unusable by a plague of frogs. As Henderson tells the villagers, "I thought I knew what it was to suffer from a plague and sympathized. I realized that they had to feed on the bread of tears and I hoped I wasn't going to be a bother here" (73).

Henderson can't resist taking on the White Man's Burden of solving the natives' problems for them. In a harebrained scheme, he makes a small bomb that he throws into the cistern, intending to kill the frogs. But the explosion breaks the cistern, and all the water is lost. Embarrassed, Henderson simply leaves. He next finds himself among the Wariri, where he briefly becomes the Sungo, or "Rain King," after moving the weighty statue of an idol whom no one in the tribe can lift; when this deed is done, rain magically appears. It eventually turns out, though, that he's been set up for this victory by enemies of King Dahfu, who want to get rid of him and decide that an ignorant outsider will be a successor they can control.

Before these events unspool, Henderson becomes attached to Dahfu, who has traveled widely, studied medicine, and is a great reader. Like Hugh Lofting's Bumpo, Dahfu speaks in an overly elaborate English ("I esteem you to be very strong. Oh, vastly," 154), but Bellow isn't making fun of the king. He uses him as a kind of oracular voice, full of psychological acuity based on extensive reading ("James, *Psychology*, a very attractive book," 222). Dahfu has deep insight into the human condition and into Henderson in particular.

"You illustrate volumes," he said. "To me you are a treasure of illustrations. I do not condemn your looks. Only I see the world in your constitution. In my medical study this became the greatest of fascinations to me and independently I have made a thorough study of the types, resulting in an entire classification system, as: The agony. The appetite. The obstinate . . .

The mad laughers. The pedantics. The fighting Lazaruses. Oh, Henderson-Sungo, how many shapes and forms! Numberless!" (205)

Increasingly, Dahfu starts to sound like Bellow's New York psychiatrist: "You show the work of a powerful and original although blockaded imagination," Dahfu tells him. "You are an exceptional amalgam of vehement forces" (254). He assigns Henderson an exhausting and dangerous series of exercises in an underground cell where he keeps a lion, forcing Henderson to strip naked and get in touch with his inner animal. This sounds like a bizarre Orientalist fantasy, but in fact it's a parodically heightened version of Bellow's experience with his Reichian analyst, who for two years made him lie naked during their sessions. Annoyed as he is by this treatment, Henderson comes to a new sense of himself, and he is able to return home to put his life in order. Enough of endless "becoming," he decides: "Time to Be! Burst the spirit's sleep. Wake up, America! Stump the experts" (153). Bellow has built his Africa out of New York, as its negative image—a reversed mirror that may shock America awake.

Bellow called *Henderson* his favorite among his books, and he said that he'd put more of himself into Henderson than into any of his other characters. This claim may seem surprising, since characters like Moses Herzog and Mr. Sammler display more direct resemblances. But as with Africa, Bellow has created his hero by inversion: where he was a poor Jewish immigrant from Canada, son of a semiliterate bootlegger, Henderson is a WASP living on the Connecticut estate he's inherited from his father, who was both a multimillionaire and the author of several books. Where Bellow was rakishly handsome, though slight of stature, Henderson is huge and ugly, a wrestler of immense strength. Whereas his Connecticut estate features well-watered fields and well-fed pigs, he travels to a drought-stricken East African savannah where the cattle are dying of thirst. By transforming New York and Connecticut into an imaginary Africa, and himself into his physical and cultural opposite, Bellow found the distance he needed to see himself and his country more clearly. He'd returned to the U.S. after trying a couple of years in Paris, where he'd become friends with James Baldwin, and now he was ready to bring the world in. As he reflects of Dahfu, "Christ! What a person to meet at this distance from home. Yes, travel is advisable. And believe me, the world is a mind. Travel is mental travel" (159).

80. J. R. R. Tolkien, *The Lord of the Rings*

Our own imagined journey reaches its end, as we return to England with our eightieth book. *The Lord of the Rings* seemed ideal for this purpose, for several reasons: as the riveting account of an epic quest "there and back again" (to recall *The Hobbit*'s subtitle); as a book very much about books (and manuscripts, tales, and legends); as the most popular novel of the twentieth century and quite likely of all time, with 150 *million* sales to date; as a book born in the aftermath of one world war and completed after the second one; and on a personal level, as the epic novel that remained the book of books for me throughout my adolescence and that has continued to unfold new dimensions as I read and teach it today.

Like More's Utopia and Saul Bellow's Africa, Tolkien's Middle-earth is an imaginary realm that is inextricably intertwined with our own. Rather than showing us witches breaking in on everyday life, as Madeleine L'Engle does in *A Wrinkle in Time*, Tolkien takes the opposite tack: he takes us into a vast world of imaginary beings in which humans are only one race among many. In one of Tolkien's many brilliant choices, his central heroes are hobbits, liminal figures with a furry foot in each realm. They seem as British as can be, and yet they aren't human beings at all, and they have to make their way in a far wider world than they're used to dealing with in their quiet little corner of Eriador. Tolkien's imaginative vision enables him to give vivid individuality within every order of Middle-earth's beings. The wizard Saruman the White, tragically seduced by power, presents a different trajectory than Gandalf the Grey, who resists the Ring's seductive power, while their colleague Radagast the Brown shows the danger of an innocence that shades over into gullibility. The Ent patriarch

Treebeard struggles to understand the minds of hobbits, whose lives are measured in decades, not centuries, and there's variety even among Ents, as we see with the impatient Quickbeam, who earned his name when he answered a question before Treebeard had even finished asking it.

Like Lofting and L'Engle, and like Lewis Carroll before them, in *The Hobbit* Tolkien had relied on a child's easy ability to enter into fantasy as soon as a parrot teaches a doctor all the animal languages, or Alice plunges down a rabbit hole. But for *The Lord of the Rings* he set himself a different task: to make his fantasy world persuasive to adults, now in the company of classics such as *Beowulf* and *Sir Gawain and the Green Knight* that he treasured, edited, and taught. He did so by grounding his fiction in the real world, or rather in three overlapping worlds in which he spent his life: his nation, racked by successive wars; his Catholic faith; and his profession, as a scholar of medieval languages and literatures.

The trilogy is centered on an epochal world war, and though Tolkien always rather implausibly denied that his story had anything to do with World War II, he did admit a connection to his traumatic experiences during World War I. He fought in the Battle of the Somme in 1916, and all but one of his close friends were killed in the trenches by the war's end. He began elaborating his vast fantasy world in 1917, after being invalided back to England, starting with a manuscript resonantly titled *The Book of Lost Tales*. The Dead Marshes in between Gondor and Mordor echo the killing fields of Flanders, and whereas in Peter Jackson's film version the orcs are horror-movie creatures with overtones of some Oriental Yellow Peril, Tolkien's orcs are more complicated, and more realistic. Crude and violent though they are, they can sound like enlisted men in the trenches, sent to die in droves by their incompetent commanders. As one orc snarls to another, as the tide of the War of the Ring begins to turn, "Whose blame is that? . . . Not mine. That comes from Higher Up." His companion agrees:

> "Ar!" said the tracker. "They've lost their heads, that's what it is. And some of the bosses are going to lose their skins too, I guess, if what I hear is true:

Tower raided and all, and hundreds of your lads done in, and prisoner got away. If that's the way your fighters go on, small wonder there's bad news from the battles."

"Who says there's bad news?" shouted the soldier.

"Ar! Who says there isn't?"[12]

Shaped by Tolkien's wartime experience, *The Lord of the Rings* is also a deeply religious work. Unlike Madeleine L'Engle, Tolkien didn't try to transplant Christianity into his alternative world, but you really can't throw a piece of elvish *lembas* without hitting a Christ figure: the man of sorrows, Aragorn; Gandalf the Grey, who dies and comes back to life transfigured as Gandalf the White; and young Frodo, who prepares to sacrifice himself to save the world. Crucially, he succeeds because he avoids the prideful temptation of power, and because he is merciful when Gollum tries to murder him to steal back the ring that he'd lost to Bilbo in *The Hobbit*. This theme is already signaled at the very outset, when Gandalf tells Frodo that Sauron's henchmen are now seeking the Ring in the Shire.

"But this is terrible!" cried Frodo. "Far worse than the worst that I imagined from your hints and warnings. O Gandalf, best of friends, what am I to do? For now I am really afraid. What am I to do? What a pity that Bilbo did not stab that vile creature, when he had a chance!"

"Pity? It was Pity that stayed his hand. Pity, and Mercy: not to strike without need. And he has been well rewarded, Frodo. Be sure that he took so little hurt from the evil, and escaped in the end, because he began his ownership of the Ring so. With Pity."[13]

Gandalf is an archetypal figure of wisdom and leader of the interspecies—I almost said interdenominational—Fellowship of the Ring, but he is also an oblique self-portrait of his creator. Crucially, Gandalf unravels the identity of Bilbo's Ring by deciphering long-forgotten documents in the royal library in

Minas Tirith. As he says at the Council of Elrond, where the Fellowship is formed, the library holds "many records that few now can read, even of the lore-masters, for their scripts and tongues have become dark to later men" (265). There Gandalf finds a forgotten scroll that reveals how the One Ring would have made its way into Gollum's hands. It's a wonder Gandalf didn't stay another year or two in Minas Tirith to prepare a critical edition.

Tolkien's creation of Middle-earth began with languages and scripts. We already see this emphasis on the title page, with a line of runes above the title and two lines of Tolkien's invented elvish script below. If you decode these inscriptions, using the tables helpfully supplied in the trilogy's extensive appendices, it turns out that these lines aren't in Middle-earth languages at all but are transliterated English: "The Lord of the Rings, translated from The Red Book of Westmarch by John Ronald Reuel Tolkien: and herein is set forth the history of the war of the Ring and the return of the King as seen by the hobbits." So the book is actually a translation of the history written by Tolkien's own creation, Bilbo Baggins. In the first chapter, Bilbo tells Gandalf that he's leaving the Shire in search of "somewhere where I can finish my book. I have thought of a nice ending for it: *and he lived happily ever after to the end of his days.*" Gandalf laughs, and replies: "But nobody will read the book, however it ends" (41). Bilbo retorts that Frodo has already been reading it. Later Frodo has to provide Bilbo with information about the unfolding saga, and finally he has to complete *The Red Book of Westmarch* for Bilbo. Frodo is both the book's first reader and its final author.

In *Utopia*, Thomas More provided his alternative world with a history, a map, and even a page showing the Utopian alphabet. Tolkien too gives us maps as well as alphabets; my 1966 British edition features two-color maps, drawn by his son Christopher, that fold out from the end of each volume, in the style of maps in Victorian travelers' accounts such as we've seen with Henry Morton Stanley (Figure 80).

Yet Tolkien went far beyond More (and quite likely beyond any writer before or since) in creating an entire world beyond the pages of his novel.

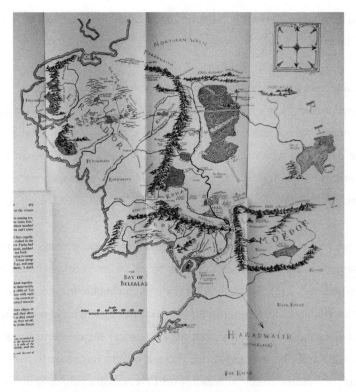

80. Christopher Tolkien, map of Middle-earth

Thomas More couldn't have conducted a conversation in Utopian to save his life, but Tolkien actually invented Elvish, an unreal but fully functioning language. In an essay entitled "A Secret Vice," Tolkien described Elvish as endlessly engrossing "in its intimacy, in its peculiarly shy individualism,"[14] as a language that no one but he could speak. He grounded his trilogy in a massive archive that he'd spent decades composing, and so he can draw with complete naturalness on a fully realized "sub-creation" or "secondary world." He used these terms in 1939, when he was beginning *The Lord of the Rings*, in a lecture—a virtual manifesto—"On Fairy-stories." There he argued against Coleridge's Romantic conception of "the willing suspension of disbelief," which Umberto Eco has described in *Six Walks in the Fictional Woods* as the necessary agreement that a reader makes with a writer.[15] Tolkien saw the fictional compact differently. What has been called "willing suspension of disbelief," he says,

> does not seem to me a good description of what happens. What really
> happens is that the story-maker proves a successful "sub-creator." He makes
> a Secondary World which your mind can enter. Inside it, what he relates is
> "true"; it accords with the laws of that world. You therefore believe it, while
> you are, as it were, inside. The moment disbelief arises, the spell is broken;
> the magic, or rather art, has failed.[16]

In Tolkien's view, it's only when a writer has failed that we have to make ourselves suspend our disbelief, "a subterfuge we use when condescending to games or make-believe" (132). Tolkien didn't want us to chuckle knowingly at the idea of elves and dwarves and then put his book on the shelf with juvenile fiction, or else read on without any serious emotional or ethical engagement. He was intent on creating a fully believable world, though unlike Byron or Joyce he wasn't trying to rival God's creation: hence, Middle-earth is a sub-creation, not to be confused with our own. In Middle-earth, "real" people like Aragorn and Boromir mingle with half-real people (hobbits), "real" fairytale figures (elves, dwarves, wizards), and newly invented beings (orcs, Ents, Nazgul). These characters collectively populate a world that we can enter without ever forgetting that we're in a world of stories that can awaken and guide our moral sympathies.

Ultimately, evil works its own destruction, but it's a very close call, and it takes the courage and resilience of Frodo and his companion Sam Gamgee to make the decisive journey into the heart of Mordor's darkness, culminating in Gollum's fortunate fall into the abyss where the Ring is destroyed. In the book's second chapter, "The Shadow of the Past," an anxious Frodo says that "I wish it need not have happened in my time." "So do I," Gandalf replies, "and so do all who live to see such times. But that is not for them to decide. All we have to decide is what to do with the time that is given us."[17]

The Eighty-first Book

So now we're finally back at the Reform Club where it all began in Verne's novel, right on schedule. You may object, though, that I've exceeded my eighty-book limit, since I began by discussing *Around the World in Eighty Days* as the inspiration for my project. But this isn't really so, any more than Phileas Fogg lost his bet, as he feared, when a last-minute delay caused him to arrive in London at 8:50 p.m., five minutes after he was supposed to appear at the Club. He calmly heads home instead, and spends the next day settling back in. That evening, though, Passepartout buys a newspaper and is astonished to find that it's still the appointed day. It turns out that since they'd circled the globe from east to west, they'd gained a day when they crossed the International Date Line. For my part, in my introduction I include Fogg and Passepartout's travel via hot air balloon among their other means. But they never use a hot air balloon in the novel. This was an addition made by the director of the 1956 movie, who wanted to take advantage of the panoramic effects it allowed. I never actually read the book as a child; it was the film that was lodged in my memory. If Verne was saved by a meridian, I'm saved by a medium.

So where do we go from here? Having notionally returned to the Reform Club's beautifully appointed library, we might take our choice from the polished oak shelves that line the library's walls. In 1884 the Reform Club published a 650-page catalogue of its 75,000 volumes. Many of them deal with social and political issues, as befits the nature of the Club, which was founded in 1836 as a place for gentlemen to smoke, play cards, and discuss governmental reforms, but they also had a good selection of literature.

One good option is always to read more by an author who has caught our eye. If *Candide* has piqued our interest in Voltaire, we can peruse the Club's 62-volume set of his *Oeuvres complètes*. Published between 1775 and 1790, this collection offers many possibilities for further reading, from Voltaire's satirical poetry to his foundational historical study *Siècle de Louis XIV* to an entire volume of his correspondence with Russia's Catherine the Great "et plusieurs Souverains." In a sign of how tastes change over time, *Candide* only appears in volume 31, folded in among his *Romans philosophiques*—far below Voltaire's epic *Henriade* and the nine volumes of his now forgotten dramas.

Alternatively, we could turn to the work that changed my life in the ninth grade, Laurence Sterne's *Tristram Shandy*, which occupies the first four volumes of the Club's ten-volume set of his complete works. We could then go on to Sterne's delightful *Sentimental Journey through France and Italy* (as I did after reading *Tristram Shandy*), and perhaps—or perhaps not—read his collected sermons. We could also follow Sterne's lead to his favorite authors, Cervantes and Rabelais (the latter available in the library either in French or in Urquhart's early translation, the one that Sterne read). Then again, we could employ some version of Doctor Dolittle's randomized technique for picking new destinations. Closing our eyes and feeling our way around the room, we might chance upon one of the Club's ten copies of novels by the reform-minded French writer Edmond About, or we might find the works of Virgil, available either in Latin or in English.

Looking beyond the Reform Club's library, my own inclination might be to return to one of the many books I was hoping to include among my eighty, but that were crowded out by other destinations or other works: perhaps the *Epic of Gilgamesh*, the poetry of Anna Akhmatova, or the *Buru Quartet* by the great Indonesian writer Pramoedya Ananta Toer. One measure of a work's greatness is that it improves on rereading and even on re-rereading. Yet there are always new possibilities to explore, a version of the remote islands that

Judith Schalansky has never seen, though unlike her I'd opt for books I *would* finally like to read—Dostoevsky's *The Double*, Musil's *The Man without Qualities*, George Eliot's *The Mill on the Floss*, Tanizaki's *The Makioka Sisters*, all of which have been sitting on my shelves for years, awaiting their turn with silent reproach.

We could also read recent works by the contemporary authors discussed here, from Margaret Atwood's Booker-winning dystopian *The Testaments* (2019)—a rare example in the history of literature of a sequel that's even better than its brilliant predecessor, *The Handmaid's Tale*, written three decades earlier. There is an entire series of new Inspector Brunetti mysteries by Donna Leon, including the enticingly titled *Transient Desires* (2021), as well as D. A. Mishani's chilling (non-)sequel *Three*, whose focus shifts from Avi Abraham to a woman detective. Or to pursue further the epidemic theme, we can turn to Orhan Pamuk's *Nights of Plague* (2021, English translation 2022), presciently set in an outbreak of plague in the Ottoman era.

Returning to London, we could proceed to works that reflect the ongoing globalization already foreshadowed in *Mrs. Dalloway*. Samuel Selvon's *The Lonely Londoners* (1954) is a key portrayal of postwar London from the perspective of postwar Caribbean immigrants; it's currently published in the UK as a Penguin Modern Classic. More recently, Andrea Levy's *Small Island* (2004) looks back to her father's immigrant experience. We could go on to the Trinidadian Nobel laureate V. S. Naipaul; his writings are often gloomy (Derek Walcott sardonically refers in a poem to "V. S. Nightfall"), but his memoir *Finding the Centre* beautifully evokes the struggle of a displaced young writer seeking to find himself in the old imperial center and to find the center of gravity of his own writing. We can also turn to another Nobel laureate, Kazuo Ishiguro, or to the novelist and film maker Hanif Kureishi, and to Zadie Smith, whose *White Teeth* (2000) centers on a family that resembles her own (the parents are a Jamaican mother and an English father), as they interact with the Iqbals from Bangladesh and the part-Jewish Chalfonts. Even in London, we're now a long way from Bloomsbury.

Whichever direction we choose, we certainly can't stop with eighty. Jules Verne didn't content himself with sending his heroes around the world in eighty days, but also propelled them to the moon and immersed them 20,000 leagues under the sea. In antiquity, restless Odysseus was said to have left Ithaca late in life, not for another sea voyage but for its opposite, a journey on land until he'd find a place where people wouldn't know what an oar was used for. The list of new literary destinations is endless. With the world falling apart in so many ways, and the pandemic's aftershocks likely to long remain with us, it's good to connect in the ways we can, over the things that matter to all of us, as we tend our gardens and perform *le tour du monde dans nos chambres*.

81. Giorgio de Chirico, The Return of Ulysses *(1968)*

Acknowledgments

This book comes as much from other people as from other books. Miss Staats, as I first knew her (now Maggie Staats Simmons), appears in these pages almost as a fairytale donor figure, complete with the requisite three gifts (a book at the outset, then a drawing and a letter from the two Sauls she introduced me to). Over the years my wife, Lori Fisler Damrosch, and I have shared many books and many travels together. Following the life-changing production of *Trial by Jury* that I've recalled in the Introduction, we've traveled to almost all of this book's venues (London, Paris, Poland, Italy, Cairo, Istanbul, Israel, Iran, India, China, Japan, South America, Mexico, and the Caribbean), pursuing our overlapping interests in comparative literature and international law, along with raising our three children—avid readers all—in New York and spending our summers on Mount Desert Island in Maine, where most of this book was written. I grew up trading books with my brother Tom, and our brother Leo has long been a model for me in writing about literature with clarity and force.

Most directly, this book owes its existence to Laura Stickney at Pelican Books in London, who asked several years ago whether I might like to do a book on world literature for general readers. She has been unfailingly supportive since then, and it's been a great pleasure to work with her, and now also with her colleague Virginia Smith at Penguin in the USA. I am very grateful as well for the eloquence and skill of my agent, Eric Simonoff, in presenting the book to publishers in the best possible way.

In its initial virtual version, beautifully designed by Smaranda Murarus, *Around the World in 80 Books* benefitted greatly from comments and queries by followers around the world, especially several people who offered repeated insights: RaNa Atef, Daniel Behar, Lux Chen, Annemarie Fischer, Szymon Gebur, Lucy He, Ashmita Khashnabish, Tadeusz Różewicz, Frank Wang, Laura Wilhelm, and Teodor-Ștefan Zotescu. I received welcome feedback from colleagues in my department and in the Institute for World Literature, particularly Luis Girón-Negrón, Martin Puchner, Bruce Robbins, Mads Rosendahl Thomsen, Galin Tihanov, Delia Ungureanu, Saul Zaritt, and Zhang Longxi. A memorable conversation in Budapest with Péter Dávidházi crystallized my approach to Auschwitz and its personal and literary legacy.

The online project also benefitted from the work of its translators: Michael Yacoub and his colleagues in Cairo for the Arabic translation; Mingwei Song at Wellesley and his team of collaborators in China; Annemarie Fischer for German; Georgeta Constantin and Monica Dobrescu for Romanian; Višnja Krstić for Serbian; Manuel Azuaje Alamo for Spanish; Deniz Gundogan Ibrisim and her colleagues for Turkish; and Olha Voznyuk for Ukrainian. I am grateful to Maayan Eitan for putting me in touch with Dror Mishani, to Mounira Hejaiej for connecting me with Jokha Alharthi, to Tarek El-Ariss for introducing me to Emily Jacir, and to Zhang Yanping for connecting me with Bei Dao. I am grateful as well to Claire Péligry for her excellent copyediting of the manuscript. First in its blog version and then as *Around the World in 80 Books* has itself become a book, my wife, Lori, read the postings and the manuscript with care and a keen editorial eye, and the resulting book has gained significantly from her involvement throughout the project.

My mother-in-law, Jean Bauer Fisler—one of the first Americans to receive a tourist visa for postwar Poland—took the photo of the Auschwitz gate which illustrates Chapter 3. Even in her final illness, which coincided with the completion of the manuscript of this book, Jean was looking forward at age ninety-five to getting back on another airplane, or in any case to reading about another journey.

Earlier versions of various entries first appeared in academic books of mine, *What Is World Literature?* (2003), *How to Read World Literature* (2009, 2017), and *Comparing the Literatures: Literary Studies in a Global Age* (2020). Some derive from my classes over the years, while in other cases, this project brought me back to writers I'd read years or even decades before, and sometimes a location's theme led me to a work I'd always meant to read. So this has been a voyage of discovery in the present as well as recovery of the past.

I feel a special debt to my great-aunt Helen Damrosch Tee-Van, two of whose drawings appear in this book. Born in 1893, she was my living link to the musical world she'd grown up in (she remembered Mahler coming to dinner), and she was an inspiration as an artist and writer, a world traveler, and a great raconteur, sharing her memories of friends as varied as Amelia Earhart, Madame Chiang Kai-shek, and E. B. White. Her final idea for a book came to her at age seventy-five, in a dream in which Batman appeared at her window and told her to write a book about bats. A newspaper profile from the 1930s shows her in the Caribbean, decked out in a diving helmet, painting fish underwater so as to get the colors just right. She told me that she used to tie her brushes to the easel to keep them from floating away. I dedicate this book to her memory: may she never rest in peace.

Credits

ILLUSTRATIONS

Figure 1:   "The Emperor of Abyssinia and his Suite," *Daily Mirror*, February 16, 1910. © National Portrait Gallery, London.

Figure 2:   Charles Dickens, *Great Expectations* (Baltimore: Penguin English Library, 1965; and London: Penguin Classics, 1996).

Figure 3:   Virginia Woolf, *Mrs. Dalloway* (New York: Harcourt Brace Jovanovich, 1981); Arnold Bennett, *Riceyman Steps* (London: Penguin, 1991).

Figure 4:   Henri Raczymow, *Le Paris retrouvé de Marcel Proust* (Paris: Parigramme, 2005).

Figure 5:   Djuna Barnes, portraits of Gertrude Stein and James Joyce. Djuna Barnes papers, Special Collections and University Archives, University of Maryland Libraries.

Figure 6:   Marguerite Duras, *The Lover* (New York: Harper & Row, 1985); Jean-Jacques Annaud and Benoît Barbier, *L'Amant: Un film de Jean-Jacques Annaud*. Paris: Grasset, 1992.

Figure 7:   Axolotl, Warren Photographic; portrait of Jorge Luis Borges by Eddie Kelly, *Irish Times*, 1982.

Figure 8:   *In Memoriam—Leopold Damrosch*, *Puck* magazine, New York, 1885.

Figure 9:   Poznań old town, photograph by David Damrosch, 2013.

Figure 10: Auschwitz entrance, photograph by Jean Bauer Fisler, 1948.

Figure 11: Anselm Kiefer, *Für Paul Celan: Aschenblüme* (2006, detail). Photo by Raphael Gaillarde / Gamma-Rapho via Getty Images.

Figure 12: Saint Petersburg map (1850), in Olga Tokarczuk, *Flights* (New York: Riverhead Books, 2018), 37.

Figure 13: Domenico di Michelino, *La commedia illumina Firenze* (c. 1465). Niday Picture Library / Alamy Stock Photo.

Figure 14: Louis Chalon, illustration for *The Decameron* (London: A. H. Bullen, 1903).

Figure 15: Karina Puente Frantzen, *Valdrada City*. © Karina Puente Frantzen.

Figure 16: Pyramid burial chamber ramp, Sakkara; el-Fishawy Café, Cairo. Photographs by David Damrosch, 2005.

Figure 17: Egyptian musicians, tomb of Djeserkareseneb, Thebes, c. 1400 B.C.E., copied in 1921–2. Metropolitan Museum of Art, New York, Rogers Fund 1930.

Figure 18: Edward William Lane, from *Description of Egypt: Notes and Views in Egypt and Nubia* (1831; Cairo: American University in Cairo Press, 2000). Harvard University Libraries.

Figure 19: Emily Jacir, *Materials for a Film (Performance)*, 2008. Courtesy of Emily Jacir.

Figure 20: Portrait of Orhan Pamuk in the Museum of Innocence, Istanbul, by Ali Betil. © Innocence Foundation-Masumiyet Vakfı, courtesy of Orhan Pamuk.

Figure 21: Jokha Alharthi, *Celestial Bodies* (New York: Catapult, 2019).

Figure 22: *"Look out. You drop that box, I'll shoot you!"* Henry Morton Stanley, *How I Found Livingstone: Travels, Adventures and Discoveries in Central Africa* (New York: Scribner, Armstrong, 1872), 642.

Figure 23: *A Map of the Emin Pasha Relief Expedition through Africa.* Henry Morton Stanley, *In Darkest Africa: or the Quest, Rescue, and Retreat of Emin, Governor of Equatoria* (New York: Scribner's, 1890), pocket insert in Vol. 1.

Figure 24: Studio photograph of Elizabeth Hammond and Leopold Damrosch, Bontoc, Philippines, 1940.

Figure 25: Elizabeth Hammond Damrosch, *Mountain Province Women* (c. 1949).

Figure 26: Yorùbá People, Egúngún Masquerade Dance Costume, early to mid-twentieth century. Collection of the Birmingham Museum of Art, Alabama; Anonymous gift.

Figure 27: Wall panel relief, South West Palace of Sennacherib, Nineveh, Assyria, c. 700 B.C.E. (detail). British Museum.

Figure 28: View from Masada, looking toward the Dead Sea. Photograph by David Damrosch, 2014.

Figure 29: Dror Mishani, *Tik ne'edar* (Jerusalem: Keter Books, 2011); *The Missing File* (New York: HarperCollins, 2013).

Figure 30: Freda Guttman, *The Earth Is Closing on Us: The Nakba.* © Freda Guttman.

Figure 31: Ali Essa, mosaic of Mahmoud Darwish's line "He thinks of the journey of ideas across borders." Madaba, Jordan, 2014.

Figure 32: Airport sign, Tehran. Photograph by Lori Fisler Damrosch, 2011.

Figure 33: Marjane Satrapi, *The Complete Persepolis* (New York: Pantheon, 2004), 142.

Figure 34: Marjane Satrapi, *The Complete Persepolis* (New York: Pantheon, 2004), 28.

Figure 35: *Zal is Sighted by a Caravan.* Attributed to 'Abdul-'Aziz, Tabriz, Iran, c. 1525. Arthur M. Sackler Gallery, Smithsonian Institution, Washington, DC: The Art and History Collection, LTS1995.2.46 (detail).

Figure 36: Left: Verses in Praise of Sultan Hasan 'Ali Shah and Verses by Hafiz, folio from an album. Right: Poet Conversing with Drinkers in a Tavern, illustrated folio 116 from a *divan* of Hafiz, c. 1550. Harvard Art Museums / Arthur M. Sackler Museum, Gifts of John Goelet. © President and Fellows of Harvard College.

Figure 37: Stacey Chase, portrait of Agha Shahid Ali. Copyright © 1990, Stacey Chase.

Figure 38: Helen Damrosch Tee-Van, portrait of Rabindranath Tagore, 1916. Collection of the author.

Figure 39: Jamyang Norbu, *Sherlock Holmes: The Missing Years* (New York: Bloomsbury, 2001); *The Mandala of Sherlock Holmes: The Missing Years* (London: John Murray, 2000); *The Mandala of Sherlock Holmes: The Adventures of the Great Detective in India and Tibet* (New York: Bloomsbury, 2003).

CREDITS

Figure 40: Carvings on the Temple of the Sun, Konarak, Orissa, India, thirteenth century. Werner Forman Archive, HIP / Art Resource, NY.

Figure 41: *La Jeunesse / New Youth* magazine, cover and sample page, 1916. Harvard-Yenching Library, Harvard University.

Figure 42: Eileen Chang, Hong Kong, 1954 (photographer unknown).

Figure 43: "The Tractor-ploughing Squadron" (1965). Stefan R. Landsberger / Private Collection. International Institute of Social History (Amsterdam), https://chineseposters.net.

Figure 44: Bei Dao, *Moment* (2013). Courtesy of Bei Dao.

Figure 45: Low-ranking geishas, Yoshiwara district, Tokyo, 1890s. Pump Park Collection / MeijiShowa.

Figure 46: Young Murasaki (Wakamurasaki), Illustration to Chapter 5 of *The Tale of Genji*, mid-seventeenth century. Harvard Art Museums / Arthur M. Sackler Museum, Gift of Charles Parker. © President and Fellows of Harvard College.

Figure 47: Painting by Morikawa Kyoriku, with calligraphy by Matsuo Bashō (1693). Tenri Central Library, Tenri University. The Picture Art Collection / Alamy Stock Photo.

Figure 48: James Merrill, 1973 © Jill Krementz.

Figure 49: James Merrill, c. 1992 (photographer unknown). James Merrill Papers, Julian Edison Department of Special Collections, Washington University Libraries.

Figure 50: Theodore Galle, after Jan Van der Straet, *Vespucci Awakening America* (early 1600s). Sarah Campbell Blaffer Foundation, Houston.

Figure 51: Johannes Janssonius, *Guiana sive Amazonum regio*, Amsterdam, 1647. Collection of the author.

Figure 52: Jean-Michel Moreau, le Jeune, illustration for Voltaire's *Candide*, 1787.

Figure 53: Left: Portrait of Machado de Assis in 1864 (photographer unknown), Acervo da Fundação Biblioteca Nacional, Rio de Janeiro. Right: Portrait of Machado in 1884 by Joaquim Insley Pacheco, Gilberto Ferrez Collection / Instituto Moreira Salles.

Figure 54: Statue of Clarice Lispector, Copacabana, Rio de Janeiro. Photograph by Simon Mayer (Adobe Stock).

Figure 55: Mask of La Malinche, Guerrero, Mexico, c. 1980. Collection of the author.

Figure 56: Aztec surrender, *Lienza de Tlaxcala*, sixteenth century. Artwork published in *Homenaje a Cristobal Colon: Antiguedades mexicanas* (1892). British Museum, Science Photo Library.

Figure 57: Palenque temples, Chiapas, Mexico. Photograph by David Damrosch, 1983.

Figure 58: Andrés de Islas, portrait of Sor Juana Inés de la Cruz, 1772. Museo de América, Madrid.

Figure 59: Miguel Ángel Asturias, headstone and portrait. Headstone photograph courtesy of Professor Jorge Antonio Leoni de León; portrait from UNESCO.

Figure 60: Derek Walcott, *Omeros* (New York: Farrar, Straus and Giroux, 1990); *Tiepolo's Hound* (New York: Farrar, Straus and Giroux, 2000).

Figure 61: Portrait of Jean Rhys as a young woman (Bridgeman Images), and in 1976 by Elizabeth Vreeland in Jean Rhys, *Smile Please: An Unfinished Autobiography* (New York: Harper & Row, 1979).

Figure 62: Helen Damrosch Tee-Van, *Sargassum Fish among its floating weed*. In William Beebe, *Nonsuch: Land of Water* (New York: Brewer, Warren and Putnam, 1932), 97.

Figure 63: Florence and Robert Dean Frisbie examining her book, in Brandon Oswald, *Mr. Moonlight of the South Seas: The Extraordinary Life of Robert Dean Frisbie* (Newport

CREDITS

Beach, CA: Dockside Sailing Press, 2nd ed. 2017), 126; *Miss Ulysses of Puka-Puka: The Autobiography of a South Sea Trader's Daughter* (Newport Beach, CA: Dockside Sailing Press, 2nd ed. 2016).

Figure 64: Judith Schalansky, *Atlas of Remote Islands: Fifty Islands I Have Never Set Foot On and Never Will* (London and New York: Penguin, 2010), 102.

Figure 65: Robert McCloskey, *One Morning in Maine* (New York: Viking, 1952), 10.

Figure 66: Robert McCloskey, *One Morning in Maine* (New York: Viking, 1952), 62–3.

Figure 67: Photograph of Annie Fields and Sarah Orne Jewett, in M. A. De Wolfe Howe, *Memories of a Hostess: A Chronicle of Eminent Friendships, Drawn Chiefly from the Diaries of Mrs. James T. Fields* (Boston: Atlantic Monthly Press, 1922), 349.

Figure 68: Marguerite Yourcenar in her kitchen at "Petite Plaisance," 1979. Photograph by Jean-Pierre Laffont, © J P Laffont.

Figure 69: Grace Frick's headstone, Brookside Cemetery, Somesville, Maine. Photograph by David Damrosch, 2020.

Figure 70: Frontispiece to Hugh Lofting, *The Voyages of Doctor Dolittle* (Philadelphia: Lippincott, 1922, 1950).

Figure 71: "The Terrible Three." Hugh Lofting, *The Voyages of Doctor Dolittle* (Philadelphia: Lippincott, 1922, 1950), 279.

Figure 72: E. B. White, *Stuart Little* (New York: Harper & Brothers, 1945), 1.

Figure 73: E. B. White, *Stuart Little* (New York: Harper & Brothers, 1945), 130.

Figure 74: Madeleine L'Engle, *A Wrinkle in Time* (New York: Farrar, Straus and Giroux, 1962), 76.

Figure 75: Saul Steinberg, *Bleecker Street*, 1970. © The Saul Steinberg Foundation / Artists Rights Society (ARS), New York.

Figure 76: Saul Steinberg, *Untitled*, 1968. © The Saul Steinberg Foundation / Artists Rights Society (ARS), New York.

Figure 77: Saul Steinberg, *Prosperity (The Pursuit of Happiness)*, 1958–9. © The Saul Steinberg Foundation / Artists Rights Society (ARS), New York.

Figure 78: Saul Steinberg, *Ship of State*, 1959. © The Saul Steinberg Foundation / Artists Rights Society (ARS), New York.

Figure 79: Sophie Bassouls, photograph of James Baldwin in Paris, 1972, via Getty Images.

Figure 80: Christopher J. R. Tolkien, map of Middle-earth. Endpaper to J. R. R. Tolkien, *The Fellowship of the Ring* (London: Allen and Unwin, 2nd ed., 1966).

Figure 81: Giorgio de Chirico, *The Return of Ulysses*, 1968. Artists Rights Society (ARS), New York.

TEXT PERMISSIONS

Ali, Agha Shahid: "Arabic," "Tonight," and "Existed," from *Call Me Ishmael Tonight: A Book of Ghazals* (New York: W. W. Norton, 2003).

Attar, Farid ud-Din: *The Conference of the Birds* (London: Penguin, 2011). Translation © 1984 Afkham Darbandi and Dick Davis.

Aztec poetry: John Bierhorst, ed. and tr., *Cantares Mexicanos: Songs of the Aztecs* (Stanford: Stanford University Press, 1985).

Bashō, Matsuo: *The Narrow Road to the Deep North: And Other Travel Sketches* (London: Penguin Classics, 1967). Translation © Nobuyuki Yuasa.

Notes

Introduction: The Voyage Out

1 Laurence Sterne, *The Life and Opinions of Tristram Shandy, Gentleman* (London: Penguin, 2003), 173.
2 Xavier de Maistre, *Voyage Around My Room*, tr. Stephen Sartarelli (New York: New Directions, 1994).
3 Apuleius, *Metamorphoses*, ed. and tr. J. Arthur Hanson (Cambridge, MA: Harvard University Press, 2 vols., 1989, 1996). *The Golden Ass*, ed. and tr. P. G. Walsh (Oxford: Oxford University Press, 1994), 3.

Chapter 1: London: Inventing a City

1 Virginia Woolf, *Mrs. Dalloway* (New York: Harcourt Brace Jovanovich, 1981), 4.
2 Ann Martin, "Sky Haunting: The British Motor-Car Industry and the World Wars," *Virginia Woolf Writing the World*, ed. Pamela L. Caughie and Diana Swanson (Clemson, SC: Clemson University Press, 2015), 52.
3 Joseph Conrad, *Heart of Darkness*, ed. Ross C. Murfin (Boston: Bedford St. Martins, 2011), 20.
4 Virginia Woolf, "The Russian Point of View," *The Common Reader, First Series*, ed. Andrew McNellie (New York: Harcourt, 2002), 182.
5 Virginia Woolf, letter to Roger Fry, *The Question of Things Happening: The Letters of Virginia Woolf, 1912–1922*, ed. Nigel Nicolson and Joanne Trautmann (London: Hogarth Press, 1976), 565.
6 Woolf, "How It Strikes a Contemporary," *The Common Reader*, 234.
7 Virginia Woolf, letter to Lytton Strachey, quoted in Michael Holroyd, *Lytton Strachey* (London: Heinemann, 1968), 2:368.
8 Virginia Woolf, *A Room of One's Own* (New York: Harcourt Brace Jovanovich, 1989), 100.
9 Virginia Woolf, "David Copperfield," *The Moment and Other Essays* (New York: Harcourt, 1948), 78.
10 Oscar Wilde, "The Decay of Lying," *Intentions* (New York: Brentano, 1905), 41.
11 Quoted in Ada Leverson, *Letters to the Sphinx from Oscar Wilde* (London: Duckworth, 1930), 42.
12 Charles Dickens, *Great Expectations* (London: Penguin, 2005), 3.

13 Virginia Woolf, "Mr. Bennett and Mrs. Brown," *The Captain's Death Bed and Other Essays* (New York: Harcourt, Brace, 1950), 103.

14 Arthur Conan Doyle, *The Complete Sherlock Holmes* (Garden City, NY: Doubleday, 2 vols., 1930), 1:19–20.

15 Patrick J. Lyons, "The Giant Rat of Sumatra, Alive and Well," *The New York Times*, December 17, 2007. https://thelede.blogs.nytimes.com/2007/12/17/the-giant -rat-of-sumatra-alive-and-well/.

16 P. G. Wodehouse, *Wodehouse on Wodehouse* (London: Penguin, 1981), 313.

17 P. G. Wodehouse, introduction to Arthur Conan Doyle, *The Sign of the Four* (New York: Ballantine, 1985), iii.

18 P. G. Wodehouse, *Jeeves and the Feudal Spirit* (New York: Harper & Row, 1954), 6.

19 P. G. Wodehouse, *Carry On, Jeeves* (Harmondsworth: Penguin, 1977), 30.

20 P. G. Wodehouse, *Something Fresh* (London: Penguin, 1979); *Something New* (New York: Ballantine, 1972), 14–15.

21 P. G. Wodehouse, *Summer Lightning* (New York: W. W. Norton, 2012), 5.

22 Wodehouse, *Something Fresh*, 7.

23 P. G. Wodehouse, "The Clicking of Cuthbert," *The Most of P. G. Wodehouse* (New York: Simon & Schuster, 1960), 394.

24 Virginia Woolf, *A Change of Perspective: The Letters of Virginia Woolf 1923–1928*, ed. Nigel Nicolson and Joanne Trautmann (London: Hogarth Press, 1977), 100–101.

25 Arnold Bennett, "Is the Novel Decaying?," *The Author's Craft and Other Critical Writings of Arnold Bennett* (Lincoln: University of Nebraska Press, 1968), 88.

26 Woolf, "Mr. Bennett and Mrs. Brown," 105.

27 Arnold Bennett, *Journals*, ed. Newman Flower (London: Cassell, 1932), 1:68.

Chapter 2: Paris: Writers' Paradise

1 Marcel Proust, *Swann's Way* (*In Search of Lost Time*, vol. 1), tr. C. K. Scott Moncrieff and Terence Kilmartin, rev. by D. J. Enright (New York: Modern Library, 1992), 60–61.

2 https://parisinstitute.org/quarantine-quill/.

3 Marcel Proust, *Contre Sainte-Beuve*, in *Marcel Proust on Art and Literature*, tr. Sylvia Townsend Warner (New York: Carroll & Graf, 1997), 19.

4 Marcel Proust, *Time Regained* (*In Search of Lost Time*, vol. 6), tr. Andreas Mayor and Terence Kilmartin, rev. by D. J. Enright (New York: Modern Library, 1993), 261.

5 Djuna Barnes, *Nightwood* (New York: New Directions, 2006), 73.

6 Marguerite Duras, *The Lover*, tr. Barbara Bray (New York: Harper & Row, 1986), 3.

7 Marguerite Duras, *Wartime Writings 1943–1949*, ed. Sophie Bogaert and Olivier Corpet, tr. Linda Coverdale (New York: New Press, 2009), 16.

8 "Les cinquante ans de 'Marelle,' livre culte de l'Argentin Julio Cortázar," *Le Monde*, May, 10 2013.

9 Julio Cortázar, "Axolotl," *The End of the Game and Other Stories*, tr. Paul Blackburn (New York: Harper & Row, 1967), 9.

10 My translation, from Rainer Maria Rilke, *Neue Gedichte* (1907), https://de.wikisource.org /wiki/Der_Panther.

11 Jorge Luis Borges, "Pierre Menard, Author of the *Quixote*," *Collected Fictions*, tr. Alexander Hurley (New York: Viking, 1998), 91.

12 Jorge Luis Borges, "Borges and I," *Collected Fictions*, 324.
13 Georges Perec, *Entretiens et conférences*, ed. Dominique Bertelli and Mireille Ribière (Nantes: Joseph K., 2003), 1:49.
14 David Bellos, *Georges Perec: A Life in Words* (London: Harville, 1999), 360.
15 Georges Perec, *W, or The Memory of Childhood*, tr. David Bellos (Boston: Godine, 1988), iii.

Chapter 3: Kraków: After Auschwitz

1   Primo Levi, *If This Is a Man*, tr. Stuart Woolf (New York: Orion, 1959), 134.
2   Primo Levi, *The Drowned and the Saved*, tr. Raymond Rosenthal (New York: Simon & Schuster, 1988), 124–6.
3   Primo Levi, *The Periodic Table*, tr. Raymond Rosenthal (New York: Schocken, 1984), 97.
4   Franz Kafka, *Diaries, 1910–1923*, tr. Joseph Kresch and Martin Greenburg (New York: Schocken, 1948, 1976), 447.
5   Walter Benjamin, "The Storyteller," *Illuminations: Essays and Reflections*, ed. Hannah Arendt, tr. Harry Zohn (New York: Harcourt, Brace & World, 1968), 94.
6   Franz Kafka, *The Metamorphosis and Other Stories*, tr. Michael Hofmann (London: Penguin, 2008), 87.
7   Franz Kafka, letter to Max Brod, 1921, *The Basic Kafka* (New York: Pocket Books, 1979), 292.
8   Ian Thomson, "The Ethics of Primo Levi," *Times Literary Supplement*, June 17, 2016.
9   Paul Celan, *Selected Poems and Prose*, tr. John Felstiner (New York: W. W. Norton, 2001), 30–33.
10 Paul Celan and Nelly Sachs, *Correspondence*, ed. Barbara Wiedemann, tr. Christopher Clark (Riverdale-on-Hudson, NY: Sheep Meadow Press, 1995), 14.
11 Celan, *Selected Poems and Prose*, 405.
12 Czesław Miłosz, *Selected and Last Poems, 1931–2004*, tr. Czesław Miłosz et al. (New York: HarperCollins, 2011), 204.
13 Czesław Miłosz, *New and Collected Poems 1931–2001*, tr. Czesław Miłosz et al. (London: Penguin, 2006), 715.
14 Miłosz, *Selected and Last Poems*, 212.
15 Miłosz, *New and Collected Poems*, 111.
16 Miłosz, *Selected and Last Poems*, 208.
17 Ibid., 275–6.
18 Miłosz, *New and Collected Poems*, 716.
19 Miłosz, *Selected and Last Poems*, 317.
20 Olga Tokarczuk, *Flights*, tr. Jennifer Croft (New York: Riverhead Books, 2018), 7.
21 Olga Tokarczuk, "The Tender Narrator." https://www.nobelprize.org/prizes/literature/2018/tokarczuk/lecture/.
22 Tokarczuk, "The Tender Narrator."

Chapter 4: Venice–Florence: Invisible Cities

1   Proust, *Time Regained*, 6:256.
2   Marco Polo, *The Travels*, tr. Ronald Latham (Harmondsworth: Penguin, 1958), 119–20.

3 Samuel Taylor Coleridge, "Kubla Khan: Or, A Vision in a Dream; A Fragment," *The Complete Poems*, ed. William Keach (London: Penguin, 1997), 252.

4 Review by "Sammycat," February 9, 2010, http://www.amazon.com/Dantes-Inferno-Divine-Playstation-3/dp/B00INX6GBK.

5 Dante Alighieri, *De vulgari eloquentia*, tr. Steven Botterill (Cambridge: Cambridge University Press, 2008), 33.

6 A good example is a reading of the first canto of the *Inferno* by the actor Roberto Benigni, in a version that conveniently gives both Italian and English subtitles as he recites: https://www.youtube.com/watch?v=dIPu090YTew.

7 Dante Alighieri, *The Divine Comedy*, Italian text with translation and commentary by John D. Sinclair (New York: Oxford University Press, 3 vols., 1979), 2:394.

8 Giovanni Boccaccio, *The Decameron*, tr. G. H. McWilliam (Harmondsworth: Penguin, 1972), 52.

9 Judith Powers Serafini-Sauli, *Giovanni Boccaccio* (New York: Twayne, 1982), 84.

10 Donna Leon, *By Its Cover* (New York: Grove Press, 2014), 69–70.

11 Donna Leon, *My Venice and Other Essays* (New York: Grove Press, 2013), 49.

12 "Private Tour on the Footsteps of Commissario Brunetti." https://www.lonelyplanet.com/italy/venice/activities/venice-private-tour-on-the-footsteps-of-commissario-brunetti/a/pa-act/v-39613P207/360029.

13 Jason Horowitz, "Picture Venice Bustling Again," *The New York Times*, June 3, 2020, A1.

14 Italo Calvino, *Invisible Cities*, tr. William Weaver (San Diego: Harcourt, Brace, 1974), 75.

15 Italo Calvino, "Presentazione," *Le città invisibili* (Milan: Mondadori, 1993), ix.

Chapter 5: Cairo–Istanbul–Muscat: Stories within Stories

1 Calvino, *Invisible Cities*, 110.

2 Translation by W. K. Simpson (with a few modifications), in Simpson, ed., *The Literature of Ancient Egypt* (New Haven: Yale University Press, 1972), 324.

3 Husain Haddawy, ed. and tr., *The Arabian Nights* (New York: W. W. Norton, 1990), xii.

4 Lawrence Venuti gives a range of illustrations of this theme in his essay collection *Translation Changes Everything: Theory and Practice* (New York: Routledge, 2013).

5 Jorge Luis Borges, *Selected Non-fictions*, ed. Eliot Weinberger, tr. Esther Allen (London and New York: Penguin, 1999), 96.

6 Wen-chin Ouyang, ed., *The Arabian Nights* (London: Everyman's Library, 2014).

7 N. J. Dawood, tr., *Tales from The Thousand and One Nights* (Harmondsworth: Penguin, rev. ed., 1973), 406.

8 Powys Mather, tr., *The Book of the Thousand Nights and One Night* (New York: St. Martin's Press, 4 vols., 1972), 4:532.

9 Emily Jacir, "Absence/Presence/Censorship," https://herbalpertawards.org/artist/absencepresencecensorship.

10 https://www.nobelprize.org/prizes/literature/1988/mahfouz/lecture/.

11 Naguib Mahfouz, *Arabian Nights and Days*, tr. Denys Johnson Davies (Cairo: American University in Cairo Press, 1995), 2.

12 Orhan Pamuk, *My Name Is Red*, tr. Erdağ M. Göknar (New York: Vintage, 2001), 51.

13 Orhan Pamuk, *Other Colors: Essays and a Story*, tr. Maureen Freely (New York: Knopf, 2007), 168–9.

14 Email communication, June 20, 2020.

15 Aida Edemariam, interview with Jokha Alharthi, *Guardian*, July 8, 2019. https://www
.theguardian.com/books/2019/jul/08/jokha-alharthi-a-lot-of-women-are-really-strong
-even-though-they-are-slaves.

16 Jokha Alharthi, *Celestial Bodies*, tr. Marilyn Booth (New York: Catapult, 2019), 1–2.

Chapter 6: The Congo–Nigeria: (Post)Colonial Encounters

1 Henry Morton Stanley, *How I Found Livingstone: Travels, Adventures and Discoveries in Central
Africa: Including an Account of Four Months' Residence with Dr. Livingstone* (New York: Scribner,
Armstrong & Co., 1872), 642.

2 Henry Morton Stanley, *The Congo and the Founding of Its Free State: A Story of Work and
Exploration* (New York: Harper and Brothers, 1885), 386.

3 Joseph Conrad, *Heart of Darkness*, ed. Ross C. Murfin (Boston: Bedford St. Martins, 2011), 25.

4 Chinua Achebe, "An Image of Africa: Racism in Conrad's *Heart of Darkness*," *Massachusetts
Review* 18:4 (1977), 794.

5 Chinua Achebe, "The African Writer and the English Language," *Morning Yet on Creation Day*
(New York: Anchor Books, 1976), 82.

6 Chinua Achebe, *Things Fall Apart* (London: Penguin, 2001), 61.

7 Bob Thompson, "Things Fall into Place," *Washington Post*, March 9, 2008. https://www
.washingtonpost.com/wp-dyn/content/article/2008/03/07/AR2008030700987.html.

8 Bill Moyers, interview with Chinua Achebe, September 29, 1988, https://billmoyers.com
/content/chinua-achebe/.

9 https://medium.com/@bookoclock/netflix-partners-with-mo-abudu-to-adapt-books
-by-shoneyin-and-soyinka-1a535a47728a.

10 Duro Ladipo, *Oba Waja*, in Wole Soyinka, *Death and the King's Horseman*, ed. Simon Gikandi
(New York: W. W. Norton, 2003), 81.

11 Soyinka, *Death and the King's Horseman*, 49.

12 Mbwil a M. Ngal, *Giambatista Viko, ou, Le viol du discours africain* (Paris: Hatier, 1984), 39.
Forthcoming as Georges Ngal, *Giambatista Viko, or The Rape of African Discourse*, ed. and tr.
David Damrosch (New York: Modern Language Association, 2022).

13 Georges Ngal, "Authenticité et littérature," *Oeuvre critique* (Paris: Harmattan, 2009), 2:197.

14 https://www.ted.com/talks/chimamanda_ngozi_adichie_the_danger_of_a_single_story#
t-5732.

15 Chimamanda Ngozi Adichie, *The Thing Around Your Neck* (New York: Anchor Books, 2009), 21.

16 Daria Tunca, interview with Chimamanda Adichie, 2005, http://www.cerep.ulg.ac.be/adichie
/cnainterviews.html.

17 Chimamanda Adichie, "Conversation with James Mustich," *Barnes and Noble Review*, June 29,
2009, http://www.barnesandnoble.com/review/chimamanda-ngozi-adichie.

Chapter 7: Israel/Palestine: Strangers in a Strange Land

1 Morton Smith, "The Present State of Old Testament Studies," *Journal of Biblical Literature* 88
(1969), 29.

2 Psalm 137:1–4, Revised Standard Version (New York: Oxford University Press, 1971).

3 "The Tale of the Two Brothers," tr. Edward F. Wente, *The Literature of Ancient Egypt*, ed. William Kelly Simpson (New Haven: Yale University Press, 3rd ed., 2003), 80–90.

4 The Song of Songs, New Revised Standard Version (New York: Oxford University Press, 1989), 8:6.

5 The Acts of the Apostles 2:5–11, New Revised Standard Version.

6 Footnote to Matthew 27:35, New Revised Standard Version.

7 D. A. Mishani, *The Missing File*, tr. Steven Cohen (New York: Bourbon Street Books, 2013), 4.

8 https://www.jewishbookcouncil.org/pb-daily/d-a-mishani-and-the-mystery-of-the -hebrew-detective.

9 Maayan Eitan, "A Missing Literature: Dror Mishani and the Case of Israeli Crime Fiction," *Crime Fiction as World Literature*, ed. Louise Nilsson, David Damrosch, and Theo D'haen (New York: Bloomsbury Academic, 2017), 181.

10 D. A. Mishani, *A Possibility of Violence*, tr. Todd Hasak-Lowy (New York: Harper, 2014), 3.

11 Emile Habiby, *The Secret Life of Saeed the Pessoptimist*, tr. Salma Khadra Jayyusi and Trevor LeGassick (New York: Interlink Books, 2002), 9.

12 Mahmoud Darwish, *Unfortunately, It Was Paradise*, ed. and tr. Munir Akash and Carolyn Forché, with Sinan Antoon and Amira El-Zein (Berkeley: University of California Press, 2013), 9.

13 Mahmoud Darwish, *In the Presence of Absence*, tr. Sinan Antoon (Brooklyn, NY: Archipelago Books, 2011), 42.

14 Mahmoud Darwish, *The Butterfly's Burden*, tr. Fady Joudah (Port Townsend, WA: Copper Canyon Press, 2007), 235.

15 Fadwa Tuqan, "Face Lost in the Wilderness," *Palestine–Israel Journal* 2:2 (1995), https://www .pij.org/articles/663/face-lost-in-the-wilderness.

16 Mahmoud Darwish, *Selected Poems*, tr. Ian Wedde and Fawwaz Tuqan (Cheshire: Carcanet, 1973), 82.

17 Edward W. Said, "Reflections on Exile," *Reflections on Exile and Other Essays* (Cambridge, MA: Harvard University Press, 2002), 137.

18 Mahmoud Darwish, "Counterpoint," tr. Mona Anis as "Edward Said: A Contrapuntal Reading," *Al-Ahram Weekly*, 30 Sept.–6 Oct. 2004. Repr. in *Cultural Critique* 67, Fall 2007, 177–8.

19 Mahmoud Darwish reading: https://www.youtube.com/watch?time_continue=683&v =G-Cxxg-D2TQ&feature=emb_title.

20 "Counterpoint," 176.

21 Ibid., 182.

Chapter 8: Tehran–Shiraz: A Desertful of Roses

1 *Persepolis*, directed by Vincent Paronnaud and Marjane Satrapi (2.4.7. Films, 2007). The trailer gives a good sense of the poetic result: https://www.youtube.com/watch?v=3PXHeKuBzPY.

2 Marjane Satrapi, *The Complete Persepolis* (New York: Pantheon, 2004), v.

3 William Shakespeare, *The Tempest* (London: Penguin, 2015), 4.1.1887–9.

4 Farid ud-Din Attar, *The Conference of the Birds*, tr. Afkham Darbandi and Dick Davis (London and New York: Penguin, rev. ed., 2011), 254.

5 Johann Wolfgang von Goethe, *West-Eastern Divan*, ed. and tr. Eric Ormsby (London: Gingko, 2019), 76.

6 Hafez, Khatun, Zakani, *Faces of Love: Hafez and the Poets of Shiraz*, tr. Dick Davis (New York: Penguin, 2013), 104.

7 Ghalib, *Lightning Should Have Fallen on Ghalib*, tr. Robert Bly and Sunil Datta (New York: Ecco, 1999), 22.

8 Quoted in Frances W. Pritchett and Owen T. A. Cornwall, ed. and tr., *Ghalib: Selected Poems and Letters* (New York: Columbia University Press, 2017), 111.

9 Pritchett and Cornwall, *Ghalib: Selected Poems and Letters*, 24.

10 Ibid., 26, with the first line adapted from Bly and Datta, *Lightning Should Have Fallen on Ghalib*, 110.

11 Bly and Datta, *Lightning Should Have Fallen on Ghalib*, 34.

12 Pritchett and Cornwall, *Ghalib: Selected Poems and Letters*, 29.

13 Ghalib, "Ghazal XXVI," tr. Adrienne Rich, *Hudson Review* 22:4 (1969–70), 622.

14 Pritchett and Cornwall, *Ghalib: Selected Poems and Letters*, 33 (first couplet); the second couplet is from the looser but eloquent translation of the poem by Adrienne Rich, *Hudson Review* 22:4 (1969–70), 619.

15 Pritchett and Cornwall, *Ghalib: Selected Poems and Letters*, 42.

16 Frances W. Pritchett, *A Desertful of Roses: The Urdu Ghazals of Mirza Asadullah Khan "Ghalib,"* http://www.columbia.edu/itc/mealac/pritchett/00ghalib/.

17 Pritchett and Cornwall, *Ghalib: Selected Poems and Letters*, 67.

18 Edward W. Said, "Secular Criticism," *The World, the Text, and the Critic* (Cambridge, MA: Harvard University Press, 1983), 1–30.

19 Agha Shahid Ali, ed., *Ravishing Disunities: Real Ghazals in English* (Middletown, CT: Wesleyan University Press, 2000).

20 Agha Shahid Ali, *Call Me Ishmael Tonight: A Book of Ghazals* (New York: W. W. Norton, 2003), 24.

Chapter 9: Calcutta/Kolkata: Rewriting Empire

1 Rudyard Kipling, *Kim: Authoritative Text, Backgrounds, Criticism*, ed. Zohreh T. Sullivan (New York: W. W. Norton, 2002), 9.

2 Rudyard Kipling, *Complete Verse: Definitive Edition* (New York: Anchor Books, 1989), 14.

3 https://www.nobelprize.org/prizes/literature/1907/summary/.

4 Rabindranath Tagore, *Gitanjali*, http://www.gutenberg.org/cache/epub/7164/pg7164-images.html.

5 Joyce Kilmer, "A Talk with Sir Rabindranath Tagore," *The New York Times*, October 29, 1916.

6 Rabindranath Tagore, *The Home and the World*, tr. Surendranath Tagore (London: Penguin, 2005), 162.

7 Salman Rushdie, *East, West* (London: Vintage, 1995), 45.

8 Salman Rushdie, "Imaginary Homelands," *Imaginary Homelands: Essays and Criticism 1981–1991* (London: Penguin, rev. ed. 1992), 17.

9 Conan Doyle, *Complete Sherlock Holmes*, 2:488.

10 Jamyang Norbu, *The Mandala of Sherlock Holmes: The Adventures of the Great Detective in India and Tibet* (New York: Bloomsbury, 2003), 86.

11 Conan Doyle, "The Adventure of the Cardboard Box," *Complete Sherlock Holmes*, 2:901.

12 Jamyang Norbu, *Shadow Tibet: Selected Writings 1989–2004* (New Delhi: Bluejay Books, 2006), 7.

13 Jhumpa Lahiri, *Interpreter of Maladies* (Boston: Houghton Mifflin, 1999), 57.

Chapter 10: Shanghai–Beijing: Journeys to the West

1 Wu Cheng'en, *The Journey to the West*, ed and tr. Anthony C. Yu (Chicago: University of Chicago Press, 4 vols., rev. ed., 2012), 4:265.

2 Wu Cheng'en, *Monkey*, tr. Arthur Waley (New York: Grove Press, 1984), 60.

3 Lu Xun, *The Real Story of Ah-Q and Other Tales of China: The Complete Fiction of Lu Xun*, tr. Julia Lovell (London and New York: Penguin, 2009), 17.

4 Eileen Chang, *Love in a Fallen City*, tr. Karen S. Kingsbury (New York: New York Review of Books; London: Penguin, 2007), 239.

5 Mo Yan, "Storytellers." https://www.nobelprize.org/prizes/literature/2012/yan/25452-mo-yan-nobel-lecture-2012.

6 Mo Yan, *Life and Death Are Wearing Me Out*, tr. Howard Goldblatt (New York: Arcade, 2012), 539.

7 Bei Dao, *The Rose of Time: New and Selected Poems*, ed. Eliot Weinberger, tr. Yanbing Chen et al. (New York: New Directions, 2009), 7.

8 Bei Dao, *The August Sleepwalker: Poetry*, tr. Bonnie S. McDougall (New York: New Directions, 1988), 121.

9 Bei Dao, *The Rose of Time*, 277.

10 Bei Dao, *Blue House*, tr. Ted Huters and Feng-ying Ming (Brookline, MA: Zephyr, 2000), 26.

11 Bei Dao, *The Rose of Time*, 99.

12 Ibid., 253.

13 Bei Dao at the 92nd Street Y: https://www.youtube.com/watch?v=oXA3hBPBOOU.

14 Bei Dao, "The Ink Point's Revelations," tr. Lucas Klein, from *Jintian* (Summer 2018, no. 118), 242.

15 Michael Palmer, "Foreword," Bei Dao, *At the Sky's Edge: Poems 1991–1996* (New York: New Directions, 1996), xi.

Chapter 11: Tokyo–Kyoto: The West of the East

1 Walter Dening, "Japanese Modern Literature," *Transactions of the 9th International Congress of Orientalists*, ed. E. Delmar Morgan (London: International Congress of Orientalists, 1893), 2:662.

2 http://www.dnp.co.jp/eng/corporate/history01.html.

3 Quoted in Robert Lyons Danly, *In the Shade of Spring Leaves: The Life of Higuchi Ichiyō, with Nine of Her Best Stories* (New York: W. W. Norton, new ed., 1992), 148.

4 Conrad, *Heart of Darkness*, 9.

5 Rei Kimura, *A Note from Ichiyo* (Phoenix: Booksmango, 2017), 83.

6 Lady Murasaki, *The Tale of Genji*, tr. Arthur Waley (London: Allen & Unwin, 1935), title page.

7 Murasaki Shikibu, *The Tale of Genji*, tr. Edward G. Seidensticker (New York: Random House, 2 vols., 1976), 1:437.

8 Sei Shōnagon, *The Pillow Book*, ed. and tr. Ivan Morris (New York: Columbia University Press; London: Penguin, 1967), 49.

9 This is one of thirty translations of this haiku at http://www.bopsecrets.org/gateway /passages/basho-frog.htm.

10 Translation by Makoto Ueda, accompanying a reproduction of the painting of the waterfall by Morikawa Kyoriku, at https://basho-yamadera.com/en/yamadera/horohoro/.

11 Matsuo Bashō, *The Narrow Road to the Deep North and Other Travel Sketches*, tr. Nobuyuki Yuasa (London and New York: Penguin, 1966), 97.

12 Ibid., 106–7, with some readings adopted from the translation by Haruo Shirane in *Early Modern Japanese Literature: An Anthology*, ed. Haruo Shirane (New York: Columbia University Press, 2002), repr. in David Damrosch et al., eds., *The Longman Anthology of World Literature* (New York: Pearson Longman, 6 vols., 2009), D:417.

13 Ibid., D:410.

14 Yukio Mishima, *Spring Snow*, tr. Michael Gallagher (New York: Vintage, 1990), 178.

15 Proust, *Swann's Way*, 64–5.

16 Yukio Mishima, *The Decay of the Angel*, tr. Edward G. Seidensticker (New York: Knopf, 1974), 247.

17 Bashō, *The Narrow Road to the Deep North*, 71.

18 James Merrill, *The Inner Room* (New York: Knopf, 1988), 53.

19 Langdon Hammer, *James Merrill: Life and Art* (New York: Knopf, 2015), 699.

Chapter 12: Brazil–Colombia: Utopias, Dystopias, Heterotopias

1 Thomas More, *Utopia*, tr. Dominic Baker-Smith (London: Penguin, 2012), 108–9.

2 Elizabeth M. Knowles, *The Oxford Dictionary of Quotations* (Oxford: Oxford University Press, 1999), 531.

3 More's epitaph is given in the original Latin as well as in this 1557 translation in https:// thomasmorestudies.org/wp-content/uploads/2020/08/TM_Epitaph-1.pdf.

4 François-Marie Arouet de Voltaire, *Candide, or Optimism*, ed. Nicholas Cronk, tr. Robert M. Adams (New York: W. W. Norton, 3rd ed., 2016), 30–31.

5 Pêro de Magalhães de Gândavo, *Tratado da Terra do Brasil* (São Paulo: Belo Horizonte, 1980), 124.

6 Joaquim Maria Machado de Assis, *The Posthumous Memoirs of Brás Cubas*, tr. Flora Thomson DeVeaux (New York: Penguin, 2020), xli.

7 "Nota da Editôra para a primeira edição," Clarice Lispector, *Laços de Familia* (São Paulo: Editôra Paulo de Azevedo, 2nd ed., 1961), 5.

8 Clarice Lispector, *The Complete Stories*, tr. Katrina Dodson (New York: New Directions, 2015), 309.

9 Lispector, *Laços de Familia*, 75.

10 Benjamin Moser, *Why This World: A Biography of Clarice Lispector* (Oxford: Oxford University Press, 2009), 126.

11 Gabriel García Márquez, "The Solitude of Latin America," https://www.nobelprize.org /prizes/literature/1982/marquez/lecture.

12 Gabriel García Márquez and Peter H. Stone, "The Art of Fiction No. 69," *The Paris Review* 82 (1981), https://www.theparisreview.org/interviews/3196/. gabriel-garcia-marquez-the-art-of-fiction-no-69-gabriel-garcia-marquez.

13 Gabriel García Márquez, *One Hundred Years of Solitude*, tr. Gregory Rabassa (New York: Harper and Row, 1970), 236.

Chapter 13: Mexico–Guatemala: The Pope's Blowgun

1 John Bierhorst, ed. and tr., *Cantares Mexicanos: Songs of the Aztecs* (Stanford: Stanford University Press, 1985), 335–7.

2 Bernal Díaz del Castillo, *The Conquest of New Spain*, tr. J. M. Cohen (Harmondsworth: Penguin, 1963), 214.

3 *Cantares Mexicanos*, folio 14v, as translated in Miguel Léon-Portilla, *Aztec Thought and Culture: A Study of the Ancient Nahuatl Mind*, tr. Jack Emory Davis (Norman: University of Oklahoma Press, 1963), 73.

4 Miguel León-Portilla and Earl Shorris, et al., *In the Language of Kings: An Anthology of Mesoamerican Literature—Pre-Columbian to the Present* (New York: W. W. Norton, 2001), 84.

5 Bernardino de Sahagún, *Psalmodia Christiana*, tr. Arthur J. O. Anderson (Salt Lake City: University of Utah Press, 1993), 7.

6 Bierhorst, *Cantares Mexicanos*, 361.

7 Martin Puchner, *The Written World: The Power of Stories to Shape People, History, Civilization* (New York: Random House, 2017), 183.

8 *Popol Vuh: The Mayan Book of the Dawn of Life*, ed. and tr. Dennis Tedlock (New York: Touchstone, 1985), 72.

9 Allen Christenson, ed. and tr., *Popol Vuh: The Sacred Book of the Maya* (Norman: University of Oklahoma Press, 2007).

10 *The Annals of the Cakchiquels; Title of the Lords of Totonicapán*, tr. Adrian Recinos et al. (Norman, OK: University of Oklahoma Press, 1953), 170.

11 *Fama y obras posthumas del Fénix de México, Decima Musa, Poetista Americana, Sor Juana Inés de la Cruz* (Madrid: Manuel Ruíz de Murga, 1700).

12 Sor Juana Inés de la Cruz, *Selected Works*, ed. Anna More, tr. Edith Grossman (New York: W. W. Norton, 2016), 110.

13 Quoted in Natalie Underberg, "Sor Juana's Villancicos: Context, Gender, and Genre," *Western Folklore* 60:4 (2001), 307; my translation of the Nahuatl phrases.

14 Luis Leal, "Myth and Social Realism in Miguel Angel Asturias," *Comparative Literature Studies* 5:3 (1968), 239.

15 Giuseppe Bellini, "Asturias y el mundo mágico de Paris," 20, https://www.biblioteca.org .ar/libros/134465.pdf.

16 Miguel Ángel Asturias, *The President*, tr. Frances Partridge (London: Gollanz, 1963), 7.

17 Asturias, *El Señor Presidente* (Madrid: Cátedra, 1997), 43; Asturias, The *President*, 7. The further quotations from Asturias come from the English translation.

18 Rosario Castellanos, *The Book of Lamentations*, tr. Esther Allen (New York and London: Penguin, 1998), ix.

Chapter 14: The Antilles and Beyond: Fragments of Epic Memory

1 Derek Walcott, "The Antilles: Fragments of Epic Memory," https://www.nobelprize.org/prizes/literature/1992/walcott/lecture/.

2 Derek Walcott, *Collected Poems 1948–1984* (New York: Farrar, Straus and Giroux, 1986), 3.

3 Andrew Pearse, "A Note for the Reader of the Poem," *Caribbean Quarterly* 1:1 (1949), 38–9.

4 David Montenegro, "An Interview with Derek Walcott," *Partisan Review* 52:2 (1990), 203.

5 Walcott, *Collected Poems*, 52.

6 Edward Hirsch, "Derek Walcott: The Art of Poetry 37," *The Paris Review* 101 (Winter 1986), https://www.theparisreview.org/interviews/2719/the-art-of-poetry-no-37-derek-walcott.

7 Walcott, *Collected Poems*, 324.

8 Ibid.

9 Derek Walcott, *Omeros* (New York: Farrar, Straus and Giroux, 1990), 14.

10 James Joyce, *Ulysses*, ed. Hans Walter Gabler (New York: Random House, 1986), 173.

11 James Joyce, "Ireland, Land of Saints and Sages," *The Critical Writings of James Joyce*, ed. Ellsworth Mason and Richard Ellmann (New York: Viking Press, 1959), 155.

12 *Selected Letters of James Joyce*, ed. Richard Ellmann (New York: Viking, 1975), 83.

13 James Joyce, *Finnegans Wake* (London: Penguin, 1999), 183.

14 Derek Walcott, *Collected Poems*, 427–9.

15 Quoted by Julia Rochester, "On the Influence of *Wide Sargeasso Sea*," https://www.penguin.co.uk/articles/2016/julia-rochester-on-the-influence-of-wide-sargasso-sea.html.

16 Jean Rhys, *Smile Please: An Unfinished Autobiography* (London: Penguin, 2016).

17 Charlotte Brontë, *Jane Eyre* (New York: New American Library, 1982), 452.

18 Jean Rhys, *Wide Sargasso Sea* (New York: W. W. Norton, 1966), 181.

19 William Beebe, *Nonsuch: Land of Water* (New York: Brewer, Warren and Putnam, 1932), 190.

20 Margaret Atwood, *The Penelopiad* (Edinburgh: Canongate, 2005), 15–16.

21 "A Chorus Line 1976 Tony Awards," https://www.youtube.com/watch?v=htLGQ3CDODY.

22 Judith Schalansky, *Atlas of Remote Islands: Fifty Islands I Have Never Set Foot On and Never Will*, tr. Christine Lo (London and New York: Penguin, 2010), 19.

23 Florence (Johnny) Frisbie, *Miss Ulysses from Puka-Puka: The Autobiography of a South Sea Trader's Daughter* (Newport Beach, CA: Dockside Sailing Press, 2nd ed., 2016), 36.

24 https://www.caribjournal.com/2013/01/13/an-island-oasis-in-guadeloupe/.

25 https://fr.tripadvisor.ch/ShowUserReviews-g644387-d6419076-r637470971-Ti_Robinson-Le_Gosier_Grande_Terre_Island_Guadeloupe.html.

Chapter 15: Bar Harbor: The World on a Desert Island

1 Robert McCloskey, *One Morning in Maine* (New York: Viking, 1952), 10.

2 Rich Hewitt, "Closing the Book on Condon's Garage," *Bangor Daily News*, July 12, 2007.

3 Sarah Orne Jewett, *The Country of the Pointed Firs and Other Stories*, with an Afterword by Peter Balaam (New York: Signet, 2009), 236.

4 Guy Reynolds, "The Transatlantic Virtual Salon: Cather and the British," *Studies in the Novel* 45:3 (2013), 358.

5 Judith Dunford, "The Ways of Maine," *Chicago Tribune*, March 27, 1994.

6 Josyane Savigneau, *Marguerite Yourcenar: Inventing a Life*, tr. Joan E. Howard (Chicago: University of Chicago Press, 1993), 197.

7 Margaret Yourcenar, *Memoirs of Hadrian*, tr. Grace Frick (New York: Farrar, Straus and Giroux, 1954), 323.

8 Savigneau, *Marguerite Yourcenar*, 197.

9 Marcel Proust, *Swann's Way*, 1:49–50.

10 Hugh Lofting, *The Story of Doctor Dolittle* (New York: Frederick Stokes, 1920), 11.

11 Hugh Lofting, *The Voyages of Doctor Dolittle* (Philadelphia: Lippincott, 1922, 1950), 150.

12 E. B. White, *Essays of E. B. White* (New York: Harper & Row, 1977), ix.

13 E. B. White, *Stuart Little* (New York: HarperCollins, 1973), 1–2.

14 White, *Essays*, 243–4.

Chapter 16: New York: Migrant Metropolis

1 Madeleine L'Engle, "How's One to Tell?" *New York Times Book Review*, May 12, 1963, BR24.

2 Madeleine L'Engle, *A Wrinkle in Time* (New York: Farrar, Straus and Giroux, 1962), 76.

3 Saul Steinberg and Harold Rosenberg, *Saul Steinberg* (New York: Knopf, in association with the Whitney Museum of American Art, 1978), 243.

4 In the Eskenazi Museum of Art, Indiana University, Bloomington.

5 Quoted in Reneé Somers, *Edith Wharton as Spatial Activist and Analyst* (London: Routledge, 2013), 27.

6 James Baldwin, *Notes of a Native Son* (New York: Bantam, 1968), 71.

7 Quoted in "Stories from Chez Baldwin: At Home and Abroad," National Museum of African American History and Culture, https://nmaahc.si.edu/blog/series/stories-chez-baldwin.

8 James Baldwin, "Sonny's Blues," *Going to Meet the Man* (New York: Vintage, 1995); *Sonny's Blues and Other Stories* (London: Penguin, 1957).

9 Jean-Paul Sartre, *Nausea*, tr. Lloyd Alexander (New York: New Directions, 1964), 174, 177.

10 Saul Bellow, *Henderson the Rain King* (New York: Viking, 1959), 46.

11 John Podhoretz, "Saul Bellow, A Neocon's Tale," *The Times* (London), April 10, 2005, https://www.thetimes.co.uk/article/saul-bellow-a-neocons-tale-8vortgj67b7.

12 J. R. R. Tolkien, *The Return of the King*, volume 3 of *The Lord of the Rings* (London: Allen and Unwin, 3 vols., 2nd ed., 1966), 202.

13 J. R. R Tolkien, *The Fellowship of the Ring*, volume 1 of *The Lord of the Rings*, 68–9.

14 J. R. R. Tolkien, "A Secret Vice," *The Monsters and the Critics and Other Essays* (Boston: Houghton Mifflin, 1983), 213.

15 Umberto Eco, *Six Walks in the Fictional Woods* (Cambridge, MA: Harvard University Press, 1994), 78.

16 J. R. R. Tolkien, "On Fairy-stories," *Tree and Leaf* (London: Allen and Unwin, 1964. Repr. in Tolkien, *The Monsters and the Critics*, 109–61), 132.

17 Tolkien, *The Fellowship of the Ring*, 60.